MW01193624

JAPAN'S CUISINES

JAPAN'S CUISINES

FOOD, PLACE AND IDENTITY

Eric C. Rath

REAKTION BOOKS

To the memory of my stepfather Philip Balsamo, who enjoyed good meals and lively conversations

Published by Reaktion Books Ltd
Unit 32, Waterside
44–48 Wharf Road
London N1 7UX, UK
www.reaktionbooks.co.uk

First published 2016
Copyright © Eric C. Rath 2016

All rights reserved

No part of this publication may be reproduced, stored in a retrieval system, or transmitted, in any form or by any means, electronic, mechanical, photocopying, recording or otherwise, without the prior permission of the publishers

Printed and bound by TJ International, Padstow, Cornwall

A catalogue record for this book is available from the British Library

ISBN 978 1 78023 643 8

CONTENTS

NOTE ON TRANSLATION

The wide variety of traditional Japanese foods means that there are many names for them, which sometimes makes translation frustrating. For consistency, I have relied on Richard Hosking's *A Dictionary of Japanese Food: Ingredients and Culture* (Rutland, VT, 1996). Readers can turn to this book for most of the Japanese culinary words that appear here in translation.

Alas, Hosking's text does not contain all of the specific terminology related to Japanese food, especially local variants. Folklorists, particularly those active before the Second World War, made it their mission to document rural life by cataloguing the different variations for names of foodstuffs and ways of eating. In 1959, one of their leaders, Shibusawa Keizō (1896–1963), published *Research on Japanese Fish Names* (*Nihon gyomei no kenkyū*), which contained 16,000 names of fish in Japanese dialects.[1] Regional names for soup that ethnologists catalogued around 1941 from different prefectures include *otsuke* (Nagasaki), *otsui* (Gifu), *otsuyo* (Nagano), *otsuyu* (Ibaraki), *otsu* (Okayama) and *tsurunoko* (Kyoto).[2] When local terms have a particularly interesting meaning, I have included these in the text with a translation alongside the common Japanese equivalent; otherwise they are omitted, such as when an *otsui* and an *otsu* can both be called soup in English.

Some culinary terms have gained greater acceptance in their Japanese form than in translation. For instance, John Keynes, author of *Japanese Cuisine: A Culinary Tour* (1966), offered 'rice sandwiches' as the translation for sushi.[3] Frequent eaters of Japanese food around the world will be more familiar with *soba* than 'buckwheat noodles' (in the text, soba refers to the noodles and buckwheat to the grain) and *umeboshi* than 'pickled apricot' (not pickled plum, as it is typically labelled), *udon* than 'thick wheat noodles' and *sōmen* than 'thin wheat noodles'. *Katsuo* is sometimes rendered as bonito, but skipjack tuna, also called arctic bonito, is the correct translation.

Katsuobushi, the fish flakes used to make stock and as a topping, is sometimes made from bonito, but the standard or proper version uses skipjack tuna. Some Japanese foods also sound tastier without translation. Blanched *warabi* sounds better for soup than 'bracken', although they are the same thing. Gelatinous cubes of *konnyaku* have become more familiar than 'devil's tongue' or 'elephant foot', neither of which seems to refer to food. A few foods, such as the asparagus-like plant *udo* or the pod-like purple fruit *akebi*, have no ready English equivalent and require definitions. References in the text to pumpkin denote the flavourful Japanese winter squash called *kabocha*, which has green, edible skin and yellow-orange flesh.

Some terms force choices on the translator that are not required in the original language. The dish *mugimeshi*, for instance, was a main staple for most of the population before the Second World War, but the term is frustratingly unclear. *Mugimeshi* can mean cooked barley (*mugi*) or it could mean barley cooked with rice. The term remains silent about the proportion of rice to barley, or whether the rice is brown, polished or semi-polished or the barley whole, cracked, polished or rolled. Cognizant of the ambiguities of such terms, Japanese food scholars will often attempt to specify this information, which sheds important light on regional differences and disparities of age, income and gender. I have included these observations when they are available and noted their absence when they are not. Chapter Three turns the spotlight on an even more slippery term: *meshi*, which can mean cooked grain, cooked rice or even a meal.

INTRODUCTION

In modern Japanese there is a rich vocabulary for referring to food. Terms such as 'local cuisine', 'tea cuisine' and 'traditional dietary cultures' suggest the depth and complexity of Japanese food. But, rather than take these terms as objective descriptions of what people in a particular location, era or situation cook and eat, this book examines how cuisines are ideological, in that those who promote them are attempting to create the very relationships between people, food and places that their cuisines purportedly describe.

There are many ways to define 'cuisine'. To name a few, a cuisine can be understood as a set of cooking habits and preferences for certain ingredients, or identified as a product of modernization and nationalism in a culture that historically gave importance to fine dining.[1] A cuisine can also be viewed as a form of fantasy involving food, whereby cooking and eating take on shared symbolic meanings for their producers and consumers.[2]

This book, however, asserts that cuisine has an ideological dimension that cannot be ignored. The comedian George Carlin joked, 'The difference between food and cuisine is sixty dollars.' He explained, 'no restaurant today would dare allow a *cook* to *cook* the *food*; instead, the *cuisine* must be *prepared* by a *chef*.'[3] Carlin reminds us that cuisines, which might appear to be innocent catalogues of cooking techniques, are actually decorative languages served up for purposes other than simply to provide an accurate portrait of what is being prepared and consumed. As the heart of Carlin's observation is the realization that cuisines benefit institutions that designate them, such as the restaurants able to charge more for 'cuisine' than for 'food'. Cuisine gives purpose to food that transcends its nutritional value.

Cuisines reveal a prescriptive language that tells populations how they should (but typically do not) eat or think about food. Japanese tea cuisine, *cha kaiseki*, consisting of the delicate and dainty meals served for the tea ceremony, is often cited as the aesthetic foundation for modern Japanese cuisine. But ever since the tea ceremony began, in the sixteenth century, the 'way of tea' has always been a pastime for the wealthy and powerful. Today less than 2 per cent of the Japanese population practises the tea ceremony, calling into question why the food served as an elite cultural pursuit for only a few people at a time in a small, darkened room should represent the culinary culture of an entire nation.[4]

There is a similar disparity between what is officially called 'traditional dietary cultures of the Japanese' (*washoku*) and the eating habits of ordinary people in Japan today. In 2013 UNESCO (the United Nations Educational, Scientific and Cultural Organization) added *washoku* to its list of arts and customs having 'intangible cultural heritage', but the vague definition of traditional Japanese dietary cultures from Japan's Ministry of Agriculture and other official agencies and on UNESCO's website, detailed later in this book, does not at all resemble either what most people in Japan once ate or what they consume today. *Washoku* is instead an idealized dietary lifestyle, focusing on foods popularized from the 1960s onwards meant to impress audiences outside Japan and guide domestic eating habits. Were most Japanese actually participant in traditional dietary cultures there would be no need to seek UNESCO designation to affirm them.

Washoku is not the first attempt by the Japanese government to define a national cuisine. At the outbreak of the Second World War, the Imperial Rule Assistance Association, Japan's effort to emulate Germany's Nazi Party, advocated 'national people's cuisine' (*kokuminshoku*) to standardize the diet, rationalize the use of scarce nutritional resources and put a positive spin on wartime rationing. Wartime national people's cuisine proved unsustainable, however, and today the term *kokuminshoku* refers to inexpensive dishes with foreign origins or 'comfort food', chiefly ramen and beef curry, without recognition of the word's militaristic past.

The *kaiseki* of the tea ceremony, the traditional dietary cultures of the Japanese, and national people's cuisine are not objective descriptions of diets but are instead ideological, in that they present an idealized version of food to serve the interest of political and social institutions. Tea cuisine narrows the discussion of cuisine to elite repasts and grants authority to the small percentage of the population that prepares, consumes and interprets them. The rubric of traditional dietary cultures showcases select heritage modes of dining – ones that were never dominant historically – as a means for the national government to try to improve Japan's balance of trade, shore up the domestic rate of food self-sufficiency, assuage fears of food safety and promote a positive image abroad. National people's cuisine disguised forced austerity as patriotic, aesthetic choices.

The rationale for a cuisine rests on 'tradition', or, more correctly, a selective interpretation of the past. As a historian of premodern Japan, I am conscious that in writing a book about modern cuisines I am trespassing beyond the year 1868, which marks the usually accepted temporal boundary into modernity in Japan. But I make these chronological incursions because in order to develop a more accurate understanding of the history of Japan's foodways, it is first necessary to confront the dominant modern definitions of 'traditional' Japanese cuisines. I discovered that many culinary traditions, such as 'local food' and the prominence of rice in the diet, have a more recent history than is typically assumed.

The visibility of Japanese culinary traditions today also rests on the fact that the Japanese diet did not change overnight in 1868. In fact, there were profound continuities in the diet from the early nineteenth century until the 1920s. The 'early modern' diet of the nineteenth century can be said to have lasted in some parts of Japan until at least the 1930s, and in other areas it endured decades longer.[5]

References to 'traditional' foods in modern cuisines do not focus on everything that was eaten until the 1920s; instead, culinary traditions are highly selective. Consequently, a secondary aim of this book is to recover the culinary diversity lacking in the dominant narratives of Japanese food history. In contradistinction to the dominant image of 'traditional dietary cultures' today, which features a bowl of white rice and side dishes such as sashimi and sometimes even slices of *wagyū* steak, Japanese people before the Second World War ate less meat, less fat and more whole grains other than rice. Rice was only rarely served in its polished, 'white' form; semi-polished and brown rice were more typical, and the grains were usually cooked with other foods, especially in rural areas. People in rural locales also relied on gathered foods such as mountain vegetables and nuts, both of which require lengthy processing before they can be eaten. Fishing communities did not feast on expensive sashimi but ate grilled herring and sardines, while villages just a few kilometres from the coast made do with salted fish, and prepared sushi as a way to preserve seafood rather than as a way to enjoy it fresh.[6] Other populations subsisted on corn or grains that today are primarily used as birdseed. The diversity of Japan's diet is largely absent today even from the local food movement, which has become a touchstone for all that is 'traditional', 'healthy' and 'sustainable'. However, as this book shows, the origin of the local food movement was anything but 'local', in that it was initiated by the policies of the central government and the scholars in its employ and not by local people. My goal in interrogating the historicity of Japanese cuisines is to bring attention to the topics, ways of cooking and ingredients that are usually 'off the table' when we typically think of Japanese food.

The approach for this book is historical, as it traces the development of different iterations of Japanese cuisine. Chapter One, covering *washoku*, traditional Japanese dietary cultures, provides an initial intervention in the topic of national cuisine by drawing on a recent example. The chapter introduces tea cuisine and rice, which are seen as exemplary of Japanese dietary cultures; and the subsequent two chapters focus on these topics separately. The remaining chapters follow a chronological order, revealing how different examples of cuisine originated and evolved.

The Japanese government's definition of 'traditional Japanese dietary cultures' offers the starting point for this book in Chapter One; it is taken as a case study to examine how the state and food scholars write culinary history not as an accurate depiction of a historical or current diet but rather as an attempt to promote nationalism and other state agendas. The UNESCO definition of *washoku* presents a timeless vision of Japan's traditional food cultures, but the reality of what most Japanese ate before the Second World War was far humbler and more heterogeneous, as this chapter shows. The rice and varied side dishes that are prominent features in discussions of Japan's traditional dietary cultures today are an invented tradition of the 1960s. *Washoku*'s promoters want to guide the population to consume more seafood and domestic produce, but Japanese consumer surveys reveal complaints about the troublesome nature of having to prepare Japanese food and explain people's preferences for other food options.

Since the Second World War, the aesthetic essence of Japanese cuisine has been considered to be tea cuisine (*cha kaiseki*), which has been attributed to the singular genius of the tea master Sen no Rikyū (1522–1591). Chapter Two reviews the historical evidence about Rikyū and concludes that he had very little if anything to do with the formation of *cha kaiseki*. The attribution to Rikyū stems from modern readings of apocryphal texts attributed to the sixteenth-century tea master, as presented by the major schools of tea ceremony that trace their artistry and lineages to him. What poses as an aesthetic touchstone for Japanese cuisine today is in fact an attempt by the schools of tea ceremony to claim authority and contend for the wider cultural relevance of their art, which has always been an elitist pastime. The chapter reassesses the history of tea cuisine and its impact on the development of Japanese cuisine by examining a prominent late seventeenth-century tea master, author and chef named Endō Genkan, who is usually ignored in these discussions but who made a lasting contribution to the foods served in the way of tea. Genkan's example demonstrates the importance of thinking of tea cuisine and its history in a wider context than the hereditary property of a few lineages, especially if tea cuisine is to be recognized as important for the Japanese cuisine of today.

Rice is not only central to modern definitions of traditional Japanese dietary cultures, but there is also more than a century of literature by folklorists, historians and anthropologists that depicts the grain as a cornerstone of Japanese civilization. Chapter Three recognizes that most Japanese ate some rice before the Second World War, but this is not the same as saying that they dined on the grain regularly or that consumption of the staple was uniform. Rice differs in the varied grades eaten and the diverse ways of processing and preparing it. Before the Second World War, rice was usually mixed with other grains, tubers, vegetables and nut meals. Standards of milling also varied. While some people in cities ate the polished 'white' variety that is familiar today, ordinary folk consumed brown rice or rice that was lightly milled – to a degree that would be unrecognizable to modern consumers. Some even ate the bran and hulls mixed in with the grain. In rural areas, undiluted polished rice was consumed only a handful of times a year, and taro, sweet potatoes, corn and other foodstuffs were the staples.

In the same way that tea ceremony cuisine is treated as a cultural monolith, rice too is given an inordinate symbolic weight in studies of Japanese culture; but an examination of the many diverse ways people prepared and consumed rice reveals the multiple, local and conflicting meanings of the grain. While rice consumption has been used as a way of imagining cultural continuities across space and time central to arguments about Japanese national identity, in fact the culture of rice shows that customs were far more diverse and far less egalitarian even into the first half of the twentieth century.

Chapter Four offers a picture of how culinary discourse gradually affected changes in Japanese eating habits over the course of the first decades of the twentieth century with the invention of 'lunch'. The notion that the noontime meal should be different from the morning and evening ones is a modern idea in Japan, one that evolved in conjunction with increased urbanization in the twentieth century, compulsory school attendance and more people working outside the home. Both pupils and male workers could eat out, but nutritionists and culinary experts contended in newspapers, cookbooks and culinary schools that wives and mothers should provide a homemade lunch for their families to take with them to school or work. Beyond being simply filling, these lunches had to be visually pleasing. The aestheticization of the Japanese lunch has its roots in the early modern period; it was popular in cities by the 1930s and has reached a culmination in the box lunches (*bentō*) that are a prominent feature of home cooking today. Other scholars have described Japan's modern bentō culture, particularly the exquisite lunches mothers now craft for their kindergarten children. This chapter traces the historical foundation of bentō cuisine.

Today, the word *kokuminshoku* refers to popular dishes like ramen and curry, but the term originated during the Second World War, as Chapter Five explores. In 1940, in response to wartime austerity measures, the Ministry of Welfare announced the development of a 'national people's cuisine' to make cooking, eating and digesting patriotic duties. The government enlisted ethnologists to develop the national people's cuisine by undertaking a survey of rural food life in 1941–2. These researchers concluded that vernacular cooking habits revealed a 'national food culture'. Their findings supported a national people's cuisine but tacitly challenged the state's fundamental assumption that a cuisine instituted from above was authentic. The notion of a 'national food culture' has endured in the ethnographic literature on Japanese food, but national people's cuisine lost salience as people on the home front simply sought to find anything to eat in order to survive in the closing years of the war. In the post-war era, the redefinition of *kokuminshoku* to refer to universally loved dishes indicates not only an amnesia about wartime national people's cuisine but also a popular repurposing of a term in an attempt to domesticate conspicuously foreign foods introduced in the modern era.

Contemporary Japan boasts many local cuisines, and Chapter Six discusses how the category of local cuisine is one of the legacies of wartime national people's cuisine. In 1943 the Ministry of Agriculture contracted the country's five imperial universities to conduct research into local foodstuffs for the war effort. What had been disdainfully called 'rural food' for its lack of rice, soy sauce and other 'modern' elements in the diet won new appreciation during wartime as 'local food', and was praised for its use of non-rationed ingredients, unconventional nutritional sources such as roots, grasses and bark, and homespun techniques for staving off starvation.

In the period of high economic growth and urbanization of the 1960s, no one was interested in foods associated with wartime deprivation, and the concept of 'local food' was reinvented as 'local cuisine' – defined as tasty dishes that could be marketed to nostalgic Japanese attempting to reconnect with their rural cultural roots. The 1980s brought a gourmet food boom and a new articulation of local food that centred on the use of heirloom ingredients – an expeditious way to commodify tradition and transform any dish into 'local' cuisine. In the last decade the Ministry of Agriculture, Forestry and Fisheries has even promoted fast foods such as hamburgers and Chinese-style dumplings (*gyōza*) as local cuisines, despite the fact that such dishes are of foreign origin and could be unhealthy if eaten daily. The main continuity driving the changing iterations of local food and local cuisine in Japan has been the role of the central government and the scholars working on the government's behalf, rather than the ordinary people who live, cook and eat in diverse parts of the country.

In opposition to the generalized view of local food found in the perspective of national dietary cultures, the concept of local food becomes more complicated and rich when it is encountered at the truly 'local' level. Chapter Seven visits locales in three areas – Saga and Kōchi prefectures and the Hida region of Gifu – places that were historically viewed as off the beaten path and divergent from the national dietary culture. Television viewers in Japan are led to believe that many people cannot locate Saga prefecture, in Kyushu, on a map, and Saga falls near the bottom in nationwide surveys of attractiveness. Kōchi, the southwest portion of the southerly island of Shikoku, was once called a 'land far from heaven', and in the twentieth century the prefecture's mountains were places where ethnologists searched for the 'forgotten Japanese'. Hida, the northern alpine region of Gifu prefecture, in the centre of the main island of Honshu, was dubbed 'Japan's Tibet' by one of the area's leading experts, and life there before the Second World War was seen as a throwback to Palaeolithic culture. Historical and ethnographic writing may treat these locales as marginal, backward and atypical, but standing in those places turns the 'periphery' into the 'centre' and enables one to see the many meanings of local food as defined by local populations.

Whether about the 'proper' diet for the Japanese people during wartime, rectifying rural life in remote hamlets, the suitable midday meals middle-class mothers should prepare for their children and spouses, or shoring up the authority of a few hereditary practitioners of elitist arts, the examples of Japan's cuisines in this book reveal that when institutions and the experts in their employ talk about cuisine, they are attempting to use food to exert control. The prouncement of the French gastronome Jean Anthelme Brillat-Savarin, 'Tell me what you eat, and I will tell you what you are', is well known, but in the case of the cuisines of modern Japan, this statement should be rephrased to make the country's institutions the speaker: 'By telling you what you eat, we tell you who you are.'

Thankfully, cuisine is not the reality that it purportedly describes. Cuisines tend to be repetitive and narrowly focused lest their messages be lost in a much more complicated actuality. They dazzle with their array of appetizing delicacies, but when we consider what is omitted from cuisines and why, they prove to be less like luxuriant gardens and more like mono-cultures that require constant intervention to keep pests, unwanted crops and weeds at bay. Understanding how the boundaries of a cuisine have been erected, by whom and why reveals the artificial nature of these partitions in the scruffy landscape of food cultures. Undertaking this investigation, we might just discover that what we have been told is a 'weed' is nothing of the sort. Today's weed may in fact have been yesterday's staple; and the distinction, which can be so important to some definitions of cuisine, hardly matters when the plant is consumed. Taking a quizzical approach to Japan's cuisines and understanding their modern history yields a greater apprecia-tion of the ideological nature of cuisine and sheds light on the richness of Japan's culinary heritage.

1

WHAT IS TRADITIONAL JAPANESE FOOD?

Possible definitions of traditional Japanese food could either be so broad that they might encompass everything ever consumed in Japan, or too narrow in their vision of idealized cuisine and exclude ways of eating, ingredients and recipes that were once prevalent. The current designation of traditional Japanese food by the government is in fact more about lifestyle than it is about food. Japanese consumers take a more concrete view of what traditional food is, identifying it in specific dishes, but that does not mean that they necessarily enjoy preparing or eating all these foods. One characteristic that both institutional and popular definitions of traditional Japanese food share is that they describe modes of eating and dishes that include white rice and meat, which are more typical of the period of high economic growth since the 1960s than of premodern Japan – or even the era before the Second World War. Concluding that these definitions fail to encompass either the breadth or the history of what the Japanese ate up to the first half of the twentieth century, this chapter offers an alternative model for conceptualizing traditional food in Japan that focuses on the diet around the country before the Second World War.

Defining Terms

A way to begin the discussion about the identity of traditional Japanese food is by examining two terms for it: *Nihon ryōri* and *washoku*.[1] These terms are translated into English in varying ways, so it is useful to explore their linguistic composition. Both *wa* and *Nihon* mean Japan. *Shoku* can refer to eating, food, meals and even to a stipend paid in foodstuffs – the equivalent of earning one's daily bread (or rice). *Ryōri* has similar meanings to *shoku* in that *ryōri* can mean prepared food or cooking; cooking for the tea ceremony is *cha kaiseki ryōri*, while the traditional cuisine of Kyoto is *Kyō ryōri*, and Buddhist vegetarian cuisine is *shōjin ryōri*. But the word *ryōri* suggests wider meanings than just cooking. '*Ryōri* is just like music and literature', explains the chef and noted food critic Abe Koryū, 'in that if one does not prepare it according to a correct grammar, one will be unable to bring forth a taste that will be perceived as good *ryōri*.'[2] Distinct conventions and the chef's artistic flair help to create *ryōri*, lending it artistic pretensions narrower in meaning than *shoku*, the Japanese way of preparing and consuming foods when aesthetics may be important but are not necessarily the primary concern. Since *Nihon ryōri* carries the nuance that the foods prepared will follow aesthetic guidelines, *ryōri* will be more probably served at distinct venues such as restaurants, or at the tea ceremony.[3]

Notwithstanding the elevated culinary nuances associated with the term *Nihon ryōri*, in 2012 the Japanese government sought international recognition for the more prosaic *washoku*, which it defines as 'traditional dietary cultures of the Japanese'. The Japanese government has been an active promoter of the country's food culture abroad since at least the turn of the twenty-first century, with agencies such as the Ministry of Agriculture, Forestry and Fisheries taking a leading role in disseminating information about the Japanese diet to enhance the country's influence globally. At the turn of the second millennium, Japan's economy, which had been the main reason behind the country's global political clout for decades, had been lagging in recession since the early 1990s, spurring the Japanese government to turn to the 'soft power' of Japanese culture to try to project a more positive national image abroad.[4] The 'Cool Japan' campaign created in 2002 promoted manga, electronics, film, fashion, music and cuisine, but with mixed results. An attempt in 2006 to certify the authenticity of Japanese restaurants globally led to cries that Japan was trying to deploy the 'sushi police'.[5] After this debacle, the Japanese government turned away from critiquing the inauthenticity of 'Japanese food' outside Japan and instead sought to promote a 'genuine' Japanese domestic food culture internationally.

Thanks to the efforts of Japan's government, in December 2013 UNESCO added *washoku* to its Representative List of the Intangible Cultural Heritage of Humanity. The listing was in response to an application in March 2012 from Japan's Agency for Cultural Affairs and the Ministry of Agriculture, Forestry and Fisheries. UNESCO's website provides a definition of *washoku*, which it translates as the 'traditional dietary cultures of the Japanese':

Washoku is a social practice based on a set of skills, knowledge, practice and traditions related to the production, processing, preparation and consumption of food. It is associated with an essential spirit of respect for nature that is closely related to the sustainable use of natural resources. The basic knowledge and the social and cultural characteristics associated with Washoku are typically seen during New Year celebrations. The Japanese make various preparations to welcome the deities of the incoming year, pounding rice cakes and preparing special meals and beautifully decorated dishes using fresh ingredients, each of which has a symbolic meaning. These dishes are served on special tableware and shared by family members or collectively among communities. The practice favours the consumption of various natural, locally sourced ingredients such as rice, fish, vegetables and edible wild plants. The basic knowledge and skills related to Washoku, such as the proper seasoning of home cooking, are passed down in the home at shared mealtimes. Grassroots groups, schoolteachers and cooking instructors also play a role in transmitting the knowledge and skills by means of formal and non-formal education or through practice.[6]

Here, *washoku* is less a designation for food and more about customs. In fact, only a few foods are mentioned: rice cakes, rice, fish, vegetables and edible wild plants. The image that emerges is of time-honoured ways of eating in harmony with nature, transmitted within the family and community organizations and manifest especially for celebrating holidays, when a variety of symbolically important foods are eaten. At the New Year, foods such as black soybeans – representing health – and prawns – evoking longevity – are prepared and served in lacquered boxes in a style of dining called *osechi ryōri*. In the UNESCO definition of *washoku*, how one should eat and with whom seems as important as what one eats, though neither is clearly designated.

Rather than as a practice, custom or activity, a more typical way of understanding *washoku* is as food. A survey undertaken in 2013 by the beverage maker Takara Shuzō asked 3,000 people in Japan ranging in age from their twenties to their sixties about the dishes they thought of when they heard the word *washoku*. Table 1 presents the name of the food and the frequency the dish was mentioned.[7]

TABLE I
Dishes Evoked by the Word *Washoku**

Dish	Percentage Respondents
Simmered dishes (*nimono*)	71.7
Sushi	68
Sashimi	66.5
Grilled or simmered fish	64.9
Miso soup	60.9
Tempura	58.6
Rice	57.1
Kaiseki cuisine	56.5
New Year's cuisine (*osechi ryōri*)	46.9
Tofu	39
Udon; soba	39
Nattō (fermented soybeans)	36.5
Tamagoyaki (Japanese rolled omelette)	36.5
Oden (winter hotpot)	32.4
Sukiyaki	26.6
Shabu shabu (beef hotpot)	18.7
Yakitori (chicken grilled on a skewer)	13.9
Other	1

*Online survey of 3,000 people (1,500 women, 1,500 men) aged 20–60, conducted by Takara Shuzō, 2013

The question about *washoku* compelled respondents to think about cooking techniques and ingredients as opposed to practices and customs; but interestingly, fewer than half of the respondents included New Year's cuisine, despite the fact that it was the only meal mentioned specifically in the government's definition for UNESCO.

Takara Shuzō's survey asked two further questions that are revelatory. One question enquired whether or not the respondents would change their views of *washoku* if UNESCO opted to add *washoku* to its list of the Intangible Cultural Heritage of Humanity. Fifty-four per cent replied that the listing would have no impact on their thinking about *washoku*. Another question was about whether or not the respondents planned to increase the frequency with which they consumed *washoku* foods: 38.1 per cent said they would, 5.7 per cent replied that they would not and 56.2 per cent were indifferent.[8]

A sample size of 3,000 people out of Japan's population of 127.6 million is quite small, but the survey is suggestive that if people are not willing to increase their consumption of one or more dishes they choose to identify as *washoku*, they might be even more reluctant to engage in customs the government associates with *washoku*. In 2013 the food scholar and cultural historian Kumakura Isao, who is listed on the Japanese government's UNESCO application as leading the 'Investigative Commission to nominate WASHOKU on the Representative List of the Intangible Cultural Heritage', spoke bluntly regarding the fact that rather than reflect the way Japanese eat today, *washoku* 'is facing its death'. Kumakura explained that the reason the government sought UNESCO recognition was to halt the deterioration of home cooking. He provided three reasons for that decline: the prevalence of eating out; purchases of ready meals; and allowing children to dictate the choice of food served at home.[9] Kumakura's observations are in contrast with the claims of Japan's application for UNESCO listing, which takes a contrary view: 'The element [*washoku*] is widely practiced in Japan and transmitted orally within families who have maintained their own ways of cooking.'[10] As long as the practices and dishes ascribed to *washoku* remain vague, it is hard to determine how widely they are practised and whether or not they are in decline. In 2015 a survey of 1,000 men and women aged 15–69 were asked if instant cup noodles could be called *washoku*, and 59.4 per cent said that they could.[11]

Washoku as Rice, Soup, Three Side Dishes and Pickles

Other definitions of *washoku* do not confine traditional Japanese food culture to vague customs and practices, but instead apply the term to designate a meal that has a particular structure: rice, miso soup, side dishes and pickles. Harada Nobuo, the most prominent scholar of Japanese food culture, writes, 'today, the organization underlying the concept of *washoku* holds that as long as there is miso soup and pickles with rice, any variety of side dishes is fine.'[12] Another leading expert on Japanese cuisine, Ishige Naomichi, concurs: 'traditionally, a meal consists of boiled plain rice, called *gohan* or *meshi*, and seasoned side dishes, called *okazu*.'[13] Kumakura Isao and the prolific food historian Nagayama Hisao agree that *washoku* indicates a meal of rice, soup, pickles and three side dishes.[14] This formula – called

'A healthy *washoku* meal of one soup and three side dishes', from *Mainichi Shimbun*, 2014.

ichijū sansai – is often attributed to the legacy of the tea ceremony, and specifically to the sixteenth-century tea master Sen no Rikyū, a problematic assertion that the next chapter examines in detail.[15]

Consensus about *washoku* begins to erode when one tries to fill the abstract structure of a traditional meal with actual ingredients and dishes. According to the responses listed in Table 1, fish and simmered dishes are more logical choices for a traditional Japanese meal than beef, notwithstanding the fact that dishes including sukiyaki and *shabu shabu* are also included in that list. The meal advocated by the Agency for Cultural Affairs in its definition of *washoku* in 2012 called for 'the fresh bounty of various mountains and seas' while avoiding fats derived from animals; and the agency's application to UNESCO does not mention meat.[16] However, beef and pork dishes are among those frequently mentioned as *washoku* foods according to an internet survey conducted in 2013 by the soy sauce maker Kikkoman. The survey asked 830 housewives aged 20–70 about the *washoku* dishes they prepared at home most frequently. Table 2 lists the top ten of these dishes in ranked order.[17]

TABLE 2

Washoku Dishes Prepared at Home*

Dish	Percentage Respondents
Grilled fish	59.8
Nikujaga (beef and potato stew)	53.7
Pork *shōgayaki* (sautéed with ginger)	51.9
Simmered squash	50.6
Udon	49.5
Simmered daikon	49.2
Pork soup (*butajiru*)	48.5
Tamagoyaki (Japanese rolled omelette)	47.5
Oden (winter hotpot)	45.1
Sautéed vegetables	44.5

*Online survey of 830 housewives aged 20–60 living in the Tokyo and Kinki [Kansai] regions, conducted by Kikkoman, 2013

Grilled fish tops the list here, but meat dishes appear to be prepared with greater frequency, since beef and pork recipes rank at numbers two and three. This list demonstrates a contrast between the foods that come to mind when Japanese respondents of both sexes are asked to think about *washoku* (see Table 1) and those that women actually prepare at home (Table 2). The former includes dishes that require technical skills to make, as exemplified by sushi and sashimi as well as tempura and *kaiseki*, and are typically enjoyed at restaurants. The latter, though also time-consuming to prepare, are more readily made at home.

The Kikkoman survey also asked housewives for their opinions of *washoku*, and the second- and third-highest ranking complaints were both about it being too time-consuming to make: 26 per cent stated that the preparations took too long and 24.6 per cent replied that the cooking required too much time.[18] Dishes such as beef stew and *oden* rely on slow simmering, a method of preparation indicative of *washoku* according to the Takara Shuzō survey and one of the most typical methods of cooking since at least the early modern period, judging by the prevalence of recipes for simmered dishes in cookbooks from that time.[19] Simmered dishes first require the cook to make stock, typically from *konbu* seaweed (kombu) and dried skipjack tuna flakes (*katsuobushi*), a process too taxing for many consumers today, who buy instant stock mixes instead; this is exemplified by the fact that the bother of making stock was the fourth most common complaint about *washoku* according to the Kikkoman survey.[20] After the stock is prepared, slow boiling of the vegetables, fish, meat and other ingredients can take several hours after everything has been sliced and prepared. Add to that the fact that a full *washoku* meal is supposed to include other dishes, as well as rice and pickles (herbs or vegetables preserved in salt, vinegar, miso or another medium), and one can see how time-consuming preparing *washoku* can be compared to boiling pasta and covering it with readymade spaghetti sauce.

Meals for special occasions such as the New Year celebrations require even more lengthy preparation. *Nishime*, the dried fish and vegetables frequently served at New Year, is made by slowly boiling ingredients in soy sauce, sweetener and ginger until the liquid disappears. *Mochi* rice cakes are also laborious to make by traditional methods, requiring the cook to steam glutinous rice and then pound it in a standing mortar repeatedly to turn it into a paste, before shaping it into cakes.

Despite agreeing that *washoku* was loaded with vegetables, that it provided for a nutritionally balanced meal and that it was healthy, the respondents' top complaint in the Kikkoman survey was that the foods tasted similar.[21] This may be why families with children, regardless of the age group, expressed a slight preference for Western dishes (*yōshoku*) according to the same survey. The difference was more pronounced in households with school-age children. Families with children in elementary school expressed a preference for Western foods 36 per cent higher than *washoku*; for those with middle schoolchildren it was 34 per cent, and for those with children in high school the difference was 24 per cent. The types of Western foods are not specified, but meat dishes, fried foods and spaghetti are typical, which may help to explain why *washoku* dishes that do use meat, as well as wheat noodles (udon), were reported as being served more often at home.[22] The results support Kumakura's assertion that allowing children to dictate the foods prepared at home has led to a decline in the preparation of fish and vegetable dishes the government defines as *washoku*.

The Japanese government in its promotion of *washoku* speaks specifically of seafood to encourage families away from consuming beef and pork (and Western foods in general), an alternative that might be healthier for individuals but not necessarily for the environment.[23] Fish for sushi and sashimi is sourced globally, and 'for nearly a century, Japan has had a major role in the depletion of fish stocks, first in certain areas of the Pacific Ocean and after World War II worldwide', write Vaclav Smil and Kobayashi Kazuhiko in their assessment of the historical changes in the Japanese diet over the last century. The authors conclude that global fish stocks would no longer be sustainable if other countries tried to emulate Japan's habit of seafood consumption.[24] Perhaps in response to such criticism, in its opening paragraph, the Japanese government's UNESCO application invokes the spirit of *washoku* as showing 'respect for nature closely related to the sustainable use of natural resources'.[25]

Rice and Washoku

One point of agreement in all the various definitions of *washoku* is the necessity of rice. Kumakura states specifically that a traditional Japanese meal must have boiled domestic short-grain, non-glutinous rice (temperate *Oryza sativa* var. *japonica*) rather than imported long-grain rice that is fried or steamed.[26] It is no coincidence that rice, the crop most closely managed by the Japanese government through its control of buying, distribution and price supports to farmers (in return for their political support), has been made integral to *washoku*.[27] Rice is one of the few foodstuffs that Japan produces in (almost) sufficient amount to feed its population. Japan grows 95 per cent of the rice needed for domestic food supplies.[28] But compare, for example, the absence of similar rhetoric about soybeans in definitions of *washoku*. Soy foods such as miso, tofu and soy sauce are essential to making Japanese food. Processed soy products might be made in Japan and called *washoku*, but Japan grows only around 5 per cent of the soybeans it consumes, and today most of the beans are imported from the United States.[29] And, despite claims about the importance of rice to *washoku*, Japanese citizens are consuming less rice than ever before. Annual per capita rice supply was 130 kilograms in 1960, amounting to one-quarter of household food expenditure, but by the year 2000, supply was less than half this amount at 60 kilograms and the grain accounted for less than 25 per cent of all food intake. The remainder is from consumption of bread, fats, protein and other foodstuffs.[30]

Rice seems inseparable from the traditional Japanese way of eating, but many experts conclude that consumption of white rice did not become commonplace until the second half of the twentieth century. 'The Japanese people have a composite food culture of eating rice along with miso soup, pickles, and consuming fish', observes Ichikawa Takeo, an expert in regional Japanese cuisine. He continues:

> But, it is correct to say that rice consumption spread throughout the country only after the Second World War; until then there were quite a few places where other grains, tubers, and grains mixed with daikon and turnips were the staple foods.[31]

Harada Nobuo wrote that farmers in Japan did not consume rice regularly perhaps until as late as the 1960s.[32] Depending on the period and location, barley, barnyard millet (*hie*), foxtail millet (*awa*), taro (*satoimo*), sweet potatoes (*satsumaimo*) and nuts have been suggested as more widely consumed staple foods for some Japanese populations than rice. Even those who champion the long history of rice consumption in Japan would have to acknowledge that the polished, boiled then steamed 'white' rice that is served at meals today has a much narrower and shorter history of consumption (measuring roughly four centuries) when compared to the previous two millennia of the history of rice cultivation in Japan, when brown rice was eaten, usually steamed or boiled and mixed with other grains. The assumption, too, that the Japanese had always craved rice despite being unable to eat it is problematic given that at the historic moment in the early 1960s when rice consumption became pervasive and reached a peak, domestic consumption of rice began to fall, and has been declining ever since. Had the Japanese really desired rice, they would be eating more of it today than ever before, but that is not the case.

Today white rice is a certain companion in *washoku* meals to side dishes such as grilled or raw fish, hearty simmered dishes and lightly cooked vegetable dishes dressed with sesame or tofu, but before the 1960s carbohydrates including rice played a more central role as a source of food energy, rather than to complement tasty delicacies. To cite one example, in rural Niigata prefecture in the 1920s, men could consume upwards of 1.3 kilograms of rice daily during the summer farming season.[33] According to government estimates for the period 1911–15, the average per capita daily diet of 2,124 calories consisted of more than 85 per cent carbohydrates, whereas in 2010 the typical diet of 2,458 calories derives only 37 per cent of energy from carbohydrates. The reason for this difference is that the amount of meat eaten increased exponentially over the course of the twentieth century: a home-cooked meal today might include rice, miso soup and pickles along with a pork cutlet, a hamburger or Chinese dumplings, but between 1911 and 1915 animal protein made up just 1 per cent of the average daily caloric intake (in 2010 meat comprised more than 20 per cent).[34] How much meat the Japanese ate historically has been 'one of the most contentious aspects in Japanese food history', writes the food scholar Katarzyna Cwiertka, but it is safe to assume that the amount of beef and pork consumed per capita was even less before the twentieth century. At the turn of the twentieth century, per capita measurements based on production levels indicated that Japanese people ate practically no pork or beef, and on average consumed about one egg and half a teaspoon of milk per month – all negligible amounts.[35] Per capita seafood consumption in the second decade of the twentieth century was also one-tenth of what it would become eight decades later. In other words, whereas the Japanese government's model of a 'traditional' Japanese meal cited earlier draws attention to the side dishes of fish and vegetables, and popular preference gives priority to beef and pork dishes, all these foods would have made relatively insignificant caloric contributions to a diet that was based largely on carbohydrates before the Second World War.

Are Foods from the 1960s Traditional Enough?

In light of the scholarly discussions of *washoku*, what Japanese people think of when they hear the term, and the vague customs and practices the Japanese government is attempting to promote as traditional dietary cultures, we can discover that what is presented as 'traditional' is actually quite modern – dating from the 1960s. This raises three concerns about whether something that is around fifty years old deserves to be called traditional.

Other prominent definitions of traditional Japanese foods take a longer historical view of Japan's food culture. The Kyoto Prefectural Government's designation of a 'traditional Kyoto vegetable' is a variety cultivated before 1868; other locales use the Second World War as a cut-off point between heirloom and modern varieties of produce.[36] Similar lines of demarcation are found in discussions of regional cuisine. Although definitions vary, 'authentic' regional dishes for most of Japan are those said to pre-date 1868, which was the year in which the last premodern warrior government fell (although dishes from Hokkaido are deemed traditional if they existed before the Second World War).[37] Such definitions of traditional foods recognize the profound changes in food production that took place after the Second World War, such as the shift to conventional varieties of fruit and vegetable better suited to the application of chemical fertilizers and pesticides than heirloom varieties.

Another problem of dating a 'traditional cuisine' to the 1960s is that this was a period when Japan had not only recovered from the Second World War but was also enjoying 'miraculous' and unprecedented economic growth – a more than 10 per cent increase in GDP annually. Economic advances allowed wider consumer access to modern appliances that revolutionized the preparation of food. By the mid-1960s, more than half of all households owned an electric refrigerator – a device that was absent from pre-war kitchens – and by 1970 the proportion of refrigerator ownership had climbed to 90 per cent.[38] This new wealth also made possible a traditional Japanese dietary culture rich in seafood, through access to a global network of food producers and markets that could bring fish from foreign waters to Japanese consumers.[39]

But it is not just fresh fish that arrived to satisfy consumers of *washoku*. In 2010, Japan's food self-sufficiency ratio – the amount of food produced domestically to meet a country's needs – was below 40 per cent, a fact that is often cited in the media and by policymakers as an economic and strategic liability.[40] The perception that Japan needs to ramp up domestic food production (and decrease imports) makes the government's promotion of indigenous foodstuffs in *washoku* understandable, but the outcome of such plans is uncertain. Urging the Japanese to eat more *washoku* would require more ingredients and would place greater demand on domestic supplies, which would raise prices and make *washoku* less affordable, and could actually spur more imports. In other words, a more traditional diet might require more ingredients to be sourced from outside the country, as has become the custom.[41]

A third problem with a definition of a culinary tradition that dates only to the 1960s is that it does not give full attention to the variety of ways of eating that existed before that time. Rice, for instance, was eaten regularly throughout Japan before 1960, but other grains such as millet and corn were also important staples, a fact that is in danger of being ignored if designations of 'traditional grain consumption' is restricted to rice. Limiting the definition of *washoku* to a rice-based diet not only denies the prevalence of other staples in the diet, but also indirectly casts aspersions on the people living in less densely populated rural areas who relied on such foods, implying that their diets were outside the mainstream and do not qualify to be part of the nation's traditional food cultures. As Chapter Six reveals, the designation of 'local food' began in the 1920s as a way to describe the non-rice-based diet of people living in the countryside as backward and non-normative, and it is unfortunate that modern definitions of *washoku* preserve this distinction.

Washoku as an Invented Tradition

As a short and narrow representation of history, *washoku* certainly qualifies as an example of an 'invented tradition', or what the anthropologist Theodore Bestor, in reference to Japan's food culture, has called 'traditionalism'.[42] Bestor defines traditionalism as 'a device of cultural ideology that wraps the present in a mantle of venerable antiquity, thereby legitimating the social present by calling attention to its presumed antecedents and origins in the culturally sacrosanct past'. Bestor notes further how, spurred by a creative and selective view of history, Japanese cuisine has become more homogeneous in recent decades, leading to the disappearance of many regional cuisines.[43]

Rather than working to critique *washoku*, most scholarly studies abide by its terms, equating *washoku* with the diet of rice and side dishes of the urban elite. In 1968 the folklorist Segawa Kiyoko criticized historical surveys of Japanese culinary culture that focus on the dining customs of the literate urban elite while ignoring commoners' diets, which do not appear as frequently in written records; and in 2008 a respected group of food scholars made a similar critique of the elitist focus of earlier Japanese food scholarship, indicating that the narrow view of food history remains unchanged some four decades later.[44] Indeed, recent histories of Japanese food and cuisine focus on the foodways of cities, particularly Edo (Tokyo), Osaka and Kyoto, presenting these sites as origins of the country's national cultural heritage while sidelining or ignoring traditions in rural parts of Japan. Such books may describe the slow foods, fast foods, gourmet foods and seasonal foods of Edo, but cast few glances at other parts of Japan in the Edo period (1600–1868).[45] These texts help to support the false notion that all food in premodern Japan was gourmet, varied and delicious. This is certainly the image one can find in culinary texts of the age, but cookbooks read by the elite do not give an accurate picture of the foods eaten by the silent majority. Scholarship that does examine varied aspects of traditional Japanese foodways explores topics in great detail, but without challenging dominant understandings of traditional food.[46]

Rethinking Washoku

For *washoku* more accurately to represent Japan's 'traditional dietary cultures', it should not be confined to an idealized meal or diet of the last half-century, but must include a longer and broader historical perspective. As mentioned earlier, 1868 has become an often used demarcation point between 'traditional' and 'modern' ingredients and recipes, and it is a convenient date for history textbooks also to demarcate premodern and modern Japan, because the last shogunate fell in that year, ushering in the Meiji Restoration and the modernization of Japanese society that followed. However, changes in diet do not necessarily conform to shifts in political history.

Granted, there were many innovations to the diet during the Meiji period (1868–1912), for example the introduction of new foods, including Western products, such as bread and beef. With the arrival of Western foods came an increased recognition of Japanese food. The Meiji period was the age in which the words for Japanese food and cuisine – *washoku* and *Nihon ryōri* – were coined, and it was also the period when particular ingredients deemed essential for 'Japanese' cooking became popularized. Mirin, a sweet alcohol indispensable in the Japanese kitchen today to make simmered dishes, pickles, sauces for grilled foods, dipping broth for noodles and other dishes, was invented at the beginning of the early modern period, but it was not in wide use until the Meiji era.[47] Two of the most popular varieties of rice today, Koshihikari from Niigata prefecture and Sasanishiki, grown in Miyagi and Yamagata prefectures, were developed in the Meiji period.[48] And in the late nineteenth century soy sauce finally eclipsed miso as the most frequently used flavouring throughout Japan.

While urban elites enjoyed exotic Western dishes in the Meiji years, the diet for most of the population, who lived in rural villages, remained largely unchanged from the nineteenth century through to the 1920s and even 1930s. During this time, outside the cities people ate what they produced locally.[49] As the historian Susan Hanley observes, 'Rather than a Westernization of the diet, the Meiji period witnessed the development of a more uniform, "indigenous" diet throughout Japan.'[50]

Instead of pointing to the Meiji Restoration of 1868 as a key turning point in the development of the Japanese diet, many scholars look to the continuities in the diet over that time and contend that there were more drastic changes after the Second World War than after the Meiji Restoration. The cultural geographer Arizono Shōichirō refers to the diet of the first decades of the twentieth century as 'early modern' to point out the continuity between what people ate then and what they consumed in the nineteenth century.[51] Smil and Kobayashi conclude that average per capita food supplies were barely unchanged during the first four decades of the twentieth century, suggesting per capita averages of between 2,100 and 2,200 calories per day. They note further that food imports in this period rose negligibly until the mid-1920s, and foreign shipments of rice and sugar did not form notable shares of overall demand until the late 1930s.[52] In other words, contrary to the situation today, whereby Japan derives 60 per cent of its food supply from foreign sources – the highest rate among affluent countries – in the first decades of the twentieth century it still relied almost entirely on its own domestic production of foodstuffs. Moreover, food production before 1930 was more similar to that of the nineteenth century than of the post-war period: farmers used organic fertilizers such as manure rather than chemical fertilizers; they threshed and milled grain largely by hand instead of using electric machines; and tenant farmers continued to pay their rent in kind, like their forbears, who had offered feudal tribute for centuries. In summary, the argument that food culture before the Second World War was 'traditional' seems easier to defend than to assume that a post-1960 diet is much older and more traditional than it is.

A longer historical perspective should be taken in tandem with the search for 'traditional dietary cultures' beyond just rice, soup, pickles and side dishes. White rice with several tasty side dishes would have been more of a rarefied ideal typical of wealthy households in urban areas than a daily reality for most Japanese before the Second World War. The very distinction between rice, soup and side dishes was meaningless for people outside the cities: rural families typically prepared a meal by cooking a pot of boiled grains, which may or may not have included rice, and adding vegetables and/or tubers and flavourings such as miso directly to the pot to create a dish that mixed grain, soup and side dishes together. Instead of viewing *washoku* as a Copernican solar system of side dishes, miso soup and pickles in orbit around rice, the definition of Japanese dietary cultures should reflect the wider spectrum of what people actually ate before the Second World War, with the daily food of commoners at one end of the spectrum and elite and celebratory dishes at the other.

The idealized version of *washoku* consisting of rice, soup, pickles and three side dishes was only one segment of the traditional diet, one more closely associated with elite culture and holidays than with daily life for most people. Urban homes were equipped with separate cooking areas with stoves that allowed grain and side dishes to be prepared separately, but in rural dwellings cooking took place at the hearth using a cauldron hanging above a fire in which grains could be boiled and additional ingredients added. *Katemeshi* is a typical example of such a dish, consisting of rice and barley or other grains cooked with additions like daikon leaves and/or the root. Before the Second World War fresh seafood was a luxury for communities even just a few kilometres from the coast.[53] Beside assessing differences, approaching *washoku* as a spectrum further enables us to judge continuities in dining patterns, such as the prevalence of pickles and miso soup as accompaniments for humbler one-pot meals and for more complicated meals of multiple side dishes.

The temptation is to view *washoku* chronologically, assuming that simpler cooking methods developed into more complex meals. However, both existed simultaneously before the Second World War, and neither was intrinsically healthy. Consider the examples of a typical urban meal from the late 1930s, consisting of a grain dish (rice alone or mixed with barley), miso soup, pickles and a vegetable or meat side dish, and a typical farmer's meal of a dish of cooked grains accompanied by miso soup, pickles or a dish of stewed vegetables. Neither meal would supply sufficient protein or energy for someone performing physical labour and an emphasis on polished grains could have led to vitamin B1 deficiency and beriberi.[54] And, just because more elaborate modes of dining have become the norm does not mean that the history of how most Japanese ate before the Second World War can be ignored or forgotten. People in mountain villages throughout Japan in the 1940s consumed some rice but relied mostly instead on barnyard millet or other grains mixed with acorns, chestnuts or chopped root vegetables, and it would be disingenuous and disrespectful to exclude their diets from *washoku*.[55]

Anything can be advertised as 'traditional', but if the term is to have any meaning in studies of the history of Japanese food, three criteria are needed. First, despite the claims of governmental promoters of *washoku*, a stronger historical argument can be made that the 'traditional' diet is better represented by dietary conditions before the Second World War than those in the period of rapid economic growth of the 1960s. Second, the traditional diet before the Second World War was far more dependent on carbohydrate-based foods] for energy than it was on meat or even vegetables, which are the main ingredients of *washoku* dishes today. Third, those carbohydrate-based foods extended beyond white rice to include other grains, tubers and sources of starch uncommon in the diet today. Such a definition of the 'traditional' diet may not be very appealing to modern consumers seeking appetizing delicacies or to a government wanting to promote the best of Japanese culinary culture and its goods abroad; but for the purposes of historical study, broadening the concept of tradition helps to contextualize the commodified versions of 'traditional food' on offer today, allows a more inclusive appraisal of the variety of foods once consumed in Japan and gives greater respect to the people who prepared and ate them.

2

TEA CUISINE AND THE ORIGINS OF JAPANESE CUISINE

The previous chapter differentiated between traditional Japanese food, defined as the everyday diet before the Second World War, and Japanese cuisine, which is a more elevated style of dining, with food prepared and consumed according to aesthetic guidelines. Anything eaten for survival could be included in the category of traditional Japanese food, but the gastronomic ideals of Japanese cuisine are harder to delimit and trace historically. Modern Japanese cuisine, especially in its most refined and tasteful forms, is often praised in comparison to the meals served at the tea ceremony, *cha kaiseki*, or tea cuisine. Tea cuisine is said to be the invention of one person, a tea master who lived four centuries ago and whose descendants currently dominate the largest institutions that teach the tea ceremony. This chapter examines how the supposed story of the origin of Japanese cuisine in the tea cuisine of a late sixteenth-century master is not only a simplification and distortion of food history, but also one that benefits the major schools of tea ceremony today. Re-evaluating the putative contributions of the so-called inventor of tea cuisine in comparison to another major, but today largely forgotten, tea practitioner who lived a century later offers a more nuanced understanding of the history of tea cuisine. This leads to the conclusion that the refined aspects of Japanese cuisine developed over a longer period of time and were accomplished thanks to countless nameless contributors rather than one genius.

Tea Cuisine, Japanese Cuisine and Rikyū

Today the word *kaiseki* refers to two types of haute cuisine: tea cuisine (懐石), which signifies the meals served at private tea gatherings, and restaurant *kaiseki* (会席), the multi-course servings of delicacies offered for lunch and dinner at the finest Japanese restaurants.[1] Tea cuisine developed from the late sixteenth century on. Restaurant *kaiseki* evolved more than a century later, as restaurateurs transformed elite forms of banqueting into fare for paying customers.[2] Both modern forms of *kaiseki* feature carefully prepared morsels of food accented by beautiful tableware, offering a high standard to judge the aesthetics of any meal. The *kaiseki* of the tea ceremony has been heralded as 'a paradigm of good taste for most Japanese'.[3] The well-worn expression that Japanese food is 'eaten by the eyes' sums up the importance of appearance and presentation in Japanese food preparation and is epitomized by both forms of *kaiseki*, which have since the late twentieth century gained international recognition and served as an inspiration for nouvelle cuisine in the West.[4] (For clarity, references to *kaiseki* here after refer to the version at tea ceremonies.)

The supposition that modern Japanese cuisine originated in the *kaiseki* meals of the tea ceremony appears in two recent authoritative histories: Kumakura Isao, *Nihon ryōri bunkashi: Kaiseki o chūshin ni* (A Cultural History of Japanese Cuisine, Focusing on Tea Cuisine, 2002), and Katarzyna Cwiertka, *Modern Japanese Cuisine: Food, Power and National Identity* (2006).[5] Both studies attribute the development of tea cuisine to just one person, the tea master Sen no Rikyū (1522–1591), who casts a long shadow in the history of the tea ceremony and Japanese culture more generally.

A *cha kaiseki* meal, 1954.

Rikyū is popularly credited with helping to make tea practice more spiritual, restrained and spartan by imbuing a 'rustic' (*wabi*) sensibility into the tea ceremony and its related arts, such as architecture and ceramics.[6] According to Kumakura and Cwiertka, Rikyū's rustic approach to tea changed the style of meals served at tea gatherings. Kumakura has asserted that tea *kaiseki* was 'perfected' during Sen no Rikyū's lifetime.[7] Cwiertka goes further to identify Rikyū as the creator of 'the fundamental rules of *kaiseki*', dubbing him the 'founding father of *kaiseki*'.[8] These views are not outliers, since the assumption that Rikyū is responsible for perfecting *kaiseki* is widely evident in both popular and scholarly publications in Japanese.[9] As the 'founding father' of tea cuisine, Rikyū would necessarily have had a lasting influence on the history of Japanese cuisine more generally, to the point that after reading these books we might be tempted to call Rikyū the 'founding father' of Japanese cuisine as well.

At stake in this discussion of Rikyū's role in the beginnings of modern Japanese cuisine is not just whom we might praise or blame for the delicate servings of food on our plate at an expensive Japanese restaurant, but how the aesthetic foundation of an important element of national culture – which might even be described as an incarnation of Japanese civilization[10] – has been credited to the creative genius of this one person. Peering at the petite arrangements of delicacies on our plate as we ponder this question, we must recall that cuisine is more than just food. 'Many Japanese assume that food habits are fundamentally related to "national character"', writes Cwiertka, 'and that they reflect people's social and cultural values.'[11] The cuisine of the tea ceremony is especially important in the discussion of national character and national cuisine because the tea ceremony has become synonymous with Japanese national identity in the twentieth century, as Kristin Surak has documented. Surak writes, 'the tea ceremony . . . played an integral role in the construction of an ideology of Japan as a nation-state' by offering a cultural practice that embodied national unity.[12] The tea schools that claim Rikyū as their founding patriarch – Omotesenke, Urasenke and Mushanokōji Senke, which today are the largest and wealthiest institutions that provide instruction in the tea ceremony – helped to transform an elite pastime into national culture, as Surak describes in her study; it was these same institutions that elevated Rikyū's role in the history of Japanese cuisine.

The idea of Rikyū's status as the inventor of tea cuisine was first articulated in tea publications in the late 1930s, but it was not until two decades after the Second World War that the notion gained currency among food historians.[13] The first modern scholarly book on culinary history, Sasagawa

Rinpū and Adachi Isamu's *Kinsei Nihon shokumotsushi* (History of Food in Early Modern Japan), published in 1935, did not give any special preference to Rikyū.[14] Instead, the authors include an anecdote about a later tea practitioner, Katagiri Sekishū (1605–1673), whom they quote as stating:

All cookery should be light cooking; if one thinks to improve the flavor, then first one must prepare heavy food, and then from that heavy food make a light taste. If one from the start seeks to make something light, the quality will turn out bad and it should not be served to guests.[15]

Instead of providing a clear definition of tea cuisine, Sasagawa and Adachi cite examples of meals they identify as tea cuisine and then provide citations that they view as indicative of good cooking in general, such as Seikishū's aforementioned comments. The reader is left with the impression that the dominant rationale for tea cuisine is that it is a simpler form of dining, rather than a way of eating connected exclusively with any one person or philosophical stance.

The idea that Rikyū invented tea cuisine was proposed in the following year in the first modern publication entirely about tea cuisine, a book of essays edited in 1936 by the leaders of the Mushanokōji Senke and Urasenke schools of tea as part of a fifteen-volume series dedicated to the history and culture of tea, *Chadō zenshū* (Complete Texts on the Way of Tea).[16] That tea cuisine is Rikyū's creation is a point made at the beginning of the volume dedicated to tea cuisine, in an essay by Sen Sōshu (1889–1953), the ninth-generation head of Mushanokōji Senke. Sen Sōshu establishes that Rikyū created tea cuisine, that his tea menus were representative of the time when he lived, and that tea cuisine changed little after Rikyū's death;[17] in other words, Rikyū invented and perfected tea cuisine. In the next essay, the fourteenth-generation Urasenke master Sen Sōshitsu (1893–1964) emphasized the spiritual dimension of tea cuisine, tracing its origin and minimalist aesthetics to Zen Buddhism.[18]

Many of the other contributors, which included the noted chef and potter Kitaōji Rosanjin (1883–1959), discoursed on tea cuisine without reference to Rikyū, but the food historian Uotani Tsunekichi (1894–1964) maintains in his essay that Rikyū was the founder of tea cuisine and that the tea master's views towards food were carried on by the Sen families, Rikyū's descendants.[19] As a chef who once owned a successful restaurant in Kobe but who left that career to become the head of a Zen temple in Wakayama, where he wrote about culinary history, Uotani had a background that lent weight to his arguments, supporting the claims and authority of the heads of the Sen schools.[20] Uotani's assertions, and those of the other writers in the volume who lauded Rikyū, helped to elevate the authority of the medieval master to the point that by the start of the Second World War, Rikyū's name had become synonymous with tea, thanks in large part to the efforts of the Sen schools' promotion of him.[21]

It took several decades after the Second World War for culinary historians to accept Rikyū as the founder of the art of tea cuisine, however. The earliest post-war food history continued the view that tea cuisine was best understood as an abbreviated mode of formal banqueting that catered to the tastes of sixteenth-century warlords. Morisue Yoshiaki and Kikuchi Yūjirō's *Shokumotsushi: Nihonjin no shoku seikatsu no hatten* (A History of Food: The Development of the Foodways of the Japanese People), published in 1952, failed to mention Rikyū in its brisk narrative.[22] But when Morisue and Kikuchi published a revised version of their text in 1965, they presented a dramatically changed version of the history of tea cuisine. In that edition, the authors state that Rikyū established a rustic style of tea embodying 'elegant simplicity' inspired by Zen Buddhism. Despite naming other tea masters who were Rikyū's contemporaries, the authors declare that none were able to surpass Rikyū in their cooking.[23] A contemporary text often used in the curriculum of high schools and women's colleges, Watanabe Minoru's *Nihon no shoku seikatsushi* (History of Japanese Foodways), published in 1964, is far bolder in its claims about Rikyū's role in creating tea cuisine, claiming that the master perfected the art of tea.[24] Watanabe did not present any additional evidence to support these claims. In fact, he relied on the same sources cited in Sasagawa and Adachi's publication in 1935.[25] His text indicates that by the mid-1960s food historians simply took for granted Rikyū's invention of tea cuisine and felt little need to prove the point.

The naturalization of the assertion that Rikyū invented tea cuisine accrued to the benefit of his descendants, the leaders, or family heads (*iemoto*), of the Sen schools of tea. Surak explains that the *iemoto* did not claim to have a genius on a par with Rikyū's, but they did not need to. The family heads 'succeeded not to Rikyū's innovative ingenuity or creative skill, but to a body of knowledge they defined and attributed to the master', a fact that nonetheless provided them with authority over techniques, the value of utensils and standards of taste, and gave them multiple sources of lucrative income such as by selling licences to students and by authenticating tea artefacts.[26] Reinforcing Rikyū's authority over tea cuisine, and by extension

Japanese cuisine, assisted the *iemoto* and their disciples in arguing for the wider saliency of the tea ceremony in Japanese culture. Far more people are exposed to some element of Japanese cuisine than the less than 2 per cent of the population that studies the tea ceremony.

Re-evaluating Rikyū

Regardless of the presumed association of Rikyū and cuisine, his specific contributions during his lifetime are hard to discern; it was an age that the historian Morgan Pitelka dubs the 'era of Momoyama [1582–1600] mytho-history' for the fact that our perception of the contributions of men of culture like Rikyū has been shaped by their later biographers.[27] Examining primary sources dating from the period of Rikyū's life and afterwards allows us to understand the structure and ingredients of a few of his tea menus as other people recorded them, but these same sources offer little information about cooking techniques beyond noting some modes of preparation, such as grilling, for certain dishes. Moreover, these sources reveal nothing about what Rikyū's meals looked or tasted like, which raises questions about the basis for the assertion that Rikyū perfected tea cuisine.

Recognizing the lack of historical information about Rikyū's views of cuisine, some scholars have tried to recreate Rikyū's approach to tea food by citing apocryphal sources dating from a century after the tea master's death, while ignoring other primary sources from the same period that reveal much more about the meaning and creation of tea cuisine. A review of the evidence of Rikyū's meals indicates that it is far easier to demonstrate Rikyū's lack of interest in cooking than to prove that he refined or perfected tea cuisine or had a major influence on the development of either tea cuisine or Japanese cuisine.

The basis for the glorification of Rikyū's place in the historical development of tea cuisine and the history of Japanese cuisine comes from three misunderstandings: first, the anachronistic dating of tea cuisine (*kaiseki*) as a cuisine to Rikyū's lifetime, when the term *kaiseki* was not even widely used for the meals served at tea ceremonies and there was no standard word for these meals; second, the overinterpretation of data about Rikyū's tea ceremony menus, which are few in number and found in just one historical record; and third, a dependence on apocryphal sources attributed to Rikyū to flesh out discussions of his tea dining and recover his philosophy of tea cuisine using ideas that more accurately reflect the preferences, a century after his death, of some of his self-appointed successors, particularly the Sen families, who claimed him as their founding patriarch. Since these three misunderstandings either stem from or are compounded by a lack of historical documentation, it is important to review the main primary sources scholars use to document Rikyū's tea menus to learn what information these texts do and do not provide. The same posthumous sources can also provide evidence about how Rikyū's fame grew a hundred years after his death and how tea aficionados in that period construed and constructed his presumed innovations in tea cuisine.

Despite the claims, the historical evidence does not show that Rikyū was a notable cook. But all that is lacking in Rikyū's approach to food – namely, an appreciation for the philosophical and sensual aspects of cooking – is found in the writings of Endō Genkan, a famous tea practitioner, expert on tea cuisine and prolific writer about tea, but one who has no modern descendants or school of disciples and hence has received far less scholarly attention than Rikyū.[28] Though he was contemporaneous with the so-called revival of Rikyū's ideas facilitated by the creation of apocryphal writings attributed to Rikyū, Endō took a completely different tack towards tea food that explored its important role in the tea ceremony and celebrated the many pleasures of dining in that setting. Previous scholarship on tea cuisine inexplicably omits serious study of Endō's work, particularly his *Guide to Meals for the Tea Ceremony*, despite the fact that this was the first printed book devoted to tea cuisine.[29] Whether Endō's work can be viewed as a missing link in the development of tea cuisine awaits further study, and perhaps depends on whether one aligns oneself with his goals for tea food or adheres to those associated with Rikyū. However, there is no dispute that Endō's thought about tea food is more developed and much easier to document than Rikyū's and consequently deserves more attention than Rikyū in histories of Japanese cuisine. Of course, to replace Rikyū with Endō as the founding father of tea cuisine would merely substitute one figurehead for another. However, evaluating the contributions of these two tea masters side by side provides a more nuanced and historical understanding of the development of both tea cuisine and Japanese cuisine than has been offered by earlier studies that attribute the perfection of the former and the origin of the latter to Rikyū alone.

Sources for Rikyū's Tea Cuisine

A paucity of historical sources makes evaluating Rikyū's interest in cooking and his possible contribution to the development of tea cuisine difficult.

We do not have any text written in his hand that provides a glimpse of what he felt about food, what he served or what he ate at tea ceremonies or ordinary meals. Menus from his tea ceremonies are found in the records of other tea masters, so we are forced to read about Rikyū's cooking through their eyes. *Matsuya kaiki* (Matsuya Record of Gatherings), for example, a tea journal assembled by three generations of the Matsuya merchant family of tea practitioners from Nara, mentions sixteen of Rikyū's tea ceremony menus.[30] Like other tea diaries of the period, the focus of *Matsuya Record of Gatherings* was on the utensils used in the ceremony. As the historian Mary Elizabeth Berry has indicated, 'Observations about the tea itself, the setting, food, conversation and etiquette – all were dispensable' and omitted.[31] Consequently, tea journals typically exclude data that might help to reconstruct Rikyū's role in the history of tea cuisine. This gap suggests a relative lack of interest in food and cooking among tea men of Rikyū's era, a time when professional chefs (*hōchōnin*) in the employ of elite warriors and aristocrats were, in increasing numbers, recording the secrets to cuisine in manuscripts.[32] The few records in *Matsuya Record of Gatherings*, and the still fewer in the tea journal maintained from 1548 to 1616 by three generations of the Tsuda merchant family from Sakai, are the only reliable historical records for Rikyū's tea gatherings.[33] Only the former, however, mentions any of the foods Rikyū served at his teas. Neither of these tea records was published until the twentieth century; in the early modern period their circulation was limited to a few handwritten copies, which severely restricted knowledge about Rikyū's style until centuries after his death.

Rikyū's clearest philosophical statements on cooking, which are few in number but often repeated in scholarship, come from an apocryphal source, *Nanpō's Record* (*Nanpōroku*), said to be a transcript of teachings Rikyū certified as authentic. Tea scholars admit that *Nanpō's Record*, which is presented as a collection of seven volumes of Rikyū's oral instructions and tea ceremonies transcribed by a mysterious (and entirely fictitious) disciple named Nanpō, was in fact a work created by the samurai *littérateur* Tachibana Jitsuzan (1655–1708), who posed as the rediscoverer of these 'lost' texts. Yet these same highly respected scholars frequently cite *Nanpō's Record* as more revelatory of Rikyū's philosophy than of Tachibana's own ideas.[34] Some of the information in *Nanpō's Record* might be based on earlier writings by Rikyū or a close disciple, but we have no basis from which to determine which parts may be authentic and which are later additions or revisions, making the entire work revealing about practices and ideas from the end of the seventeenth century but anachronistic for those of Rikyū's lifetime a century before.[35]

Nanpō's Record contains both pithy statements on tea food and a record of tea gatherings with menus; the latter was based in part on another historically problematic record, *Rikyū hyakkaiki* (Rikyū's Hundred Teas).[36] Published a decade before the compilation of *Nanpō's Record*, *Rikyū's Hundred Teas* documents 87 tea ceremonies by the master in the final years of his life.[37] The original compiler of the writings is unknown and the earliest version remains preserved as a 'hidden text', a manuscript held by a private owner who does not make it available to scholars.[38] The dates of the ceremonies are especially in need of clarification because the years listed in the existing versions are considered inaccurate, which casts doubts on the entire work's reliability.[39] *Rikyū's Hundred Teas* appeared in print in 1680, on the cusp of the 'Rikyū revival', the efforts of Rikyū's self-appointed artistic descendants to infuse rusticity into tea, a style they credited to Rikyū. The date of publication provides circumstantial evidence that the text, either in full or revised form, dates from after Rikyū's lifetime, meaning that, like *Nanpō's Record*, it is in fact indicative of preferences in the tea world of the late seventeenth century and not of the sixteenth.

Designating a Tea Cuisine

Although Rikyū is called the founding father or perfecter of tea cuisine, the term 'tea cuisine' (*kaiseki*) was not widely used to describe the meals at tea ceremonies in his lifetime. Today, the *kaiseki* meal served at the tea ceremony is usually written with the kanji for 'warming stone' (懐石), reflecting what is said to be a time-honoured custom among Zen monks to place a heated stone in the front of their robes to stave off hunger. Despite suggesting a possible origin of tea food in a strange monastic custom, the writing of *kaiseki* as 'warming stone' actually dates from a century after Rikyū's death and appears first in the apocryphal *Nanpō's Record*.[40] The text includes several famous pronouncements Rikyū allegedly made about tea cuisine, and is relied upon by modern tea scholars such as Tsutsui Hiroichi for reconstructing Rikyū's philosophy on tea food. Tsutsui directly associates the way of writing *kaiseki* as 'warming stone' with Rikyū's Zen Buddhist practice and his spartan attitudes towards food.[41] In reading these two characters, Tsutsui thereby takes the inventive word choice – or misspelling – by Tachibana in *Nanpō's Record* as an indication of Rikyū's spirituality and concern for tea cuisine; in fact, there is no evidence that Rikyū even knew this word, coined a century after his death, or that he would think that a hot rock would be worthy of mention. Moreover, though *Nanpō's Record* introduced the way of writing *kaiseki* as 'warming stone', this spelling of the word *kaiseki* was not popularized until the Meiji period (1868–1912).[42]

In Rikyū's era there was no generally accepted term for the meals served at tea ceremonies, and the association between the word *kaiseki* and tea food was hardly solidified.[43] The term *kaiseki* did exist in Rikyū's time, but was written with the kanji for 'sitting together' (会席). While this way of writing *kaiseki* is synonymous with the *kaiseki* meals served in Japanese restaurants today, in the medieval period it was a term closely associated with gatherings for composing poetry. For instance, the tea text *Yamanoue Sōjiki* (Yamanoue Sōji's Record, 1588) compares the layout of the tea room to a gathering place for composing poetry (会席).[44] In one of the first appearances of the word, the fourteenth-century war tale *Taiheiki* (Chronicle of Great Peace) refers to a poetry gathering as a *kaiseki* (会席). This word *kaiseki* did not refer to dining until about 200 years later, when it appeared in the 1560s to describe the meals at tea gatherings. Written this way, the word *kaiseki* continued to be used throughout the early modern period to refer to get-togethers to compose poetry.[45] Thus, *kaiseki* did not refer consistently to the meals at tea ceremonies until well after Rikyū's lifetime.[46]

Lacking a standard term for tea cuisine, tea masters in Rikyū's time referred to the meals at tea gatherings as 'the menu' (*kondate* or *shitate*) or 'the meal' (*furumai*), among other terms.[47] In *Rikyū's Hundred Teas*, there is no term used to introduce the menus: dishes are simply listed along with the utensils and participants in the description of the tea event. Kumakura Isao suggests that this absence of terminology indicates the lack of a 'tea style of cuisine' until Rikyū's time, which he also suggests was when tea cuisine crystallized.[48] But, following the same logic, it is hard to say that Rikyū created or even refined *kaiseki* when that term was not in general use during or shortly after his lifetime to distinguish tea cuisine, and when there was no standard term for the meals served at tea ceremonies in his lifetime. If Rikyū did do something innovative with tea food, it is hard to imagine why he or one of his disciples did not put a name to it, perhaps even being so bold as to name it after Rikyū himself to indicate his contribution. After all, many other tea objects bear Rikyū's name to reflect his supposed preferences or inventions, including types of tea containers (*natsume*), combs, pillboxes (*inrō*), sandals, chopsticks and shades of colours, as well as types of pottery, kettles and sweet filled buns (*manjū*). It is hard to imagine why Rikyū's culinary innovation, especially one so important and revolutionary, would not be recognized in a similar way with a new name. The lack of consistency in the terminology for tea ceremony meals suggests that tea cuisine had not taken full form as a cuisine during Rikyū's lifetime. Additionally, since tea writings from Rikyū's age do not speak to the artistic or philosophical underpinnings of tea cuisine, some tea scholars avoid using the term *kaiseki* cuisine for that of Rikyū's time, prefering other terms instead.[49]

Determining when and how *kaiseki* became a cuisine requires an aesthetic judgement, but one important step in the creation of a widely recognized cuisine is the establishment and dissemination of the parameters for that cuisine through popular media such as print.[50] Rikyū died on the eve of Japan's print revolution, at the turn of the seventeenth century, which made available for the first time artistic writings – including culinary ones – that had previously been the preserve of closed lineages of professionals who guarded their secrets in manuscript form. Print also enabled many more authors to create new texts for a wider readership. Consequently, in tracing the genesis of *kaiseki* as a cuisine, attention should be given to the role of printed texts in establishing the foundational principles of tea cuisine and informing the public about them. Beyond several apocryphal works attributed to Rikyū, which had appeared in print by the late seventeenth century, one of the most important yet inexplicably under-studied books for the history of tea cuisine is Endō Genkan's *Guide to Menus for the Tea Ceremony* (1696). As described in further detail below, this book provided recipes, serving suggestions, guidance on manners and a wealth of information beyond the terse listing of menu items found in records of tea gatherings. Moreover, Endō's text demonstrates a profound artistic sense and a philosophical basis for tea cuisine, which are lacking in the data for the meals attributed to Rikyū. In order to place this observation in more concrete terms, the following section examines the meals attributed to Rikyū before introducing by way of comparison the serving suggestions for tea food in Endō's *Guide*.

Reading 'Rikyū's' Tea Menus

Though we can never know what his tea cuisine tasted like, a sense of what Rikyū supposedly served, and any claims regarding his role in the development of tea cuisine, might be inferred from evaluating the 87 meals dating from between 1590 and a month before his death in 1591 that are listed in *Rikyū's Hundred Teas*. Though an apocryphal writing, it is nevertheless the most complete statement about Rikyū's culinary agenda for tea, and after its publication would have been central to discussions of the tea master's approach to tea cuisine. Such apocryphal texts helped to popularize the authority of the tea master a century after his death, but, far from showcasing

Rikyū's culinary genius, the 87 tea menus in *Rikyū's Hundred Teas* provide little indication that Rikyū took much of an interest in meal preparation; the menus tend to be repetitive and suggest that he usually stuck to the same ingredients. We find that ingredients for grilled dishes, fish salad (*namasu*), a forerunner of sashimi, and other side dishes were: salmon (appears 27 times), sea bream (22), fermented sea cucumber intestines (*konowata*, 22), carp (21), abalone (18), black kombu (*kurome*, 16), fishcake (*kamaboko*, 11), tofu (7), small bird (*kotori*, 6), crucian carp, burdock, eel (4), shiitake mushrooms, miso mixed with yuzu, goose, turbo (3), wheat gluten (*fu*), pigeon, *fuhichi* (?), harvest fish (*managatsuo*), ark shell (*akagai*), quail (2), ayu (sweetfish), stew (*nabeyaki*), anchovy, spiced miso (*horomiso*), sea cucumber (*tawarako*), salad of dried fish (*mizuae*), *yakimiso*, song bird (*unjaku*, 1). Ingredients for soups were: miso-coated items (*misoyaki*, 16), goose, vegetables (12), fermented soybeans (*nattō*, 10), swan (8), cod, oysters (5), small birds, shiitake mushrooms, taro (3), blowfish, sea bream, duck (2), crane, *atsumejiru*, sliced ingredients (*tataki*), carp, pheasant (1).[51]

Tsutsui Hiroichi, who tabulated these numbers, credited Rikyū with infusing Buddhist vegetarian cooking into tea cuisine.[52] However, a strict vegetarian diet is not indicated by this list of ingredients, which includes a variety of fish and fowl dishes that far outnumber the few non-meat ingredients such as shiitake and wheat gluten. The method of preparing the vegetable dishes is unspecified, and may have included the use of stock made from fish or bird flesh and bone.[53]

When compared with modern tea cuisine, the ingredients listed in *Rikyū's Hundred Teas* make us cognizant of the huge gap between what Rikyū is said to have served and the cuisine found in tearooms and restaurants in Japan today. Besides Japanese crane, which is now an endangered species, Rikyū allegedly served fowl including goose and swan, which one would be hard-pressed to find on any modern Japanese menu, but these birds were favourites at warrior banquets in the late medieval period.[54] Two of the fish species served most frequently at banquets for samurai – carp and crucian carp (*funa*) – were both popular in the medieval period but were later superseded by ocean fish, particularly sea bream. For tea 'sweets', *Rikyū's Hundred Teas* indicates a preference for savouries such as wheat gluten, chestnuts, roasted Japanese nutmeg, kombu, grilled rice cakes, soymilk skin (*yuba*), persimmons and rice crackers.[55] These savouries mark a clear distinction between the tea refreshments in Rikyū's period, when sugar was still an expensive import, and the sugary, soft or hard tea confectionery popular since the late seventeenth century. In sum, we cannot ignore the medieval preferences in the selection of ingredients attributed to Rikyū, which many diners today would find unpalatable. Clearly, tea cuisine in Rikyū's period – as described in an apocryphal work that appeared nearly a century after his death – had a long journey to travel before it became anything like modern tea cuisine or modern Japanese cuisine.

Judging from the above list of ingredients, *Rikyū's Hundred Teas* reveals that Rikyū was a chef who favoured a limited repertoire of foodstuffs, which is surprising considering that in the period supposedly covered by the book, the tea master was employed by the most powerful person in Japan, the warlord Toyotomi Hideyoshi (1537–1598), who unified the country in 1590 after more than a century of civil war. Hideyoshi's patronage would presumably have allowed Rikyū access to the best ingredients money could buy and provided him with delicacies from around the country, offered in tribute either to Hideyoshi or to Rikyū himself. Nevertheless, almost one-third of the 87 meals listed feature salmon and one-quarter include sea bream or use fermented sea cucumber intestines. The repetition of dishes is exemplified by fourteen meals in the first month of 1591. Ten of these fourteen meals, more than 71 per cent, include fermented sea cucumber intestines, which was a delicacy, but too much even of a good thing can become tedious.[56] In the eleventh month of the previous year, Rikyū had allegedly used black kombu in eleven out of 24 meals; on one occasion he used black kombu for four meals in a row and on another for three in a row.[57] From Rikyū's choice of black kombu, we might conclude that he had a rustic approach to tea cuisine, but he – or those writing on his behalf – could have easily taken further steps towards rustic humility by using more vegetables instead of fish and fowl; or, had he truly thought that meals should evoke spirituality, he could have served the humble grain gruel with pickles that sustains Zen monks.

Beyond the repetition of ingredients, the same text shows that Rikyū often repeatedly served the same dishes for several days. For example, the meals for the twentieth to twenty-second days of the eleventh month of 1590 are virtually identical: they featured fishcake, carp salad in a vinegar miso dressing (*nuta-ae*) and a soup of oyster mushrooms (*hiratake*). On the twenty-first, a dish of duck cooked in a pot was added.[58] These meals do not give the impression that Rikyū was interested in culinary exploration, especially if he was directing someone else to cook for him, which may have been the case given his status as tea master to the powerful. Perhaps Rikyū was repetitive in his choice of foods and tea implements because his meals demonstrated perfection. However, a decision to repeat foods and ingredients could also betray the attitude of someone who was conservative and unable to think inventively with food, which is hardly a characteristic one would apply to someone who perfected a cuisine.

Another distinction between Rikyū's menus considered thus far and modern tea cuisine is the lack of attention in the descriptions to the pairing of ingredients. The 'artful selection and arrangement' (*toriawase*) of ingredients and pairing of prepared foods is a defining characteristic of Japanese cuisine today, especially of restaurant and tea *kaiseki*.[59] *Nanpō's Record* suggests that Rikyū anticipated the importance of the artful selection of foods for a meal with his proclamation: 'The arrangement of the meal, its strong and light [flavours], is of course as important as the selection of tea utensils.'[60] Yet the rationale for the pairings of dishes and ingredients in *Rikyū's Hundred Teas* is hard to divine. For the menus from the eighth month to the tenth month of 1590, some fourteen of the 21 meals contain a fish salad (*namasu*).[61] Fish salad usually included one or more types of sliced fish with garnishes of vegetables and fruits typically in a vinegar dressing. *Namasu* were central to medieval and early modern banqueting cuisine, occupying the middle of the main tray in meals, which might have two, four, six or more additional short trays, each bearing more soups and side dishes.[62] Omitting the ingredients of the *namasu* leaves a huge gap in the record of Rikyū's meals and makes the rationale for his selection of ingredients impossible to know. Similarly, Rikyū's favourite soup in these menus, *misoyaki*, is something cooked in miso, but we have no idea what. Had harmonization – or even taste – been critical to the unknown scribe who recorded these occasions, then the ingredients and methods of preparation of these central dishes would have been included. Indeed, if Rikyū cared about his reputation as a chef, he might have been insulted by the attribution of *Rikyū's Hundred Teas* to him because the text depicts him as someone whose cooking favoured repetition over innovation and was memorable more for its frequently appearing ingredients than for its culinary innovations.

In *Nanpō's Record*, Tachibana Jitsuzan, the author who posed as the work's alleged transmitter, demonstrated familiarity with *Rikyū's Hundred Teas* by plagiarizing parts of it; and he appears to have anticipated the criticism that Rikyū's tea menus were repetitive and lacklustre. However, Tachibana presents redundancy not as a flaw but as a virtue of Rikyū's approach; he included a colophon to the list of tea gatherings in which Rikyū chastised his disciple Nanpō, the alleged compiler of *Nanpō's Record*, for focusing on different tea gatherings and not recognizing the rationale for repetition:

The tea gatherings excerpted here are only the occasions when things like the utensils and conventions were different, and I am opposed to that. I would like you to review these and understand my true intentions. I never desire change: when everything is just the same day after day, one's process of thinking is constantly revised, and everything is as it should be. A focus on the rarity of the procedures, decorations and combinations of utensils results in a distasteful tea gathering.[63]

While affirming Rikyū's presumed preference for monotony over innovation, Tachibana did not have Rikyū pass comment on the meals served for the tea gatherings in *Nanpō's Record* except to imply that there were even more repetitive or less remarkable meals that Nanpō failed to record. Since the menus in *Nanpō's Record* were derivative of the tea meetings described in *Rikyū's Hundred Teas*, which were noted previously for their repetitive nature, one can only guess at how much more tedious were the more typical meals that Rikyū – as channelled by Tachibana – had in mind.

Like the flowers in the tearoom alcove, which must be changed frequently, food cannot be reused indefinitely, and the tea menu can also serve as a reminder of the change of season, as in modern Japanese cooking. Unfortunately, the connection between food and seasonality escapes anyone's notice in *Nanpō's Record*. Tachibana did not allow Rikyū to recognize that, in contrast to other items such as tea utensils, which can remain static day after day, food must be replaced at every tea meeting. Tachibana, who mentions *kaiseki* by name only twice in *Nanpō's Record*, missed the opportunity to allow Rikyū to recognize the effervescent quality of culinary ingredients, the practical needs of the chef and the potential of food to express and evoke larger ideas, such as the change of season. *Nanpō's Record*'s silence on the potential for cuisine to be an object of intellectual and artistic creativity or contemplation suggests either that Tachibana lacked the knowledge or the sensitivity to portray Rikyū as realizing the full possibilities of tea food, or that the unknown sources Tachibana used to compose *Nanpō's Record* reveal that the full understanding of the potential of tea food to reflect seasonality and suggest larger ideas post-dated Rikyū's lifetime.

Besides an assumed preference for repetition, Rikyū developed a reputation in the early modern period for disliking rare gourmet foods, an image that is contradicted by the aforementioned menus attributed to him. One famous apocryphal story in *Chawa shigetsushū* (Tea Stories: The Moon

Pointing Collection, 1701) presents an episode in which Rikyū criticized the use of fishcake at an impromptu tea ceremony meal because it was a 'luxury'.[64] Rikyū's criticism seems rather petty, since fishcake can be made using any fish – even a prosaic one like catfish. Rikyū allegedly served fishcake eleven times, on four more occasions than when he served tofu, according to *Rikyū's Hundred Teas*. According to the same text, he offered more luxurious foods including crane soup, which was reserved for high-ranking warriors and nobles. He went so far as to garnish one dish with gold leaf as part of a menu from the thirteenth day of the ninth month of 1590.[65] But the image of Rikyū as parsimonious chef is reinforced by a famous passage from *Nanpō's Record* where he is reported as saying, 'rare tastes are to be avoided . . . and [tea] meals should be just enough so that the guests avoid starvation.'[66]

The command to avoid rare tastes is hard to reconcile with the list of ingredients in *Rikyū's Hundred Teas*. Rarity is relative and less of a concern for someone working for the elite. Certainly by early modern standards, Rikyū's menus featured some rare tastes prominently. For example, fermented sea cucumber intestines, which became one of the top three delicacies in the early modern period, rank number two in the list of commonly served items in Rikyū's tea ceremony menus according to *Rikyū's Hundred Teas*. Although Rikyū's censure of rare tastes can be viewed as indicating a preference for simplicity, exemplifying his efforts to promote a rustic style of tea ceremony, the same passage could also reveal the lack of a coherent philosophy of food to the point that the success of a meal for Rikyū could be judged by the ability to prevent guests from fainting from hunger, which is a very low bar for measuring the qualities of any meal or the perfection of a cuisine.

Cuisine as Structure over Food

Historians do not dwell long on the ingredients of Rikyū's tea menus because they view the way Rikyū structured those meals as having made the most lasting contribution to the development of tea cuisine and Japanese cuisine. The following section presents the idea that Rikyū refined or perfected tea cuisine by reducing the structure of a tea ceremony meal to just one soup and two or three side dishes. An evaluation of the data used to support this theory reveals that the conclusion that Rikyū promoted a particular style of tea dining is based more on guesswork than on historical evidence.

Tsutsui Hiroichi provides the most detailed exposition of the observation made by several scholars that Rikyū preferred to serve just one soup with two or three side dishes at tea gatherings.[67] Tsutsui's words echo the late seventeenth-century *Nanpō's Record*, which presents Rikyū as stating that the foundation of tea cuisine is precisely this structure, or an even simpler one: 'The type of food to be served in a small tea room is one soup and one or two side dishes with a little sake. It is inappropriate to have a grand meal for a rustic tea sitting.'[68] Tsutsui forms his conclusions by reviewing the tea menus in *Rikyū's Hundred Teas* to find that, with several exceptions, Rikyū stuck to a pattern of offering just a soup and two or three side dishes to his guests. The structure of tea menus in *Rikyū's Hundred Teas* and the number of their occurrences reported by Tsutsui were: one soup, two side dishes (44); one soup, three side dishes (32); two soups, two side dishes (3); one soup, four side dishes (2); two side dishes (2); two soups, three side dishes (2); one soup, one side dish (1); and one soup, five side dishes (1).[69] Thus, by Tsutsui's tabulation *Rikyū's Hundred Teas* demonstrates a preference for a single soup with a few side dishes, but the text also reveals that Rikyū was not wedded to that structure all the time, which suggests a greater diversity in his modes of tea menus to suit different occasions. On two occasions, he did not offer a soup at all.

Based on the fact that extant versions of *Rikyū's Hundred Teas* date from well after Rikyū's lifetime, the tea scholar Tani Akira challenges the conclusion that *Rikyū's Hundred Teas* actually reveals Rikyū's approach to tea cuisine. Tani explains that *Rikyū's Hundred Teas* may have been reworked by a later editor seeking to create an idealized version of what was assumed to be Rikyū's preferred style.[70] In other words, the menus may have been edited so that most reflected the style of one soup and two or three side dishes. Thus, we cannot know if the text is truthful to Rikyū's preferences or to the assumptions of later editors.

However, Tsutsui also turns to a less historically problematic source, the *Matsuya Record of Gatherings*, for insight into Rikyū's preferred meal structure. These menus include the earliest we have for Rikyū, dating from the second month of 1544, when he was just 22 years old, and another from 1590, when he was 68. In nine of the sixteen menus in *Matsuya Record of Gatherings*, Rikyū preserved the pattern of one soup and two or three side dishes. On five occasions, he offered two soups with between one and three side dishes, and at two tea gatherings he served a soup with four side dishes. Thus, more than half (56.3 per cent) of these meals followed a format of just one soup and two or three side dishes.[71] When more than half of the meals reliably attributable to Rikyū follow the same pattern, it is tempting to try to identify his preference for menu structure. Nevertheless, these nine meals appear in just one historical record and span a period of more than four and a half decades of Rikyū's career. Nine meals represent simply too small a sample size to judge his preferences regarding tea cuisine from the course of his lifetime. Instead of making a philosophical statement about the correct form of cuisine, his choice of serving style on these nine occasions might reflect his attitude towards his guests, or it might indicate that the ingredients that he wanted to serve were not available or had spoiled. Moreover, the *Matsuya Record of Gatherings* indicates that on five occasions (over 31 per cent of the meals) Rikyū offered two soups, a fact that is hard to reconcile with an assumed preference for serving just one soup.

Adding the sixteen reliable records in *Matsuya Record of Gatherings* to the 87 historically problematic ones in *Rikyū's Hundred Teas* yields only 103 tea menus from the entire course of Rikyū's career, and we are left to wonder what he served the rest of the time and to people outside the presence of the composers of these texts. Assuming that Rikyū held a tea ceremony with a meal every five days, that would leave 3,431 tea menus unaccounted for from his 47-year career from 1544 to 1591.[72] This is a conservative estimate for a tea master who served powerful warlords and other members of the elite, as well as their humbler associates. Rikyū hosted 61 teas in three and a half months – roughly two ceremonies every three days – with up to four ceremonies on a single day, according to *Rikyū's Hundred Teas*.[73] In other words, even with a conservative estimate of a full tea ceremony every five days of his tea career, the tea menus recorded in *Matsuya Record of Gatherings* and *Rikyū's Hundred Teas* combined would comprise just 3 per cent of the total number of meals Rikyū served at his tea ceremonies, requiring a qualification to the assertion that the meals in these writings are representative of his style of tea in any way.

To express more concretely the composition of Rikyū's tea menus, Tsutsui selected from *Matsuya Record of Gatherings* one menu from the nineteenth day of the first month of 1583 as 'representative of Rikyū's tea cuisine'.[74] On this date, Rikyū served sea bream, fermented sea cucumber intestines, something (perhaps a rice cake or vegetable) grilled and served with sweet miso topping, a soup made from greens and quail, and five different tea sweets: sweet filled bun, Japanese nutmeg, roasted chestnuts, shiitake and arrowhead. As interesting as this menu of one soup and three side dishes may be for its several savoury tea sweets, Tsutsui presents no rationale for why it is particularly representative when viewed against the potential number of Rikyū's meals during his career that are not recorded in this source or any other. Indeed, it is difficult to rationalize how any of Rikyū's meals in

Matsuya Record of Gatherings could be called 'representative of Rikyū's tea cuisine' when that meal was only one of thousands of Rikyū's tea menus during his career. Although *Matsuya Record of Gatherings* could be suggestive of Rikyū's approach to tea menus, any conclusions drawn from it need to be cautious and qualified, which is not the approach adopted in prior studies.

Rikyū's menu structure of one soup and two or three side dishes was typical rather than innovative among late sixteenth-century tea practitioners. Whereas medieval banquets for the court or warrior elite typically had three, five or seven trays of food per person, reducing the amount of food served at tea gatherings became customary among tea practitioners of the time. Records of tea gatherings of the sixteenth century reveal that the most basic form of a tea menu consisted of a tray with rice, soup and a side dish accompanied by another, more elaborate side dish, followed by sweets served before the tea. In other words, the 'one soup, two side dish' format on a single tray was standard, but, as Tani writes, 'the tea cuisine recorded in sixteenth-century records of tea gatherings can be thought of as variations on the theme of the aforementioned single-tray style; and according to the occasion this format might be drastically altered to create something grandiose.' For example, menus for the tea ceremony were elaborated for special occasions to include other dishes prepared in various ways, or with the use of additional trays with soups and more side dishes when the meals were for someone of high rank.[75] In sum, while tea practitioners in Rikyū's era already shared the view that the minimal amount of food to be served at a tea gathering was one soup and a few side dishes, that did not prevent them from adjusting the size of the menu depending on the occasion and guests present.

Though he is credited for this innovation, there does not appear to be much evidence to support the theory that Rikyū was a forceful advocate for a tea menu of one soup and three side dishes. Other tea masters before Rikyū have been incorrectly credited with creating a tea ceremony meal with one soup and three side dishes. Rikyū's teacher Takeno Jōō (1502–1555), for example, is alleged to have written, 'one soup and three side dishes are suitable to tea cuisine. One should not exceed that amount even for special guests.'[76] In contradiction to this statement, Jōō's actual tea menus usually involved two or three trays of food per person with serving dishes covered in gold and silver leaf.[77] The fiction of Jōō's directive suggests an attempt to create a genealogy for a certain structure of tea menu all the way back to Rikyū's teacher. If Rikyū had advocated strongly that tea menus should consist of no more than one soup and two or three side dishes, one would expect his associates and disciples to have adopted that pattern, yet by and large they did not. The Matsuya family, who provide the only historical records of Rikyū's tea menus, continued to enjoy a variety of types of meal at their tea ceremonies varying in size and complexity during Rikyū's lifetime, and their tea feasts became even more lavish after his death. The culinary historian Harada Nobuo has explained that only a minority of Rikyū's disciples, including his sons and the warlord Furuta Oribe (1543–1615), used a meal structure of one soup and two or three side dishes.[78] Based on a study of records of tea gatherings from after Rikyū's lifetime, Tani concludes that the meal format of one soup and a few side dishes did not become the main style of tea cuisine until the mid-eighteenth century, and that tea practitioners in the years following Rikyū's death preferred to serve two soups and multiple side dishes.[79] In other words, a century and a half elapsed after Rikyū's death before most tea practitioners adopted the custom of serving just one tray with a soup and a few side dishes.

Assumptions about Rikyū's preferred structure of tea menus have given rise to suppositions about the philosophical basis for this type of menu format. After citing an example of a meal from *Rikyū's Hundred Teas*, Kumakura Isao writes:

> The menu was not limited to one soup and three dishes because of an insufficiency of food, however, but rather to allow for better appreciation of the taste of the food that was served. It was a humanistic meal . . . I say humanistic because *kaiseki* cuisine was the first cuisine to reflect a sense of season and a sensitivity to human feelings.[80]

Kumakura's elegant appraisal may apply to modern tea cuisine, but it is hard to substantiate for Rikyū's period for several reasons, the first of which is the problematic nature of defining *kaiseki* as a cuisine in Rikyū's lifetime, as mentioned earlier. Second, none of the sources about Rikyū's tea menus, even the apocryphal ones, records the taste of the dishes. Third, the importance of seasonality is not only omitted from even apocryphal texts attributed to Rikyū, but is also a modern concern – one born in a period when it became possible to eat non-seasonal foods, such as watermelon in winter, thanks to improvements in transportation, refrigeration and other technology. As Kumakura himself observed in a different context, it was not until the late nineteenth century that tea masters in published writings paid attention to rules of seasonality in creating idealized tea menus.[81] Finally, we cannot presume to know what Rikyū or any of his diners felt when they peered at a plate of sardines, or any other dish they were served, especially since no one recorded these thoughts. They may have been concerned about 'human feelings', or they may have been glad that they had already eaten before attending Rikyū's tea, where the only purpose of the food was to prevent starvation. All this makes Kumakura's suppositions about the philosophical dimension of Rikyū's mode of serving tea meals hard to swallow.

Even menus that follow the prescribed pattern of one soup and two or three side dishes can vary enough to indicate that it would be reductionistic to deduce that meals in this pattern follow a unified culinary philosophy. For example, the menus of Endō Genkan, whose views on tea cuisine are described in further detail below, follow the same pattern of one soup and two or three side dishes. The difference between Endō's menus and those attributed to Rikyū is that rather than restrict his side dishes to a single item, Endō included several ingredients prepared separately or combined as one side dish. For the seventh day of the eleventh month, he suggests a simmered dish, a side dish and pickles as the accompaniment to rice and soup, which follows a structure of one soup and two side dishes, not counting the pickles. However, Endō's soup is made from blowfish, which would have been a challenge to prepare and titillating to eat owing to the deadly poison for which the fish is famous. The simmered dish contains abalone, yam, freshwater seaweed and umeboshi, and the side dish consists of a small grilled fish and steamed flounder. He follows this with sake and a soup of sea bream and yuzu, accompanied by snacks consisting of a small grilled bird and 'sake-drenched wheat gluten with kombu.'[82] Endō's mouth-watering menu proves the point that structure is only one of the features that give meaning to a meal. Indeed, the choice of ingredients filling the structure could be said to be the most prominent aspect, since dishes and ingredients varied while the structure itself remained relatively constant.

Endō Genkan: Connoisseur of Tea Cuisine

Further assessment of Rikyū's legacy can be gained by studying the views of Endō Genkan, who lived a century after Rikyū's death. Endō demonstrated his familiarity with the tea menus attributed to Rikyū by dismissing them as dated: 'A long time ago there was a text called *Rikyū's Hundred Teas* that was something worldly people carried in their pockets. However, this has old practices not suitable for the meals for the tea ceremony today.'[83] Endō sought to fill this perceived gap by creating the first published book about tea ceremony cooking, *Guide to Menus for the Tea Ceremony*. In it, he reflected further on the style of tea menus in the era of the ceremony's beginnings, writing about a meal reminiscent of one served by Rikyū in order to illustrate its shortcomings:

> In the past, things were exceedingly simple: brown rice, a traveler's soup with grilled, salted sardines in it served on a folksy wood tray. In those days that style was interesting, so the tea ceremony became popular. Today, however, is a period when society is peacefully governed, people have grown fat around the middle, and the cooking of the past is, conversely, not thought to be appropriate to the tea of today.[84]

Although Endō criticized members of contemporary society for becoming a little chubby, he did not advocate returning to the austere diet associated with Rikyū. In Endō's opinion, ideas about food that could be attributed to Rikyū's era were clearly outmoded. In fact, he told a personal anecdote as a warning against rustic tea practitioners who carried their philosophy too far when they served tea food:

> There was a rustic tea practitioner whose name was well known in society, and he was fond of eccentric habits. One day he invited a high-level warlord [*daimyō*] [to tea]. On that occasion he served rice drenched in soup, a grilled salt-cured fish on a small plate, and pickles [all] served on a tray. The warlord became uneasy and wondered what was going on, but he did not say anything and thereafter he consumed his tea in a good mood, and the gathering concluded . . . I attended that same tea gathering . . . and I thought how terrible it was to make someone eat something that looked like somebody's leftovers . . . Later I heard that the warlord was furious; he was invited to tea again, but he never went back to that tea master's house.[85]

Clearly the master of rustic tea made too much effort to demonstrate simplicity by serving rice covered with a soup or sauce and other dishes 'that looked like somebody's leftovers', and, for his terrible error of etiquette and good taste, he lost a patron. To drive home his point about the importance of serving appropriate tea ceremony meals to high-ranking guests, Endō included a second anecdote about a master of rustic tea who made the mistake of offering fried rice to aristocrats at a morning tea, something that would sicken even commoners, according to Endō.[86]

Since Endō clearly maligned the rustic style of tea menus he associated with Rikyū, scholars who uphold the rustic style to be central to the development of tea cuisine omit Endō from their histories. Kumakura Isao's *A Cultural History of Japanese Cuisine, Focusing on Tea Cuisine* traces the development of tea cuisine in the private tea records of aristocrats and Rikyū's descendants, the Sen family, without any reference to Endō's work.[87] In his book on the history of tea cuisine, Tsutsui Hiroichi mentions Endō's ideas in passing while discoursing on ingredients for tea menus, but does not provide a sustained discussion of Endō's ideas.[88] Thus, Kumakura and Tsutsui, who contend that the development of tea cuisine was foundational to the rise of modern Japanese cuisine, relegate Endō's writings to outlier status and ignore them. If Endō's book on tea cuisine were little more than a denunciation of Rikyū or rustic tea food, one could be justified in ignoring it; but *Guide to Menus for the Tea Ceremony* demonstrates his considerable knowledge about food preparation and presents sophisticated ideas about dining that far surpass contemporaneous works attributed to Rikyū (namely, *Rikyū's Hundred Teas* and *Nanpō's Record*). Consequently, even a cursory evaluation of Endō's book on tea cuisine reveals what is lacking in writings attributed to Rikyū and what may be gained in terms of understanding the history of tea cuisine and Japanese cuisine by considering evidence beyond texts associated with Rikyū.

Endō's style of tea cuisine is evident from his statements and his menus. In contrast to Rikyū's alleged preference for repetition in tea gatherings, Endō advocated changing menus – even for tea ceremonies performed on the same day, as exemplified by his guidance for tea ceremony menus for the celebrations of *kuchi kiri*, the ceremonial opening of the jar containing new tea leaves that marked the beginning of the tea ceremony calendar:

Many people perform tea ceremonies morning and evening from the tenth month for the ceremonial opening of the tea jar, and it is essential to have different meals for morning and evening. Since tea practitioners socialize with one another, before long they will meet up and critique the meals at a certain tea ceremony by a certain person. So, on occasions when one or two types of dishes that were served in the morning are also used in the evening, the evening guests will certainly want to know why. Even if they do not say it, they will wonder the reason at the bottom of their hearts, which is not a very good feeling.

Endō reassures his readers that they will have a wide variety of menus to choose from in his book so that they will not commit the error of duplicating meals.[89] His implication, which is encountered earlier in his book, is that other texts that warn against novelty and promote repetition for tea cuisine provide bad advice that will offend guests and harm a tea master's reputation.

Another reason Endō advocated changing foods from menu to menu was to use the freshest available ingredients: 'Meals must make use of fish and fowl that are at the peak of seasonality; and it is best to avoid varieties of vegetables and greens unsuitable for the season. It will be awful if a guest gets food poisoning.' If a host offers seasonal foods, he could simply apologize if a guest takes ill, but 'it will be the fault of the host if he uses seasonally inappropriate ingredients or strange fish and birds.'[90] Endō's concern for seasonality indicates a wish to protect the health of his guests and the reputation of the host by using the freshest foods rather than a desire to reflect the seasons with appropriate food choices in the way a modern chef must remind diners of what season it is in an age when any foodstuff is available year-round. Such observations reveal that Endō was as familiar with how to cook as he was with which foods should be served.

Endō provides 72 tea menus in volumes four to seven of his eight-volume *Guide to Meals for the Tea Ceremony*, a work that also covers instructions for hosting a visit by a high-ranking warlord or shogun and provides additional information about food preparation and entertaining elite guests.[91] Endō arranged his menus seasonally, beginning with menus for the tenth month, since that marked the 'tea masters' New Year' with the aforementioned ceremony of *kuchi kiri*. He provides both morning and evening menus, including eight that are entirely vegetarian. Not only are the menus in month order, but they are meant to coordinate with seasonal observances. For example, he includes menus for the first and fourth days of the New Year, the former characterized by its inclusion of chilled sake and *daifukucha* – hot water with umeboshi, *sanshō* (Japanese pepper), black soybeans and kombu – a customary tonic consumed in the New Year for health and to ward off malevolent spirits.[92] The first day of the fourth month marks the traditional start of summer, with a switch to summer clothing and a change in tearoom procedure from the use of the sunken hearth to the brazier for heating water for tea. Endō cautions, 'from this season on, fish quickly spoils, so it is of absolute importance that one uses the freshest ingredients when fish and fowl are required.' The advent of summer also marks the arrival of fresh vegetables and, he reminds us, 'use of the first produce of the season is a singular delight to be anticipated.'[93]

In contrast to the menus attributed to Rikyū, Endō's work is defined by variety, luxury and careful attention to preparation. Each menu is different, and he includes cooking and serving notes. Guests for a meal prepared following guidelines attributed to Rikyū would escape starvation, but anyone enjoying one of Endō's meals would be assured of a carefully devised culinary experience with many tastes to pique enjoyment, as the menu below illustrates. The attention Endō gave to this meal is remarkable for its use of seasonal foods such as carrots and matsutake mushrooms, one of the great delicacies of autumn. His use of persimmons is both luxurious and radical, for not only would these fruits have been expensive at that time of year because they were just coming into season, they would have been categorized as the 'first fruits of the season', which the author expressed delight in, and as such, according to sumptuary legislation promulgated a decade before Endō's book was published, it would have been illegal for commoners to consume them.[94]

VEGETARIAN MENU FOR AN EVENING TEA CEREMONY

Eighth Month, Twenty-third Day

A flat, wide dish [*hirazara*]: simmered dish of fried tofu purse [*kinchaku tōfu*], matsutake mushrooms, Akita *warabi* [bracken]
Soup of grated yam [*tororo*], green nori, spicy mustard
Barley [instead of rice]

Two-tiered box:
Upper tier: pickled green beans and thin daikon
Lower tier: grilled matsutake mushrooms, fried kombu

Sake
Snacks of parboiled and pressed carrots, deep-fried [perilla?] leaves
Soup of umeboshi, nori, arrowhead
Tea sweets for thin tea: grilled wheat gluten, shiitake simmered in herb broth
Tea
Sweets for thick tea: Imperial Palace persimmons

Endō provides a few notes about how these foods should be served:

Wild yam is the best variety to use for the grated yam in the soup. If crushed chestnuts are added when warming the grated yam, then the mix becomes too hard. The fried tofu purse is also called a tofu roll. Enquiries at a tofu shop revealed that a cloth is used to compress the tofu into a round shape. The tofu purse is fried in oil and put into the simmered dish. The grilled matsutake mushrooms are sliced thinly, basted with soy sauce, and then grilled.[95]

Endō's notes indicate that he took an interest in gathering and preparing food, even if he may not have done these tasks himself. He knew about the pitfalls and variations for specific recipes, and he augmented his menus by purchasing prepared foods such as the 'tofu purse', which may have contained other delicacies tucked inside the fried tofu. Endō did not describe the taste of his dishes, but we can get a sense of the flavouring from his addition of spicy mustard to one soup and umeboshi to another, and by the shiitake mushrooms simmered in herb broth. We can almost glimpse what the meal looked like, with pieces of green fried kombu paired with thin slices of brown matsutake mushrooms, evoking the pine trees where the mushrooms are found. Long green beans with slices of thin white daikon provide further indication of his sense of visuality. Endō liked to stimulate the reader's imagination and appetite, as exemplified by this menu.

In contrast to the perceived views of Rikyū that appear to direct the mind away from food, the tea master Endō clearly relished food as an integral part of any tea ceremony, to the point that he asserted that meals at a tea ceremony were more stimulating even than banquets. 'When one attends a typical banquet, it is not interesting to tell others about it after returning home,' he wrote. 'But, when someone takes his place at a tea gathering, it is proper to discuss the varieties of utensils, the flower arrangement and the dishes of food served as part of the positive and negative qualities of the tea.' At the same time, Endō cautioned his readers against enjoying too much of a good thing, because tea ceremonies require restraint. 'Even people who might normally consume things they desire to eat according to their own habits – and who eat until they have overeaten and consume so much that they even steal food from other people's trays – they will not take more than two or three bowls of rice at a tea ceremony.' Endō, who in addition to writing and teaching about tea worked as a paediatrician, recognized the health benefits of eating in moderation. Tea food, he asserted, was especially good for the health because of its avoidance of bony fish and ingredients that might cause food poisoning.[96]

The Development of Tea Cuisine

Future research should endeavour to trace the impact of Endō's ideas about tea cuisine in contrast to the notions attributed to Rikyū; however, a few preliminary observations can be made. Some tea masters contemporaneous with Endō found inspiration in Rikyū's work, but they did not uphold the idea that Rikyū perfected tea cuisine. Yabunouchi Chikushin (1678–1745), the fourth-generation leader of the Yabunouchi tea school, advocated for what he viewed as Rikyū's precedent of serving just one soup and a few side dishes. At the same time he qualified Rikyū's achievement, indicating that Rikyū had taken one step in refining the service of tea food but had not concluded the journey. Yabunouchi noted that, 'after Rikyū reformed the serving of tea food (*kaizen*), even the aristocratic and wealthy limited themselves to one soup and three side dishes or to one soup and two dishes. Rustic tea practitioners finally reduced it to one soup and one dish.'[97]

Yabunouchi's remarks must be circumscribed by what we know of actual tea menus from tea records, which indicate that the style of serving just one soup and two or three side dishes did not become standard until after Yabunouchi's death, as noted earlier. However, his point that subsequent tea practitioners proved to be more rustic in their approach to serving food than Rikyū deserves attention. Rikyū's descendants preferred a style of tea food even more rustic than was attributed to Rikyū, as evidenced by what we know of the tea menus of Rikyū's grandson Sen Sōtan (1578–1658), whose sons founded the three Sen lineages of Omotesenke, Urasenke and Mushanokōji Senke. Sōtan's cuisine was much more rustic than Rikyū's – to the point that he was nicknamed 'Rustic' (Wabi) Sōtan.[98] The rustic style was also pronounced in the tea menus of Sōtan's son Sensō (1622–1697), founder of the Urasenke lineage. Sensō lived in the age of the publication of *Rikyū's Hundred Teas* and the creation of *Nanpō's Record*. Although he did not write these texts, he did contribute in many ways to the late seventeenth-century revival of Rikyū. The tea scholars Gary Cadwallader and Joseph Justice write in their study of Sensō's tea menus:

> Sensō was a major figure in the revival of the tea style of his great grandfather Sen Rikyū. This style, called *wabicha* [rustic tea], favored the simpler, more spiritually oriented way of tea. Sensō's menus not only reveal a debt to Rikyū's style of tea, but Sensō also consciously evoked Rikyū with food, laying the groundwork to establish both Rikyū and his style of *kaiseki* as the dominant forms of *tea cuisine* today.[99]

In other words, Sensō's contemporary style of rustic tea was projected backwards to Rikyū's time to affirm affiliation with the founder of his family's artistic lineage at a time when Sensō was endeavouring to establish his own branch of that lineage.

Sensō's conscious effort to evoke Rikyū with tea food suggests another meaning of the word *kaiseki*, when written as 'warming stone' (懐石). As noted earlier, this way of writing *kaiseki* first appeared during Sensō's lifetime, in the apocryphal *Nanpō's Record* during the late seventeenth-century 'revival' of Rikyū's ideas, and evokes Zen Buddhism to suggest that tea food is a device for spiritual training. Yet the kanji *kai* (懐) in *kaiseki* also has the meaning of nostalgia. Consequently, it is tempting to refer to the tea cuisine of Sensō and *Nanpō's Record*, which consciously evoke Rikyū, as 'memorial stones', indicating a way of serving food created in tribute to Rikyū and not invented by him. Sen Sensō raised a monument to his ancestor, the Rikyū Hall, which he completed exactly 100 years after Rikyū's death. A 'memorial stone' is just as unappetizing as a stone used to warm a belly, and that too might call to mind features of Rikyū's tea food described in this chapter.

Prominent scholars reinforce Rikyū's imposing legacy in the history of the tea ceremony and Japanese culture by their statements that he perfected or refined tea cuisine, which they uphold as foundational to the historical development of modern Japanese cuisine. This chapter, however, has made clear that there is no evidence to prove that Rikyū had any impact on the history of Japanese foodways during his lifetime. *Kaiseki* in Rikyū's lifetime could hardly be called a cuisine, because there was no standard term for the meals served at tea gatherings. Cuisines, like other fields of cultural activity, require widespread acceptance of common assumptions regarding their production and reception, and in Rikyū's era knowledge of cuisine was restricted to tea records in private circulation and handwritten manuscripts maintained by hereditary lineages of chefs. The popularization of knowledge about *kaiseki* and other types of dining was made possible only by the development of publishing businesses in the seventeenth century, which means that knowledge of tea cuisine was not widespread until after Rikyū's death. By then, Rikyū may have become an authority on tea menus and other aspects of the tea ceremony in some circles, but his fame was caused in large part by the popularization of apocryphal writings, which present him as a fussy eater and a parsimonious tea master whose interests in tea cuisine reveal a preoccupation with repetition rather than culinary innovation. The connection between the content of these posthumous writings and Rikyū's actual deeds is pure supposition, combined with wishful think-ing and an uncritical acceptance of conventional wisdom on the part of the tea master's successors and cheerleaders.

Beyond establishing the lack of proof to support the assertion that Rikyū perfected or refined tea cuisine, this chapter has demonstrated that there is insufficient evidence to draw conclusions about Rikyū's own pref-erences in tea menus or his ideas about gastronomy. The historical evidence of his tea cuisine, drawn from sixteen menus from a single source, indicates that in over half of his tea ceremony meals he offered just one soup and two or three side dishes. But Rikyū did not invent this style of serving tea food. Instead, he followed a custom that was typical of his era and one that he and other tea masters often deviated from and did not even have a common name to describe. The same historical source indicates that Rikyū served meals with two soups approximately 30 per cent of the time. However, the sample size of sixteen meals is too small for us to draw any definite conclusions about Rikyū's style of tea cuisine, especially in light of the thousands of other meals he provided for tea guests during his lifetime and that we know nothing about. Other tea records indicate that the custom of serving one soup and two or three side dishes declined after Rikyū's death and did not become widespread until a century and a half later, which further discounts the assumption that Rikyū popularized this style of tea dining. Unless new documents are discovered, it is impossible to know with certainty Rikyū's preferred format for tea menus and whether he created his meals to express his artistic views and spiritual convictions, or if he simply preferred smaller meals.

The dearth of historical documentation from Rikyū's lifetime forces scholars who champion Rikyū to turn to apocryphal texts such as *Nanpō's Record* while ignoring writings such as Endō's book *Guide to Meals for the Tea Ceremony*, which challenges the centrality of rustic tea food but nevertheless provides much more specific information about cooking and the meaning and enjoyment of tea cuisine, including reflections on how to avoid food poisoning and directions on how to prepare certain dishes. Scholarship that overemphasizes Rikyū's historical contributions while downplaying the paucity of sources to support them and ignoring richer historical materials probably reflects the respect that academics have for Rikyū, as well as their possibly unconscious acceptance of his towering place in Japanese culture. One can also observe that the most prominent schol-ars who champion Rikyū are closely affiliated with the Urasenke school of tea, whose leader, the family head, traces his lineage to Rikyū and his rustic style of tea ceremony back through the first Urasenke master, Sensō. Tsutsui Hiroichi, who provides the most information purporting to reveal Rikyū's culinary genius, is head librarian of the Konnichian Archive in the Urasenke headquarters in Kyoto. Both Tsutsui and Kumakura Isao have collaborated on scholarly projects with the retired head of the Urasenke school, their writings appear in publications funded by Urasenke, and their books have been published by its press, Tankōsha.[100] Promoting Rikyū's contribution to tea cuisine bolsters institutions such as Urasenke and their leaders who claim descent from Rikyū or purport to offer his authentic teachings, implying that a genetic connection with a long-dead tea master translates into expertise on an aspect of modern national culture – Japanese cuisine – that is respected internationally and encountered daily in Japan. No comparable institutions exist that lay claim to Endō Genkan's legacy, and so his contributions have been relegated to a footnote in standard histories of tea cuisine and are omitted entirely from similar narratives of Japanese cuisine.

Rikyū's position as a font of knowledge about Japanese cuisine is a matter of faith rather than fact, which makes historiography that promotes Rikyū's contributions a type of evangelism, conscious or not, for a view of tea cuisine, modern Japanese cuisine and national culture that mythologizes Rikyū and his supposed contribution and empowers those who can successfully lay claim to his legacy. An essay on Rikyū that appears in the volume *Tea in Japan: Essays on the History of Chanoyu*, edited by Paul Varley and Kumakura Isao, compared *Nanpō's Record* to the Gospel of John in an attempt to establish the authority of *Nanpō's Record* as a source for Rikyū's ideas.[101] The implied comparison of Rikyū with Jesus Christ draws attention to the sacrosanct status of the martyred tea master in historiography on Japanese culture and the posthumously recorded wisdom statements attributed to him. One is reminded of the term 'Japanese Tea Cult', which is a bygone translation for 'tea ceremony' (*chanoyu*) but a designation that could be revived to draw attention to 'evangelical' scholarship that expounds Rikyū's supposed feats to the exclusion of other people, texts, trends and facts.[102]

Diminishing or deleting Rikyū's role in the development of tea cuisine reduces or eliminates his perceived place in the foundation of modern Japanese cuisine and national culture. Simultaneously, it allows consideration of the contributions of other individuals and acknowledges that something as complex as a cuisine in its premodern or modern form is not the product of one genius but developed through the labour of many individuals, men and women, working in kitchens, writing about food and enjoying their meals. A national cuisine or even a culinary genre such as tea cuisine cannot arise without the involvement of many different people and institutions over time.

3

RICE AND ITS IDENTITIES

Definitions of 'traditional' Japanese food, as we have seen, vary from the standpoint of the Japanese government, which defines *washoku* as 'dietary cultures', to Japanese consumers who use the same word to refer to prepared foods such as grilled fish, tempura and sukiyaki. Two points these interpretations have in common are, first, that their parameters of 'tradition' more closely approximate the diet of the period of high economic growth in the 1960s than that of the era before the Second World War, and second, that they view rice as inseparable from the traditional Japanese diet. Rice is one of the only foods named in the government's official definition of *washoku,* and rice is the accompaniment to traditional side dishes such as grilled fish. Per capita rice consumption reached an all-time peak in 1962; it has declined since then to the point that the per capita supply of rice is now less than half of what it was a century ago, and a typical Japanese person today derives three times more food energy from sources other than rice. Yet for many, a meal would be neither 'traditional' nor 'Japanese' if it did not include a bowl of white rice.

It has been argued that rice is desirable because it is naturally delicious.[1] Despite the continuing fall in per capita rice consumption since the early 1960s, 'tasty' brands of rice such as Koshihikari remain in demand. Yet buying rice for taste is a post-war phenomenon, observes the agronomist Suge Hiroshi. Suge explains, 'until around the end of the Second World War, for people suffering from a lack of foodstuffs, rice was rice – there was no regard for which varieties tasted good and which tasted bad.'[2] Suge attunes us to the fact that delicious food is a luxury reserved for good economic times for people with plenty to eat. Moreover, if taste provides the motivation to consume rice, then one would expect rice consumption to be at an all-time high today rather than to have crested fifty years ago.

Rice's cultural importance stems not from its role as a staple foodstuff but from the fact that the grain is said to be a time-honoured symbol of Japanese identity, as the anthropologist Emiko Ohnuki-Tierney explained in her acclaimed book *Rice as Self: Japanese Identities through Time* (1993).[3] Reiterating Ohnuki-Tierney's ideas, the scholars Vaclav Smil and Kazuhiko Kobayashi write, 'rice had a prominent place in the nation's cosmology, identity, self-perception, and culture for centuries before it became an indispensable staple.'[4] White rice in particular has long been a necessary part of celebrations, for example the rice cakes made for the New Year, mentioned in the UNESCO definition of 'traditional dietary cultures of the Japanese'. But before the Second World War much of the population ate white rice only on rare occasions, to the extent that outside festival days, if someone heard that white rice was being prepared, they knew they were being invited to a funeral.[5]

Food changes when it enters the privacy of the mouth. Likewise, the symbolic meanings of rice that might be perceived to resonate throughout a country across time are understood and experienced individually through the intimacy of eating. Japanese populations that shared the habit of eating rice before the Second World War – and not all of them did – reveal great diversity in the ways they processed and prepared the grain, and these ways are elided in contemporary discussions that equate 'traditional' Japanese food with consuming white rice. Rather than serving as a means to reinforce national identity, variations in rice consumption expressed inequalities of wealth and differences in status and gender, and differentiated rural from urban populations, exposing some people to discrimination based on the quality, amount or absence of rice in their diets.

This chapter demonstrates how before the Second World War, rice was not considered a uniform foodstuff, either when it was growing in a paddy or field, or when it was processed, cooked or served; and rice's lack of uniformity had implications for the identities of the people who prepared and consumed it. First, the chapter explains how rice was never believed historically to be a singular plant but rather recognized as having multiple varieties and even different genders. Second, it examines the distinction between glutinous and non-glutinous forms of rice and how milling differentiates 'white' rice from partially polished varieties and brown rice. A third way in which rice became even more varied was in the different methods by which it was prepared. Today, rice cookers provide a uniform and virtually foolproof way of making white rice, but before the Second World War there were many techniques using a variety of utensils that yielded results from soft and watery to hard and dry. Fourth, as part of a traditional meal nowadays rice is typically served separately and in its own bowl, but populations that ate rice in the first half of the twentieth century usually consumed it in a blend of other grains, vegetables, tubers and foodstuffs, sometimes to the point that rice could no longer be considered the main food, either because it was lost in a mash of other ingredients or because it was simply meant as a binding agent for delicacies. Fifth, even a household that might cook a daily grain dish one way might still serve it in different ways to family members depending on their age, status and gender (of which more below). Finally, rice was not the only important staple. Some regions of Japan grew high-quality rice, which farmers sold, in turn subsisting on rice of lower quality or other staples. Other regions could not readily grow rice and their populations relied on different grains and other sources of carbohydrate. In these instances, populations eating foods different from rice sometimes faced discrimination.

A compelling case has been made that rice in Japan as a foodstuff and as a symbol is a mechanism for fostering group identity throughout time, but, far from being a unified experience, the different modes of processing and eating rice – even within a single family – before the Second World War reveal distinctions between people along urban and rural lines, and according to gender, social status, wealth and locality. Such diverse experiences with rice were rooted in the practices of daily life, and therefore had a more prominent effect on forming identities than abstract notions about the collective self far removed from lived experiences.

Varieties of Rice

Rice may be said to be central to Japanese national culture and the diet depending on the locale and era, but historically all rice was not considered the same. Rice is the 'spirit of the sun, which becomes replete with that virtue when it is full of water', wrote Miyazaki Yasusada in *Nōgyō zensho* (Encyclopaedia of Agriculture), published in 1697. But Miyazaki affirmed that all rice was not identical. 'There is an unlimited variety of early and late ripening types,' he explained; 'some taste bad and others taste good.' Miyazaki advised the farmers who were his readers to select the variety of rice most suitable to local conditions. The earliest agricultural manual, *Seiryōki* (Seirō Chronicles), compiled between 1629 and 1654, distinguished varieties of rice by the season in which they could be harvested, delineating twelve types each of early rice, early middle rice and late middle rice, and

24 varieties of late rice. The same text further noted sixteen varieties of glutinous rice, twelve types of upland rice – meant to be grown in fields, not paddies – and eight types of 'red rice', a variety with a reddish hue.[6] In 1734 the shogunal doctor Niwa Seihaku recorded twenty varieties of rice grown in Shinano province (Nagano prefecture) that had been selected to suit local conditions.[7] By the end of the early modern period there were hundreds of varieties of rice, and that number has grown to thousands today.[8]

In early modern Japan, rice came in different genders and colours, and the grain was grown for different functions. Agricultural manuals taught farmers how to distinguish between 'male' and more fecund 'female' types of rice, because rice, like most plants, was believed to have male and female aspects.[9] The *Aizu nōsho* (Agricultural Text from Aizu), written in Aizu province (modern Fukushima prefecture) by Sase Yojiemon and printed in 1684, delineated different varieties of rice on the basis of maturation period, providing some types with names after the locales where the rice was grown (paddy or upland field), or giving them more fanciful designations that alluded to fertility and femininity, such as 'young wife' (*konyōbō*) and 'Kyoto courtesan' (*Kyō jorō*).[10] *Tamon'in nikki* (Tamon'in Diary), which details life at Kōfukuji temple in Nara from 1478 to 1618, offers insight into the many ways that rice was traditionally processed and thereby differentiated depending on function. The record mentions polished rice, non-glutinous rice, non-glutinous polished rice, glutinous rice, polished glutinous rice, glutinous rice flour, new polished rice, new rice, old rice, early rice, daily rice, winter rice, rice for brewing sake, Bizen rice and Kizu rice (named after locations), black rice, rice flour, rice flour for tea refreshments, rice flour from non-glutinous rice, rice for *chimaki* (a confection of rice cakes wrapped in leaves of bamboo grass) and rice for making miso.[11] The black rice (*kurogome*) mentioned here is another term for unpolished brown rice.[12] Red rice (*akagome*), aforementioned in the *Seirō Chronicles*, came in glutinous and non-glutinous varieties and was rice of inferior quality with a reddish hue; it was poor-tasting but hardy and economical, since it expanded well when cooked.[13] Besides noting different colours of rice, by the end of the early modern period consumers came to esteem the merits of regional differences in rice varieties depending on their place of origin, and would pay more for rice from famous areas.[14]

Despite the profusion of varieties, not much effort was made to improve the taste of rice in the early modern period: farmers lacked the know-how to do so until the modern era.[15] Locations that had once produced poor-quality rice at the turn of the twentieth century are now home to famous brands, as farmers and prefectural agricultural specialists have worked to improve quality, giving rise to the high-end varieties such as Koshihikari and Sasanishiki from Tohoku and Hokuriku, Niigata prefecture's Uonuma Koshihikari and Akitakomachi from Akita prefecture.[16] Special varieties of rice have higher starch content, larger grains and less fat and protein than conventional types.

Viewed in comparison to other types of rice globally, a shorter grain distinguishes the Japonica grown in Japan from the longer, non-sticky Indica and the longer, somewhat sticky Javanica. Within Japan the major distinction in varieties of Japonica rice is between non-glutinous (*uruchi*) and glutinous (*mochigome*). The distinction does not refer to gluten, the proteins in wheat, but to the proportion of the starches amylose and amylopectin in the rice. The more glutinous – stickier – forms of rice contain a higher percentage of amylopectin.[17] Glutinous rice is generally less productive than non-glutinous rice, but it is better able to withstand cold so it can be grown at higher elevations and in cooler locales.[18] Glutinous rice is best steamed to make rice cakes (mochi), as described below, or cooked with azuki beans, which impart a red colour to the dish known as *sekihan*, which is served at celebrations. Non-glutinous rice is tastiest when boiled, or when simmered with a lot of water to make porridge. When glutinous rice is boiled, it becomes pasty, but when it is steamed it becomes hard and sticky.[19] Sake making relies on non-glutinous rice exclusively, but the sweet liquid flavouring mirin is made from glutinous rice mixed with distilled spirits (*shōchū*).

Harvesting and Processing

The most important distinction for consumers today is between brown rice and white rice, a transformation that occurs by milling, which is part of the process of making the rice grown in the fields palatable – a series of simple tasks that are nevertheless laborious when undertaken without the advantage of modern machinery.[20] Before the introduction of modern farming technology, depending on the variety and locale, rice seedlings were planted by hand in May and transplanted also by hand to the paddy in June; the grain was harvested in October, but sometimes as early as mid-August. Farmers cut the rice stalks using sickles, gathering the stalks into bundles and hanging them on poles, with the grain heads facing down, to dry in the fields. After several days' drying, the rice was ready for threshing to remove the grain from the stalk. At the beginning of the early modern period, farmers threshed rice by dragging the stalks between long bamboo chopsticks (*kokihashi*), but by the end of the seventeenth century an implement called a *senbakoki*, a device resembling a vertical rake, was invented and came into use in the provinces around Kyoto. Farmers dragged the grain stalks through the teeth of the *senbakoki*, separating grain from chaff in a process ten times faster and more efficient than using *kokihashi*.[21] Threshing machines had taken over this task by the late 1920s. The unhulled rice was usually sun-dried on straw mats that could be rolled up to store the grain until it was hulled. The leftover stalks could be used as animal feed, kindling or fertilizer or woven to make rope, rice bags or sandals.

Hulling rice removes the chaff, creating brown rice; this task was traditionally accomplished by pounding the grain in a large mortar with a pestle, but in the latter part of the early modern period the use of a lathe mortar (*kizuriusu*) became prevalent as a method to accomplish the same task more efficiently. The upper portion of a lathe mortar rests on a cone-shaped, serrated lower mortar, which serves as an axis for the upper part to rotate. Two farmers, one seated on each side of the lathe mortar, used a rope to rotate the top portion of the mortar back and forth a half-turn each way. Unhulled grain was poured into a hole in the top mortar, and hulled grain and chaff would emerge from the space between the upper and lower mortars.[22] In contrast to the lathe mortar, which makes only half-turns back and forth, a more vigorous revolving mortar (called a *tōusu* or *suriusu*) allowed the upper mortar to rotate fully on top of a lower mortar set inside a wooden frame for stability. However, the more vigorous grinding of the revolving mortar damages more of the rice, resulting in some 2 per cent of the grain becoming 'broken rice', lowering its quality – a fact that impeded the spread of the revolving mortar.[23] Such broken rice was pulverized further to make flour for dumplings or used in porridge, serving as an important food source for farmers.[24]

After hulling, the farmer is left with a pile of grain and chaff that must be separated by winnowing. Rice has a considerable amount of chaff, and removing the hull reduces the volume by half.[25] Traditionally, winnowing was accomplished by tossing the mix of pulverized hull and grain into the air to allow the pieces of hull to blow away. In the early modern era, a winnowing machine (*tōmi*) was invented to accomplish this task; the farmer poured the mix of grain and chaff into a box with a revolving fan inside. After passing through the winnower, any remaining chaff clinging to the grain was separated in a sieve or by pouring the mix through a vertical sieve called a *man'ichi dōshi*.[26]

Threshing scene, undated photograph, attributed to Kashima Kiyobei. After pounding the rice in the wooden pestle, the rice is winnowed in the mechanism on the left, called a *tōmi*. The man at the back holds a large winnowing fan to blow away debris.

Milling

With the husk removed, the rice can be consumed as brown rice or milled to remove the bran. The bran (*nuka*) consists of the peel, seed coat and the outer portion of the endosperm. Rice bran amounts to between 5 and 6 per cent of the rice's volume and contains most of the B1 vitamins and minerals. The core of the rice is mostly starch.[27] Milling rice reduces the vitamin content and results in a higher percentage of starch. Brown rice is 70 per cent starch, 8 per cent protein and 3 per cent fat. Polished rice, meanwhile, is 75 per cent starch, 1 per cent fat and around 6 or 7 per cent protein.[28] Milling rice also reduces by 50 per cent the amount of thiamine, a B1 vitamin; and thiamine deficiency can induce beriberi, a condition that can cause weakness, pain, cardiac damage and heart failure.[29] Beriberi was called the 'Edo sickness' in the early modern period, suggesting that the disease was endemic in particular locales (thanks to the prevalence of white rice in the diet there). It could be cured by travelling to the countryside, where eating less polished rice and other grains was the norm. The exact causes of beriberi were debated until scientists synthesized thiamine in 1936.[30] More vitamin B1 and protein is lost when milled rice is washed before cooking to remove any residual bran.[31]

Milling rice is a very simple but time-consuming process. After 1942, when the Japanese government created a national distribution and rationing system for rice, it distributed only brown rice to civilians; some people proved how easy it was to mill their own by pouring the brown rice into the ubiquitous 1.8-litre bottles that were used for sake and soy sauce, and using a stick to polish the grain, pounding the stick up and down like a butter churn.[32] A far older method of milling using a mortar is celebrated in pictures of the 'rabbit on the moon', who stands by a large hourglass-shaped mortar with a long, straight pestle in his paws. Until the early modern period, both mortar and pestle were made from wood, but from the middle part of that period, thanks to technological advances in stone carving, stone mortars became more common in farm households. The late seventeenth-century farm manual *Hyakushō denki* (Reports from Farmers) refers to a stone mortar as the most important treasure of a farm household.[33] By that period, most farmers had substituted the straight pestle for a more efficient one shaped like a hammer.[34] Besides milling grain, mortars served many purposes, including mashing soybeans for tofu or fish for fishcake (*kamaboko*), and grinding any broken rice leftover from hulling and other grains into flour for porridge, noodles (udon or soba) or dumplings.[35]

Due to the effort involved (and the other chores demanding farmers' time), milling rice was an unnecessary task, especially since it reduced the amount of rice left to eat, but urbanites in the early modern period developed a taste for polished rice. At the turn of the seventeenth century nearly all of the rice available in cities was brown rice, but by 1650 the first milling shops appeared in Edo. Early mills probably served specialized food makers such as confectioners, who needed rice flour. But within a century, the growth of the milling trade in Edo and other technological advances made consuming polished rice possible for any city-dweller who could afford it.[36] Rice millers switched to standing mortars (*fumiusu, ashibumi usu*) that used foot power to operate two pedals to lift and drop the pestle. Waterwheels automated the process, and waterwheel-driven mortars came into widespread use in cities late in the early modern period.[37] Both standing mortars and waterwheels were used in sake making, for which large amounts of highly milled rice were needed. Breweries in Nishinomiya and Imazu, between Osaka and Kobe, in the cradle of the sake making industry, employed standing mortars until the middle of the Edo period, before replacing them with waterwheels, which proved much more efficient. A standing mortar can be used to mill rice to the equivalent of modern table rice, reducing the grain size by 8 per cent in the process, but a waterwheel can mill away 25 to 35 per cent – the amount needed to make the lowest grade of premium sake by modern standards. A waterwheel also automates and speeds up the milling process, producing up to around 2,725 litres of milled rice a day compared to only about 95 litres with a standing mortar.[38] Steam-powered milling machines were adopted in the modern period, allowing even more highly polished rice, and at the same time causing more instances of beriberi.[39] Statistics from the Japanese navy reveal that in 1878, some 1,552 out of 6,366 sailors contracted beriberi in the course of duty that year.[40] The navy eliminated beriberi by changing sailors' diets, but the disease continued to plague the army, which sought bacteriological causes for it. During the Russo-Japanese War (1904–5), some 250,000 Japanese soldiers were hospitalized with beriberi and upward of 27,000 died from the affliction.[41] Since the cause of beriberi was debated through the first decades of the twentieth century, the cost of milled rice rather than health concerns prompted many urban residents to eat brown rice or mix rice with other grains such as barley, as described below – practices that prevented beriberi.[42]

'Threshing with a Standing Mortar [*fumiusu*]', photograph by Raimund von Stillfried-Rathenitz, taken before 1886.

Differences in Refinement

The milled rice consumed in early modern cities was different from modern table rice. Owing to the fact that highly polished rice cost more, most urban commoners in the early modern period consumed rice that was only partially milled.[43] In mid-nineteenth-century Edo, eight cups of the most highly milled rice (unfortunately, we do not know the exact milling rate in this instance) cost 3.5 times more than the least polished rice.[44] Highly milled rice was needed for brewing sake. Other varieties were meant for daily consumption as cooked grains. Such partially milled varieties retained the germ (and more vitamin B1) and had a slightly darker appearance than the table rice eaten today.[45] Besides their darker colour, the grains of partially milled varieties were slightly larger than those of modern table rice.[46] 'Half-milled rice' (*hantsukimai, gobutsukimai*) left 4 per cent of the bran and 96 per cent of the kernel (see Table 3), resulting in one-third more B1 than was found in fully polished rice.[47] The consensus among scholars is that early modern commoners ate '70 per cent milled rice' (*shichibumai*, also called *shichibu tzukimai*), which removed all but 30 per cent of the bran and left the endosperm intact.[48] Less milled rice and brown rice saw a resurgence with the advent of rationing in the Second World War. In 1939 '70 per cent milled rice' became the national standard for rice milling under the Rice Milling Regulation Law.[49]

TABLE 3
Milling Rates

Type	% Bran Remaining	% Kernel Size
Brown rice	100	100
Half-milled rice	50	96
Milled to 70 per cent	30	94
Modern table rice	0	92

During wartime, milling laws were not always obeyed, as the earlier example of urban residents using sake and soy sauce bottles and sticks to mill their own rice illustrates. In conversations with ethnologists, some farmers reported in 1941 that they processed the '70 per cent milled rice' they received as rations. They gave several reasons for wanting to eat more highly polished rice, including that white rice increased in volume when cooked;

that they needed the bran for animal feed and pickling; and that the taste of white rice was better, declaring that less polished versions, which they dubbed 'red rice', were 'tasteless'.[50] Brown rice needs to be soaked for longer than more polished rice and requires a longer cooking time.

Production levels of rice are known from the turn of the twentieth century, but the statistics do not reveal how much rice was officially or privately milled, so how much rice was consumed as brown rice and how much as white rice remains unknown. One estimate places the amount of rice polished for foods including sake making, confectionery, *kōji* (the mould-inoculated rice used in the brewing of sake and the making of miso and soy sauce) and mirin at just under 0.92 per cent of the amount of rice produced between 1880 and 1940.[51] Less than 1 per cent for sake making seems a gross underestimate. In some areas in the early modern period 15 per cent of the rice was destined to be milled for sake production, an amount also true for the Meiji era.[52] Higher estimates of polished rice dedicated to non-food purposes such as sake would mean a corresponding reduction in the amount of any rice, polished or brown, available per capita.

After milling, glutinous rice could be steamed, drained, returned to the mortar and pounded further to make rice cakes (mochi), a recipe that probably dates from the prehistoric period.[53] The term *mochi* derives from the glutinous rice (*mochigome*) used to create it, although foodstuffs, especially confectionery called mochi, can be made from non-glutinous rice, rice flour made from glutinous or non-glutinous rice, and other ingredients. Mochi is the basis for Japan's traditional confectionery (*wagashi*); and mochi, especially those made from rice, have a variety of ritual uses, particularly when shaped into large round 'mirror rice cakes', a traditional New Year's offering to the deities of the household and the field, and ancestral spirits.[54] While urban consumers enjoyed mochi sweets, savoury types were important staple foods in rural areas. A survey by the Home Ministry published in 1881 described how people in rural areas made mochi from wheat flour, rice husks, barley, buckwheat, foxtail millet, barnyard millet and ordinary millet. The cakes were usually made in advance and then grilled and eaten as a quick breakfast or snack.[55] In Meiji-period Niigata prefecture, rice hulls were mixed with the flour of other grains and formed around vegetables cooked in miso. The gigantic dumplings, called an *anpu* or *yakimochi*, were grilled and eaten as a breakfast food in mountain villages.[56] In mountainous regions, mochi were also made with ground chestnuts and acorns, which were important staple foods in some locales, as Chapter Seven describes.[57]

Leftovers from milling rice and other grains were not discarded but instead pounded further into flour to make other foods. The advent of the revolving mortar made it easier for peasants to make soba and udon noodles, dumplings, crackers and suchlike.[58] In rural areas until the early 1940s, grilled dumplings made from rice, wheat or barley flour made for an easy breakfast called 'morning tea' (asacha) in parts of Shimane prefecture and 'tea snacks' (chanoko) in Nagasaki. Though rice and wheat were the preferred ingredients for dumplings, buckwheat dumplings were found in some parts of Japan.[59] But rice, unless it was damaged, was often too valuable to use for dumplings. A common expression had it that it took four times as much rice to make dumplings as it did to make porridge.[60]

In summary, the quality of the rice eaten before and during the Second World War varied from damaged kernels and even hulls ground into flour for dumplings to polished varieties that are nonetheless different from the table rice eaten today. Rice was understood to be a heterogeneous plant that became even more differentiated by the various ways it was processed. Cooking, as explained below, also dramatically transforms rice into a range of dishes, both crude and elegant.

Traditional Methods of Cooking Rice

Besides differing rates of milling, the varied methods for cooking rice show the diverse ways in which the grain was consumed, revealing variations by region and economic status. Today, cooking rice usually consists of the simple task of combining rice and water in an electric rice cooker and pressing a button, but before that device appeared on the market, in 1955, there were many more methods of preparing rice, and all were more labour-intensive.[61] One primitive way to cook rice is to dig a hole in the ground, place the rice inside a cloth bag drenched in water, cover the bag with rocks and then build a fire on top to steam the rice.[62] However, the two most typical and ancient techniques for cooking rice, which both date from the prehistoric era in Japan, were steaming to make 'hard rice' (kowaii) and boiling to create 'soft rice' (himeii). Steaming was the preferred means of making glutinous rice and boiling the best way to make non-glutinous rice, as noted earlier.[63]

Steaming to make hard rice requires using a ceramic, metal or wooden steaming basket (koshiki) lined with a damp cloth and placed over a heat source. The resulting steamed rice is so hard that it can be piled into pyramids or cones, as it still is today in ceremonial offerings at Shinto shrines.

'Taking a Break' (*Hito yasumi*), photograph by Mugishima Masaru, 1949, Kotoko Higashimachi, Yatsushiro City, Kumamoto prefecture. The photo shows a central hearth in a rural home.

Hard rice is crumbly, and in the ancient period, when that mode of cooking rice was typical, aristocrats ate it with a spoon.[64]

Boiled 'soft rice', also called 'princess rice' (*himeii*), requires a metal pot or *nabe*, and before the medieval era pots were expensive utensils which only the wealthy, aristocrats or monastics, could afford – although a samurai's helmet could serve for cooking during military campaigns.[65] With the spread of metal pots after the medieval era, boiling gradually became the preferred method of cooking non-glutinous rice in rural areas, by placing a pot either over the fire in a central hearth or over a portable stove called a *shichirin*. Since peasants usually added other grains such as barley to their cooked rice, as described below, cooking in a pot without a lid made it easier to skim off any slime in the water produced by the added starchy grains. Cooking grain in a lidless pot meant that the rice did not steam well, so boiling worked best for making watery porridges (*okayu*), flavoured gruels (*ojiya*) or cooked grain with the sticky consistency of oatmeal.[66] Rice porridges and gruel are soft and easy to eat, so have long been considered ideal for the infirm and infants.[67] Rice gruel was also eaten on ritual occasions, such as at New Year, and before planting rice seedlings. In Gifu prefecture rice porridge was made with azuki beans as a year-end offering to persimmon trees, as a prayer that they will bear fruit in the coming year.[68]

Hard rice can be too hard and soft rice can be too watery; so the optimal way to prepare non-glutinous rice, and the one that became the preferred method of making rice in cities in the early modern period, combines boiling and steaming. One way to accomplish the process of boiling and steaming is called 'cooking rice and then removing the boiled water' (*yutorimeshi*) or 'twice-cooked rice' (*futatabimeshi*). Initially, plenty of water is boiled with the rice – one recipe called for using twice as much water as rice. After boiling, the rice is strained to remove any sticky, glutinous sludge. The rice is then returned to the same pot to steam briefly. This method of cooking rice is ideally suited to a pot over a hearth, and was prevalent in rural areas until the 1950s.[69]

However, the preferred way of cooking non-glutinous rice, which combined boiling and steaming, was a technique called 'cooking and drying rice' (*takiboshimeshi*), and this was most common in urban areas. It relied on a rice cauldron (*kama*), which is taller than a pot (*nabe*). The height of the rice cauldron is designed to trap steam. The *kama* has a thick wooden lid that helps to control the temperature of the rice as it boils and then steams. Rice boiled in a cooking pot is soggier than that cooked in a heavy-lidded *kama*. The heavy wooden lid of the *kama* not only allows pressure to build inside the cauldron without over-boiling, which is essential to make brown rice more palatable, but also absorbs water so that the rice does not become too watery.[70] As the steam builds in the cauldron, the water content of the rice decreases and the rice fluffs up as steam replaces water between the kernels. At this point the temperature is reduced moderately so that the rice can steam fully without burning. The final steaming is critical: Japonica rice must steam for fifteen minutes in order to taste good. The rice is 65 per cent water at this point, and steaming helps to distribute the water evenly.[71] The method of 'cooking and drying rice' therefore requires strict control over the cooking time, heat and amount of water used. According to an early modern folk saying, one has to intuit the proper temperature and timing by the sound and appearance of the boiling pot: 'When cooking rice, andante (*chorochoro*) for the beginning, allegro (*gungun* or *poppo*) for the middle, and moderato (*sukoshi yurumeyo*) after the steaming.'[72] Initiating a slow simmer marks the andante passage, allowing the rice to absorb water slowly as the water temperature climbs to boiling point. If the boiling point is reached too soon, the rice will be undercooked in the centre, so the rice must boil slowly. The allegro movement of the boiling water indicates that the temperature is sufficiently high to allow the rice to become plump. Patience is required especially at this point. Instructions warn the cook 'not to remove the cover of the rice pot even if the baby cries', that is, even if the lid rattles, because doing so allows steam to escape. As a final step, rice straw was sometimes added to the fire under the pot to raise the heat briefly, so that the rice burns just a little to become more aromatic (today, cooks sometimes do this by turning up the heat for a short time). Then the cauldron is removed from the heat and allowed to rest and continue to steam for five more minutes before the rice is transferred to a serving vessel.[73]

Although cauldrons could also be used for boiling and steaming other foods, such as noodles and vegetables, the main function of any *kama* was to cook rice, making the cauldron a specialized kitchen device in the early modern period found mostly in urban areas and some wealthier homes in rural locales.[74] The size of the cauldrons varied depending on the amount of grain they were designed to cook. The largest cauldrons had a capacity of around 1,760 litres, but the standard sizes ranged between 45 and 100 litres. There was also a small-sized *kama* with a capacity of just 22 litres.[75]

Besides their heavy wooden lids, *kama* are differentiated from other pots by the metal lip found around the middle of the container, allowing the cauldron to fit snugly into the hole of a cooking stove (*kamado*) and prevent any liquid from seeping from the pot and trickling down into the fire below. For this feature *kama* are often referred to as 'winged cauldrons' (*hagama*), a design innovation that is said to have originated in the area around Kyoto, Osaka and Nara. Marking the approximate midway point in the pot, the wings also serve to indicate the maximum level to which the pot may be filled with rice and water; the area above the wings is left empty so that it can fill with steam during cooking.[76]

The preferred cooking surface for a rice cauldron was a *kamado*, an enclosed stove made of brick, stone or earth with holes in the top designed to fit cauldrons and other pots. Evidence of *kamado* dates from the Colossal Tomb period (300–552), and the device is probably an import from Korea: the earliest examples have been found in northern Kyushu and the area around Kyoto and Nara.[77] At the beginning of the seventeenth century, only the wealthy in western Japan used *kamado*, but the cauldron spread to the homes of merchants by the eighteenth century, and wealthier families had *kamado* with three, five or even seven holes for pots.[78] With one hole dedicated to a rice cauldron, the others could hold pots for cooking side dishes and soups, allowing a more varied diet than was possible with a single cooking pot over a hearth, as in a farmhouse.[79] Before the 1920s, when a separate kitchen became typical of newer middle-class homes in urban areas, *kamado* were usually constructed near the entranceway of a dwelling, taking advantage of the pounded earth or stone floor as protection against fire and relying on the ventilation of a nearby doorway, since *kamado* traditionally lack chimney flues.

In *Ryōri tebikisō* (Introductory Writing on Cooking), the cookbook author Shimoda Utako (1854–1936) provided detailed instructions on how to cook rice in a cauldron on a *kamado*. Published in 1898, *Introductory Writing on Cooking* was the first culinary book written by a woman as the sole author, and Shimoda intended her text for female students taking courses in home economics.[80] Acknowledging that some of her middle-class readers might have grown up in households where the servants had prepared the rice, Shimoda wrote, 'because boiled grain is the staple food of our country, everyone needs a general knowledge about it.' She continued, 'I have set forth methods for boiling various types of grains, but first I will begin by explaining ordinary cooked rice.' Shimoda listed 47 methods for preparing rice with other grains such as barley and millet or in combination with vegetables such as aubergine (eggplant), lotus or fresh or dried daikon, or with seafood such as *katsuobushi*, sardines or oysters. She gave most of her attention, however, to the basic recipe for cooking rice. Her recipe begins by describing the process of washing the rice in water to remove any bran and other impurities:

> First, rub the rice together thoroughly until the water is completely clear all the way to the surface, and then rinse and drain it. Next, place the rice in the pot and add water. The boiled rice will be good or bad depending on the amount of water and on the strength of the fire. So, please pay attention. Depending on its quality, rice either absorbs a lot of water or it does not. Generally speaking, you should

'A renovated *kamado* installed in farm household kitchen', Kumamoto prefecture, 1961. The cauldron for cooking rice (*kama*) is on the stove (*kamado*) in the foreground; this *kamado* includes a flue.

remember that new rice only absorbs a little water and older rice absorbs a lot. Additionally, water absorption differs depending on high heat or low heat. As for the amount of water to use, the water should typically measure about three centimetres over the surface of the rice. When softer rice is desired, wash the rice and leave it to soak in water for a few hours.

The fire belongs directly under the cauldron so that it heats evenly. Use low heat initially, but towards the middle of cooking raise the heat, and then use low heat to finish cooking. Bank off some of the firewood when a lot of steam pours out of the space between the pot and the lid. Bank off the firewood, but let some embers remain and allow the pot to sit for a while. Then, remove the pot; and when the contents have settled, transfer the rice to a covered rice tub. If the rice burns while cooking, sprinkle sake on it, and place it [in the cauldron] over the fire for a while, leaving it there until the contents settle. Usually that makes tasty cooked rice.[81]

Besides mastering the use of heat and timing, according to Shimoda a successful chef needed to develop an eye for the quality and age of the rice, both of which affect the amount of water to use. Traditional guidance is found in the *Meihan burui* (Collection of Famous Grain Dishes) published in 1802, which recommends using an equal proportion of water to washed rice, provided the rice has been soaked beforehand. If the rice is not soaked, then 10 per cent more water is needed. The same text further indicates that 10 per cent more water is required for cooking older rice. To clarify these matters, *Collection of Famous Grain Dishes* advises readers to obtain advice from someone experienced in cooking rice.[82] For a more savoury version, an early modern culinary text by Shōsekiken Sōken, *Ryōri mōmoku chōmishō* (Collected Writings on Cuisine and an Outline on Seasonings), published in 1730, recommended substituting one-third of the water used for cooking the rice with stock made from kombu, or adding a dash of sake or soy sauce for every 2 litres of rice for flavouring.[83] Until after the Second World War, the usual source for any water for cooking was the local well – in 1935 less than a third of households had indoor taps in the kitchen.[84]

To make really good-tasting rice – and to avoid making other common mistakes – there were even more matters to pay attention to, as Murai Gensai (1863–1927) explained in *Daidokoro chōhōki* (Treasury of the Kitchen, 1905). Murai was the most famous food writer of the early twentieth century and author of the novel *Kuidōraku* (The Gourmet's Delight), which was published in newspaper instalments in 1903 and later collected as a four-volume book. In *Treasury of the Kitchen* Murai uses a fictional device to frame cooking advice, setting up a dialogue between an unnamed housewife and her maid, Miso, who is in need of constant advice and direction. Maids, like the fictional Miso in Murai's book, were often portrayed in the literature of the period as potential obstacles to the operation of clean kitchens and healthy cooking.[85] Miso has to be told how to do every task around the kitchen. The housewife warns the gullible maid that rice shops are unscrupulous, since they will sell good-quality rice one day and bad the next. Her instructions to Miso offered Murai's readers insight into how to buy rice: 'When you look at the rice, the most important thing to check is whether or not the grains are similar in size. If the grains are not the same size, then when you cook the rice, the larger grains won't become soft and the smaller grains will overcook, then the rice won't taste good at all.' Having learned the pitfalls of buying rice that is improperly milled, Miso thereafter purchases short-grain rice, with a smaller germ remaining and a transparent lustre.[86] The housewife reminds Miso not to waste the water she used to wash the rice, but to save it to water houseplants or to boil octopus or abalone.[87]

The attention and time needed to cook rice well were reasons for busy and frugal households to cook rice just once a day, a fact that was as true in the early twentieth century as it was 100 years earlier in the early modern period, as Kitagawa Kisō (Morisada, 1810–?) observed in *Morisada Mankō* (Morisada's Voluminous Sketches), thirty volumes of observations about daily life compiled around 1853. Kitagawa wrote that in Edo people cooked rice only once a day, in the morning, and so ate cold rice for lunch and dinner. Residents of Osaka and Kyoto, he reported, ate for breakfast rice porridge made from the previous day's rice, and prepared fresh rice for the midday meal.[88] Once prepared, rice could be eaten cold or reheated as 'twice rice' (*futatabi meshi*), or consumed by pouring hot tea on top to make *chazuke*. Boiling leftover rice made porridge. Adding just a dash of miso or soy sauce to the porridge created 'flavoured gruel' (*ojiya*), or with the addition of vegetables, sweet potatoes, yams or other ingredients the dish became a 'mixed boil' (*zōsui*).

Since urban commoners in Edo ate cold rice for lunch and dinner, culinary texts from the early modern period provided clues about how to preserve rice, methods that endured in Japan into the twentieth century.[89] One method was to dry out the cooked rice to create parched rice (*hoshiii, kareii*), which could be prepared quickly by adding hot water. Another time-honoured technique is to press boiled rice into balls called *onigiri* or *omusubi*. Kitagawa noted a preference in Osaka and Kyoto for rice balls topped with black sesame seeds and shaped into miniature rice bales (*tawara*), while in Edo most people made round or triangular rice balls, fashioned either by hand or in wooden moulds.[90] Today, a wide variety of rice balls is commercially available with different toppings and stuffings, and simple ones are still made at home.

Another reason to cook rice only once a day in urban areas was to save on the cost of firewood.[91] Gas-burning rice cookers were introduced in Tokyo in 1904, but even two decades later, two-thirds of homes in that city still lacked gas and relied on firewood for cooking.[92] (Charcoal was too weak a heat source to use for a *kamado*.) The wood-burning *kamado* remained the most important means of cooking rice in cities until after the Second World War, while a pot over the hearth served that function in the countryside, especially in the northern and mountainous central parts of the country, where the hearth was an important heat source for the home.[93] Thus, premodern differences in the methods of cooking rice persisted until the first half of the twentieth century.

Barley Rice

Beyond the various ways of making rice by itself, it was also typical to cook rice mixed with other grains, chiefly barley. *Mugimeshi* (also called *pakuhan*) refers to barley mixed with rice or cooked barley by itself. The term appeared in the historical record frequently in the Muromachi period (1336–1573), and the dish was a staple food for commoners from the seventeenth century.[94] Whole barley is relatively simple to prepare once it has been hulled by pounding it in a mortar, like rice.[95] The one complication is that boiling whole barley produces a slimy starch that coats the kernels, so barley is usually drained once and then re-boiled. Most early modern culinary texts called for barley that had been soaked in water for a long time or boiled first until the kernels 'laugh' – that is, split open.[96] With the spread of rotating stone mortars in the early modern period, farmers could create cracked barley (*hikiwari mugi*), which needed to be cooked only once.[97] The *Collection of Famous Grain Dishes* offers an early nineteenth-century recipe for preparing 'barley which had been milled, dried, then cracked', which could be added to rice for cooking without having to be soaked overnight.[98] The cookbook directs the reader to wash the barley carefully before adding it to the rice.[99]

Barley was an important supplemental foodstuff because it could be grown as a second crop in a paddy after the rice was harvested, a practice that began in the medieval period where local climate allowed it – colder regions, such as Yamagata and Akita, proved too inclement for this second cropping of barley. Barley had also been grown on dry fields since the ancient period.[100] The *Tamon'in Diary* (1478–1616) from Kōfukuji temple in Nara, indicates that barley was planted in the tenth month, after rice had been harvested, and then reaped in the fourth month. The monks keeping the record wrote that barley was served blended with rice, by itself or ground into flour.[101]

Because of the labour needed to crack barley or to spoon off the slime from cooking whole barley, the grain could be more troublesome to make than rice, a fact that contributed to its image as a less sophisticated and more rustic foodstuff – according to the gourmands living in early modern cities, at least. The early nineteenth-century *Collection of Famous Grain Dishes* offered a recipe for Half-barley Rice, describing it as 'a typical meal of farmers', but the author admitted that 'even among urban populations there are thrifty and health-conscious households and many others who consume Half-barley Rice.' The recipe for half-barley rice combines equal proportions of rice and cracked barley, finishing with a touch of salt sprinkled over the cooked grains or added to the cooking pot.[102] Kitagawa confirmed the rustic image of barley in the early nineteenth century, writing: 'There are places in the countryside where rice is consumed undiluted, but in most instances it is eaten there mixed with barley.'[103] One eighteenth-century comic poet from Edo turned the association between barley and rural life into a joke, quipping, 'The bride who is expert in cooking barley comes from sturdy rural stock.'[104]

Kitagawa observed that some commoners in cities ate barley for health reasons or because they liked it, but most city dwellers consumed barley without rice only on seasonal occasions, dressing it up with grated yam (*tororo*), pieces of dried nori and *katsuobushi* or other toppings to transform the humble dish into a luxury.[105] Urban commoners preferred rice to barley, serving only three parts barley to seven parts rice.[106] The custom of eating rice mixed with barley in these proportions remained widespread in Tokyo in the first half of the twentieth century not just for the lower classes and labourers but also among thrifty merchant households.[107] Likewise, in rural areas up to the late 1920s, rice was often diluted with other grains such as wheat, millet and barnyard millet and vegetables such as daikon, in a portion of seven parts grain or vegetables to three parts rice – the opposite of that in cities.[108]

Draftees in the 1920s would discover that barley mixed with rice was also a feature of military catering. When the military 'modernized' its food services in the 1920s, barley rice became recognized as an important staple. The navy had introduced it in the 1880s as a means to counter beriberi, even before the causes of the condition were understood. Suzuki Umetarō identified the cause of beriberi as the result of a deficiency in vitamin B in 1910, but it took the army until 1925 to mandate rations of barley mixed with rice in the same ratio of seven to three prevalent in rural areas.[109]

That the middle class in Tokyo also ate barley is supported by the appearance of recipes for the grain in cookbooks meant for affluent households, which would have been able to afford modern appliances such as gas stoves.[110] The cookbook author Akiho Masumi (1864–1921) in *Katei wayō hoken shokuryō: Sanshoku kondate oyobi ryōrihō* (Nutritious Japanese and Western Foods for the Home: Menus for Three Daily Meals and the Rules for Cooking, 1915), provided a recipe for Cracked Barley Rice with three parts barley to seven parts rice, and he included a separate recipe for whole barley that followed the same proportions. Barley remained important enough to include in this book of modern culinary techniques, which provided exact cooking times down to the minute – an innovation derived from Western cookery texts introduced from the late nineteenth century onwards. Akiho calculated the cost of the gas needed to cook different dishes, despite the fact that two-thirds of homes in Tokyo at this time lacked gas stoves, as noted earlier. The author, who had studied in England through the sponsorship of the Japanese navy, explained that Western methods of cooking were important. His text introduced Western roasting (*rōsutingu*), baking (*bēkingu*) and frying (*furaingu*). But the author asserted that his readers should also know the fundamentals of Japanese cooking, which included making barley rice.[111]

Three years after the publication of Akiho's cookbook, in 1918, rice riots occurred throughout Japan in response to the doubling of the cost of rice from the previous year, an event that some scholars have interpreted to mean that Japanese had come to view access to affordable rice as a necessity.[112] However, a national survey conducted the same year found that urban populations continued to eat rice and barley, while in areas near cities few people consumed rice alone. Besides barley, people in rural locales also relied on foxtail millet, barnyard millet and buckwheat in their diets.[113] Early modern methods of mixing barley with rice thus continued into the twentieth century, as did the association of barley with rural lifestyle and poverty, a point affirmed in Nagatsuka Takashi's novel *Tsuchi* (The Soil, 1910), about tenant farmers in Ibaraki prefecture:

> Faint with hunger they ate anything, however unsavory it looked or smelled, just to fill the gaping void they felt inside them. Not even pausing to chew, they washed down great mouthfuls of moldering barley with water, for only by getting as much into their bellies as possible could they get their strength back. Although not even a horse or cow will eat hay when it can graze on green grass, poor farmers had no alternative but to consume old, decaying food.[114]

Seven years after the publication of *The Soil*, a 1917 survey by the Home Ministry described rural villages where diets were based on barley, with potatoes, daikon and other vegetables mixed in, revealing that the further one travelled from urban centres, the less prominent rice was in the diet.[115] Though eating barley was associated with rural lifestyles, it was also affected by economic status. Surveys conducted in rural Iwate and Yamanashi in 1913 and 1915 indicated that barley rice was a typical foodstuff for even the wealthiest members of a village, although the wealthy ate proportionally less of it. In Fujisatomura village, in Esashi district in Iwate, for example, the village elite ate barley with rice and side dishes of fish and tofu; they even drank sake at dinner. But poorer farmers diluted their barley with foxtail millet, not rice, and rarely consumed any side dishes. Some farmers in the area subsisted on foxtail millet or barley alone. Villages in Yamanashi prefecture reveal a similar dispersion of wealth, with the upper-level farmers eating fish to accompany their barley rice and the poorest farmers unable to afford even miso for soup.[116]

In Niigata prefecture, which is famous for its rice, farmers in the 1920s ate rice mixed with barley, except poorer tenant farmers, who consumed foxtail millet, barnyard millet and ordinary millet, which they ate mixed with rice, chopped daikon and other greens to make a porridge called *katemeshi*. In other regions that also became famous for their rice, such as Yamagata prefecture, barley remained a staple.[117]

Chiba prefecture followed the ratio of rice to barley of seven to three more typical of urban areas, but in some instances domestic rice was diluted with less desirable imported rice. Villagers near Nagasaki mixed their rice with barley, foxtail millet and sweet potato.[118] It was not until 1929 that rice could be grown throughout Hokkaido, thanks to the development of hardier varieties suitable to local conditions. Thus Hokkaido's farmers subsisted on white potatoes from September to April, when other foods became available; pumpkin and boiled corn were other important staples there.[119]

In the same period in rural Fukushima prefecture, 'households often chose to sell all or most of the rice they harvested in order to meet an immediate need for cash', as the historian Kerry Smith has written. Wealthier farmers could sell rice when prices were high, but tenants often had to sell immediately after harvest and could purchase rice only after the price had risen.[120] A Home Ministry survey from 1929 of 2,519 farm households in 134 villages throughout Japan found that less than 20 per cent of the households consumed rice as the main staple, while 79 per cent ate a rice-barley mix in the typical blend of seven parts barley to three parts rice, which they served accompanied by pickles but few if any animal products.[121]

In the 1920s, rice amounted to over 70 per cent of the grains supplied per capita, the equivalent of about 180 litres per person yearly, including rice used for sake and other purposes, but wide geographic and economic diversity in rice consumption remained. Consumption of millets fell, but barley remained a significant staple in rural areas and in less affluent sections of cities.[122] One attempt to use interviews to reconstruct the typical diet for Tokyoites of the 1920s and '30s determined that in eight of twelve households barley was an important staple to augment the rice, in the familiar ratio of seven to three.[123]

Rice Consumption on the Eve of the Second World War

Through the 1930s and 1940s, the typical way of eating rice, depending on the region, was to dilute the grain with other foodstuffs.[124] The military continued to serve rice mixed with barley to troops.[125] Barley also remained an important second crop from the Kantō region westwards, while barnyard millet and foxtail millet were key staples elsewhere.[126] In areas famous for producing rice, farmers continued to sell the rice they grew. Cultivators in Yamagata prefecture in 1930, for example, sold the high-quality rice they farmed, and purchased less expensive rice grown outside the region and wheat for their personal consumption.[127] After selling the best rice they had grown, farmers also turned to third- or fourth-rate rice and rice damaged in processing; the truly desperate ate rice chaff and unripened kernels. The scholar Masuda Shōko comments on these circumstances, writing that, 'although this was rice, it cannot be thought of in the same way as the rice sold today.' In other words, the increased prevalence of rice in the diet in the first decades of the twentieth century should not disguise the fact that there were wide differences in the quality of rice eaten.[128]

Hori Ichirō (1910–1974), a noted scholar of Japanese folk religion, participated in conducting a survey of regional dietary culture in 1941–2 with the aim of determining food sources and means of economizing that would be useful to the regime of wartime rationing that had recently begun.[129] The survey indicates that by the early 1940s, rice had become a main staple throughout the country, thanks to the government's wartime distribution system, but there were only a few places where rice alone was eaten.[130] Hori wrote that the amount of rationed rice people received in 1941 amounted to less than two cups per day, and that was the same amount a typical farmer would have eaten for just one meal. Thus, Hori was quick to explain that people could not subsist on rice alone. He wrote that in Miyagi prefecture, for instance, farmers mixed their rice with barley, seven parts to three. In other locations, millet, sweet potatoes and other grains were added to rice; and dumplings made from various flours were also important supplements to the diet.[131] Folklorists working on the same study of rural diets as Hori reported that in the northern Tōhoku region one particular rural family of five shared only 9 litres of rice per month, amounting to about 300 ml – less than a bowl of rice – per day per person, an amount three to four times less than was typical for the same type of household in the 1930s.[132] The researchers reported that the same family seemed to eat and smoke tobacco throughout the day, making the difference between meals and snacks hard to distinguish; 'tobacco' was often a euphemism for snacks in some locales. The family in Tōhoku augmented their rice allotment with wheat dumplings in soup, azuki bean porridge, pumpkin and white potatoes. According to the same survey, in Gifu prefecture sweet potatoes were an important supplemental food and were eaten grilled, mashed then shaped into dumplings, pulverized and mixed with flour to make a dish called *dēwa*, added to rice or porridge, mixed with buckwheat flour and consumed in dry form.[133]

'One-pot' Meals (Katemeshi)

Mixing rice with barley was one way to economize on food, as was the creation of *katemeshi* (also called *kate* and *kateme*), a one-pot meal that was a traditional staple of farm households throughout the Second World War. In the ancient period, *kate* referred to grains and other provisions for travelling, and by the medieval era the term meant stored foodstuffs. By the early modern period the word was used for foodstuffs – especially daikon roots and greens – that were cooked with other grains. The term *kate* appears in *Shikinichi kahō* (Household Rules for Festivals), which describes how a farm family in rural Echigo (modern Niigata prefecture) in the 1850s ate rice (or barley mixed with rice) for a few meals around the New Year, but typically subsisted on rice porridge or *kate*.[134] A Home Office survey in 1879 noted that city-dwellers consumed 33 per cent more rice than their counterparts in rural areas, and provided a detailed analysis of rural diets. The survey found that in Shizuoka, for instance, diets varied according to four broad economic levels, and the amount of rice consumed by the poorest group amounted to just 20 per cent in a diet augmented by barnyard millet and ordinary millet consumed as a porridge or mixed with other foodstuffs as *katemeshi*.[135] The mixture of grain and chopped greens was much less desirable than a diet of white rice and side dishes, according to Shibuya Teisuke, a farmer from the Kantō region who in the 1920s reflected on his dinner of *katemeshi* made from rice mixed with wheat and yam leaves, complaining: 'Wealthy villagers and city people throw these things away, or else feed them to oxen or pigs.'[136] In the same decade, in Yokogoshi, a village that is now part of Niigata City, servants struck back at their employers, who dined on white rice while serving them poor-quality *katemeshi*. They wrote their employers' names and the quality of the grain dish they served on a local bridge for all to see.[137] Folklorists charged by the government in 1941 to travel to rural areas and document local diets were stunned to find how locals in Fukushima prefecture mixed anything available in with their rice, writing, 'as long as the vegetable is not poisonous, it can be added [to the *katemeshi*].' *Katemeshi* made with chopped daikon root and leaves was ubiquitous, but in eastern Japan white potatoes were added, while sweet potatoes were more common in the west. In Mie prefecture, locals added potato leaves and chopped daikon to *katemeshi*. Other additions to *katemeshi* around Japan included taro, carrots, burdock, pumpkin, turnips, mushrooms, chestnuts, soybeans, azuki beans and kidney beans. Tofu or the lees (*okara*) from making tofu could be added when available, as well as *konnyaku* (konjac). Coastal regions included seaweeds such as hijiki and wakame in their *katemeshi*. The dish did not necessarily include just rice or barley as the main grains; foxtail millet and barnyard millet were also used, alone or in a mix of other grains.[138]

Blended Rice Dishes

One-pot meals of greens and grains were associated with poverty, but other mixed grain dishes had a more positive image, as exemplified by blended rice dishes known as 'mixed rice' (*mazemeshi*), 'rice boiled with other ingredients' (*takikomi gohan*) and 'five items rice' (*gomoku meshi*). In sharp contrast to *katemeshi*, which typically had only one ingredient added to rice, all three of these dishes made use of multiple ingredients, which were typically far more luxurious than chopped tubers, greens and daikon leaves. Rather than a means of economizing on rice by mixing it with whatever was available, blended rice dishes were prepared for special occasions and to be served with soup and side dishes. The ingredients could be cooked with the rice, as in the case of *takikomi gohan*, or stirred in after the rice was cooked, as with *mazemeshi* and *gomoku meshi*. In Kyoto, *gomoku meshi* was made with burdock, taro, tofu or chicken.[139] Shimoda Utako's recipe for the dish in *Introductory Writing on Cooking* (1898) called for bamboo shoots, butterbur in the spring, whole peas in the summer and matsutake mushrooms in the autumn – combinations that remain seasonal favourites. Shimoda added that fried tofu, *konnyaku*, shiitake and cowpeas were other possible ingredients.[140] Blended rice dishes could be quite lavish, as in the medieval recipe for Fragrant Rice (*hōhan*), a dish mentioned in the Japanese-Portuguese dictionary *Vocabulario da lingoa de Iapam* (1603). Rice is mounded on a plate and covered with simmered foods to the point that the rice can no longer be seen, then a sauce is poured over it, turning the rice from a complement to side dishes into a main dish. In its recipe for Fragrant Rice, *Ryōri monogatari* (Tales of Cookery, 1643) recommends topping the rice with fishcake, chestnuts, ginger, grated daikon, fried egg, greens, fried kombu, myoga ginger, finely shaved *katsuobushi* and nori.[141] About a century later, Shōsekiken Sōken offered an even more complicated version of the dish in *Collected Writings on Cuisine and an Outline on Seasonings*, suggesting that the rice should be cooked with duck, pheasant, prawns, rockfish or bamboo shoots. He wrote that the dish could be served cold in the summer with a topping of nori, chestnuts, ginger, grated daikon and pureed yam.[142] Fragrant Rice was the most elaborate way of serving rice for special occasions with other ingredients cooked separately or added later. It was a rice dish, but one in which the rice disappeared, covered by other ingredients.

Gendered Servings

Families before the Second World War may have prepared rice or barley rice, but that does not mean that everyone in the household had an equal share of these grains, since age and gender determined the amount and type of foods served to each person. Children and the elderly would have had less need for food energy and consumed less, but women in a household might receive less rice regardless of how hard they worked. When mixed grain dishes are boiled, the non-rice portions float to the top of the pot, and unless the grains are mixed together, they can be served separately and often were, depending on a person's gender or status in a household. Before the Second World War, in rural Aomori and Iwate, for instance, the white rice portion of a grain dish from the bottom of the cooking pot was called the 'man's meal' (*otoko meshi*) and the remaining top portion of mixed grains and vegetables the 'woman's meal' (*onna meshi*).[143]

The scholar Masuda Shōko has written extensively about gendered and social distinctions in grain consumption, documenting numerous cases throughout the pre-war era of discrimination associated with consuming grains other than rice. In mountainous parts of the Tanba region of Kyoto prefecture, for instance, locals subsisted on a dish of 80 to 90 per cent rice and 10 to 20 per cent barley, called 'older brother's grain' (*animeshi*). When the grains boiled, the barley rose to the top of the cooking pot and was scooped out and served to the women and second and third sons in the household; the household head and his heir ate pure rice from the bottom of the pot. In the Kuji area of Iwate, men in fishing villages with nearby rice paddy ate unadulterated, polished rice that was the 'man's meal', while women consumed rice mixed with other grains as well as less desirable side dishes. Masuda found similar gendered disparities in eating in Aichi, Fukui, Nagano, Tochigi, Kanagawa, Kagoshima and Okayama prefectures, suggesting that sexist consumption habits were once widespread.[144]

Besides gender-based discrimination, Masuda documented many instances of class chauvinism based on the distinction between people who consumed rice and those who did not. She explained that it was not clear when the negative associations of eating mixed grain dishes of barley and millets first appeared, but concluded that the notions were rooted in the long-held perception that mixed grains were rural foods, which the aforementioned references from the early modern period confirm. The folklorists involved in the 1941 survey surmised that discrimination against people who consumed non-rice grains intensified as more people incorporated rice into their diets.[145] To cite some examples from Masuda's research, Hamura City in Tokyo prefecture was noted for its dry field farming in the 1920s, and its residents were pejoratively called 'barley farmers' by outsiders. Hamura's farmers were the butt of jokes; the derogatory phrase 'the lad who grew up on foxtail millet has never heard of a rice tree' implied that the city's residents were so ignorant that they might believe that rice grew on trees. In Nakanojōchō in Gunma prefecture mixed grain dishes were called 'beggar's food', since householders gave the poor a mixture of barley, foxtail millet and rice. In Suginami Ward in Tokyo many farmers grew foxtail millet and barnyard millet until the 1920s, reserving these foodstuffs to feed servants and thus calling foxtail millet and barnyard millet 'servants' grains'. In Chiba prefecture before the Second World War, to prepare the dish called *sanpuku meshi*, which consisted of rice, barley and foxtail millet, the grains were cooked separately and then mixed together before serving – except for the head of the household, who dined on unadulterated rice. The servants received mostly barley and foxtail millet for their meals. In Ichihara City in Chiba, common wisdom held that foxtail millet tasted worse than barley and that it was servants' food; one servant from Ishihara described this situation at mealtime: 'when I opened my lunch pail, the crows cry "cheap!, cheap!"'[146]

Gender and status distinctions were as much a part of when and where members of a household ate as of what they consumed. As the historian Jordan Sand explains, customs of dining separately prevalent in early modern households endured past the Meiji Restoration of 1868 and into the modern period:

In some households, children, apprentices, and servants were grouped apart from the patriarch and his wife and allowed to eat only after they had finished their meal; elsewhere, the room in which the husband dined was off limits to his wife. Even for modern professionals whose lives were less bound by these status taboos, there was no general expectation that dinner would be taken together with the father present.[147]

From the first decades of the twentieth century, urban families gradually took to using a shared dining table, but that did not mean that eating immediately became egalitarian. The patriarch maintained his authority in the household by choosing a preferred seat at the table, such as in front of the decorative alcove (*tokonoma*), and the matriarch continued to control the amount that family members ate by sitting near the rice container. Similar customs were evident in rural households in the 1950s, where men and women ate together but the latter 'were served last and skimped when food is short'. In such households, hierarchy determined where family members sat during the meal to the point that 'only priests and fools [would dare] sit in the master's place.'[148]

The 'traditional' way of consuming rice today in Japan, in a separate bowl as the accompaniment to savoury side dishes, should not allow us to forget all the frugal and fancy ways that grain has been prepared, served and consumed that affected its meanings in the past. Rice can take many forms: brown, white, glutinous and non-glutinous; served in whole kernels or ground into flour; steamed hard, soft-boiled or pounded into cakes; cooked by itself or in a mixture of grains, tubers, leaves, vegetables and other ingredients ranging from the prosaic to the rare – rice can even be drunk as sake or used to make miso and the cooking flavouring mirin. Ohnuki-Tierney observes, 'the symbolic power of rice derives to a large degree from the day-to-day sharing of rice among the members of a social group and its use in the discourse.'[149] But even though many communities ate rice and may have shared abstract ideas about the grain, when they actually consumed rice, they did so in different amounts and by diverse methods that marginalized members of their own households. Eating or not eating rice was as much about reinforcing divisions between people on a day-to-day basis as it was a possible means to foster group identity. Rice can still be argued to be an important symbol, but attempts to ascertain communalities in the diet – or in the national character – should not be at the expense of recognizing the great diversity of Japan's traditional dietary cultures and of the identities of the people who participate in them when any food is considered, especially one that is viewed as being so essential and symbolically important as rice.

4

THE MAKING OF THE MODERN
BOXED LUNCH

'Holding a bentō mom cried making'[1]

One of the frequent complaints about traditional Japanese food by Japanese people is the time and difficulty involved in preparing it: simmering foods for hours, cutting slices of fish precisely or deep-frying in hot oil. Cooking is even more demanding when the meal not only has to taste good, but also must look good and be nutritious. The UNESCO definition of *washoku* describes 'beautifully decorated dishes using fresh ingredients, each of which has a symbolic meaning'. Packed lunches called bentō (or more politely obentō) epitomize and intensify the challenges of making traditional Japanese food because they typically incorporate many different types of food – some fried, others boiled, pickled, grilled, roasted or raw. All these ingredients are cleverly and appealingly arranged as accompaniments to rice. Bentō making can be called a cuisine; according to one commentator, 'if we were to analyze to the profoundest limit the history of this lunchbox – the spirit of its form and aesthetics – we might discover the secret essence of that technology which has made it possible for Japan to survive in the world.'[2] Such an estimation presents bentō boxes as expressions of the uniqueness of Japanese culture, but bentō have a diverse past, which reveals how difficult it is to achieve the high standards of beauty, variety, nutrition and taste expected for the best bentō today.

There are many categories of bentō, but today the ones that are perhaps the most difficult to create – or, to cite the poem above, those most likely to cause a mother to cry in preparing them – are the ones crafted for kindergarten-age children.[3] Kindergarten bentō not only have to please finicky five-year olds, they also have to pass muster with their teachers, who require that the packed lunches be visually appealing, healthy and designed so that the child will consume the contents quickly. In her noted article 'Japanese Mothers and Obentōs: The Lunch-box as Ideological State Apparatus' (1991), the anthropologist Anne Allison observes:

> Much of a woman's labor over *obentō* stems from some agenda other than that of getting the child to eat an entire lunch-box. The latter is certainly a consideration and it is the rationale as well as cover for women being scrutinized by the school's authority figure – the teacher.[4]

In order to be able to prepare a boxed lunch that will meet the standards of school officials, Allison explains that bentō making requires mothers to conform to ideological and gender norms. The historian Tomoko Onabe concurs, 'In the world of kindergarten a bentō becomes a legitimate and crucial symbol of whether or not motherly affection is genuine.'[5] With one's aptitude as a parent at stake, it is no wonder that a mother might burst into tears making a bentō.

The poem cited above resonates well with the anxiety many mothers face when making bentō today, but the poem actually dates from the early modern period, which prompts a different interpretation. Long before the launch in 1872 of a compulsory system of education, bentō were made for special occasions, picnics, outdoor excursions, travelling and for members of the family working outside the home – as they still are today. Since the mother in the poem cried making the bentō, we can infer that the reason she made it was neither pleasurable nor routine, but rather that the bentō was for an extraordinary event such as a family member leaving on a long and potentially dangerous journey. Comparing modern and early modern interpretations of the poem suggests that a mother's stress when preparing a meal for a loved one for a singular occasion has now become a daily occurrence.

Besides the boxed lunches for young children, many other varieties of bentō are found in Japan today. *Ekiben* ('railway-station bentō'), for example, come in thousands of variations, with hundreds of new ones debuting each year. *Ekiben* have been sold on trains and at stations throughout the country since 1883 – eleven years after Japan's first railway opened.[6] One can also find bentō at convenience stores, and some high-end restaurants even specialize in serving gourmet *kaiseki* bentō.

Leaving aside the history of mass-produced and professionally made bentō such as those sold on trains and in restaurants, this chapter focuses on the development of home-made box lunches, of which kindergarten boxed

'Boxed lunch for a child entering kindergarten', 2010.

lunches are the most prominent example today. Homemade bentō have a history that can be traced to the foods carried by travellers since at least the eighth century, but the aesthetics of making boxed meals crystallized in the early modern period. The 'ideological state apparatus' that guides mothers in bentō making, which Allison delineates in her article about contemporary Japan, took shape on the eve of the Second World War. Homemade bentō evolved from a prepared meal created out of necessity into a gourmet repast for special occasions before taking one of their most conspicuous forms as an artful and nutritious lunch for schoolchildren.

The evolution of bentō is part of the history of lunch in Japan. The custom of eating at midday can be traced back centuries, but the notion that the noon meal should be distinct from other meals during the day evolved out of necessity, when work required that food be made portable to be eaten outside the home. The creation of a compulsory system of education, along with changes in the nature of work at the turn of the twentieth century, meant that more people studied or laboured away from where they lived; and they had to eat their midday meals away from home, a fact that helped to domesticate further the practice of bentō making. Reflecting the influence of Western food culture, lunch – a category of meal absent in early modern

Japanese cookery writings – gained definition in early twentieth-century cookbooks, which confirmed that the noon meal was supposed to be a discrete type of repast, distinct from the morning and evening meals. Lunch required different foods from other meals prepared during the day, and therefore demanded more labour from housewives, who were the people in the household required either to prepare lunch at home or to make bentō for their family to take to work or school.

Early Travel Foods

The word bentō can refer to a container or to the food within it, but the literal translation of the term is something that is 'truly convenient', which is an apt way to refer to a portable meal. The scholar Kitamura Nobuo (1783–1856) traced the origin of the term bentō to the word *mentsū*, referring to a type of food container intended for one person. However, the term bentō originated in Song dynasty China (960–1279), designating something useful. Its association with food in Japan was clear by the period of the publication of the Japanese–Portuguese dictionary *Vocabulario da lingoa de Iapam*, printed by Jesuit missionaries in Nagasaki in 1603. The dictionary offers two definitions of bentō: as something convenient and as a portable meal.[7] The association of bentō with a food container appears to be more recent, because during the first half of the twentieth century people carried their meals in a variety of vessels with different names.

In prehistoric times, the Palaeolithic peoples of Japan doubtless took food with them to eat while travelling away from their homesteads, but histories of bentō usually begin by describing the portable foods consumed from the eighth century onwards, since these are the earliest that appear in historical records. At banquets and special occasions in the Nara (710–84) and Heian (794–1185) periods, aristocrats distributed to their retainers snacks called *donjiki* – glutinous grain moulded by hand into egg-shaped balls. *Donjiki* were also travel foods; heartier, harder and stickier versions of the modern rice balls called *onigiri* or *omusubi* made from polished, non-glutinous white rice today.[8] Another ancient travel food was dried grain created from glutinous varieties of rice, millet or foxtail millet that had been steamed and then dried in the sun. Placed in a bag, the dried grain could be eaten directly using the hands or added to hot water to make porridge.[9] Rice was also toasted in the hull and then hulled to make another travel food called 'toasted rice' (*yakigome*). Travellers also took umeboshi, miso and salt to eat along with their grain foods.[10] To make carrying all these foods easier, travellers slung from their waists, long, narrow sacks made from rice straw – a mode of transporting rations that was used by troops in the Sino-Japanese War (1894–5).[11]

Such travel foods are mentioned in passing in the eighth-century *Nihon shoki* (Chronicles of Japan) and *Man'yōshū* (Collection of Myriad Leaves), the earliest extant collection of Japanese poetry.[12] The latter contains a verse suggesting how travellers used leaves to wrap up their provisions:

At home
grain is served in a vessel,
when taking grass for one's pillow
traveling
it is served on an oak leaf.[13]

In the poem, the oak leaf serving as a plate complements the grass pillow, a term synonymous with travelling.

Foods served on or wrapped in leaves remain ubiquitous in Japanese traditional food culture. Harking back to the aforementioned poem are oak-leaf rice cakes (*kashiwa mochi*), a confection made from rice flour dough stuffed with sweetened azuki paste and served inside a folded oak leaf, traditionally eaten to mark the fifth day of the fifth month to fortify the body before the start of summer. Besides oak leaves, sticky confections such as rice cakes are still served on or between cherry, persimmon and plum leaves as well as chrysanthemum leaves, cedar needles and lotus leaves. Practically any foliage that is not poisonous can be used.[14] These leaves are generally not consumed, but they do serve an important culinary function by adding visual, tactile and aesthetic appeal.

Many regional forms of sushi originated as portable foods that feature whole or sliced fish stuffed with rice and wrapped in the large green blades of bamboo grass or in the thin brown outer leaves of bamboo shoots. In Kii, the mountainous southern part of present-day Mie prefecture, locals once took cooked barley and rice and moulded the grain into balls, which they wrapped in pickled leaf mustard (*takana*) to make *takanazushi*, a lunch convenient when working away from the home. The dish is also called 'eye-popping sushi' (*meharizushi*), suggesting a physical reaction to the enormous size of the wrapped rice balls. In Iga, which is in the western part of Mie prefecture, balls of rice mixed with soybeans were wrapped in butterbur leaves, three balls per leaf, to create a delicacy that was offered to the spirit of the fields at the start of the planting season.[15]

Travellers and people working away from home also used leaves to cook food, and these dishes have survived in regional cuisine. In Urahara in Niigata prefecture, locals working in the mountains once caught ayu (sweetfish) or cherry salmon, wrapped the fish in magnolia leaves (*hoba*) slathered with miso and placed them in the coals of a fire pit to bake. *Hoba miso*, a similar recipe, is found in Takayama City in Gifu prefecture and calls for placing the magnolia leaf directly on top of a portable brazier to serve as a cooking surface. After an obligatory smear of miso and a garnish of green onions, the magnolia leaf is used as a surface to cook vegetables, fish, meat or eggs. In pre-Second World War Iwafune in Niigata prefecture, when farmers went to work in the mountains in the summer, they carried the ingredients for soup: miso to be dissolved in cold water, to which they could add a cucumber and perilla leaves or gathered herbs such as mizuna. The cold soup was an accompaniment to rice and barley and pickles.[16]

Leaves may be the earliest means of transporting prepared foods, but references to vessels meant to carry foods for travelling date from the ancient period. 'Dried grain containers' were another way of holding the dried grains mentioned earlier. A lidded box, typically made from thin strips of cypress, called a *warigo* could contain cooked grain and other foods. Such boxes had internal dividers to keep the foods separate in the manner of modern bentō boxes.[17]

The containers used by farmers and workers for their lunches varied by location and function in the first half of the twentieth century. In the Urahara region of Niigata, besides the magnolia leaves used for cooking mentioned earlier, locals enjoyed a more elaborate boxed lunch during the spring planting season, called a *yachigari bentō*, which had two parts: a bottom container for rice and an upper portion for the side dishes, which were typically vegetables pickled in miso, salted salmon, fermented soybeans (*nattō*) or other preserved foods.[18] Wealthier workers in cities before the Second World War could expect to find better foodstuffs in their lunchboxes, but these too were plain by today's standards. In the Fukugawa area of Tokyo in the household of the plasterer Andō Fukumatsu, for example, the matron of the home prepared a large pot of barley rice in the morning so that there would be enough for lunch. Andō's lunchbox had two parts: a bottom box for the barley rice and a separate container for side dishes, which typically included a piece of salted salmon, a Japanese-style omelette (as used in sushi) and pickles.[19]

Premodern customs of using leaves and a variety of containers for portable meals endured in parts of Japan past the first half of the twentieth

Farmers in Yatsushiro City eating lunch, photographed by Mugishima Masaru, 1948.

century. Farmers in the 1960s retained the ancient practice of using magnolia leaves or the outer bark of bamboo shoots to wrap their lunches when they went off to work in the mountains. Kotani Kanekichi, a teacher born in 1892 in rural Wakayama prefecture, recalled how he would go for long walks in the mountains as a youth carrying with him a lunch of *onigiri* made from a mix of rice and barley around umeboshi, which he wrapped first in bamboo leaves and then in a cloth.[20] Leaves were ideal for sticky grains like glutinous rice or millet, which could be compressed into a small ball and would hold their shape. But barnyard millet is not glutinous and would crumble if made into a ball, thus requiring the use of a container, usually a bag. Hemp bags were used for barnyard millet in Aomori and Iwate for this purpose until the early 1960s.[21] Farmers consumed the barnyard millet by pressing on the bag to clump the grain into lumps that could be eaten by hand; any remaining grains could be eaten directly from the bag, eliminating the need for chopsticks and giving concrete meaning to the words 'sack lunch'.[22]

A Brief History of Lunch

Bentō and other portable foods marked a departure from eating at home, where there was not a ready distinction between the contents of the meal and the time of day. Traditionally, the midday meal was a lot like the first meal of the day and similar to the evening one. Culinary texts written before the twentieth century fail to distinguish meals according to the time of day. Early modern recipe collections are instead organized by ingredients, listing ways to prepare certain recipes, or by types of dishes such as soups, simmered foods, sweets and so on. The words for breakfast (chōshoku, asameshi), lunch (chūshoku, hirumeshi) and dinner (yūshoku, yūhan) were not fixed until the end of the early modern period.[23] 'Lunch' (ranchi) was a foreign import. The Western-style bakery Fūgetsudo introduced a 'lunch service with a glass of wine' to diners in Tokyo in 1877. That same year, the bakery, which had its origins as a Japanese-style confectioner, began serving French cuisine and Western dishes such as omelettes, steak, beef curry and ice cream.[24] Wealthy urbanites could enjoy exotic lunches in cities in the late nineteenth century, but in terms of the meals served in homes in both rural areas and cities in the first half of the twentieth century, it is often difficult to discern much of a difference between the morning meal, the one eaten at midday and the one in the evening except when one of those meals is prepared in advance to be eaten away from home at a workplace or school. Since the latter was usually the midday meal, the history of bentō is connected to the history of lunch in Japan.

In the ancient period, the ruling elite ate only twice a day, and it is generally, but erroneously, believed that the rest of the population followed the same practice in the medieval period.[25] Scholars surmise a shift from two meals a day to three for most of the population by the turn of the seventeenth or eighteenth century, but in either case their evidence appears to be based on elite dining patterns, which are the only ones that have survived in the historical records. All these propositions assume that the general population imitated the habits of the elite. To summarize the argument, in the ancient period aristocrats ate twice daily while monastics, owing to their clerical vows, ate only breakfast. Kamakura period (1185–1333) artisans and warriors adopted a midday meal to sustain themselves, and by the end of the fourteenth century it was customary even for monastics to snack during the day.[26] Yet the assumption is that the rest of the population was content with eating just twice a day until the seventeenth or eighteenth century, an idea that takes for granted that commoners were guided in their meal choice by a desire to emulate the elite rather than the more logical proposition that they ate when they were hungry. Farmers in the early twentieth century consumed four, five or even six meals a day, so it is illogical to assume that their premodern forebears, who laboured equally hard, would have restricted themselves to just two meals per day. Unfortunately, we do not have the documentary evidence to know how often the general population ate in the premodern era, but the evidence for the early twentieth century offers compelling reason to argue that most people followed their stomachs rather than the habits of the idle elite, and so ate more than twice a day.

Meal frequency varied by location and season, with a major distinction being between main meals and snacks. Ethnologists surveying food habits in the countryside in 1941 observed that while people in the cities ate three meals daily, inhabitants in agricultural regions and mountainous areas ate four or five times daily in the summer and three or four times in the winter. In the summer, the day began with a pre-breakfast. In Nagasaki the pre-breakfast was called a 'tea snack' or 'tobacco', while in Shimane it was 'morning tea'. An afternoon snack was also typical in rural areas. In the winter, farmers could sleep later than in the summer and so they often snacked less during the day, but when they did handicraft work late into the night they added a 'night meal' after their usual dinner.[27] A concrete example of what people ate for these meals comes from an oral history project conducted under the direction of the Ministry of Agriculture, Forestry and Fisheries in the early 1980s, in which elderly people were asked about their typical meals in the 1920s and 1930s.[28] In Iwafune in Akita prefecture in the summer, farmers ate five times daily: a breakfast of rice cooked with barley, miso soup containing aubergine (eggplant) and white potatoes, and a salad of green beans, chestnuts, miso and a little sugar, along with cucumber and aubergine pickles. Their mid-morning snack was watermelon or melon. The midday meal was barley rice served with miso soup, a grilled fish, sautéed aubergine, pickled spring onions (scallions) and umeboshi. An afternoon snack of edamame came before the evening meal of wheat noodles; shiitake, dried gourd and green onion soup with a soy sauce broth; and a salad made from gourd, pepper and miso, accompanied by pickles.[29] The folklorist Ema Mieko, who in 1932 moved to Takayama in Gifu prefecture with her husband, the author Ema Shū, described how locals in the mountainous Hida region of Gifu ate seven meals a day in the summer: breakfast, morning snack, lunch, tea break, snack, dinner and the night meal. These meals consisted of similar dishes. The chief staple was a grain dish combining rice, barnyard millet, foxtail millet and the bran from the barnyard millet. The cooked grain accompanied miso soup, pickles, dumplings made from horse chestnuts, and dumplings or porridge made from the flour of a variety of millet called Shikokubie. Lunch might include the addition of boiled pumpkin, and the night meal might include boiled white potatoes. In the winter, the people of Hida ate six meals, according to Ema, skipping the snack after breakfast.[30]

In other locales, a snack supplemented the three main meals of the day, but that snack was often the equivalent of a meal. In the south, on the Pacific coast in the Ise area of Mie prefecture, a typical spring menu for a farm household in the 1920s and '30s consisted of a breakfast of rice and barley or rice mixed with soybeans, miso soup with dried daikon, and pickled daikon. For the midday meal, barley and rice and miso soup were repeated and served with boiled peas, dried sardines and daikon pickles. The afternoon was punctuated by a snack of rice crackers, dried rice cakes, buckwheat dough or *tanohana* – parched barley and brown sugar on top of barley rice. For the evening meal, barley mixed with rice appeared yet again, with boiled onion with miso dressing and boiled peas.[31] On the central plains near Saga City in Saga prefecture, afternoon snacks for farmers included steamed sweet potatoes in the winter, boiled white potatoes or boiled corn on the cob in the summer and steamed sweet potatoes or persimmons in the autumn.[32] The folklorist Segawa Kiyoko observed that for farmers,

> snacks were different from the snacks for people in the cities. They were not treats for the mouth. They were something to eat once someone had depleted all their energy and needed fuel to return to work, so they had to provide energy.

Accordingly, she writes, it was often difficult to differentiate a snack from a meal.[33]

As the previous examples indicate, for the rural population before the Second World War, there was often little to distinguish the noonday meal from those at other times of the day, and the distinction between snacks and meals was also sometimes hard to discern. To illustrate further the lack of difference between meals, we can turn to an example cited by the noted food scholar Ishige Naomichi of his grandmother's household in the 1930s.

Ishige's grandmother lived in an agricultural area that is now part of Yamagata City in Yamagata prefecture. He writes:

> There was not much difference for the meals every day, breakfast, lunch and dinner. The usual staple was barley rice cooked in a ratio of four parts rice to six parts barley. With the barley rice for breakfast would be miso soup, one vegetable dish and pickles. When people returned home for lunch there was only leftover barley rice, miso soup and pickles; dinner was miso soup and one vegetable side dish such as vegetable soup, vegetables in sesame dressing, or parboiled and pressed spinach. Vegetable side dishes were the norm and there was fish only once a week.[34]

Work in the fields demanded more attention and energy than the need to prepare separate foods for each meal, especially when enough rice and barley could be made in the morning to last the day. Busy farm households were often empty during the noon hour with everyone working outdoors, so miso and pickles were left on hand to accompany the leftover grain dish and serve as a midday meal for anyone who needed it. Folklorists in the 1941 food survey noted that housewives would not be embarrassed by the lack of side dishes on offer for a midday meal, but they did take pride in their miso, explaining that farmers would be ashamed to admit to eating new miso when miso three to four years old was preferred.[35] The older miso was an indication that the family could afford to stockpile the seasoning rather than consuming it immediately after it was made.

Cooking rice in the morning and then eating the leftovers was once the norm in Edo during the early nineteenth century, and that custom continued into the twentieth. Although residents of Osaka and Kyoto made rice for their noonday meal, they too made it just once a day, consuming rice porridge for breakfast made from the previous day's batch.[36] Many households in Tokyo in the 1920s and 1930s retained the habit of cooking rice just once a day since it was less time-consuming and more economical, saving on fuel. The family of Yanaka Kami, a performer of ballads (*ryōkyoku*) living in Shitamachi, had white rice and miso soup for breakfast and leftovers for lunch, which depending on the season, might have been accompanied by a boiled vegetable, such as daikon in the winter and bamboo shoots in the spring. Even in the more fashionable Yamanote section of the city, in the same period the middle-class household of Nozawa Mitsue ate reheated rice for lunch, although she enjoyed better side dishes: for breakfast miso soup with daikon along with pickled napa cabbage and simmered soybeans; and for lunch leftover rice with a piece of grilled salted salmon and any other foods remaining from breakfast.[37]

The Art of the Lunchbox

With their varied and often gourmet ingredients and beautiful presentation, bentō today are far removed from the foods taken to work sites before the Second World War – to the point that one might assume that bentō are post-war innovations. However, there is a long historical precedent for elaborate boxed lunches that dates from the early modern period. For example, *makunouchi* ('between the scenes') bentō were part of the enjoyment of attending the Kabuki theatre. In the first half of the nineteenth century these boxed meals typically included grilled rice balls and side dishes such as fried egg, fishcake, boiled *konnyaku* and grilled tofu. Arranged in a box, the meals were delivered to the audience members' seats.[38]

Wealthy urbanites and samurai in the early modern period devoted extraordinary attention and resources to their portable meals, as is clear from the beautiful food containers they used, made from lacquer, wood, porcelain, metal and bamboo. The finest examples of these, meant for the highest-ranking warlords, are embossed in gold lacquer, but even the simplest show masterful craftsmanship and clever design that catered to individual preferences.[39] The largest are sturdy boxes holding multiple lacquered containers, plates, vessels for sake and serving utensils. Pushing a button near the top on one side of some bentō holders allows a narrow box to slip out, to contain chopsticks. For travelling or eating at work, samurai took 'hip-bentō' (*koshi bentō*), curved containers designed to sit comfortably when secured to the waist. Other bentō boxes are made like Russian dolls: five separate boxes that fit snugly inside one another for storage. The workmanship of bentō boxes shows the pride that their owners placed in these containers and in creating the proper ambiance when taking a prepared meal on trips outside the home.

Instead of being meant for a working lunch, elaborate bentō boxes were usually for special occasions. The culinary text *Ryōri hayashinan* (Ready Guide to Cooking) describes how sumptuous meals could be created to match the beautiful portable food containers. *Ready Guide to Cooking* also deserves attention as the earliest expression of the aesthetics of the boxed lunch that are so prominent today, offering the first articulation of the rules about what should be included in a container of food and how the contents should be arranged.

'Hip bentō': lunchbox of cinnabar lacquer with paulownia and chrysanthemum motifs in gold *makie*. The design of this bentō allows it be carried comfortably at the waist, so it is called a 'hip bentō' (*koshi bentō*).

The Beautiful Bentō of 'Ready Guide to Cooking'

Daigo Sanjin's *Ready Guide to Cooking* was published in two instalments of two volumes each. The first instalment appeared in print in 1801 and the second in 1804. Volumes one to three are devoted to different styles of dining: the first covers banquet cuisine and *kaiseki* meals for the tea cuisine; the second focuses on portable meals including bentō. Volume three offers an interpretation of meals in mountainous rural areas, providing a chance for the author to discourse on salted and dried seafood; the same volume also describes table dining in the Chinese style (*shippoku ryōri*). The final tome lists recipes for soups, salads with vinegar dressings and grilled foods; it also provides general culinary advice. The four-volume text proved quite popular, and was reprinted in 1822, 1835 and 1915.[40]

The boxed meals of volume two of *Ready Guide to Cooking* are not typical lunches, nor do they specify which meal during the day they are meant to replace – a reminder of the fact that lunch was not yet an established part of the culinary lexicon in the early nineteenth century, even for the wealthy readers of Daigo's text. The meals are instead meant for special occasions, as suggested by the author, who lists menus for outings to observe the change of seasons, for cherry blossom viewings, boat excursions, visits to a holiday home, paying respects to someone taken ill and for celebrations of the doll festival in the third month. For most of these examples, Daigo provides menus of top, middle and lower quality for his readers to choose from. He also includes vegetarian versions of some meals.

In *Ready Guide to Cooking* nearly all the menus are for multi-tiered boxes of food intended to be shared by a group – a style of eating that continues today in the elaborate containers of foods served at the New Year. The boxes of prepared fish and vegetables are meant to accompany a separate case containing rice or another grain dish. Daigo directs his readers to package the foods into separate containers according to their type:

> The first box contains a selection of fish, the second is vegetarian, the third has preserved fish and pickles, and the fourth steamed sweets [such as stuffed buns and sweet azuki jelly]. Alternatively, the first container can be a combination of fish and vegetables, and the third can be varieties of sashimi.

The difference in packing the boxes, he explains, depends on the occasion: 'For boxes of food to be sent to other people or those for the doll festival, one should separate the fish from the vegetables following the earlier rule, but for pleasure excursions and flower viewing one can do as one wishes and arrange the fish and vegetables together.' Daigo adds to his introductory remarks a word of caution: to avoid using raw foods for meals meant for travellers or intended for the infirm. The latter, he states, should not be given simmered or grilled foods either.[41]

Daigo does not describe how to make the dishes in his menus, but he does provide a few occasional notes about them, such as variations of seasonal ingredients that can be used, and he adds suggestions about how to serve the foods. In one example, he offers that it is attention-grabbing to cut a watermelon in half, hollow it out and serve slices of melon in the fruit's shell instead of a bowl.[42] Such statements provide reasons for inferring that the author intended his boxed meals to be unpacked, rather than eaten directly from their containers as modern bentō are.

Daigo goes so far as to recommend the use of found objects in unpacking and serving a premade meal. His menu for travelling to a holiday home instructs the reader to incorporate flowers and fruits from the host's garden:

> When you are invited to stay at a holiday home or to have a meal there, take a moment and examine the seasonal fruits and flowers in the host's garden and the produce in the vegetable plot to see if they might be used as a garnish for a soup or as a decoration for the meal.

Reproduction of a menu for a bentō for flower viewing from Daigo Sanjin's *Ready Guide to Cooking*.

> If someone has rare flowers and vegetables, do not act thoughtlessly and use them haphazardly. Praise them and request to select them for use in the dining arrangement, and then display them prominently.[43]

Daigo's preoccupation with creating a boxed meal that is artful and tailored to the recipient foreshadows the homemade bentō of today, which are generally made with care to please the person who receives them both by their taste and by their appearance. The major difference from modern bentō is that Daigo not only tells his readers how to make the bentō – or supervise their construction – but advises on the orchestration of their unpacking and display before eating. Early modern bentō containers often included individual serving plates that would allow a more elegant mode of dining than eating directly from a box.

Most of Daigo's menus are meant to be unpacked, but he also includes advice for creating individual boxed meals that are visually appealing.

He indicates that individual bentō are meant for 'festivals, banquets and other occasions with many people'. To make preparation and clean-up easier, he advises using boxes made from Japanese cypress that can be thrown away after eating. His menus for two different bentō both delineate one box for a grain dish and another for prepared delicacies. One version has fish; the other is vegetarian:[44]

Selection of Refreshments

Teriyaki tilefish	Vegetables pickled in sake lees
Chinese yam	Pickled greens
Abalone	Boiled green bell pepper
Royal fern	Ginger
Fried egg	Cedar toothpicks
Large shiitake	
Lower box: Grilled rice balls	

Vegetarian Refreshments

Dried tofu	Vegetables pickled in sake lees
Arrowhead	Pickled greens
Dried gourd	Boiled green pepper
Shiitake	Cedar toothpicks
Wrapped wheat gluten	
Lower box: Grilled rice balls	

Daigo notes the addition of toothpicks but omits chopsticks, which no one would have forgotten, so they must have been assumed.

Beyond merely listing the foods, Daigo gives guidance for packing the individual boxed meals, explaining how a single square box can be divided into three, five, seven or nine geometrical parts, each meant to hold a separate item of food:

Depending on one's thoughts for the individual bentō, it is fine to pack them as one wishes, but it is better if the left and right sides are symmetrical. The most important aspect is the balance of colours. Make sure that similar colours are not crammed in the same place. It is better if red is placed in the centre. Many of the contents of the box will bleed colours, and it's distasteful if the colours blur together.[45]

Just as it would be ill-advised to have two foods of the same colour next to each other, Daigo instructs readers to cut the morsels into different shapes and sizes to provide a pleasing visual contrast:

> When packing the boxes, whether it is nine, seven, five or three varieties of foods, it is best if the flavours and the way the foods are cut are contrasting. But that does not mean that one should cut the foods willy-nilly. Pay attention that the morsels are not all the same shape, whether they are big, small, long, short, round or crooked. Unless you also keep in mind the dimensions of the container and fill it in an appropriate manner from the beginning, cutting the pieces and constructing it accordingly, when you pack the box it will end up looking strange. You have to cut the pieces so that they fit the proportions of the box's interior.[46]

Daigo articulates aesthetics of bentō packing that are still used in the creation of bentō today, but in his era, crafting gourmet bentō was for people who could afford to celebrate well on special occasions. It would be a century before the aesthetics of lunchbox making became a daily practice of the middle class, necessitated by family members commuting to work and school. By that time bentō had become synonymous with lunch.

Preparing the Modern Lunch

The category of lunch entered the lexicon of cookbook authors after the turn of the twentieth century, but initially in terms of contents the midday meal differed from breakfast and dinner largely in name alone. English and American cookbooks provided the inspiration for Japanese authors to organize their volumes according to the three meals of the day. Examples of Japanese cookbooks patterned after Western prototypes include Anzai Komako's *Shiki mainichi sanshoku ryōrihō* (Culinary Guide to Three Meals a Day in Season, 1909), Nishino Miyoshi's *Katei jitsuyō kondate to ryōrihō* (Practical Home Menus and Culinary Guide, 1915) and Akiho Masumi's *Katei wayō hoken shokuryō: Sanshoku kondate oyobi ryōrihō* (Healthy Japanese and Western Foods for the Family: Menus of Three Meals and Culinary Guide, 1915).[47] These three cookbooks were published as instructional materials for women's cooking schools and girls' higher schools (equivalent to a boys' middle school) which taught home economics courses and were growing in enrolments in this period. The number of female students in post-primary education increased sixfold between 1910 and 1926, to the point that almost as many girls gained an education beyond primary school as did boys.[48]

The menus these pedagogical cookbooks suggested were not elaborate. After providing some general advice about the kitchen and some basic culinary tips, Anzai's *Culinary Guide to Three Meals a Day in Season* guided readers on how to make one or two different dishes for each meal on a given day. Soups and simmered dishes prevail for Anzai's suggestions for breakfast, but the distinction between the types of food and amount prepared for lunch and dinner is hard to discern. For instance, grilled fish and meat dishes appear as often for the midday meal as they do for the evening one. Anzai's proposed menu for 27 March lists a breakfast of clear soup with bean sprouts and dried sardines; lunch of a salad of daikon, kombu and lotus root that had been lightly simmered in soy sauce, with sesame dressing; and dinner of grilled fish, a greenling basted with soy sauce and simmered carrot.[49] A grain dish would have been the natural accompaniment to these foods. Learning to create three meals a day provided a way for students to study how to cook a variety of dishes while also learning to budget and plan ahead. Cost, according to Anzai, is the primary concern in creating any menu, for it determined the amount that needed to be devoted to seasonings including soy sauce, sugar and miso; the remainder could be spent on vegetables and meat.[50] The readers of these texts and the students in cooking classes came to understand that it was insufficient simply to serve leftovers for lunch, despite the fact that this was the norm.

The cooking pedagogue Akiho Masumi (1864–1921) helped to foster the idea that lunch should be a distinct type of meal worthy of as much attention as dinner. In 1904, he opened a cooking school in Kanda in Tokyo, where he taught women how to cook both Japanese and Western dishes; in 1907 he renamed the institution Tokyo Women's Cooking School.[51] The didactic tone of his cookbook *Healthy Japanese and Western Foods for the Family* is unmistakable. He set out by advising his readers about the necessity of thinking about health and economy, which extended not just to the ingredients but also to the kitchen, which must allow in sufficient light and clean air lest the cooking space attract cockroaches and cause health problems for the chef or the people who eat the food. Akiho referred to the high standards of cooking areas in Europe and America and lectured, 'Westerners who are accustomed to bright and clean kitchens would raise their eyebrows if they saw a gloomy kitchen and they would not be able to stay half a day in it.' Meals must also be served at the correct time, necessitating a clock in the kitchen, 'otherwise mealtimes will be absurdly early or late or dinner too late'.[52] Situated within a proper arena for cooking with an apron, soap, a modern gas stove and ample amounts of MSG seasoning (monosodium glutamate, sold under the brand name Ajinomoto), which Akiho dubbed a 'blessing of modern civilization', the reader of Akiho's cookbook can embark on his recipes, which followed Anzai's early work by beginning with the fundamentals of making stock, cooking rice and preparing pickles, and then gave pointers for preparing specific ingredients, Western soups and salad dressings.[53]

Akiho devotes most of his text to the daily menus, which consist of directions to make a different single serving of breakfast, lunch and dinner each day. The menus do not follow a seasonal order as in Anzai's cookbook, but they are composed to include what the author viewed as the proper 'amount of foods for optimum health', namely, 3 cups (700 ml) of white rice, approximately half a pound (225 g) of meat and about a pound (450 g) of vegetables, including potatoes, per person each day.[54] That he provides exact measurements, cooking times, temperatures and advice on plating underscores the fact that Akiho's work is an instructional cookbook meant to be used by students who might be unaccustomed to working in a modern kitchen.

As modern as Akiho's pretensions are, his menus nonetheless are largely Japanese, augmented with Western dishes, such as chicken cutlets, omelettes and meatballs, and a few dishes that may be of his own invention, such as cucumbers stuffed with beef. He makes sure that his students follow centuries-old custom in serving the finished products by supplying a diagram for each meal showing a tray with the rice in the bottom left-hand corner, the soup in the bottom right-hand corner, pickles in the centre of the tray and two side dishes occupying the top corners. Readers who may have missed the fact that this arrangement of dishes follows time-honoured precedents would nonetheless see the same format repeated for every meal.

There is a preponderance of egg dishes included with breakfast, but little else distinguishes that meal from lunch and dinner. Like Anzai's *Culinary Guide*, Akiho's menus appear to be exercises in creating a variety of recipes with an emphasis on Western dishes and ingedients, as the following example illustrates:

Breakfast Menu

Rice
Miso soup with aubergine and white potatoes
Curried eggs
Grilled aubergine
Pickles

Each of the dishes listed includes the amount of ingredients to be used; and after each meal, the author tabulates the cost to facilitate an understanding of how such meals could fit into a household budget. In all his menus, Akiho provided concise directions referring readers back to earlier chapters, should they need a reminder about how to prepare miso soup. He even tells his readers how thickly to slice the aubergine and potatoes for the soup. His curry sauce is made by sautéing diced onions in butter until they are browned and adding curry powder with a teaspoon of flour.

The lunch menu for the same day in Akiho's cookbook substitutes dark miso for white miso for the soup and adds an intriguing French recipe:

Lunch Menu

Rice
Soup: white miso, fish roe, vegetable
Côtelettes Champvallon: chicken, vegetables
Salad: ayu (sweetfish), vegetables
Pickles

The miso soup is made with diced sea bream roe and tofu and the 'vegetable' is a garnish of mitsuba. Côtelettes Champvallon is usually prepared with lamb on a bed of potatoes, but the variation here calls for chicken, as Akiho indicated:

For Côtelettes Champvallon, cut the meat of a pullet into long, thin slices; sprinkle with salt; coat with egg yolk, then roll in soft breadcrumbs to coat. Next, heat butter in a frying pan and place the chicken in the centre of the pan to fry. Cut into three pieces and serve on a plate garnished with white potatoes with a topping of butter and milk.[55]

Directions for the salad indicate steaming the ayu for ten minutes, allowing the fish to cool and serving alongside potatoes and cherry tomatoes with an 'oil dressing', which from its ingredients of olive oil, eggs, vinegar, milk, salt, pepper and sugar sounds similar to mayonnaise. To use milk in a recipe at this time was quite novel given that 99 per cent of the Japanese population at the beginning of the twentieth century never drank milk. Chicken and eggs also marked the meal as elite, since per capita consumption of the former was negligible and consumption of the latter amounted to one egg per month per person in this period.[56] Yet, Akiho advocated consuming 225 g of meat daily. The use of imported olive oil and sautéing in butter also marked the menu as Western.

A typical dinner returns to the familiar pattern of rice, soup, pickles and side dishes:

Dinner Menu

Rice
Soup: sea bream, vegetables
Fried fish: ayu, ginger
Sesame-vinegar salad: fish, small kudzu crackers, mitsuba

The stock for the evening soup is made with MSG, which is added to water, salt and sugar with pieces of sea bream that were previously cooked separately. The ayu is grilled whole on a skewer and the ginger is meant as a garnish. The salad combines five or six slices of sea bream with boiled mitsuba in a sesame-vinegar sauce, but how the kudzu crackers are to be prepared and served remains unstated, which might suggest that they are purchased.[57]

Cookbooks such as *Healthy Japanese and Western Foods for the Family* imparted to their readers – the middle- to upper-class girls attending women's higher school and cooking academies in major cities – that lunch was as important a meal as any other served during the day. Lunch demanded attention, creativity and even expensive ingredients worthy of dinner. Later authors took this message to heart in their writing of the first modern bentō cookbooks.

Entering the Age of Bentō Cookbooks

In the first decades of the twentieth century more people in cities ate their midday meal outside the home because of school or work. As the Japanese economy diversified, urbanization advanced, and people left the country-side for employment in the cities. Tokyo's population doubled in the first decades of the twentieth century and there was an especially sharp rise after the First World War in the ranks of middle-class white-collar workers.[58] In 1907 the government mandated six years of compulsory education and by 1908, some 98 per cent of children attended school. Ten per cent of these students – those whose parents could afford it – went on to middle school. Making a lunch bentō for schoolchildren or for a salaried employee did not have to be a complicated process. A typical bentō for a middle-class white-collar worker in Osaka in the 1920s was leftover rice from breakfast and one or two side dishes, such as fried egg, salted salmon, boiled fishcake or whatever was left uneaten from dinner the previous evening.[59]

For those who could afford the time and the money to make better-quality meals, cookbook authors provided guidance, preaching that lunchtime bentō should be more than simply a meal of leftovers. Bentō cookbooks indicated that boxed lunches should include original dishes tastefully arranged. Fujimura Munetaru's *Nichiyō benri bentō ryōri annai* (Convenient Daily Guide to Bentō Cooking, 1905) provides the earliest example of a modern cookbook dedicated to bentō. His work began a boom in recipes for bentō from the second decade of the twentieth century in articles in newspapers and magazines that catered to middle-class housewives.[60] Despite its novelty, Fujimura's cookbook followed prior models of culinary writings. The volume opens with cooking tips, which included methods of making stock, how to remove the bitterness from *warabi*, techniques to cut dried fish, and the best way to boil white potatoes and cook 'wild animals'. The techniques speak to the age in which the cookbook was written, when salted fish, gathered foods and game still figured prominently even in the urban diet. Fujimura divided his recipes according to the four seasons, a long-standing mode of organization dating back to early modern cookery texts and followed in the twentieth-century cookbooks mentioned above. Fujimura wrote about thirty recipes for each season, half of which were for vegetable dishes and the other half fish recipes. He suggested bamboo shoots and whitebait dishes for spring, and aubergine, abalone and ayu recipes in summer. Meat dishes – chicken, beef and pork – were included in a miscellaneous section, followed by separate chapters on egg recipes, tempura, dried foods, tofu, sushi and rice dishes.

The novelty of Fujimura's cookbook was its specificity to bentō. Fujimura indicates that bentō must adhere to special rules, such as avoiding gooey foods and ingredients that have a tendency to spoil.[61] Above all, he directs readers to pay attention to the appearance of the bentō. He did not provide any photographs of bentō as models, relying instead on written descriptions. 'The increase or decrease in people's appetites depends upon their impressions of the food,' he explains, 'and will rise and fall dramatically according to that.'[62] In other words, bentō have to look good to taste good.

Like his predecessor Daigo Sanjin almost a century earlier, Fujimura states that bentō making starts with an appreciation for the container. Containers must change seasonally and should consist of two boxes: one for rice and the other for side dishes.[63] The latter must be packed with extreme care so that even an ordinary lunchbox is beautiful:

> In bentō cooking one must pay absolute attention to the appearance of any bentō, including the lunches for low-paid office workers, even if no one values these or even criticizes the need for something that looks so beautiful. In essence a bentō is a single container with all the foods placed inside it, and sometimes the contents may become disordered. One packs a bentō in the morning and arranges the contents carefully, but when the bentō is opened to be eaten, if everything looks like a complete mess, there will not be any incentive to touch it with one's chopsticks. So, one must pay utmost attention to these matters for bentō.[64]

Contrary to Daigo, Fujimura extended the art of making beautiful bentō beyond special events and day trips to the country to include the prosaic lunches entry-level white-collar workers would carry with them to work each day. It would only be a matter of time before the same standards were applied for boxed lunches made for schoolchildren.

Beyond appearance, the recipes in Fujimura's *Convenient Daily Guide to Bentō Cooking* required the inclusion of appetizing ingredients such as lobster, ham and matsutake mushrooms – the last described by the Japanese food scholar Richard Hosking as 'one of the great experiences of life' to consume.[65] Fujimura's recipes for autumn provide a glimpse of the delicacies he thought appropriate for boxed meals:

Vegetable Dishes

Roasted Matsutake
Grilled Matsutake
Pan-fried Matsutake
Simmered Matsutake
Matsutake in Fried Egg
Matsutake Pan-fried with Tofu
Stewed Matsutake
Grilled *Hatsutake* Mushroom
Hatsutake Pickled in Sake Lees
Teriyaki Sword Bean
Teriyaki Yuzu
Yam Grilled with Miso Topping
Perilla Buds Boiled in Sweet Syrup
Fresh Lotus Root with Egg Filling
Crushed Arrowhead
Crushed Gingko Nuts
Tiny Taro Tubers Grilled with Black Sesame

Fish Dishes

Teriyaki Ayu with Roe
Grilled Salted Yellowtail
Steamed Shrimp Cakes
Halfbeak Grilled with Salt
Halfbeak Grilled with Egg
Teriyaki Halfbeak
Miso Teriyaki Pacific Saury
Pacific Saury Simmered with Yuzu
Yellowtail Pan-fried with Vinegar
Young Stripped Mullet Grilled with Salt
Boiled Whole Tiger Prawn
Teriyaki Pike Conger
Burdock Wrapped in Pike Conger Skin
Yuzu and Soy Sauce Teriyaki Skipjack Tuna
Catfish à la Rikyū [sesame and soy sauce teriyaki]
Pan-fried Duck Breast
Duckling Boiled on the Bone

Autumn Mackerel Dish
Teriyaki False Halibut [*hirame*]
False Halibut Fish Paste
Miso Teriyaki Minnow
Goby Wrapped in Kombu
Butterfish Grilled with Salt

Fujimura intended his readers to pack more than one of these delicacies into a lunch, and he suggests food pairings in several of the recipes. Perilla buds, he explains, are an ideal match for a grilled fish or venus clams boiled in a soy sauce and sugar syrup. Arrowheads are suggested as a good complement to fish or fowl. Yuzu teriyaki is best served with grilled matsutake or with a fish.

Fujimura's recipes are not necessarily complicated, but they are expensive for these lavish ingredients such as fresh fish and matsutake, and are also time-consuming to create. The kombu for the goby recipe is steamed for an hour; the Pacific saury needs to be bathed in saltwater for two to three hours; and the yellowtail must be covered lightly in salt overnight.[66] For a bentō to be ready for someone when they walked out of the house in the morning, several hours of labour in the kitchen were required.

Gourmet bentō also typify Nishino Miyoshi's *Wayō shiki bentō ryōri kazugazu* (Bounty of Japanese and Western Seasonal Bentō Cooking, 1916). Nishino was a prominent home economics educator at women's higher schools in Tokyo in the 1920s and early 1930s, becoming in 1929 the first female official in the Ministry of Education's Board of Inspection.[67] Her background in home economics is evident in the variety of dishes in her bentō cookbook, which borrowed from both Japanese and Western recipes. She betrays a fondness for sandwiches made from beef, ham, egg, cucumber and chicken (the last served with mashed potatoes), and she includes several jam sandwich recipes made with peach, apricot, jujube and apple.[68] In her brief prefatory remarks Nishino divulges that her book is meant for ordinary households and for the edification of women studying cooking. She further states that she arranged her 'easy-to-make' recipes according to the four seasons, and that she chose dishes drawn from the daily meals people eat at home, excepting foods that are so juicy as to be inappropriate for bentō.[69]

Like Fujimura's earlier book, *Convenient Daily Guide to Bentō Cooking*, Nishio's cookbook lacks illustrations and the author's guidelines provide information for making complete lunches consisting of two separate dishes paired together. For example, she lists kidney beans boiled with sugar and soy sauce in the same entry as a recipe for venus clam simmered in broth until dry. Her Teriyaki Flying Fish has a side dish of Spicy Turnip Pickles. She suggests accompanying Strawberry Jam Sandwiches with Fried Fish; and she includes directions for making several boxes of food to take to flower viewing, showing how to create a lunch for a special occasion.[70]

Nishino proves to be an inventive chef with a fondness for recipes with clever names: God of Fortune Pickles (made with burdock, aubergine, cucumber and kidney beans) and Two-tone Ayu (two pieces of ayu, one fried in egg yolk with flour, the other fried in egg white without flour).[71] She has a flair for presentation, as revealed in recipes such as Spanish mackerel steamed with pickled cherry leaves served with a sesame miso dressing; and boiled spinach wrapped in nori accompanying flounder grilled with vinegar then simmered in a syrup. She even makes drab fishcake into a gourmet dish by grilling it with sea urchin roe. She pan-fries *udo*, a stalky plant similar to asparagus, with truffles. And she creates a flavourful tempura with sweet potatoes and dried persimmons.[72]

It would be erroneous to conclude that everyone could afford the time, energy and ingredients to make the bentō dishes that Fujimura and Nishino described in their cookbooks. What child could expect lobster in their school lunch, even if both authors include recipes for it?[73] Fujimura and Nishino had raised the bar on the acceptable boxed lunch to the point where most bentō paled in comparison.

Mizōe Yasuko (1903–1990), a professor at Shimane University who grew up in rural Hiroshima prefecture, recalled her usual school lunch, which was far removed from the descriptions found in Nishino's text published in the same period.

> Except for the winter, I didn't bring a lunch to school. I ran home more than a half-mile along a crooked road. In the autumn when it was harvest time, I would eat a rice ball outdoors in the fields where my parents were working, then I would run back to school. When I think about it now, it was like a race eating a rice ball at an aid station in a marathon.

In the winter, when she did not have to run the distance home, Mizōe brought to school grilled mochi or soy sauce-flavoured rice cakes her mother had wrapped in paper.[74] Such were the simple homemade delicacies in her school lunch.

School Lunches

By the 1930s the problem was not what schoolchildren ate at home or brought to school in their bentō but rather the fact that some children did not bring any lunch to school at all and arrived hungry. Newspapers illustrated the dire conditions in the north in the wake of poor harvests in 1931 and 1934 by spotlighting the plight of undernourished children turning up at school with nothing to eat.[75] In response, the Ministry of Education created a school lunch programme for impoverished children in 1932. As early as 1889, a private elementary school in Yamagata prefecture provided a midday meal for students from poorer households six days a week, consisting of a bentō containing rice, vegetables and fish. Similar lunch programmes began in the first decade of the twentieth century in Hiroshima, Akita, Shizuoka, Okayama and Iwate prefectures. By 1934 the national school lunch programme fed almost 600,000 pupils, which was still less than 7 per cent of the entire school-age population, meaning the rest of the children still brought whatever lunch they could from home.[76] Kurihara Masu (b. 1921), who grew up in a farm household in Tochigi prefecture, recalled the bentō she ate while attending a girl's higher school in the mid-1930s. Every morning the girls in the boarding house took turns preparing and packing a simple lunch. 'The side dishes in our bentō were things like fried sweet potatoes, pinto beans, and nori', explained Kurihara. 'These were quite poor by the standards of today.'[77]

School lunches of simple, prepared foods from home had to suffice for many, but housewives in middle-class urban households were prompted to a higher standard for school lunches in the aforementioned bentō cookbooks and in magazines such as *Culinary Companion* (*Ryōri no tomo*), which debuted in 1913. The magazine was a publication of the Greater Japan Culinary Research Group, which in 1936 also published its own bentō cookbook, *Tsūgaku jidō eiyō bentō jūni kagetsu* (Twelve Months of Nutritional Boxed Lunches for Schoolchildren). The text acknowledged the accomplishments of the school lunch programme, but intimated that homemade bentō provided a better form of motherly nurturing and nutrition. 'The recent lunch programmes for students have seen some success, but we hope to have people demonstrate just a little more concern for children with a bentō made with loving hands. The purpose of a nutritious bentō is salvation from a lack of nutrition and an unbalanced diet.'[78] School lunch, in other words, was for children's nutrition the most important meal of the day, so it required a mother's careful attention and intervention. Some mothers were failing in those duties, according to the cookbook's authors:

Reproduction of a child's 'soybean rice' boxed lunch: rice with soybeans, grilled salted cherry salmon, pickled daikon, simmered daikon and taro. The chef created the school boxed lunch based on the recollections of her grandmother, who was born in 1931.

> Bentō are made with inappropriate side dishes because mornings are so busy, or simply out of blind love for darling children. Things are chosen because they are delicious, or the snacks that a child likes are casually added, which only strengthens the child's habitual snacking. Leftovers from last night's dinner or anything else on hand without any regard are included, with the only desire simply to fill the child's belly with the boxed lunch. Such are the things one sees more often than not.[79]

The sermonizing tone of *Twelve Months of Nutritional Boxed Lunches for Schoolchildren* is a contrast to earlier publications about bentō, which emphasize the joys, gourmet qualities and creative potential of making lunchboxes. Lack of diligence or too much of an emphasis on taste had to take a back seat to the science of nutrition, according to *Twelve Months of Nutritional Boxed Lunches*. Lack of flavour could be solved by the liberal use of MSG. All the recipes in the cookbook included Ajinomoto in their list of ingredients.

If readers took to heart the messages in *Twelve Months of Nutritional Boxed Lunches*, they would never see making lunch for children as a simple task, but one instead filled with pitfalls, with the child's health and one's suitability as a mother hanging in the balance. In a single sentence that lasts a paragraph and takes up more than a page, the authors provided a list of potential crises that need to be mitigated every day in making a bentō. These problems included balancing nutrition against a child's likes and dislikes; resolving a child's unhealthy food preferences by modifying ingredients; taking into account the flavours that some children might not like and then using techniques to disguise them; weighing a child's personal tastes against the fact that a bentō for a child should be simple; taking into consideration individual partiality while keeping in mind age differences among children, and the change of seasons; and so on. Such a long list of potential problems left impressionable readers needing professional guidance, and the authors cited an unnamed doctor of nutrition who preached about the need not just for sufficient calories, protein and vitamins from meat, fish and other foods in any child's lunch, but also the importance of avoiding smelly foods, packing grilled items rather than boiled ones, and using a bentō box only after it had been properly washed and dried.[80] Anyone who fretted about having to make a healthy lunch for their child every day would probably have become even more anxious after reading this book.

Readers of *Twelve Months of Nutritional Boxed Lunches* could study the discussion of the required daily allowance of protein, vitamins, carbohydrates and fat needed for growing children, then refer to the ten-page appendix that listed 108 foods and their nutritional content; or they could simply refer to the recipes, all of which listed the amount of protein, nutrients and calories they supplied and were written in a more approachable manner than the pedantic and worrisome tone of the introduction. The recipes are arranged from January to December with each month allotted about eight different dishes, each on its own page. At the top of each page is a list of ingredients by weight, accompanied by a tiny sketch meant more as an illustration of the foods used than as an aid to creating the recipe.

Earlier bentō authors had prioritized making any recipe harmonize with the specific lunchbox, and *Twelve Months of Nutritional Boxed Lunches* was no exception, promoting the use of anodized aluminium containers:

> These days enamel and aluminium bentō boxes are being adopted, but the contents of these will cool too easily, and it is very unhealthy if umeboshi, salted foods, or those with a vinegar dressing come in

contact with them at all. So the trend is to use anodized aluminium for lunchboxes for the children we care so much for.

Similar health concerns still prompt cooks to choose anodized aluminium, which unlike conventional aluminium is chemically treated to prevent corrosion and leaching of the metal into the food. The authors of the book warned that readers should be wary because the excellent properties of anodized aluminium had led to many forgeries of crude manufacture. They advised buying containers only from reputable dealers.[81]

Readers of *Twelve Months of Nutritional Boxed Lunches* could learn where to purchase authentic anodized aluminium lunchboxes from an advertisement in the cookbook. The authors offered for sale lunchboxes in different sizes with round or square corners and with or without chopsticks. Two pages of black-and-white photos showed how the aluminium bentō could be used, revealing a smaller compartment within the lunchbox to hold side dishes separate from the rice, which comprised about four-fifths of the lunch in the examples.

Where earlier bentō authors had included both meat and vegetable dishes sometimes in equal amounts, healthy eating for the authors of this book meant consuming animal protein. Few of the 91 recipes feature vegetables and fewer still are wholly vegetarian. Western vegetables are more evident as well than in earlier cookbooks. White potatoes, boiled spinach and canned green peas make more frequent appearances than *konnyaku*, taro and arrowhead. The predilection for meat even in vegetable dishes is evidenced by the recipes for Vegetables Simmered in Miso, which includes fishcake; Soy Bean Bentō, which adds sardines or whitebait; and a recipe for cucumbers stuffed with salmon.[82] Sardines, salted or canned salmon and dried cod appear to be the most frequently used fish, but the rest are hardly exotic: pond smelt, tuna, *katsuobushi*, mackerel and horse mackerel appear. Pork is the most often used meat, but chicken and beef recipes are also included, as in the example of a recipe for Beef with Simmered Vegetables. Dairy products are also used in the recipes. Traditional flavourings are augmented with butter, which is used as a dressing for squid and for cooking salmon.[83] The taste of the dishes would have been predominantly salty (from the soy sauce, miso and salted fish) and sweet (thanks to the use of sugar and mirin). Ajinomoto would have contributed its savoury MSG flavour to all the dishes.

A large variety of canned foods and sauces had been available to consumers by the 1920s, and the authors of *Twelve Months of Nutritional Boxed*

Lunches promoted the use of canned foods such as green peas and salmon, except when these were 'too expensive', such as in the case of canned bamboo shoots.[84] The recipes revealed that processed foods could be used in recipes, and even provided encouragement to housewives to try canned foods by tacitly affirming their safety and alimentary quality.

Canned foods, premade sauces and MSG are inexpensive shortcuts to making bentō more affordable and perhaps easier to create, but the lunch-boxes still had to look appealing to children. Where earlier writers had made their boxed lunches attractive by including gourmet ingredients such as lobster and matsutake, the authors of *Twelve Months of Nutritional Boxed Lunches* suggest how to dress up ordinary rice in clever ways. Their recipe for a Cherry Blossom Bentō owes its pink colour to shrimp, peas and rice mixed with tomato sauce. A New Year's lunchbox dubbed Pine Green relies on spinach and nori mixed with rice for its colour.

And the authors incorporate nationalist themes in their cookbook. Japanese Flag Fish-flake Bentō uses a circle of red fish flakes on top of strands of white kombu to evoke the national flag on a bed of rice. The recipe for Mount Fuji Pressed Sushi with Green Leaves constructs the quintessential peak with white kombu on top of rice and uses slivers of carrot to suggest rays of light shining from the summit.[85] Japanese Flag Fish-flake Bentō harks back to Daigo Sanjin's advice dating from the early nineteenth century to put red foods in the centre of a bentō, but it is also a forerunner of the *Hinomaru bentō* or Japanese Flag Bentō, consisting of white rice with just one red ume-boshi in the centre, a nationalist recipe popular in the Second World War. Compared to the gourmet bentō in previous cookbooks, the recipes in *Twelve Months of Nutritional Boxed Lunches* represent a type of subterfuge, using design and inexpensive foods to mask a paucity of ingredients, which would become even more dear as Japan became more deeply engaged in warfare on the continent and in the Pacific theatre in the late 1930s and early 1940s.

The examples in the book were the poor cousins of earlier versions of bentō cookery and of suggestions for lunch found in cookbooks dating from the first two decades of the twentieth century. Yet, the recipes demonstrate the evolution of lunch from leftovers into a craft of making an original meal to satisfy a family member's physical needs (and perhaps even their need for emotional nourishment) – as well as one to be judged according to aesthetic and nutritional standards by institutions outside the family, the 'ideological state apparatus' for contemporary Japan described by Anne Allison.

A few years after *Twelve Months of Nutritional Boxed Lunches* was published, wartime rationing and mobilization prompted the government and cookbook authors to take an even stronger stand against luxurious foods and to promote healthy eating with even greater vigour. Wartime scarcity and rationing also changed bentō cooking, making even the white rice necessary to create a *Hinomaru bentō* into a luxury. The return to gourmet boxed lunches would have to wait until the period of recovery after the war, but the foundation of Japan's bentō culture as both high cuisine and a practice of daily life had been established by the 1930s.

5

NATIONAL PEOPLE'S CUISINE

The official designation of 'traditional Japanese dietary cultures' (*washoku*) for UNESCO in 2013 was not the first effort of the Japanese government to define a national cuisine. In response to accelerated changes in the Japanese diet brought about by wartime austerity, on 5 October 1940 Japan's Ministry of Welfare announced the planned development of a 'national people's cuisine' (*kokuminshoku*).[1] The Imperial Rule Assistance Association (IRAA), Japan's attempt at creating a mass political party emulating Germany's Nazi Party, took up the task of delineating a national people's cuisine by enlisting nutritionists, ethnologists, teachers of home economics and other experts to create a cuisine that would inculcate a common identity in wartime, make the best use of diminishing food resources and ensure the health of the population on the home front. If 'traditional Japanese dietary cultures' can be described as an exercise of 'soft power', an attempt to use culture to affect Japan's image abroad positively while guiding eating habits at home towards native dishes that make greater use of domestic ingredients, wartime 'national people's cuisine' represents a 'harder' approach, with the goal of turning all domestic cooking, eating and digestion into patriotic duties.

Nowadays, the word *kokuminshoku* refers not to wartime foodways but to so-called people's food, inexpensive popular dishes such as ramen and beef curry. Wartime national 'people's cuisine' had little to commend it compared to the widely popular ramen and curry dishes that are sold in specialist restaurants and as easy-to-make processed foods. The change in meaning of the term reveals an amnesia about *kokuminshoku*'s wartime origins.[2] This forgetting of the history of *kokuminshoku* is understandable because the wartime cuisine was a state-sponsored, reified programme for dietary lifestyle, which quickly lost its saliency, even before the war ended. Yet the legacy of Japan's wartime cuisine is still apparent because it finds prominent echoes in recent government rhetoric about the 'traditional dietary cultures of the Japanese' (*washoku*). Both *kokuminshoku* and *washoku* emphasize local food; in fact, the local food movement developed alongside and abetted the invention of national people's cuisine in the early 1940s (see Chapter Six). Further, besides encouraging people to eat locally, both campaigns emphasize nutrition. And one can also find the emphasis of *kokuminshoku* on seasonality and tradition rearticulated in the government's promotion of the 'traditional dietary cultures of the Japanese' today. Finally, both culinary programmes attempt to put a brave face on crises in the food supply to improve public perceptions, whether in response to wartime scarcity and mobilization on the one hand, or as disaster recovery and combatting the actual and perceived fallout of the March 2011 Fukushima nuclear disaster on the other.[3]

Complicit in defining a national people's cuisine, but ultimately yielding different definitions of national culinary identity, was a survey of food culture by native ethnologists from 1941 to '42.[4] The Imperial Rule Assistance Association directed an academic association of ethnologists to conduct research to help define 'national people's cuisine'. The government's order exemplifies how *kokuminshoku* was a form of culinary identity shaped from the top down. But the ethnologists' approach to their study, which they had developed in previous research on rural communities, constructed an image of Japanese foodways from the bottom up and from the periphery looking in. In their collection of data about vernacular cooking habits, food routines, taboos and accepted wisdom regarding eating, the ethnologists saw revealed a culinary identity that they identified as 'Japanese food culture' (*Nihon no shokubunka*).[5] Their diffuse model of national identity, produced in the unspectacular aspects of everyday life, offered only a brief nod of support to the government's formulation of *kokuminshoku*, and it could even be said to challenge tacitly the state's fundamental assumptions that a cuisine instituted from above was legitimate. The post-war redefinition of *kokuminshoku* as 'people's food' supports the ethnologists' assertion that an authentic national food culture stems from the people and not from the state – a point that the recent Japanese government itself admits, by translating *washoku* as a plurality of 'dietary cultures'.

The Early Days of Rationing (1939–40)

The history of Japanese food in the late 1930s and early 1940s can be told in terms of how wartime rationing restricted the diet, although double-digit inflation also greatly diminished purchasing power to the point that from 1934 to 1945, real wages fell by 60 per cent.[6] Limitations on polishing rice and price controls on brown rice began in 1938 with the enactment of the National General Mobilization Law.[7] By the end of 1939 department stores substituted barley for rice in their meals; restaurants replaced actual displays of food with photographs to attract customers; and price controls were instituted on the core ingredients needed to make Japanese recipes: miso, soy sauce, salt and fresh fish, and matches to light the cooking fire. In 1940 rationing of sugar, charcoal, firewood and milk began,[8] and price limits for sweets, jam and bread were instituted that year. And from 1940 to 1950 no cocoa beans were imported, dooming the nation's chocolatiers and Western-style confectioners.[9] The neon lights went out in bars and cafés in Osaka in January 1940; in April, monthly meatless days began and by June, cafés and restaurants were told to stop serving lavish dishes. In July rationing of fresh fruit began, and the following month restaurants in Tokyo prefecture were told to stop serving rice as the government exhorted civilians to view 'luxury as the enemy'.

Kokuminshoku (1940–43)

These restrictions on consumption preceded the announcement by the Ministry of Welfare on 5 October 1940 that launched the development of national people's cuisine. News about the ministry's announcement appeared in the morning edition of the *Asahi shimbun* newspaper on 6 October. One is tempted to detect a note of sarcasm in the headline 'Now it's National People's Cuisine: The Same Things for All Classes.'[10] National people's cuisine, according to the article, followed in the wake of the government's attempt to create a 'national people's dress', which was officially launched in November 1940 but had been previewed beginning in January by a series of articles in the *Tokyo Nichinichi Shimbun* showing government bureaucrats posing in prototypes of the drab national uniform.[11] Like national people's dress, national people's cuisine was meant to conserve resources and direct them towards the war effort while 'ensuring nutrition and provisions for civilians during wartime', according to the *Asahi Shimbun* article. The article's subtitle further indicates that national people's cuisine was meant to be a uniform diet. According to the article, the government

planned to engage in research and to enact measures on many fronts, such as the stabilization of prices and rationing of essential resources with the aim of standardizing consistently as national people's cuisine the meals in schools, factories, dormitories for schools and companies and public cafeterias as well as all varieties of meals made for the public and the meals in all households regardless of wealth.

The campaign to define a national people's cuisine was quickly taken up by the newly founded IRAA. That the IRAA, a conglomeration of political parties and other institutions meant to create a national network of support for government policies, began work on the definition of a cuisine in the same month as its own inception in October 1940 demonstrates the importance of food to the war effort and to the perception that eating could serve as a means to mobilize and unify the population.[12] But national people's cuisine would also be as much about how one ate (or was supposed to eat) as about what one ate.

The term 'national people's cuisine', *kokuminshoku*, was coined as an abbreviation of *kokumin shokuryō*, 'civilian rations'. The phrase 'civilian rations' pre-dates 'national people's cuisine' by more than a decade, and was popularized by translations and references to the ideas of the Latvian demographer Kārlis Balodis (Carl Ballod, 1864–1931), who helped to shape Germany's rationing system during the First World War.[13] At the end of the war, references to Germany's wartime civilian rationing became anxiety-producing for Japan, given that Britain's successful blockade of Germany led to more than 400,000 civilian deaths from hunger and proved pivotal in Germany's defeat. The historian Lizzie Collingham writes, 'The German request for an armistice . . . was the result of failure on the battlefield. But to many of those who witnessed these events, it appeared as though hunger was the victor and that it was starvation among the army and civilians which had brought about a humiliating defeat.'[14] Thus, national people's cuisine attempted to give a more uplifting meaning to a wartime diet that was becoming ever more constrained by rationing in Japan. Rather than define a cuisine for the home front in negative terms by listing what was to be eliminated and reduced, portrayals of national people's cuisine appealed to abstract sensibilities such as the importance of seasonality, celebratory and local foods and nutrition, which are more reminiscent of a cuisine than of a system of rationing.

National people's cuisine had several different iterations because factionalism within the IRAA often resulted in vague and contradictory policies.[15] One can detect in the three different definitions of national people's cuisine a gradual lowering of expectations about what the reified cuisine could achieve regarding mobilization and with diminishing food resources. Lofty ideals about creating foods for celebrations gave way to attempts to make limited ingredients more pleasurable, which in turn fell by the wayside when the goal shifted to making the best use of anything edible.

Timed with the official launch of national people's cuisine, Joshi Eiyō Gakuen (Women's Nutrition School, now called Kagawa Nutrition University), a women's college of nutrition founded in Tokyo in 1940, held a three-day symposium starting on 9 March 1941. The graduates of the college were entering employment with the IRAA; therefore the event's message can be interpreted as reflecting government policies. The event articulated five guidelines for the cuisine:[16]

1. The purpose of a national people's cuisine is self-sufficiency without reliance on foreign countries.
2. In the national people's cuisine the serving amounts are determined according to age and physical activity.
3. National people's cuisine gives careful consideration to calories, protein, vitamins, salt and to the sources of proteins to determine the servings of fish, legumes and vegetables. Deficiencies in calories are supplemented by rice.
4. National people's cuisine is the food for all citizens. It is possible to have a superlative national cuisine based on grains and tubers even without rice.
5. Based on seasonal ingredients, there is a distinction between ordinary and celebratory foods and a continuation of the joys of seasonal festivities.[17]

Self-sufficiency for the nation, mentioned in point one, is sustained by the discipline of the individual, who eats only the amount of food appropriate to their needs, as point two states. The second and third characteristics provide a role for professional nutritionists, such as the Women's Nutrition School graduates, as the arbiters of the new cuisine for their expertise in knowing the scientific composition of foods and the appropriate amounts that people need. The third point also indicates that rice is supposed to make up for insufficient fish and vegetables in the diet, but the fourth point claims that the new cuisine does not need rice at all, recognizing that potatoes and other grains were playing an increasing role as replacements for rice in the wartime diet. Given the supposed prominence of rice in Japanese cuisine and culture, it is significant to note how the earliest definition of a modern national cuisine discouraged rice consumption. The final point promises that national people's cuisine will still allow for the creation of speciality dishes to coincide with the enjoyment of seasonal holidays, promising consumers some change of pace and continuation of culinary traditions. To illustrate all these points, the symposium featured displays of local foods, foods for ceremonies and recipes for Western-style dining, and provided instructions on making nutritious dishes, such as a sardine and daikon salad.[18]

Two months later, in May 1941, the Keio University professor and doctor of medicine Ōmori Kenta spoke at a government-sponsored exhibition on national people's cuisine. He echoed the first three points from the previous definition: emphasizing self-sufficiency, matching food intake to age and workload, and highlighting the importance of nutrition. Ōmori combined the science of nutrition and portion size in his first point. In his second point, he reduced the scope of self-sufficiency from the national to the local level by referencing urban 'block associations'. From 1940, the government distributed food rations in cities through block organizations and compelled people within them to cook together to save resources.[19] The need to conserve if not de-emphasize rice consumption Ōmori discussed elsewhere in his talk. He concluded his list of the five characteristics of *kokuminshoku* by introducing two new points (four and five):

1. The level of nutrition should be scientifically adjusted to match age and occupation.
2. As much as possible the food should be native at the lowest level of the neighbourhood block, making it the goal to obtain locally all possible food consumed every year.
3. Menus should have the flexibility to be allowed to incorporate modifications in foodstuffs according to the change in seasons and the particulars of a locale.
4. Ingredients should be inexpensive and in abundance so that they can be distributed to citizens.
5. The menu and taste of the food should be tailored to every person's preference; it should display originality and be made into an enjoyable meal.[20]

Despite encouraging community cooking, Ōmori's final suggestion, that national people's cuisine should acknowledge individual taste rather than reflect a standardized diet, represented a shift away from the almost impossible task of creating a uniform diet for all citizens. National people's cuisine,

after all, means using locally inexpensive, seasonal ingredients, which necessarily recognizes that communities will source ingredients, cook and eat
differently depending on the locale. Personal preferences could also be
allowed, as long as the foods were affordable and served in amounts corresponding to age and workload. As in the previous iteration of national
people's cuisine, at the Women's Nutrition School, recognition of seasonality was important, but Ōmori indicated that the change of seasons would
determine the availability of certain foodstuffs, rather than providing a
rationale for celebration. Instead of enjoying special food for special reasons, Ōmori told his audiences to take the inexpensive ingredients at hand
and make them into something pleasurable to eat.

The definition of national people's cuisine was hardly consistent, and
evolved further over the course of the war, as is shown by an IRAA publication from 1942, which largely follows the previous points except for the
last one:

1. The portions for national people's cuisine are determined according
   to age, gender and the amount of physical labour.
2. The ingredients for foods and their amounts are determined
   following the food policies of our nation and with the goal of
   self-sufficiency.
3. It is essential that the national people's cuisine as the food of all
   the people is in accord with the climate and natural conditions of
   various places and that it has the ability to adapt so that it can use
   ingredients that are appropriate to the seasons.
4. The price should be affordable so that it is widely available to the
   general populace.
5. The goal is to use all resources. Thus, one tries to reduce the amount
   discarded and attempts to prevent the loss of nutrients in processing
   and cooking.[21]

The first point of this definition adds gender to age and occupation as the
basis for allocating servings of food, and it reiterates that local availability
and cost should be defining factors in creating national people's cuisine. The
plea to use available and affordable ingredients is tacit admission that more
expensive foodstuffs might perhaps be available (as on the black market) but
that authentic national people's cuisine was inexpensive. The pronounce-
ment thereby grants culinary virtue to rationed and inexpensive foods and to
ingredients such as daikon leaves and fruit peel that people would normally

discard but that they might be forced to consume in an effort to waste nothing (or simply to survive in wartime, as described below). Gone are the celebratory dishes and the acknowledgement of personal taste, replaced by a focus on using every available scrap of food, prepared so as to prevent any loss of nutrients.

One of the contradictions in national people's cuisine was that the uniform dietary guidelines drew distinctions based on age, occupation and gender, and these divisions were more boldly drawn in the popular press. In March 1941 the *Asahi Shimbun* ran a series of articles dedicated to a different form of national people's cuisine, tailored for specific age groups and occupations. Elementary schoolchildren (and their mothers) were exhorted to 'eat healthy national people's cuisine and go off to public schools'.[22] Housewives were cautioned to make national people's cuisine for the elderly to prevent high blood pressure and heart disease.[23] One article grouped women into different categories depending on whether they were pregnant, engaging in 'light work' (such as housework, department sales, office work and tailoring) or involved in 'heavy labour', which could also include housework, domestic service as a maid or operating a printing press.[24] Young men aged 17 to 29 were advised to consume 2,500 calories and 100 grams of protein per day, while women of the same age were told that 2,100 calories and 90 grams of protein was sufficient.[25] The amounts accorded with the Ministry of Welfare's 1941 estimates of 2,500 calories needed daily for adult working men.[26] And the amounts nearly matched the average per capita food supply for 1935, which was 2,200 calories per day; but by the year 1941, when these caloric estimates were publicized and national people's cuisine was officially launched, only some 2,000 calories of food supply was available per capita. This was the underlying reason why nutritionists sought to tailor menus by age group, occupation and gender – so that strained food resources would go to people who were perceived to need to eat the most.[27] Male labourers apparently deserved larger servings of national people's cuisine than did housewives and children.

Besides newspaper articles, civilians learned about national people's cuisine through public exhibitions and publications including cookbooks.[28] The three-day symposium at the Women's Nutrition School was timed to coincide with the official launch of *kokuminshoku*.[29] The following month, an exhibit in the Japanese Red Cross Museum in Tokyo's Shiba Park attracted a large audience. 'Overcoming Difficult Times: An Exhibition of National People's Cuisine for Wartime' drew over 46,600 visitors, according to the event's organizers, the Japanese Red Cross, which worked in conjunction

'Recommendations to Eat Everything', book illustration from *Chochiku o umidasu seikatsu no gōrika* (Finding Savings: Rationalizing Lifestyle, 1942). The captions exhort viewers to make culinary use of fish heads, bones and entrails as well as daikon leaves and fruit and vegetable peelings.

with the Imperial Rule Assistance Association, the Ministries of Education, Agriculture and Welfare and the Tokyo prefectural and city governments to hold the month-long event (27 April–31 May). Advertised by handbills; newspaper articles; posters in train stations, factories, social clubs and major stores; and leaflets distributed to schools, women's organizations and government offices, the exposition employed guides to explain the displays. It presented a bewildering array of information relating to national people's cuisine that included forums on community gardening; displays of model menus and sample dishes; presentations on hygiene and unhealthy teeth; dioramas of methods of food preservation; introductions to edible grasses; descriptions of the nutritional value of grasshoppers; specimens of fish that could be caught or raised; pie charts showing the production targets for sweet and white potatoes; flow charts about how rationed sugar went from producer to consumer; displays about how to cook without wasting food; photographs of infirmities caused by malnutrition; explanations of communal kitchens; lecture demonstrations on home bread baking using wheat and soybean flours and powdered fish and seaweed; posters about keeping chickens and goats in one's garden; and a talk on children's nutrition.[30]

Promoters of national people's cuisine sought to make a national duty out of personal food choices under a regime of wartime scarcity. Cookbooks for national people's cuisine reminded readers that their digestive systems had patriotic roles to play: 'The practice of assisting imperial rule originates in the kitchen and goes to the depths of the stomach', as the preface to one cookbook indicated.[31] But the recipes in the same cookbook, though frugal, nonetheless sound appealing, making the governmental culinary guidelines more palatable. Katō Toshiko's *Kokuminshoku: Eiyō kondate sanbyaku rokujū go nichi* (National People's Cuisine: Three Hundred and Sixty-five Days of Nutritious Menus), published in 1941, suggests the following dinner menu for the fourteenth day of February: Oyster Porridge with Green Onion, Bath-bubbled Daikon, Dried Sardines in Sesame Miso Dressing.[32] Like today's recipes for oyster rice porridge (*kaki zōsui*), the directions indicate adding stock to rice or another grain before cooking and then adding the oysters.[33] Bath-bubbled Daikon (*furofuki daikon*) is a well-known winter dish in which vegetables are boiled until soft, then eaten warm slathered in miso. The dish with sesame dressing is a relative of the familiar *goma'ae* recipe usually made with spinach and a sweet sesame dressing, but served here without the rationed sugar and as a topping for small dried sardines, which were typically reserved for soup stock. The way to citizens' hearts was through their stomachs – or at least through their imaginations, because these cookbooks presumed the availability of ingredients such as rationed miso and fresh oysters.

Cookbooks published at the end of the war offered menus at the level of subsistence rather than gourmet sustenance, illustrating how the reality of wartime scarcity forced advocates of national people's cuisine to lower their culinary standards. The title of the cookbook *Kessen shoku seikatsu kufūshū* (Collection of Strategies for Food-life for the Final Battle), published in 1944 by the government of Kanagawa prefecture, warns readers that dietary culture has reached a moment of crisis. The essays in *Collection of Strategies for Food-life for the Final Battle* were overtly critical of previous 'gourmet' versions of national people's cuisine and those that assumed access to more copious amounts of rationed foods. One of the contributors to the volume, Kinoshita Shigeru of the Yokohama Nutritionists Cooperative, wrote, 'Those things called nutritious menus that have appeared up until now in women's magazines, I want you to throw all of those away without any exception.' He continued, 'Viewed from the restrictive food situation and current rationing system of today, I want to get rid of the study of nutrition up to this point.' The author explained how previous nutritionists had presumed

a 2,400-calorie diet in constructing their menus, allocating 1,700 calories
to rice. But with only some 1,150 calories of rice available per capita daily by
1944, older recipes, he explained, were now worthless, and he endeavoured
to create menus for a diet of 1,500 calories per day. Kinoshita spoke with
authority as a chef who operated a rice-porridge cafeteria in Yokohama and
claimed to feed more than 2,000 people a day. A sense of the type of low-
grade meal he served is suggested by his warning, 'I want you to give up the
feeling of wanting something tasty to eat or trying to get something good for
yourself.'[34] It is little wonder that Japanese people were feeling hungry trying
to survive with 100 fewer calories available per capita daily, by Kinoshita's
estimate, than during China's Great Leap Forward, when some 30 million
people died of starvation.[35] *Collection of Strategies for Food-life for the Final
Battle* promised in its preface to include recipes that used only the rationed
ingredients available.[36] After a chapter on nutrition, the cookbook devotes
five chapters to how to reduce food waste with suggestions on how to consume fruit peel, fish guts and fish heads and how to conserve cooking fuel.
Recipes instruct how to make food from used tea leaves and how to brew
homemade soy sauce. That the cookbook ends with guidance on how to
grow pumpkins and potatoes is revelatory about where the ingredients are
supposed to come from. The cookbook signals how national people's cuisine
disappeared during the closing years of the Second World War as people
simply struggled to find enough food to survive.

Ethnologists and National Food Culture

In the 1940s, the search for ways to economize on existing resources and
discover new things to eat led many people from the cities to rural areas to
buy food from farmers, and when the Imperial Rule Assistance Association
sought to create a national people's cuisine, it enlisted experts on rural life.
In 1941 the IRAA's Department for the Direction of National Lifestyle contracted with the professional organization of native ethnologists to contrive
a national people's cuisine inspired by rural foods.[37] An IRAA directive reads:

> With the aim of providing correct directions for national nutrition
> during a time of war, committees on national people's cuisine will
> be constituted of specialists in the capital, while in all the prefec-
> tures committees on rural food will be organized. The committee
> members will compile national food guidelines indicating the stand-
> ards for national people's cuisine; additionally the committees will

commission the Popular Traditions Association with the task of discovering and popularizing emergency foodstuffs from rural locales.[38]

While experts in the capital laboured to define a national people's cuisine, ethnologists in the countryside from the Popular Traditions Association were ordered to discover survival foods that could be incorporated into it. The ethnologists' survey occurred half a year after the formal launch of national people's cuisine in 1941.

The Popular Traditions Association was the academic organization for professional ethnologists in Japan, a group known today as the Folklore Society of Japan. Hashiura Yasuo (1888–1979) established the association in 1935 to celebrate the sixtieth birthday of his mentor, Yanagita Kunio (1875–1962), the founding father of folklore studies in the country. Ethnographic study of rural foodways began in Japan in the mid-1920s, but Yanagita undertook sustained research on food folklore from the early 1930s, spurring other scholars to consider ways in which food could illuminate religious and social dimensions of popular life.[39] Yanagita was less interested in what Japanese people actually ate than in the spiritual dimensions of foodways.[40] Hashiura had also begun publishing on the subject of food in the mid-1930s in the pages of the folklore organization's journal, *Minkan denshō* (Popular Traditions). Initial discussion of a plan to research rural food began on 8 December 1940 when Fukamizu Seisaiku (1900–1972) facilitated a discussion among members of the Popular Traditions Association, including Yanagita, about the society's plans for the coming year and the role of the group in the war effort. Fukamizu was an artist, English-language teacher and author of children's literature, and he later found employment with the IRAA.[41]

Yanagita did not participate in the IRAA-funded survey directly, but his control of native ethnographic studies and the overbearing power he exercised over his disciples is well known.[42] Even without his direct participation, the ethnologists' study owed a huge debt to his premise that remote areas of rural Japan preserved traces of the nation's past. According to Yanagita's viewpoint, 'local differences, rather than being the products of distinct local histories, were redefined as different evolutionary points along the single line of national history', as Tessa Morris-Suzuki has commented.[43] The preface to the ethnologists' study of rural food reiterates Yanagita's premise, stating, 'the country's culture of ages past is preserved in the remoteness of every mountain village even today.'[44] Thus, the survey was meant to illuminate national culture rather than create a new category of local rural foodways.[45]

The ethnologists' study also followed Yanagita's methodology in terms of the format for the interviews, the number and types of questions asked and the way the data would be compiled. Beginning with his 1934 survey of mountain villages, Yanagita generated a scripted list of 100 questions, which he printed in booklets and gave to fieldworkers for interviewing one or more 'local tradition keepers', informants who due to their age or social standing were viewed as the best source of information about local lore. A question was printed on the left-hand page of the booklet and the right side was left blank to record the respondents' replies.[46] Using a similar format, the Popular Traditions Association titled its food questionnaires *Notebooks on Investigating Foodstuffs*. Each booklet contained 100 questions covering three broad categories: daily foods, festival meals and foodstuffs consumed during famines.[47] The first two categories reveal a debt to Yanagita's approach to analysing culture by discerning the boundaries between ordinary life (*ke*) and celebrations (*hare*).[48] Only the final category on survival foods, which numbered just five questions in total, had immediate bearing on Japan's needs in wartime. A few examples of the survey questions can provide a sense of the sweeping scope of the study. The following questions are numbered according to the order that they appear in the survey:[49]

1. Generally what variety of grain is used in your village as the everyday staple food?
5. To what degree do you mill that grain?
11. What kinds of noodles are there?
17. What is the ingredient most commonly used in side dishes?
23. What types of seasoning do you use?
29. What kind of soup do you make?
31. Do you make sushi? What types of fish do you use?
36. What is the typical serving size for food? Do you have a word to refer to that?[50]
39. Do you use tables?
45. Is there some kind of prayer or chant that is said before or after a meal?
48. Is there anything you dislike seeing when you are eating?
55. What kind of food do you use as daily religious offerings?
65. Please tell me the general types of meal there are for non-auspicious occasions.
69. What are the special rules of etiquette for a drinking party?

84. Are there types of food that are prepared only by men?
90. What kinds of luxury items are there? What do you call them?
95. What kinds of food are usually eaten during a famine?
96. In times of famine, what sort of knowledge is needed about food?[51]

Judging from these sample questions, the ethnologists interpreted their charge to 'discover and popularize emergency foodstuffs from rural locales' quite broadly. The questions reveal how the ethnologists hoped to penetrate beyond the artefacts and practices of daily consumption to discover the psychology of local communities. By asking the same questions of people in all the locales surveyed, the ethnologists could make regional comparisons and define norms. The ultimate goal in this and similar research projects was to understand the interiority of the rural citizens, which provided a means of understanding the subjectivity of the country's past.[52] Rural food customs, in other words, revealed the foundations of national culinary culture.

Unable to select researchers and send them into the field during wartime lest they be mistaken for spies, Hashiura had to recruit volunteers who were already in place, and he advertised in his group's academic journal for assistance. It was up to the volunteers to determine the site for research and whom to interview. Potential fieldworkers were directed to select nearby communities that preserved 'old-fashioned foodways'. In the late autumn of 1941, Hashiura sent out surveys and asked that they be completed by early spring the next year.[53] Despite this haphazard approach, some 85 surveys survive from 38 different locations including Okinawa and Hokkaido.

Following Yanagita's methodology, the surveyors did not consider the need to contact a large number of informants in each locale. Often a single person was the sole spokesperson for an entire area.[54] Fieldworkers were supposed to record the full name, age, gender and occupation of each informant, but they sometimes neglected to do that. Fieldworkers were also tasked with appending two tables to the responses: one describing typical daily eating habits for the locale surveyed and the other the amount of food a person ate in a year in the location.

Collecting all of the data from the volunteer surveys, Hashiura Yasuo took on Yanagita's customary role as editor, compiling the results. How Hashiura reported his study to the Imperial Rule Assistance Association remains unknown.[55] Only the title of his essay survives, *Nihon no tabe-mono to tabekata (dai ichi shū)* (Japanese Food and Ways of Eating [Report

Number One]), which suggests that Hashiura framed his results according to a national scope – and that he planned to write more reports.[56] Fifteen unpublished synthetic essays created by researchers provide an indication of how the survey's data may have been collated.[57] The essays include discussions of how to mix grains with other foodstuffs in porridges; noodles such as soba, udon and sōmen; substitutes for staples; food preservation; sources of starch; wild plants; uses for salt; sweeteners; side dishes; pickles; soups; meal frequency; amounts of food served at meals; famine foods; and the contents of typical daily meals.[58]

The ethnologists' study yielded some data about foods that might have been useful in coping with wartime shortages, but not all of the information was germane to the war effort. The synthetic essay about famine foods describes how the bark and roots of pine trees can be made into cakes (*mochi*) or added to grain porridge.[59] However, many responses about famine foods were less than enlightening. Asked about famine foods, one informant from Kyoto replied, 'there were no significant famines in the past so there was little thought given to how to prepare for them.'[60]

Left unanswered in the ethnologists' survey is the question of how these rural foods should be incorporated into national people's cuisine, and that term does not appear in their surveys or reports. On the one hand, the ethnologists were merely supposed to document local foods, not develop mechanisms for promoting their production and consumption. On the other hand, the ethnologists' methodological assumptions raise fundamental questions about how their study's results could be reconciled with the government's national people's cuisine. Instead of counting calories, as did the advocates of national people's cuisine, the ethnologists applied their own methodology to record the names of foodstuffs in different dialects. Moreover, the premise of native ethnography that held that rural foodways were 'old fashioned' versions of a modern national cuisine drew attention to the artificiality of national people's cuisine. By documenting a culinary culture grounded in time-honoured practices of daily life in the country's rural heartland, the ethnologists revealed the arbitrariness and lack of authenticity of the central government's national people's cuisine, which was less than a year old at the time of their survey. Charged to abet the development of a national people's cuisine, the ethnologists revealed instead a pre-existing national food culture in the countryside.

Understandably, the ethnologists did not dare challenge national people's cuisine or the war effort directly in their reports, especially since their research had been possible only with the wartime government's financial support. However, some involved in the study could not deny the effects of war on the diet. Hori Ichirō, who would become a noted scholar of Japanese folk religion and Yanagita Kunio's son-in-law, wrote in one of the synthetic essays that the amount of rice in a person's daily ration was less than what a typical farmer ate for a single meal.[61] Hori's implication was that people were simply not receiving enough food to eat from the government.

But not all the effects of the war on the diet were negative. One of the findings of the survey was that the government's system of grain purchasing and distribution enacted with the February 1942 Food Control Law introduced rice into the diet of many rural areas for the first time – though at the same time people in other locales had to make do with less rice.[62] Clearly the diet of the rural countryside was transforming, and it was hard for the ethnologists to ignore the accelerated standardization of the Japanese diet by rationing, price controls and the proposed adoption of a national people's cuisine. Such developments provided further encouragement to the native ethnologists' existing scholarly impulses to document the diverse diets of rural areas before the basis of Japan's authentic national food culture disappeared.

A Culture of Deprivation (1944–5)

Also shaping the meanings of nation, people and food in Japan during the Second World War was the culture of deprived adaptation exemplified by 'substitute foods'.[63] These foods were foodstuffs meant to replace typical staples and side dishes. They included lotus leaves, pumpkin stalks, carrot leaves, yam peel, spinach roots, sweet potato vines, cherry stones, fish heads, fish bones and a wide variety of other things not generally eaten: grasses, locusts, bee larvae, insect pupae, frogs, snakes, sparrows, acorns and flour made from persimmon peel. Publications in the closing month of 1944 gave instructions on how to turn leftover tea leaves, mikan (satsuma) peel and corn cobs into food.[64] The state tried to put a positive spin on 'substitute foods' by presenting them as part of a national people's cuisine, but the term substitute food, which had a longer history of usage than national people's cuisine, became more commonplace in discourse by the end of the war. Ethnologists viewed substitute foods as aberrations of daily life, but nonetheless listed them in their reports. Contrary to both reified versions of cuisine – the invented national people's cuisine and the scholars' vision of a popular food culture – substitute foods played a concrete and critical role in the everyday food practices people used to survive in wartime. By the end of the war substitute foods had come to define personal identities as measures of what hungry people would be willing to eat to survive, as reminders of all that was lacking in the diet and as a traditional or ad hoc means of coping with constrained consumption patterns, which by 1942 had turned daily life into a 'dismal grind of scarcity and restriction'.[65]

From National People's Cuisine to People's Food

As noted at the outset of this chapter, today the word *kokuminshoku* refers not to wartime experience but to inexpensive, popular dishes such as beef curry and ramen, indicating not only an amnesia about wartime cuisine but also the Japanese culinary appropriation of conspicuously foreign foods introduced in the modern era. Curry came to Japan as a legacy of British colonialism and is said to have arrived via a British vessel perhaps as early as 1859.[66] The word itself is Tamil in origin, but for the Japanese, the beef sauce is synonymous with Western culinary culture, since Japanese people generally eschewed eating beef before the modern era. In the late nineteenth century the Japanese navy adopted British-style meat dishes as a successful means to counteract beriberi, even without fully understanding the causes of that condition. During the 1920s, beef curry was a quintessential military dish, consisting of a spicy roux made with beef stock to which potatoes, vegetables, greens and anything else could be added.[67]

Today ramen is gaining popularity globally as a 'Japanese' food, but its origins in the early twentieth century point to the fare of inexpensive Chinese restaurants in Japan that invented the dish once known by the derogatory name *Shina soba* ('Chink soba') and sometimes still called *Chūka soba* (Chinese soba).[68] In the Occupation period, ramen became popularized as a cheap, fatty dish, with noodles made from wheat imported from the United States, and sold by Korean and Chinese pedlars.[69]

Despite now being available in high-end gourmet versions, both curry and ramen are generally inexpensive, and their low cost is one of the qualities they shared with the goals articulated for wartime national people's cuisine. Where national people's cuisine marked an effort to put a positive spin on rationing, the application of the term 'people's food' to curry and ramen represents a rebranding of conspicuously foreign foods as Japanese. The shift in the meaning of *kokuminshoku* was not by government fiat, as was the imposition of a wartime cuisine, but instead constitutes a gradual assimilation of recipes, ingredients and cooking methods into a national dietary culture shaped, as the wartime ethnologists had described, more by

Tilling the soil in a burned area of Kanda, Tokyo, 4 May 1945.

what people liked to eat and identify as their own than by what they were told they should consume as citizens. Today, some prominent food scholars go so far as to claim that ramen and curry are not just people's food but have become part of traditional Japanese cuisine.[70] And in a survey in 2015 that asked 1,000 people to identify *washoku* foods, 54.8 per cent of respondents included ramen in that category.[71]

In contrast to the forced wedding of nation and food in the wartime government's invention of national people's cuisine, native ethnologists presented a broad vision of Japan's food culture purportedly based on widespread and time-honoured domestic patterns. Despite their dissimilarities, both the proponents of national people's cuisine and the ethnologists who supported the idea of a national food culture created reified versions of culinary culture as a means to assert stability in an era of great and dire change for Japan. Backers of national people's cuisine sought to reassure people that counting calories, measuring vitamins and serving foods in the correct amount depending on age, gender and work would compensate for inadequate food supplies. Ethnologists contended that gathering details of rural foodways, from the names of soups to taboos about eating, would preserve a common cultural past and yield insights into national psychology at a time when everyone's personal life was severely disrupted by warfare. Viewed against one another and in regard to popular survival strategies as exemplified by the consumption of substitute foods, these wartime cuisines serve as reminders that a national cuisine is not simply a side effect of nationalism evolving in a series of steps that can be ticked off on a checklist, such as the effect of industrialization or improvements in transportation; instead, the making of a national cuisine is an ideological struggle born of an ongoing and usually contested process.

6

WHEN LOCAL FOOD BECAME
LOCAL CUISINE

Obtaining food locally was not only a guiding principle of wartime national people's cuisine; it also quickly became a necessity for survival in the early 1940s when city-dwellers sent their children to the countryside to barter for vegetables and cleared bombed areas in order to grow potatoes and pumpkins. Today, most of Japan's food is anything but local. Measured in terms of food energy, which includes the imported grains fed to domestic livestock, in 2010 Japan produced only 39 per cent of the food its population consumed.[1] Politicians have since at least the late 1990s made food self-sufficiency a major policy concern, and the more recent governmental promoters of *washoku* as the 'traditional dietary cultures of the Japanese' advocate greater reliance on domestic food sources. As a measure of the authenticity of a cuisine, the prominence of local food has endured since the Second World War, but the meaning of 'local food' has radically changed over that time, as this chapter examines.

At the surface, the category of local food seems to define itself: the ingredients available for consumption in a given area in contrast to foodstuffs that are either ubiquitous or are found elsewhere. Discovering local foods would appear to be as easy as following the contours of a map or simply drawing new boundaries. Some scholars of Japanese dietary cultures keep within the borders of ancient provinces or modern prefectures to delineate local food; others have created their own maps of the locations where special ingredients or distinct methods of preparation flourish.[2]

Despite the understandable tendency to define local food simply on the basis of geography, the terms for local food did not appear in Japan until the 1920s, around the period that Japan became a significant importer of sugar, wheat and rice.[3] In other words, 'local food' emerged at a time when Japan was becoming increasingly dependent on foreign food imports. The

Shirakawagō, Gifu Prefecture, the quintessential nostalgic location for a Japanese hometown and a UNESCO World Heritage Site, 2013.

novelty of local food should not be surprising, since the conditions the words describe would have been meaningless in an earlier age, when nearly all the foodstuffs were produced and eaten locally.[4]

Though people had been eating locally for generations, the category of local food that evolved in the twentieth century was not really local at all: it emerged through the intervention of state and national actors responding to international events. Wartime shortages, themselves the product of shipping blockades and the reallocation of food resources for military use, prompted the central government to identify and promote local foods, defined as a rural diet of coarse grains, rustic ingredients and folk recipes that most urbanites found unpalatable. During the period of rapid economic growth after the war, wartime local foods were no longer appetizing, and government researchers, food scholars and cookbook authors redefined local food as a collection of delicacies and special recipes that together comprised local cuisines and that evoked nostalgia, nature and sustainable agriculture and carried other positive nuances. Local food went from being considered largely uniform, backward, bland, rustic and peripheral to being a panoply of delicacies expressing distinct local cuisines, and was now seen as integral to Japan's traditional dietary cultures.

Early Modern Japan: Local Delicacies without Local Food

Local food is alluring because it appears to offer an authentic historical connection to time-honoured methods of harvesting, fishing, gathering and eating. Japan's traditional dietary cultures, according to its official UNESCO description, 'favors the consumption of various natural locally sourced ingredients such as rice, fish, vegetables and edible wild plants'.[5] In this view, local food is a building block of a national food culture. One can easily imagine that Japan's local foods and cooking styles helped to form a modern national cuisine in the same way that regional and ethnic foods are said to have given rise to Indian cuisine.[6]

Yet in Japan the categories of local food and regional cuisine are more recent than the construct of a national cuisine. Terms for Japanese cuisine first appear around 1880, pre-dating the use of words referring to local food by more than four decades.[7] The first designations of regional styles of cooking – even such prominent examples as 'Kyoto cuisine' – date from the modern period, while the term for Kyoto cuisine (*Kyō-ryōri*) was not widely used until the 1920s.[8] Regionality was not associated with Japanese cooking until after the mid-1930s.[9]

Far from being a national cuisine that has incorporated regional foods equally, Japanese cuisine today reveals a conspicuously urban bias in its most prominent dishes. Sushi (hand-pressed *nigirizushi* and rolled *makizushi*), soba and tempura, for instance, were representative of the diet of Edo, not of outlying provinces.[10] Even the preferred method of first boiling and then steaming rice that is programmed into Japanese rice cookers today was an urban style of preparation. As we have seen, in rural homes, rice was usually boiled in a pot with other grains and ingredients to make porridge.

Of course, the absence of a national, regional or local cuisine does not mean the absence of any cuisine. Early modern Japan saw the development of a complex cuisine based on a recognition of the power of food to signify religious, literary and artistic meanings, with rules for cooking and etiquette grounded in and disseminated by a prolific publishing industry that printed hundreds of volumes about cooking, menus and other writings on gastronomy.[11] The most elaborate articulation of premodern cuisine was found in the banquets for the aristocratic and warrior elite and the texts that described these feasts, but the culinary rituals associated with seasonal observations practised by people at all levels of society in both urban and rural areas reveal how foodstuffs in traditional Japanese culinary cultures, even before they were lumped together in the modern category of a national cuisine, could take on multiple symbolic associations while still providing nourishment.[12]

Writers in the early modern period generalized freely about the foods in different provinces and mentioned the specialities there, but they stopped short of describing regional or local cuisines, just as they did not refer to these cooking styles as 'Japanese'. In a text from 1697, *Honchō shokkan* (Mirror to Native Foodstuffs), the author Hitomi Hitsudai, a physician working for the central warrior government, described regional food differences, noting, for example, the places that grew the best buckwheat for making noodles.[13] Collections of poems and poetic terminology, such as *Shokoku meibutsu ōrai* (Tour of the Famous Products of the Provinces, 1727) and a different text with the same name printed in 1824, listed the noted goods of various places, such as shiitake from Izu (Shizuoka), dried daikon from Owari (Aichi), pears from Kai (Yamanashi), matsutake from Yamashiro (Kyoto) and persimmons from Yamato (Nara). However, some prominent regions – Izumo (Shimane), Tosa (Kōchi) and Kaga (Ishikawa), among others – are omitted from these texts, as if they had no local specialities at all.[14]

Novelists drew attention to some local specialities, but not always in positive ways. Takizawa (Kyokutei) Bakin (1767–1848), the author of *Nansō Satomi hakkenden* (Tale of the Eight Dog Warriors of the Satomi Clan, 1814–42), made a few observations about local food in his travel diary *Kiryo manroku* (A Meandering Account of a Journey), completed in 1820. He wrote, 'the only things that taste good in Kyoto are wheat gluten, soymilk skin (*yuba*), taro, mizuna and udon. Everything else is unpalatable for the people of Edo.' Bakin delivered an even less charitable view of food in Osaka: 'There are three good things in Osaka: the merchants, the seafood and gravestones. There are three bad things: the sake, eel and the cooking.'[15] Bakin's contemporaries from Osaka could counter with folk sayings about how their city was the 'country's kitchen' and that Osaka was a place where 'one could become impoverished by spending too much money on good food'. The comic novelist Jippensha Ikku (1765–1831) took a more charitable approach to Kyoto's most famous local delicacies in his comic travel tale *Tōkaidōchū hizakurige* (Shanks's Mare). He wrote, 'the Daibutsu rice-cakes of Maruyama, the spikenard shoots of Daigo, the leaf buds of Kurama . . . the turnips of Tōji, the vegetables of Mibu – these are some of the things of which the Kyōto people are proud.'[16] The local specialities that Bakin derided and Ikku lauded could be found in Osaka, Kyoto and numerous other cities, towns and villages, but these noteworthy ingredients did not add up to a complete inventory of a local food supply – nevermind a local cuisine. Instead, published lists of local specialities reflected noted agricultural products known outside a locale, rather than the everyday foods consumed within it.

Rural Food

Lacking a premodern equivalent, the Japanese terms for 'local food', *kyōdo ryōri* and *kyōdo shoku*, were coined to describe the foodstuffs not just in any locale but in rural areas, reflecting the original meaning of *kyōdo*, a word that dates from as early as the eighth century and refers to the countryside. In the early twentieth century *kyōdo* came to suggest a personal connection to lands outside the urban core: the locale where one was born and raised.[17] The exact boundaries of the area expressed by the word *kyōdo* are undefined, but refer to a larger setting than a 'native village' (*kyōri, furusato*). One is tempted to hypothesize that the change in meaning of the term *kyōdo* is connected to the doubling of the urban population in Japan in the first three decades of the twentieth century, as people who left the farm for the city reflected on the rural life they had left behind.

Beginning in the 1910s with the work of the founding father of the study of Japanese folklore, Yanagita Kunio, and reaching a culmination in 1934 with the organization of the Centre for Research of Rural Lifestyles (Kyōdo Seikatsu Kenkyūjo), native ethnologists following Yanagita identified the rural *kyōdo* – particularly the most remote mountain and fishing villages – for ethnographic surveys. Yanagita and his colleagues averred that vestiges of Japan's national past lingered in places far from the influence of advanced urban centres.[18] Areas designated as 'local' were backward and the same was true of the diet of these places. So-called local foods (*kyōdo shoku*) were defined in negative terms by the absence of soy sauce and sugar, and of rice as a staple grain.[19] Local foods, in other words, lacked the ingredients that people in cities considered necessary for a 'civilized' life.[20] Rural staple grains such as millet, barnyard millet and foxtail millet were 'discriminated foods', marking those who consumed them as stupid and contemptible, as Chapter Two described.[21] For city-dwellers, the rural diet might appear to have little to recommend it other than the inventive but unappetizing ways that farmers coped with deprivation.

The monthly magazine *Ie no hikari* (Light of the Household), founded by the National Agricultural Cooperative in 1925, however, presented the diet of the countryside in a more positive light, respectful of the publication's rural readership. In 1932 *Light of the Household* undertook a study of rural diets by convening a panel of six experts, who surveyed the spending and consumption habits of thirty farm households in Tokyo prefecture. The specialists determined that rural cooking was nutritious and could provide inspiration for improving the diet in other non-urban parts of Japan. Based upon such observations and with input from the burgeoning field of nutritional science in Japan, *Light of the Household* sought to foster a 'new rural cooking' that would combine rustic culinary knowhow and local ingredients with modern cooking habits and the science of dietetics.[22] Articles in the magazine suggested that vitamin-rich locusts, a local delicacy in Nagano prefecture, might be adopted in other places to enhance the diet, while at the same time finding a use for a pest.[23] New rural cooking was intended to transplant to the countryside the culinary dexterity and concern for nutrition found in middle-class urban households, while at the same time providing a way to disseminate folk wisdom about foodstuffs and their uses from one rural area to another.[24]

Local Food and the Second World War

Knowledge of the use of native ingredients, ways of economizing on rice and the effort to maximize the nutritive values of foods were key principles of national people's cuisine, as noted in the previous chapter. Such ideals notwithstanding, the diet on the home front gradually came to be defined solely in negative terms by the reduction of rationed foodstuffs, including white rice, soy sauce, miso and sugar. A publication of the Imperial Rule Assistance Association (IRAA) in 1942 advocated that rice should be replaced in the diet with other grains and potatoes as staple foods, but that was already occurring by 1940.[25] Rationing of eggs, fish, rice and wheat, which began on a large scale in 1941, became systematized in the 1942 Food Control Law, which gave the central government power over the purchase, distribution and sale of foods including sugar, rice and other grains. In 1943 the IRAA undertook to increase potato production, and as white and sweet potatoes became increasingly important sources of food energy, the tubers were re-categorized from vegetables to staple foods.[26] Wartime deprivation meant that the diet of the general population was becoming closer to the way that the rural diet had been described in terms of what was lacking.

It was rural diets, defined as 'local food', that the wartime government turned to in response to the crises in the domestic food supply. In 1943 the

Ministry of Agriculture established the Association for the Centralization of Food Resources, which in the year of its creation charged the agricultural economics departments of the five imperial universities with carrying out a study of rural food to last for six months, beginning in the autumn of 1943.[27] The aim of the project was not simply to report on food culture in the countryside but also to mobilize local food for the war effort. The introduction in the publication of the findings of the project announced, 'we undertook a survey of local food to clarify an ideal form of regional cuisine, which when augmented through improvements from the field of nutrition will be appropriate to the conditions of warfare.'[28] In contrast to the earlier IRAA-funded study by folklorists described in the previous chapter, which examined a diverse range of food customs, the imperial universities had a much more narrowly defined mandate for their research, in different regions of Japan. For each local foodstuff, the universities were required to record: 1) its name; 2) the social, economic and political factors that gave rise to it; 3) methods of preparation; 4) how the food was gathered; 5) how it was distributed locally; 6) methods of cultivation; and 7) its nutritional value in local diets.[29]

The emphasis on practical outcomes over theory is evident in the report by Tokyo Imperial University (now the University of Tokyo), which explained in its preface: 'in our survey, we avoided establishing a fixed definition of local food; instead we looked to various customs existing as time-honoured traditions in every locale and we limited ourselves to staple foods that were substitutes or supplements for rice, which is the national staple food.' While purporting to deny a definition of local food, this particular study nonetheless affirmed that local food was characterized by a non-rice diet, harking back to depictions of rural food from the 1930s.[30] The study reveals an urban bias in the assumption that a non-rice diet was not the norm.

After introducing the general area where the study occurred, Tokyo Imperial University organized its findings by foodstuff and how each was prepared, designating the categories of cooked grains, tubers and flour-based foods such as noodles. Later sections of the report made observations about these foods according to the seven aforementioned directives; then the report introduced the twelve specific sites surveyed. Kyushu Imperial University took a similar approach in its study, introducing foodstuffs and following up with descriptions of the locales. Besides staple grains, it described how to cook snakes, locusts and silkworms, which its report presented as 'local foods' of Hiroshima prefecture.[31]

The researchers from the five imperial universities interpreted local food as deviations from the presumed national norm of eating rice as a staple, and saw geography as the cause for these variances. Local foods, according to their reports, reflected a symbiosis between native foods and the adaptation of the Japanese to different environments. The discussion of local food by the survey team from Tōhoku Imperial University in Sendai explained:

> From the beginning food takes on particular characteristics depending on race, and these set characteristics are closely related to such things as the climate where the foodstuffs are produced and the topography. For instance, rice, which is the staple food of our Yamato race, certainly has an intimate relationship to the weather and geography of our land, making it something that did not appear by accident. Consequently, the more closely we examine this point we find that in our country there are many regional gradations of not only staple foods but also subsidiary foodstuffs according to various regional climates and topographical conditions.

In contrast to diets found in cities, which were sites of consumption but not food production, 'local foods are created from the foodways that arise from places where production and living are intertwined', according to the report.[32] Report authors from Tōhoku Imperial University stated that the most significant local foods in northern Japan were barnyard millet, foxtail millet and buckwheat. The university's study explicated methods of cultivating, harvesting and cooking these grains, describing their nutritional value.[33] Kyoto Imperial University selected the mountainous Hida region in northern Gifu prefecture due to the variety of well-known indigenous food customs there. In the scholarly literature of the period, Hida was synonymous with a non-rice diet, a place where locals relied on grains such as barnyard millet, foxtail millet and buckwheat and sources of starch that included chestnuts, horse chestnuts and acorns.[34] At a popular level in the 1930s and 1940s, the rugged mode of living in mountainous Hida, nicknamed 'Japan's Tibet', was associated with a lifestyle described as 'simian'.[35] If the 'Yamato race' relied on rice as a staple, by implication Japanese living in remote mountainous areas like Hida, where rice cultivation was not possible, lived in forced adaptation to a lack of rice and could therefore be deemed 'primitive'.

The efforts of government-sponsored food researchers to publish their work in the final phase of the Second World War did not solve the country's food problems. More than half of Japan's war casualties died from starvation.

Conditions at home worsened even after surrender, as the historian Barak Kushner describes: 'When Japan surrendered in August 1945, its food supply, perilously dependent on rice, reached only sixty percent of its prewar levels. Conditions continued to decline in 1946.' He elaborates, 'In the first year after the war ended, people died at Tokyo and Ueno rail stations at an average of about twenty a day. In Osaka, about sixty people a month perished from starvation.'[36] Japan's GDP did not return to pre-war levels until 1953.

The Rise of Local Cuisine in the Post-war Era

The category of local food, which was synonymous with rural food before and during the Second World War, took on new meanings in the 1950s and 1960s, in the period of Japan's recovery and 'miraculous' economic growth, when many Japanese left the countryside and agricultural work. From 1960 to 1975, each year approximately 70,000–80,000 workers found jobs outside the agricultural sector, reducing the number of people engaged in farming over the course of those fifteen years by some 58 per cent.[37] Japan's urban population grew from 38 per cent of the total in 1950 to 75 per cent by 1975.[38] Not only did these urban arrivals modify their eating habits, but over time they developed new attitudes towards the foods in the countryside that they had left behind. The nutritionist Ura Riyo, who participated in wartime government-sponsored studies of local food, wrote one of the first post-war books on local food – not by travelling around Japan but by interviewing colleagues from different parts of the country while studying at the Institute of Public Health in Tokyo in 1951–2.[39] From the late 1950s, researchers like Ura became acutely interested in trying to document local foods given the rapid and profound transformation of the Japanese diet, as measured in the increased quality and variety of food consumed.[40]

The sense that Japan's entire dietary culture and especially local ways of eating were entering a new phase of development is evident from an Agency for Cultural Affairs survey conducted from 1962 to '64. The foreword to the study states:

> There is greater consciousness of the protection of the properties of folk culture in the general public, but due to rapid social developments in recent years, daily life is transforming and the traditional lifestyle and customs of our country are swiftly changing; tangible and intangible cultural properties are quickly disappearing.[41]

With the aim of cultural preservation, researchers conducted fieldwork in thirty areas in each of Japan's prefectures. The remarkable accomplishment of the survey was the creation of twelve maps of Japan's regional food culture, which gave a name to the study: *Nihon minzoku chizu* (Atlas of Japanese Folk Culture). The maps separately display local variations in the consumption of staple grains; foods made from flour, such as noodles; the ratio of rice to other grains consumed; the different names for lunch; the contents of morning meals; of afternoon meals; and of boxed lunches (*bentō*); and local occupations. These variations were explored in further detail in an interpretive essay that was followed by descriptions of foodways in the localities surveyed.

Even as the study was undertaken, the data in the *Atlas of Japanese Folk Culture* was quickly becoming an anachronism. In the very year that the study began, the amount of rice consumed annually per capita in Japan reached its highest point ever, at 171 kilograms.[42] Distinguishing local food on the basis of how much rice as opposed to other staple grains was consumed became meaningless after rice became Japan's main staple grain nationally. From the late 1950s regional and class differences in the diet were much less pronounced than before the Second World War and the daily diet was becoming standardized, notes the prominent food scholar Ishige Naomichi.[43] Knowledge of many local foods was also fading, according to a major study from 1972 by the food scholar Matsushita Sachiko and Yoshikawa Seiji, an employee of the Ministry of Agriculture, Forestry and Fisheries. The authors asked 677 food researchers, educators and students taking courses about food and home economics to identify 712 local foods. The study concluded that only 201 local foods were well known and that just 162 more were barely known, prompting the authors to call for further research into the 349 local foods (almost half of the foods surveyed) that were becoming extinct.[44] Many local foods were produced using time-honoured methods of preserving raw ingredients, such as through pickling, and these traditional recipes had become less necessary by 1970, by which time some 90 per cent of households owned electric refrigerators.[45]

Another attempt to reassess local food in the midst of these dramatic changes in the diet was the geographer Kōsaka Mutsuko's influential survey published in 1974.[46] Criticizing wartime studies of local food as simply the search for ways to relieve famine, Kōsaka shifted focus away from local foods to local cuisine, which she defined as dishes dating from before the Meiji Restoration in 1868 and distinct to a specific locale. She acknowledged that Hokkaido became part of Japan only in 1869, and allowed that recipes invented there after 1868 could be considered authentic regional cuisine. Yet she refused to include Osaka and Tokyo, since these urban centres were sites of food consumption but not production – an assumption similar to the wartime studies that equated local food with rural food. Dispatching researchers who were students at Risshō Women's University (now Bunkyō University) in Tokyo, Kōsaka instructed them to conduct interviews in different prefectures enquiring about foodstuffs such as local ingredients and seasonal speciality dishes. Collating the data, she produced maps showing regional variations in ingredient use and cooking methods, noting, for instance, that 64 per cent of local dishes were made by simmering.[47] Unlike those of pre-war and wartime folklorists, who surveyed local foods and assumed that they offered an accurate picture of age-old customs, Kōsaka's study attempted to use interviews to reconstruct elements of food culture from more than a century earlier, which by definition pre-dated the lives of any informants surveyed.[48]

Kōsaka's methodology, for its naive faith that oral testimony can somehow bridge a hundred years of history, was part of what the anthropologist Millie Creighton has dubbed the 'retro boom' of the 1970s, 'involving a renewed interest in Japanese traditions and nostalgia for the past . . . that has romanticized Japan's agrarian heritage'. Creighton describes how the domestic tourist industry capitalized on the nation's fascination with nostalgia by promoting travel to rural hamlets 'that were formerly considered unsophisticated and boring'.[49] The nostalgia associated with native place as expressed by the term 'local' (*kyōdo*) and by the related but more familiar 'home town' (*furusato*) intensified in the 1970s as many people's actual personal links with rural life had faded when they moved to the city.[50]

Virtual culinary travel to the countryside was part of the romanticized journey into Japan's agrarian past, and cookbooks in the late 1960s and early '70s offered detailed descriptions of local cuisines. Local food writing coincided with a gourmet boom that began in the mid-1960s as the mass media focused on the pleasures of eating, as seen in television programmes including *Gochisōsama* (That Was Delicious), which began in 1971, and *Ryōri tenkoku* (Culinary Heaven), first broadcast in 1975.[51] Significantly, Matsushita and Yoshikawa's 1972 study of local food, mentioned earlier, was one of the first to ask respondents whether or not they ate local foods and if these dishes tasted good. Such information was valuable for cookbook authors seeking to compile collections of favourite local delicacies, which besides representing authentic local identity also had to be delicious. The cookbook *Nihon no kyōdo ryōri* (Japan's Local Cuisines), published first in

1966 and then in a revised edition in 1974, promised in its introduction: 'fresh Japanese cuisine that can reveal home towns [*furusato*]' – the proto-typical destinations for tourists to the countryside seeking to reconnect with their cultural and emotional roots.[52] *Japan's Local Cuisines* was composed by teachers from cooking schools throughout the country and described the regional dishes of Japan's 47 prefectures. Departing from previous studies that denied a local cuisine to cities, the cookbook included Tokyo, where examples of local cuisine included sushi, loach, horsemeat sashimi, tempura, grilled eel, soba and beef sukiyaki.[53] All these dishes, excepting horsemeat, are familiar staples of modern Japanese cuisine – an acknowledgement of the profound impact of urban foods on the shaping of national cuisine. That the cookbook was also meant for the armchair traveller is evident from the prefaces to the different regions. The section for foods from Gifu promised 'the taste of authentic mountain country' and described famous tourist sites in the prefecture, such as Takayama, Gifu's 'little Kyoto'. The delicacies of Kōchi, which represented 'chic southern country cuisine', were introduced with a short essay about the prefecture's geography and history and its famous Sunday markets, described as 'the most representative thing about Kōchi'.[54]

Makers of processed food also attempted to capture the budding interest in local cuisine in the 1970s. In 1970 Nissin Foods, founded by Momofuku Andō, the inventor of instant ramen, introduced Country-style Soba followed by Ramen Family, two products that were 'testaments to the depopulation of the countryside and the decline of extended kinship ties in Japan during the same period', according to the historian George Solt.[55]

Trends to identify and promote local cuisines continued and inten-sified in the 1980s, reaching a pinnacle with the Ministry of Agriculture, Forestry and Fisheries' (MAFF) fifty-volume series *Nihon no shoku seikatsu zenshū* (Collected Writings on Japanese Foodways), a countrywide sur-vey of regional food lore advertised as a 'catalogue of 15,000 types of local food'.[56] The MAFF's series used oral interviews to reconstruct the diet in the Taishō (1912–26) and early Shōwa periods (1926–89) preceding the Second World War – a much more recent past than in Kōsaka's earlier oral history of the pre-Meiji period, but a past equally difficult to recover, as the folk-lorist Fukuta Azio pointed out contemporaneously in 1987: 'There is what amounts to a delusion that folklore surveys can reconstruct the situation of the Taishō and early Shōwa periods, over fifty years ago.'[57] Yet the MAFF's volumes replicate the past to the point that the descriptions of conditions in the 1920s are written in the present tense. A note in each of the volumes indicates that the photographs attempt to recreate scenes from half a century earlier.[58] If the decontextualized home town 'is frequently portrayed by images of rustic landscapes, dilapidated shrines and remote anonymous train stations' in travel advertising, as Creighton describes, then the corresponding image in the MAFF's books about local food is the photos of elderly women in period costume making straw sandals or squatting in front of mud stoves.[59] The images supply a human connection to the culinary past while testifying to its authenticity. Descriptions of local diets are interlaced in the volumes with vignettes of country life and snippets of unattributed folksy dialogue to complete the portrait of home-town foodways. For example, readers learn that when the paddies are flooded on the Kachō plain in Kōchi prefecture, 'one hears people greet each other by saying, "are your paddies started?", and where moles have dug holes in the paths between the paddies the routes are spread cleanly with mud indicating that their repairs are done.'[60] Work on a muddy field never sounded so romantic.

Ambiguity between the present and past is similar to the blurring of the concept of the local in the MAFF volumes. Each book examines a different prefecture, dividing it into about half a dozen sub-regions. Niigata prefecture is reported as having six culinary sub-regions, Kōchi has four, Gifu has seven and Saga six.[61] Synthetic essays at the end of each volume describe what sets the prefecture apart from the rest of Japan. Each book is organized with chapters on the prefecture's sub-regions. Like Kōsaka's study, *Collected Writings on Japanese Foodways* makes use of oral interviews, but the fact that the foodways described were those of the childhoods of the informants gives the findings more credibility. However, the informants, whose names and biographical information appear in the volume, are never quoted directly. Their testimonies are instead woven together into unattributed narratives presenting an idealized version of local food culture in the 1920s and '30s, including typical daily meals, festive dishes and the ways in which special foods are used to celebrate moments in people's lives. The fifty volumes, each divided into about six separate sub-regions and containing essays synthesizing interviews with dozens of informants, show the diversity of Japan's food culture even as they undermine the idea that regional or local food or cuisine is a meaningful rubric for all this information. Consequently, the terms local food and local cuisine do not appear prominently in the MAFF's series, which use place names instead, making food entirely local by linking it to specific locations on a map. The study also renders local food entirely historical, because the diets in the locales surveyed had obviously changed drastically in half a century – otherwise the authors could have reported on conditions in the 1980s. Photographs in the text of elderly informants dressed in period costume and making and consuming their native foods serve as a reminder of the fragility of traditions that might disappear when the guardians of tradition die.

Traditional Dietary Cultures and Native Foods

The MAFF's approach of associating local food so closely with the 1920s suggests that local food has largely disappeared today; but the term local food saw a resurgence in the 1980s, with consumers interested in 'eating locally' and public and private efforts to promote regional ingredients. Foods that have received particular focus since the 1980s are heirloom vegetables: traditional varieties that existed before the advent of modern hybrids. Kyoto's regional governments designated certain 'traditional Kyoto vegetables' in 1987, and two years later Kanazawa City in Ishikawa prefecture labelled some of its heirloom produce 'Kaga vegetables', named after the prefecture's ancient province.[62] The scientist and food scholar Ichikawa Takeo coined the term 'native food' to refer to cooking that relies on local ingredients such as heirloom vegetables.[63] He writes,

> native foods are largely the effect of their ingredients, which include vegetables, gathered herbs, wild animals, wild fowl, domesticated animals and marine products.[64] Among these, heirloom vegetables are intimately intertwined with the conditions of the local environment including the weather, geography and the soil.[65]

By Ichikawa's estimation, then, it no longer matters that the diet has changed since the 1920s, because one can create authentic local cuisine simply by adding native foods to a recipe. Thus chefs in Kyoto include the leafy vegetable mizuna in noodle soup to make Kyoto-style ramen, while other restaurateurs serve 'Kyoto cuisine' prepared using heirloom Kyoto vegetables transported to their restaurants in Tokyo.[66]

Ichikawa's portrait of native foods resembles pre-war definitions of rural food that emphasized the primacy of geography in distinguishing the local diet, but with two important distinctions. First, by Ichikawa's definition, post-war native foods are not grains, but side-dishes containing meat, reflecting the shift away from rice consumption in the Japanese diet since the mid-1960s. In the 1960s, staple grains still supplied half of the food energy of a typical Japanese household, but by the time Ichikawa wrote his essay, at the end of the twentieth century, the average household derived more energy from meat and fat than from grains.[67] The domesticated and game meats that Ichikawa highlights as native ingredients would not even have been on the tables of most Japanese citizens in the first half of the twentieth century. Beef, pork and other meat comprised less than 1.7 kilograms per capita in the food supply in 1925. By the year 2000, however, meat supply had reached 45 kilograms per capita annually, indicating a 25-fold increase over 75 years.[68] Foods may be native to a place, but they also reflect modern preferences for meat dishes. Meat and heirloom vegetables are thus simultaneously expressions of the modern diet and embodiments of tradition, without any of the stigma of wartime rural dishes associated with poverty and deprivation.

A second point that distinguishes native ingredients, such as heirloom vegetables, popular since the 1980s from pre-war rural foods is taste. During the Second World War city-dwellers complained about having to eat foods that were typical of rural diets.[69] In contrast, the more variegated and luxurious diet of the post-war era not only allowed more opportunities to consume meat and other delicacies, but also enabled consumers to reflect on taste; and gourmandism has now become central to defining the authenticity of local foods. Gone are the days of wartime austerity when side dishes included 'crow snake' in some locales.[70] The advertisement for the MAFF's *Collected Writings on Japanese Foodways* series equates local foods with gourmet delicacies, explaining: 'local foods developed within the native setting [*fudō*] of a locale and they are tastes that are found nowhere else. That "taste of nowhere else" has the highest value in the age of gourmet food.'[71] Here the 'value' of the local dish is not measured in the daily nourishment it provides for the local consumer, but instead as a potential delight for the gourmand who arrives to try new delicacies. Locals benefit from reading the MAFF's series by learning which indigenous food products to sell to outsiders.[72]

In a move that further emphasized that local foods should taste good, in 2007 the MAFF convened a panel of eight experts in 'culinary research, food culture, the relationship between urban and rural areas and women's movements' to select the top 100 best local dishes, for a project dubbed: 'I Want to Eat! I Want to Serve! The Taste of Home Towns'. According to the project's website, local food 'is premised on the distinct natural features, foodstuffs, eating habits and the historical-cultural background of each locale and inevitably arises from an original idea of the people's lifestyle of that area.' Yet local foods must also taste good to qualify as 'I Want to Eat! I

Want to Serve!' foods. The MAFF panellists selected from a list of local foods gleaned from publications and suggestions from prefectural and municipal governments as well as an Internet poll.[73] Japan's wartime government contracted with scholars to speak to people directly about what they ate, but the current government employs expert panels with only minimal input from ordinary people to determine that dishes such as salmon roe on rice, curry soup, pork *shabu shabu* and Hiroshima *okonomiyaki* are representative local delicacies for national enjoyment and reflections of Japanese culture to be promoted internationally.

In appealing to foreign audiences, taste has taken priority over place in determining the authenticity of local foods, as evidenced by the pamphlet *Japan's Tasty Secrets*, offered on the MAFF website, which features the words 'local cuisines' (*kyōdo ryōri*) on its front cover. The brochure showcases, according to its subtitle, *Local Food that Satisfies the World's Most Demanding Eaters*. The dishes listed include Chinese dumplings (*gyōza*) from Utsunomiya and the Sasebo Burger from Nagasaki, two obviously foreign additions to the Japanese diet.[74] Local foods may not survive unless people consume them, but the pamphlet reveals a perception that local food must adapt to modern tastes to include cheap, high-calorie foods that might appeal to foreign tourists, such as those served by fast-food restaurants.

Attention to local delicacies supports the MAFF's efforts to promote tourism and the agricultural and fishery sectors, and assists the efforts of the Japanese government to advance the country's dietary cultures internationally, as exemplified by the 2012 application by MAFF and the Agency for Cultural Affairs to have Japan's traditional dietary cultures (*washoku*) receive UNESCO Intangible Cultural Heritage status. According to a press release from the Agency for Cultural Affairs that year, *washoku*:

> 'Utilizes various fresh ingredients' depending on such factors as the four seasons and the locale; has distinguishing characteristics including a 'presentation style that reveals the beauty of nature'; follows a spirit of 'respect for nature', which is fundamental to the Japanese people; is intimately connected with seasonal observances such as the New Year's, rice planting and harvest festivals; and has social customs that strengthen ties within families and members of a local community.[75]

In a rejection of wartime definitions of local food as linked to specifics of place and race, and post-war studies that present local cuisine largely in

Y koso APAN

JAPAN'S TASTY SECRETS

Local food that satisfies the world's most demanding eaters

MAFF
Ministry of Agriculture, Forestry and Fisheries

Japan's Tasty Secrets, cover of an online booklet.

historical terms, traditional dietary cultures are by the MAFF's definition rooted in timeless communities whose diet is natural, tasty and beautifully presented. Japan's traditional dietary cultures are, in other words, said to be found in the local cuisines of anonymous socially engaged communities that interact harmoniously with the environment for sustenance.

Such a benign definition of national dietary cultures composed of various regional cuisines directly confronts fears of more problematic interventions between man and nature, such as that witnessed in the nuclear disaster at Fukushima in March 2011, which prompted the evacuation of many communities in the northeast, devastated agriculture and fisheries in the region, and sparked international and domestic fears about the safety of Japan's foodstuffs. In fact, the Japanese government's application to UNESCO called for the designation of *washoku* with heritage status as a 'symbol of Japan's recovery' from the March 2011 disasters, requesting that the international community reaffirm the purity and refinement of Japan's traditional dietary cultures despite the fact that ongoing fear about radiation in the food supply was prompting continued international prohibition on imports of foodstuffs from irradiated areas.[76]

In Japan, local food, which was once synonymous with a backward diet of coarse grains found in remote villages, has become in recent years a cornucopia of gourmet dishes justifying the designation 'local cuisine'. The transition in meaning from food to cuisine mirrors developments in the Japanese diet since the 1960s, particularly the shift away from grains as the main staples and towards more diverse and luxurious sources of food energy such as meat dishes, as consumers have sought to make daily dining a more varied and pleasurable experience.

The shift in meaning from local food to local cuisine also reflects a change in attitudes about the places that produce food. After the war, the remote villages of pre-war Japan became sites of disappearing cultural assets, romanticized home towns and tourist destinations. Similarly, the inhabitants of rural locales were no longer viewed with scorn or pity for their humble diets, but were seen as endangered resources themselves, valorized for their engagement in traditional communities, especially as purveyors of authentic ingredients.

For scholars, the means of discovering local food shifted away from interviews with local residents about contemporary conditions in the 1930s and '40s to attempts to use oral history in the 1970s and '80s in the hope of recovering conditions of fifty or 100 years ago. Even as more recent iterations of Japanese dietary cultures promise benign sourcing of seasonal, native ingredients such as heirloom vegetables, the hamburgers, Chinese dumplings and other 'B-grade'[77] dishes that are among the newly designated 'tasty' local foods, are often fatty concoctions less healthy to eat daily.

From the standpoint of the consumer, eating locally in Japan or elsewhere can be a strategy for supporting nearby producers and possibly obtaining fresher foodstuffs; and by other definitions eating locally might simply describe what people in a specific area do without giving much thought to the food's origin, historical resonances or cultural dimensions.[78] Eating locally can also be a type of gourmandism, especially when heirloom foods and delicacies are more expensive than conventional varieties – which is usually the case.

But, as this chapter has shown, rather than being created locally from the ground up, the categories of local food and local cuisine in Japan have taken their meanings in relationship to the policies of central government, which mobilized elements of the rural diet to fit the exigencies of wartime and sought in the post-war era to find and promote regional delicacies to bolster the domestic economy, the rural sector, tourism and Japan's image abroad.[79] Although Japan can now boast about its delicious local cuisines, heirloom ingredients and even the quality of its hamburgers, the main continuity driving the changing iterations of local food has been the role of central government and scholars, many of whom were working on the government's behalf – as opposed to the ordinary people who live, cook and dine in diverse locations.

7

LOCAL FOOD CULTURES IN SAGA, KŌCHI AND HIDA

In the panoply of traditional Japanese dietary cultures (comprising *washoku*), any local cuisines might be considered interchangeable, but when viewed individually in the areas where they are from, local delicacies are not homogeneous but reflect the contexts that gave rise to them. This chapter spotlights three locations: Saga and Kōchi prefectures and the mountainous Hida area of Gifu prefecture. Situated on different islands, the three areas share the fact that they have long been presented as peripheral to nationwide culinary trends. The intent of this chapter is not simply to examine local dietary culture in these places as examples of what is omitted, marginalized or homogenized in narratives of national culinary discourse, but to visit a few specific places to show how local actors designate their indigenous culinary traditions in reaction to comments by outsiders about their culinary lives and in reflection on the gastronomic legacies of the places where they live.

The local diets in Saga, Kōchi and Hida have changed so much since the 1960s that distinct foods once consumed daily in these regions are no longer to be found. Today, 'local' food designates delicacies that are sold to visitors. Turning a diet into a delicacy involves searching through alimentary traditions to find or create items that are marketable to outsiders. In some instances, specific ingredients used in new recipes form the basis for the elevation of local food cultures to the level of cuisine. In others, styles of banqueting described in local publications and modified for tourists serve as testimonies of indigenous gastronomic customs. Local food cultures in Saga, Kōchi and Hida all emphasize sake, Japan's traditional alcoholic drink, which is surprisingly absent from discussions of the country's national dietary cultures. The local food cultures of Saga, Kōchi and Hida one finds today represent a narrowing of the inventory of all that was

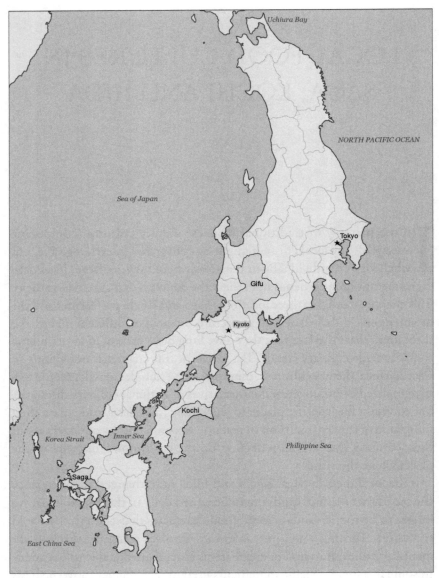

Map of Japan noting the locations of Gifu, Saga and Kōchi prefectures.

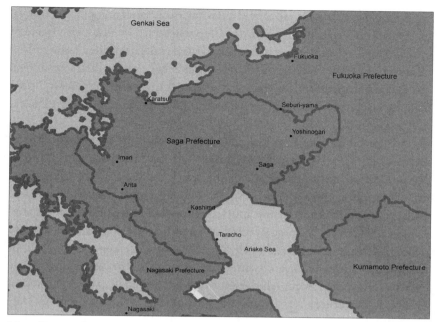

Map of Saga prefecture.

once consumed in these areas, but they also reveal how locales present their indigenous dietary cultures in the best possible light.

Saga Prefecture

Saga prefecture (population approx. 830,000) is bordered in the north by the Genkai Sea, a designation given to the Sea of Japan off the northern coast of Kyushu. Nagasaki prefecture adjoins Saga's western border and Fukuoka prefecture is to the east. The islands of Iki and Tsushima lie off Saga's northern coast as stepping-stones to the Korean peninsula. The chain of islands between the two nations always kept Saga in close contact with the continent, making the prefecture a likely candidate for the place where rice was first introduced to Japan, by the fifth century BCE.[1] Evidence of dry field farming of barley and buckwheat in Saga dates to the Yayoi period (300 BCE–300 CE) and Saga is home to Yoshinogari (thirty minutes from Saga City by train), the site of a reconstructed Yayoi-period settlement, replete with moats, wooden palisades, burial mounds and multistorey buildings.[2] Saga's southern border is the Ariake Sea, a more placid body of water than the northern coast and no more than an average of 20 metres deep.

Today, Saga devotes more land than any other prefecture (some 100 sq. km/25,000 ac.) to the production of Nijō wheat, which is favoured in beer brewing, and the prefecture is also noted for its sake breweries, as described below.[3] Important fruit crops include strawberries and mikan (satsumas), both grown in greenhouses. Saga may also be the place where tea was introduced to Japan; the prefecture currently ranks eighth in terms of national tea production.

Mount Sefuri (1,054 m/3,460 ft), just over the border in Fukuoka prefecture, marks the division between the more mountainous northern part of Saga centred around the port city of Karatsu and the flatter southern portion demarcating the Saga Plain. Northern and southern Saga were different political domains in the early modern period. Karatsu domain, located around the Genkai Sea port of Karatsu, encompassed the northern coastal region and was administered by the Ogasawara family, hereditary vassals of the Tokugawa warrior government. Hizen domain, of the Nabeshima family based in Saga City, occupied the southern part of Saga as well as most of Nagasaki prefecture.

Some food scholars divide the traditional foodways of Saga prefecture according to these early modern political divisions, explaining that the warlords of Karatsu in the north enjoyed a far more lavish diet than the Nabeshima house, the rulers of Hizen domain in the south.[4] The two parts of Saga provide different local delicacies. From the Genkai Sea in the north come sea bream, horse mackerel, squid and wakame. Whaling boats once set out from ports on the Genkai Sea and female divers (*ama*) caught abalone, sea urchin and other delicacies along the coast.[5] A decade after the 1986 International Whaling Commission moratorium on commercial whaling, Nagasaki and Saga still ranked the highest in per capita consumption of whale meat in all of Japan.[6] In southern Saga, freshwater fish – carp, crucian carp, catfish and eels – once thrived in the waterways of the Saga Plain around Saga City, while oysters, octopus, pen shell, crab, cockles and gizzard shad can be taken from the Ariake Sea. Today, the Ariake is the famous source of red nori, a red algae, which is flattened into sheets for use in sushi making and other dishes. Saga produces more nori than any other prefecture, with gourmet brands selling for up to ¥500 ($4.50/£3.50) for a single sheet. Mudskippers, mantis shrimp and other edible creatures also live on the Ariake Sea coast.[7]

The Saga Plain was an area distinguished by its 'creek agriculture', due to the prevalence of canals and waterways that flow through and irrigate its paddies.[8] Two major watercourses flow through the Saga Plain: to the north and east is the Chikugo River, which meanders through four of Kyushu's prefectures before it reaches the Ariake Sea in Saga; the Rokkaku River forms the plain's southern and western boundaries. Between the plain's major rivers are numerous streams and irrigation canals. Traditionally, communities worked together to maintain the creeks, keeping them clear of debris. The waterways were drained each March for cleaning and again after the autumn rice harvest, when the silt was removed and used as fertilizer. Draining the water provided a chance to catch carp, catfish and eel.[9] Other parts of the prefecture, such as the slopes of Mount Hachiman near Karatsu, and Arita, are famous for their terraced rice paddies, the former having received special recognition by the Ministry of Education as an important cultural landscape.

Thanks to its geography, Saga had become a leading prefecture for rice production by 1938, when it exceeded the national average for yield by 96 kilograms per 1,000 square metres, due to local improvements in irrigation, such as the use of electric pumps to replace waterwheels and the introduction of chemical fertilizers.[10] Saga's farmers also replaced longer grain Indica with shorter grain Japonica varieties of rice, despite the fact that the former was faster growing and heartier. The change was caused by the preference for Japonica, which in Japan is considered tastier when prepared by boiling and steaming.[11] In 2014 Saga ranked tenth among all prefectures for rice production.[12]

Since rice was a valuable cash crop, farmers in Saga before the Second World War economized on their own consumption of it. Brown rice eaten with other grains was the dominant staple in rural areas in the 1920s and '30s, and was generally consumed mixed with barley in a ratio of four parts rice to one part barley. Pure white rice was a treat enjoyed only a few times a year, such as to celebrate the New Year. Cropping of staples besides rice occurred after the rice had been harvested. Farmers planted winter wheat, rye and barley. They grew soybeans and azuki on the footpaths between paddies and their home gardens contained broad beans, green vegetables and white and sweet potatoes.[13]

Saga's ports of Imari and Karatsu (literally 'China port' or 'the port to China'), never rivalled Dazaifu in Fukuoka, the main departure point for the continent since the ancient period; but when the warlord Toyotomi Hideyoshi launched two attempts to conquer China through Korea in the 1590s, he established a military headquarters in the town of Nagoya, on the Saga coast. Saga's warlords expatriated Korean artisans, helping to establish the world-famous ceramic centres in Arita and Imari, which gave their names to colourful painted porcelain, and in Karatsu, noted for its more subdued stoneware. Saga's ceramics industry flourished thanks to the proximity of nearby foreign ports. The warrior government handled trade with the Dutch and Chinese in the port of Nagasaki, which it controlled directly. Iki and Tsushima islands, which were separate domains, engaged in limited trade with Korea.

Many of the leaders of the Meiji Restoration, which brought the downfall of the Tokugawa military regime in 1868, came from Saga. The fall of the last warrior government brought an end to the samurai, but did not diminish the 'way of the warrior', which informed the ethos of the modern Japanese military. *Hagakure*, a seventeenth-century code of warrior behaviour, sometimes called the 'Bible of the samurai', was written by Yamamoto Tsunetomo (1659–1719), who hailed from Saga. The confectionery shop Hagakuredō in Saga City now makes a Hagakure cracker, flavoured with sweet ginger, in honour of this text.[14]

Despite Saga's importance historically, its prominent role in Japan's foreign relations and its noted ceramics, the prefecture suffers from an image problem today. Saga ranked near the bottom of a 2012 national survey that rated the attractiveness of prefectures based on their public image, appeal to tourists and degree of familiarity. In that poll Saga numbered 45 out of 47 prefectures. Neighbouring Nagasaki and Fukuoka, in contrast, were in the top ten. To highlight Saga's plight further, in a story about the national rankings broadcast on 27 September 2012, reporters from TV Asahi stopped people on the street in Tokyo asking them if they could find Saga on a map of Japan: none could.[15] Unfortunately, in the same survey the following year Saga fell to second from bottom.[16]

The Wonder Granny of Saga

Saga's low public image and supposed lack of appeal presents a challenge for the prefecture in promoting its local food culture to a wider audience, but these same negative qualities have worked to the benefit of one author who writes about his life and diet in Saga. The comedian Shimada Yōshichi (b. 1950) is a Saga native who has benefited from the prefecture's image as being off the beaten track while at the same time working to draw attention to the prefecture through his tales, which began with the book *Saga no gabai bāchan* (The Wonder Granny of Saga, 1987).[17] This book was the first in a series of texts in which Shimada recounts tales of life with his grandmother in Saga. In 2006 *The Wonder Granny of Saga* became the basis for a film by the same name, followed by a television series broadcast nationally in 2007 and 2010, stage productions in 2007 and 2010 and another film in 2009, titled *Shimada Yōshichi no Saga gabai bāchan* (Shimada Yōshichi's Wonder Granny from Saga). Tying in with the films were a cookbook in 2006, a Nintendo DS game that hit the shops in 2009, and goods bearing the grandmother's likeness.[18]

Shimada explains in *The Wonder Granny of Saga* that his life in Saga with his grandmother, Tokunaga Sano (1900–1991), began unwillingly. During the Second World War, his parents fled Hiroshima for Saga before the atomic bombing in 1945. His father returned to Hiroshima immediately after news of the city's destruction. Having witnessed the devastation first-hand, he returned to Saga. That trip shortly after the atomic bombing, Shimada believes, was the cause of his father's sudden illness and death. The family later returned to Hiroshima but Shimada's mother struggled to raise her two sons. Worried about having to balance work with caring for both children, especially her younger son, Shimada's mother made the decision to entrust his care to his grandmother in Saga.

One day in 1958, when he was around seven years old, Shimada and his mother accompanied his aunt to the station to see her off. Just as the train was about to leave, Shimada's mother pushed him through the train doors and into his aunt's arms. Shocked and crying, Shimada looked to his aunt for an explanation, and she said through her own tears that his mother was sending him to live with his grandmother in Saga. 'How my life completely changed when my mother pushed me,' Shimada reflected.[19] He described the separation from his mother as a trauma, one that haunts him to this day. But *The Wonder Granny of Saga* focuses more on the life lessons of his grandmother than the pain of separation from his mother.

From the prelude that begins the book it is clear that food helps define Shimada's grandmother's character and his relationship with her. The book opens with the following dialogue:

'Granny, for two or three days all we've had is rice without any side dishes.'
Laughing, she replies, 'Tomorrow we won't even have rice.'[20]

Having raised seven of her own children as a single mother working part-time as a cleaner, Shimada's grandmother was not well-off. But her way of living showed how someone could find happiness even without money, a lesson that Shimada suggests has been forgotten in the focus on materialism in the age of Japan's economic success.[21] Shimada's grandmother made frugal living sound fun. She walked around town dragging a magnet tied to a rope behind her to collect nails and pieces of iron, which she could sell as scrap.

But the way in which Shimada's grandmother provided food for the family is what really sets her apart. She called the river near her home a 'supermarket', because every day the vegetable sellers upstream would throw irregularly shaped daikon or curly cucumbers that they could not sell into the river. Shimada's grandmother fished them out, gathering more than half of her fruit and vegetables that way. Local women would also wash their vegetables in the same river and sometimes lose them to the current; she would collect those as well. 'Other households would consult a cookbook and decide what to make,' Shimada observed, 'but Granny looked in the river.'[22] So much of his grandmother's way of living was tied to food that writing a cookbook of her recipes was a natural extension of the initial book, one timed for the release of the film version of Shimada's first book.

Saga no gabai bāchan no reshipi (Recipes from the Wonder Granny of Saga, 2006) is more of a homage to a simple lifestyle than a book for learning culinary technique or a discussion of cooking in Saga. The book provides instructions for making simple dishes such as 'Tomato As Is' – sliced tomato flavoured with sesame oil and vinegar; watermelon rind pickles; and a few desserts such as shaved ice topped with sugar. Grandmother's frugal cooking, explains Shimada, was meant to accompany and facilitate the consuming of rice, the main staple.[23] The cookbook includes photographs of the author in a rural setting – presumably Saga – to establish the idea of a location that is not reflected in the ingredients and recipes.

Recipes from the Wonder Granny of Saga reveals the fact that local Saga cooking has less name recognition than cuisine from other parts of Japan. In Kanazawa and Kyoto, for instance, one can make a 'local dish' simply by including one of the noted heirloom vegetables from the area, but that is harder to do in Saga. Large-scale commercial vegetable plots date in Saga only from the 1970s, when they were built on repurposed paddies and on reclaimed land in the Ariake Sea. Moreover, there are only two heirloom vegetables in Saga: a variety of long, blush-coloured daikon called *onnayama*, and Saga pickling melon.[24] This is a paltry number compared to other prefectures, and neither vegetable features in Shimada's cookbook. Neighbouring Fukuoka and Nagasaki prefectures claim eight varieties each of traditional vegetable, but that is one-third of the number of varieties found in some other prefectures, such as Kagoshima, Nagano and Niigata.[25]

Saga prefecture can boast more loudly about its seafood than its vegetables, but seafood recipes are also absent from the cookbook. The two
sardine recipes that appear do not do justice to the variety of seafood available in Saga, but they do reflect the outlook of Shimada's grandmother, who
quips: 'Because someone is said to eat sardines does not mean that they are
poor. Long ago people would look at a sardine but call it a sea bream, so a
sea bream was a sardine!'[26] Not content with eating sardines, in the early
modern period, the lords of Hizen domain regularly gifted 83 different local
products, including some sixty foodstuffs, to the Tokugawa warrior government and to other domains, and the list of these foodstuffs provides a record
of Saga's famous seafood and other delicacies. Foodstuffs that appear more
than once in domain records include, in order of their frequency: the shell-
fish *umitake* preserved in sake lees, salt-cured jellyfish, crucian carp, goose,
stripped mullet, oysters, sea bream, carp, gourd, abalone, duck, turbo and ayu
(sweetfish).[27] Recipes for goose would be atypical for any Japanese cookbook
today, but *Recipes from the Wonder Granny of Saga* also eschews more pedes-
trian ingredients, including ayu and carp.

Absent too from the cookbook are several of Saga's hallmark dishes: a
vegetable soup called *noppeijiru*; *okunchi nigomi* (a stew from Arita made
of fish, chicken and vegetables slow-simmered in a dark-miso stock); and
vegetables or seafood pickled in sake lees. But the most surprising omission
from Granny's cookbook is pickled mustard greens (*okomoji*), a condiment
that even a penny-wise grandmother could afford and one typical of the
fare of the most humble households in the area of Saga where she lived.[28]
Salty and spicy, the strong-tasting pickled mustard greens are too provincial
for contemporary readers. One never finds fancy gift packs of the pickle
marketed to tourists in Saga today.[29]

The lack of Saga-specific fare in *Recipes from the Wonder Granny of Saga*
corresponds to the absence in the text of other pointers that would allow
readers to pinpoint locations specific to the prefecture or indicative of it,
apart from a map of Kyushu on the front cover that marks Saga's location.
Candid profile shots of elderly women stooping to select vegetables at outdoor markets or riding away on their bicycles are juxtaposed with landscapes
of wild flowers, a steep staircase leading to a shrine and shots of the author
sitting on a bridge and in front of an old-fashioned stove. However, there is
nothing distinct to Saga in any of these images – they could be scenes of the
countryside from countless other places in Japan – and that might be the
point. Shimada's narrative as it plays out in books and other media focuses
on his relationship with his sagacious grandmother living in the middle of

nowhere. The fact that they lived in Saga seems inconsequential. Shimada's Saga prefecture is less a portrait of a specific locale and its food and more an archetype of a home town imbued with a familiar patina of nostalgia, maternal nurture and proximity to nature.

Other food writers are more specific than Shimada when it comes to describing Saga's food culture, but they face a similar challenge in making the prefecture's traditional cooking appealing to wider audiences. The book *Saga no kakure aji* (Hidden Tastes of Saga), published in Saga in 2001, is a compilation of articles written for the *Saga Shimbun* newspaper in 1998 by a specialist in agriculture, Sadamitsu Mitsuo. Sadamitsu's essays describe 'hidden tastes' but do not present detailed recipes for readers to replicate. He also includes short entries from historical sources that mention the prefecture's foodstuffs, such as the aforementioned list of products exchanged by early modern warlords, which adds to the impression that the distinct features of Saga's food culture have faded over time. He identifies pickled mustard greens as an integral part of the traditional diet, dubbing Saga 'the home of mustard greens'.[30] Yet the fact that he feels that readers need to be reminded of mustard greens illustrates that this once ubiquitous pickle is no longer a familiar part of the local diet. Sadamitsu focuses on the exoticism of traditional ways of eating. He describes crucian carp wrapped in kombu, a dish once eaten only on festival days that features a now unpopular bottom-feeding river fish. Another dish, called *gōkonbata*, combines grated daikon with rabbit and is named after the tool used to grate daikon. And he explains how bee larvae were once roasted with soy sauce and sugar.[31] Such traditional tastes have become rarities in the contemporary Saga diet to the point that they are 'hidden' even to the prefecture's inhabitants.

Saga's Famed Sake

Arguably, Saga prefecture's most globally famous agricultural product today is not its food but its sake. Rice from the fertile paddies of the Saga Plain and the prefecture's many waterways supply the primary ingredients for sake brewing. Though the number of Saga's breweries has declined to 27 in 2016 from 80 in 1995, sake can still be said to be the prefecture's favourite traditional alcoholic beverage. Kyushu is noted for the production and consumption of distilled spirits (*shōchū*), but Saga lacks even a single dedicated *shōchū* maker, though some sake breweries make it as a sideline.[32]

The traditional heart of Saga's brewing culture is the small town of Hamamachi, better known by its older name Hamashuku, now part of

Hamashuku, Saga Prefecture, 2013.

Kashima City (population 31,000). Before it became part of Kashima in 1954, Hamashuku, literally 'Shore Station', was an important stopping point for travellers on the Nagasaki Coastal Road, which passed through Saga to connect the port of Nagasaki with northern Kyushu. Today Hamashuku is accessed by train; the ride takes about an hour from Saga City on the Nagasaki Mainline, which follows the Ariake Coast and is the modern route connecting Saga with Nagasaki. Hamashuku is fifteen minutes' walk from Hizen Hamashuku railway station.

Hamashuku was once a centre of the fishing industry on the Ariake Sea coast, but the town's claim to fame today is its sake breweries; there are six of these in close proximity and the most famous is Fukuchiyo Shuzō, producers of the brand Nabeshima, named after the family of warlords that once ruled southern Saga. Nabeshima Dai Ginjō, a highly refined variety of sake from Fukuchiyo Shuzō with a fruity bouquet reminiscent of Japanese pear (*nashi*) and melon, won the top award at the International Wine Challenge in London in 2011, earning the brewery pride of place among Saga's other noted brands, which include Amabuki, Azuma Ichi, Kumo no Mado and Tenzan.

Hamashuku's breweries line its historic main street, nicknamed 'Sake Brewers' Row'. A stone's throw away are a few restored early nineteenth-century residences of farmers and samurai. Walking down Sake Brewers' Row and looking at the whitewashed merchant buildings and shops, one is able to imagine what the community was like as a stopping point on the road to Nagasaki – a place where the fish of the Ariake Sea were brought up the Hama River from the coast to be traded by wholesalers and where merchants brought loads of rice to the breweries to be polished, steamed and made into sake.

Only four of Hamashuku's breweries currently produce sake, but one of these provides free samples for tourists and also dedicates a few of its back rooms to a 'Shōwa-era Household', a collection of furnishings and bric-a-brac from the late 1950s and early 1960s. Other varieties of sake can be purchased for tasting at the nearby establishment Iki Iki Kan ('Chug Chug House'). Tourists come to Hamashuku to see the old town and sample the sake rather than the food, although the adventurous can try charcoal-grilled mudskipper sold from stands. The crucian carp dish mentioned in Sadamitsu's book is famous in Hamashuku, but will not be found on the menu of the local restaurant just off Sake Brewers' Row. Prepared for the festival of Ebisu, patron of fishermen and deity of fortune, in January, the carp is rolled in kombu and simmered with large slices of carrot, daikon and burdock until the liquid evaporates, leaving the meat and vegetables infused with flavour. Locals offer the dish to Ebisu and Daikoku, another god of fortune, before consuming some themselves.[33]

Local Food at the Treasure House of Tara

Travellers on National Route 207, which runs south from Hamashuku out of town, can see signs for 'local food' on motorway billboards. Ten minutes by car from Hamashuku is the Tarafukukan, a shop located in Tarachō (population 8,721), a community on the Ariake Sea coast.[34] Tarafukukan, the 'Treasure House of Tara', carries farm produce, pickles, eggs, nori harvested from the Ariake Sea and juice made from the prefecture's famous mikan (satsumas). (Saga grows more mikan in greenhouses than any other prefecture in Japan.) Also locally famous and sold at Tarafukukan are sweetcorn from May to July and mangoes in July and August. The shop issues a monthly flyer, *Tarafukukan tsūshin* (Tarafukukan Report), which lists the specials, profiles local suppliers and advertises events such as the shop's annual harvest festival in November. The June 2013 report introduced two local farmers:

Shitagawa Asayo, who with her husband has farmed in Taracho for 54 years and grows potatoes, mikan and taro; and the Hayata family, growers in Tara for 25 years and who provide Tarafukukan with sweetcorn, tomatoes, aubergine (eggplant) and other vegetables.[35]

Tarafukukan, which opened in 2005, is an example of a national phenomenon of 'roadside stations' (*michi no eki*) that developed in the early 1990s. It is one of 72 such locations recognized and promoted by Saga prefecture as offering local food direct from the producers. Tarafukukan would not be possible without its car park, which can fit up to 200 cars and thirteen buses, enabling groups to stop.

The concept of *michi no eki* grew out of a meeting in 1990 in Hiroshima of groups involved in the economic sustainability of local communities along with representatives of the Ministry of Construction (now part of the Ministry of Land, Infrastructure, Transport and Tourism, MLIT). The idea was to enhance the typical amenities of motorway rest stops – parking areas, toilets, telephones and waste bins – with retail space to sell goods and services to travellers. In 1991 the Ministry of Construction collaborated with local governments in Tochigi, Gifu and Yamaguchi prefectures to open twelve *michi no eki* as experiments. As of April 2014 there are 1,030 *michi no eki* nationally, 123 of which are in Kyushu and Okinawa.[36] The success of these establishments gained the attention of the World Bank, which presents *michi no eki* as models for community economic growth in the developing world, and pilot projects of *michi no eki* have been launched in China, Kenya and elsewhere.[37] The term 'michinoeki' has recently entered English usage, indicating the globalization of a Japanese institution that attempts to turn a motorway rest stop into an economic opportunity for a local area.

A World Bank paper of 2004 gave four reasons for the success of michinoeki in Japan. First, michinoeki provide a model of government and private partnership. Local municipalities propose building a roadside station, typically along a major route and the public sector covers construction and part of the administrative costs. Establishing a michinoeki requires permission from and adherence to the policies of MLIT, and applications usually come from local governments. MLIT stipulates the parameters of the facility, such as the minimum number of parking spaces and lavatories. Construction of the roadside station is financed locally or in collaboration with MLIT, which pays for facilities such as the car park and buildings.

A second reason for the success of michinoeki is that, rather than its being a top–down initiative of central government, local residents are involved in planning and operating the roadside station, providing them with a stake in its success. Depending on local circumstances and the size of the michinoeki, the stations are managed by the prefectural government or municipality with staffing or assistance from the chamber of commerce, fishing co-op, farmers' groups, women's organizations, the tourist board, forestry board, volunteer groups and private businesses. The involvement of local residents is crucial to the financial success of the michinoeki to ensure that it is more than a glorified rest stop.

Travellers appreciate the facilities offered at michinoeki, which is the third reason for their success. Besides the obligatory toilets and telephones, michinoeki include restaurants and 24-hour shops for purchasing items, such as local vegetables and regional products, beyond the typical rest-stop snacks and knick-knacks. Some michinoeki have hot springs for bathing as well as gyms, libraries and museums.[38] The facilities allow travellers the chance to develop a deeper appreciation of the areas they are visiting.

The chance for a traveller to use a bathroom or stretch their legs becomes an economic opportunity for locals to develop and market distinctive local products, which is the fourth reason for the success of michinoeki, according to the World Bank. Michinoeki showcase and sell goods produced nearby and they provide information about neighbouring attractions and businesses. Farmers selling produce at michinoeki can make upwards of ¥10 million ($95,000/£65,000) each annually in sales, while at the same time introducing their goods to local and visiting consumers. The World Bank's guidelines observe, 'When residents earn profits from these endeavours, their motivation is heightened and the result is better quality in their products.'[39]

In sum, michinoeki are a scheme to provide infrastructural support to travellers so that they will stop in a community, but at the same time they help and encourage residents to work together to define the representative products of their locality and in the process strengthen their own identification with their local place and its goods. 'When large numbers of stakeholders participate in a michinoeki, they gain profits as well as a sense of their own identity. An improved identity and higher profits lead to greater motivation and this has led to the success of michinoeki projects in Japan', according to the World Bank report.[40] Michinoeki contribute to the infrastructure of provincial community building and economic vitality, with local food playing a central role.

Local food is one of the mainstays of michinoeki sales. A visit to Tarafukukan in July 2013 revealed that the shop sells crates of

Tarafukukan, Saga prefecture, 2013. This structure burned down on 28 October 2013 and a new building was dedicated on 21 September 2014.

greenhouse-grown mikan and locally made fishcakes in different flavours and shapes, made from such regional fish as cutlassfish (*tachiuo*), white croaker (*ishimochi* – called *guchi* locally) and even crab. Taracho is a noted fishing area, and customers can purchase fresh fish packed whole or in fillets and even Saga mudskippers grilled with salt. Local vegetables are on offer, including Saga 'long aubergine' and asparagus – these varieties may not have official designations as heirloom types, but that does not stop farmers from advertising them by local names. Out near the parking area, vendors at temporary stands sell pickles and salted fish.

Of all the local seafood available in Taracho, none is more famous than crab. Visitors arriving at Taracho railway station might miss the Tarafukukan, which is far from the station, but when the train doors open they will see an advertisement for Takezaki crabs, a variety of blue crab caught nearby. The name Takezaki refers to the southern section of Tara, another stop down the line from Tara, near Hizen Ōura station, a small building with only a few seats and the last stop in Saga before the line enters Nagasaki prefecture. The village of Takezaki became part of Ōura in 1872 and was incorporated into Tarachō in 1955. The Ōura Fishing Cooperative established a centre to promote crab cultivation in 1989, raising fry to release nearby in the waters of the Ariake Sea, where the adult crabs are netted or captured in traps. Takezaki crabs can reach almost 30 cm in length, but most are half that size. Male specimens are said to be in peak season in summer and the females in winter.[41]

Traditional inns in the area clearly see dishes made from Takezaki crabs as a draw for tourists. One *ryokan* in Takezaki served a whole male and female crab for dinner with a Chinese-style crab dumpling as one of the side dishes. Breakfast included rice cooked with crab, crab in the miso soup (made also with slices of fried tofu, carrots and cabbage) and a small dish of crab salad. Slices of Saga beef, another noted product from the prefecture, cooked on a small grill at the table substituted for the crab for dinner the second night, but breakfast the next morning was the same as the day before. Except for small pieces of grilled local fish – white croaker and tongue sole (*shitabirame*, called *kuchizoko* in Saga), which were both in season – two nights in the inn made it clear that crab was one answer to the question of local food. Blue crabs were once plentiful throughout Japan, but their numbers have sharply declined in recent years, making fresh blue crabs a luxury that this area of Saga is happy to supply to visitors.[42] Other inns and restaurants in Tarachō advertise crab rice porridge, boiled whole crab, crab steamed in premium sake, crab hotpot and set menus featuring crab.

Though it is noted for seafood today, life was harder in Tara in the era before the Second World War. Four kilometres from coastal Tara are the settlements near Tara peak (980 m/3,225 ft) still noted for their terraced rice paddies in the highest part of Saga prefecture, forming the boundary with neighbouring Nagasaki prefecture. The mountain paddies were not the source of staple foods before the war, though; tenant farmers paid the rice they grew as rent, while farmers who owned land typically sold the rice. Both groups subsisted on barley and sweet potatoes with some millet and buckwheat, reserving white rice for special occasions. Seafood was also a rarity in this mountainous area. Local rivers supplied catfish, ayu and river crabs, but farmers living in the mountains made the trip to the Ariake Sea only four or five times a year as their farm work permitted to gather oysters and short-neck clams and to eat fish that were otherwise available in their community infrequently, when brought by a fishmonger. Eating fish was such a rarity in the mountain villages in Tara that men typically consumed the fish heads, children the body of the fish, and women whatever was left. Pheasant, boar, rabbit (sometimes eaten raw as sashimi) and raccoon dog (*tanuki*) were other sources of animal protein available to hunters. Household gardens provided cucumbers, pumpkins, string beans, peas, burdock and sesame. White potatoes, taro, watermelon and Baker's garlic (*rakkyō*, a type of green onion) were grown in fields in the mountains. But starch was the main source of calories, and barley cooked with a small amount of brown rice and sweet potatoes (called *imonettakuihan*) was the standard fare in autumn, winter and spring. Cooked barley and rice, a recipe called *buttsuihan*, was the main summer dish. Pickled mustard greens were an accompaniment to meals all year round, providing a point of continuity for the traditional diet throughout Saga prefecture, yet one not well suited to appeal to the tastes of outsiders, as noted earlier.[43] Neither the inns in Taracho nor the Tarafukukan offers mustard green pickles to visitors.

Katsuo in Kōchi

Crab has become a recognized local product of the southeastern part of Saga prefecture, but it has a long way to go before it can be seen as on a par with seafood in other prefectures, as exemplified by skipjack tuna (*katsuo*) in Kōchi prefecture (population 757,914). Kōchi rests on the shores of the Pacific Ocean on the southwest corner of the island of Shikoku and its coastal waters are noted for grunt, horse mackerel, bastard halibut, a variety of mackerel called *gomasaba*, tuna, tilefish, alfonsino, cutlassfish, squid and sea bream. But skipjack tuna is the star of Kōchi's food culture.[44] In 1988 Kōchi named *katsuo* its official prefectural fish.

Skipjack tuna enjoyed raw, seared or processed into flakes (*katsuobushi*) has been an important food since ancient times. The flakes were an indispensable ingredient for soup stock for the wealthy and powerful since the medieval period, and their use gradually spread to the rest of the population in the first decades of the twentieth century.[45] In Edo, the first *katsuo* of the season was considered a prize of spring celebrated in verse and demanding exorbitant sums to obtain. One early nineteenth-century source lists the price of skipjack tuna early in the season as two or three *ryō*, the equivalent of £1,300–£1,950 ($1,850–$2,800) at a time when a bowl of soba cost the equivalent of £2.50 ($3.75).[46]

Katsuo has been synonymous with Kōchi since the early modern period when the Yamanouchi house, the warlords of Tosa domain, as the prefecture was then called, hired their own boats to catch the fish.[47] Today, raw *katsuo* eaten as sashimi and seared (*tataki*) – lightly grilling the fish to leave the inside still pink – are quintessential foods of Kōchi for both tourists and

Seared skipjack tuna (*katsuo tataki*).

natives of this prefecture. Kōchi's residents consume more *katsuo* than those of any other prefecture.[48]

Katsuo can be found all over the world, but they swim along Kōchi's coast twice a year. In the spring, they follow an ocean current known as the Black Tide, which originates in the Philippines, passes the eastern coast of Taiwan and brings the fish to Kōchi around the beginning of March. The months of April to July are the peak season to catch *katsuo*. Fishermen travel out to the schools of *katsuo* in twelve-person boats and throw sardines into the water to attract the fish; using poles and hooks baited with sardines they catch them in quick succession, filling their small boats with the flapping fish.[49] Skipjack tuna migrate south in late autumn, passing again along Kōchi's coast around November and December, allowing fishermen a second chance to take them.

It has been suggested that the process of making *katsuobushi* was invented in Kōchi, although the technique is more likely to have originated in Southeast Asia, arriving in Japan by the turn of the sixteenth century via the Ryukyu Islands.[50] Heian period (794–1185) texts mention dried skipjack tuna, which was the form in which the ocean fish had to be consumed in the landlocked capital of Kyoto. The word *katsuo* was written with Chinese characters with the literal meaning of 'hard fish', indicating that *katsuo* was synonymous with a dried form. Another way of writing *katsuo* was as 'victory fish', adding to its appeal for samurai. The distinction between raw and dried skipjack was finally clarified in the early sixteenth century when the word *katsuo* came to be used for the raw form and *katsuo-bushi* was coined to indicate dried skipjack created by a new method. Not simply dried, *katsuobushi* relies on repeated inoculations with the fungus *Aspergillus glaucus* (*kōji*, the mould used in sake brewing and miso making, is also in the genus *Aspergillus*).[51]

The process of making *katsuobushi* begins with cleaning the fish: the head, internal organs and back fin are removed and the fish is cut into three or four fillets depending on its size. The fillets are removed to a basket that is placed inside a cauldron for simmering at 97–98 degrees Celsius. After an hour, the fish are removed and allowed to cool enough for the bones and skin to be removed. The fillets are then moved to a different basket and placed in a smoking room, in which aromatic woods such as oak, willow and cherry are burned. The fish is smoked for an hour, which dries it. Then it is allowed to cool for a day. To create a uniform and pleasing appearance, any abrasions on the fillets are filled with a mix of smoked and raw *katsuo* using a small spatula. Then the fish is returned to the smoker where it is smoked six to twelve more times depending on the size of the fillet. Afterwards, the fish is dried in the sun for several days. Workers then use knives to pare off any remaining soft spots caused by fatty deposits left on the fish's surface; a smoother surface helps preserve the fish and facilitates application of the mould and is said to therefore improve the taste. The fillets are then dusted with the *A. glaucus* fungus, then packed and sealed in a box and placed in a drying room for two weeks. When the box is opened, the fish are covered with a tar of blue mould. The fish are dried in the sun and then wiped clean of the mould. The process of inoculating fish with mould, sealing them in a box, sun-drying the fillets, removing the mould and replacing the mould takes place four more times. During the course of the process, the colour of the mould gradually changes from greenish to darker grey as the fat and moisture content of the fish decreases – taking three to four months in total.[52] At this point the fish has become a dense, solid block that resembles a smooth chunk of wood. Most consumers purchase bags of *katsuobushi* that are pre-shaved from these blocks of fish, but higher-quality restaurants and gourmands prefer the preserved *katsuo* in its solid form. They judge the quality of the preserved *katsuo* by its appearance and by striking the fillets together to hear the sound they make – to see how traditional technology has transformed a fresh fish into what appears to be a block of wood. The hard *katsuobushi* can be freshly shaved using a box with a blade in the lid that conveniently catches the flakes, for use as the basis for *dashi* stock for miso soup or as a topping for various dishes.

Katsuobushi may be fundamental to traditional Japanese cooking, but the most delicious way to eat fresh *katsuo* is as sashimi or seared (*tataki*); the latter preparation also called Tosa sashimi in homage to Kōchi's ancient name. *Katsuo* fillets are pierced with skewers and briefly grilled over a straw fire. The straw burns quickly, flaring up to sear the outside but preserve the distinctive pink flesh inside. Visitors to Hirome Ichiba, the famous indoor food court in Kōchi City, where residents and tourists eat and drink from 8 am to 11 pm, can watch the preparation of *katsuo tataki* at shops that prepare the delicacy. (Cooking the fish directly over the burner of a gas stove produces a similar effect, albeit one less dramatic.) After searing, the *katsuo* is quickly removed from the flame, sliced into pieces slightly thicker than typical sashimi, sprinkled with salt and vinegar made from local yuzu, then lightly pounded with the palm of the hand or the flat side of a knife to drive in the flavour – giving an explanation for the literal meaning of *tataki*, 'beating'.[53] In Kōchi, *katsuo tataki* is eaten with slivers of garlic and dipped in yuzu vinegar (another hallmark of Kōchi cuisine), in soy sauce, or in a combination of the two flavourings. The succulent flavour of *katsuo tataki* is reminiscent of the meatiness of rare beef sirloin. Some have asserted that the dish began in the late nineteenth century as a substitute for steak to serve to Western visitors, but records of its preparation date from 1582. *Katsuo tataki* is synonymous with Tosa cuisine, but the recipe may have originated outside the prefecture, since similar *tataki* dishes can be found in Shizuoka, Kagoshima and Mie prefectures. *Tataki* made with moray eel is an autumn delicacy in Kōchi.[54]

The Mountains of Kōchi

For a prefecture famous for its seafood, the most surprising aspect of Kōchi's geography is its mountains. Approximately 85 per cent of Kōchi is mountainous, and the Shikoku Karst that forms Kōchi's northwestern boundary with Ehime prefecture reaches nearly 1,500 metres (5,000 ft). Kōchi is also Japan's most heavily forested prefecture, with nearly 85 per cent of its landscape covered in trees.[55]

Kōchi has been considered a faraway place since ancient times, when it was known as Tosa. The eighth-century classic of imperial poetry *Man'yōshū*

(Collection of Myriad Leaves) refers to Tosa as a 'land far from heaven'.[56] The tenth-century manual of imperial laws, ritual and seasonal observances *Engishiki* (Procedures of the Engi Era) calls Tosa 'a far country', while the *Shoku Nihongi* (Supplementary Chronicles of Japan) dubs the province 'Enryū', literally a place where people are exiled far away.[57] Kōchi's distance from the capital gave the prejudicial impression to outsiders that the area was backward, or, more positively, that it was a place where old culinary customs were preserved. Kōchi was not linked with other prefectures by train until 1935.[58] Even as recently as 1999, the food culture of the mountains of Shikoku was described as having retained Neolithic features until the early 1970s.[59]

For folklorists seeking the roots of Japanese culture in distant places in the 1930s and '40s, the mountains of Kōchi were an ideal place to visit. In 1941, responding to the call of the Popular Traditions Association to report on local food, as described in Chapter Five, Katsurai Kazuo offered the only report about conditions in Kōchi prefecture based on a survey conducted from 1 October 1941 to 28 February 1942 in a mountain village called Tosayamamura (now Tosayamamura Tosayama), located some

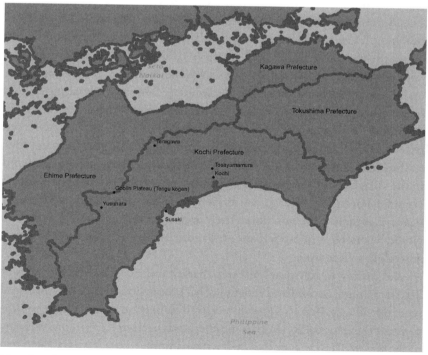

Map of Kōchi.

13.5 kilometres north of Kōchi City.[60] In contrast to the other wartime surveys in this study, which listed informants, Katsurai either neglected to include this data, or he served as his own informant. He had been living in Tosayamamura since the spring of 1935 conducting ethnographic research. After the war he established a reputation as one of Kōchi's most prominent native ethnologists, with a particular expertise in folk religion. The fruit of his nine years of research in Tosayamamura appeared in his book *Tosayama minzokushi* (Account of the People of Tosayama), published in 1955.[61]

Katsurai reported that the farmers of Tosayamamura ate four or five meals a day, except in the winter when there was not enough daylight or hard labour to require eating as much. Breakfast was usually at 6 am. The midday meal was around 11 am. A snack called 'second tea' was at 3 pm, supper was at 7 pm and dinner at 10 pm. The midday meal and snacks were usually taken outdoors as a break from work or eaten standing in the cooking area, but the rest of the meals were prepared and consumed at home around the hearth, where families took their place according to their status in the household. Seating places varied by household, but women usually sat closest to the cooking area and served everyone the grain dish. The contents of all the meals were the same except for the snack, which was usually a steamed sweet potato. Meals consisted of miso soup, small salted fish and pickles to accompany a grain dish. For lunch farmers poured hot tea on the grain to reheat it, and ate the leftovers for breakfast the next day. Supper included an extra dish such as noodles, sardines, boiled vegetables or, infrequently, whale meat. All side dishes were to facilitate eating cooked grain rather than meant to replace it. Men consumed almost 2 litres of grain daily and women ate 70–80 per cent that amount. Children were served between one-third of a litre and a litre of grain depending on their age. Due to these copious amounts, Katsurai recorded that there was some concern in the village about receiving enough government-distributed grain during wartime. For eating at home, family members used squat lidded boxes called *hakozen* as tables. The box stored their utensils, plates and bowls, and these would be put back in the box after the meal, usually without being washed, according to Katsurai.

According to Katsurai's research, barley and rice were main staples of Tosayamamura, cooked and eaten in equal proportions. He added that until recently villagers had also grown barnyard millet and foxtail millet to supplement these foods. As in other mountainous parts of Kōchi, corn was part of the autumn and winter diet in Tosayamamura, where it was cracked in a mortar, simmered for an hour until the kernels became plump, then added to rice to cook further. Corn was also ground to make flour that could be added to rice or eaten alone. Cornflour was used to make a snack typically consumed by women and the elderly when they made rope or sandals or did other work in the evenings. The flour was roasted in a pan and then ground into a meal that was formed into dough with tea and eaten. Ground buckwheat and taro, harvested in November, were added to cooked grain. Taro was also prepared by impaling the tuber on bamboo slivers, slathering it with miso and setting it to grill on the hearth. On rainy days, farmers had time to make dumplings from cornflour and taro. Sweet potatoes, also harvested in November, were dried and crushed into a powder that could be wetted and worked into dough to make dumplings, although typically sweet potatoes were steamed and eaten as a snack – a favourite of the village children, according to Katsurai. Both taro and sweet potatoes were preserved in holes dug in the ground then covered with straw and mounds of earth or they were stored in rice bran for the winter months.

Besides mixing rice with barley, Katsurai explained that until about 1940 villagers ate a higher proportion of corn to their rice – about seven parts corn to three parts rice – but by 1941 the proportion had either been reversed or had reached a fifty–fifty split. His observation suggests that Japan's wartime rice distribution system had brought more rice to the Tosayamamura diet. However, Katsurai was quick to point out that there were no farmers in the area who relied solely on rice as their main staple. Thanks to the recent construction of a waterwheel, villagers could polish their rice more easily than they had in the past using a hand-powered rotating stone mortar or standing mortar. The waterwheel provided polished white rice, 70 per cent milled rice and half-milled rice. Some of the local rice also went towards sake making. At one time every household made its own home brew, which would be shared with friends and neighbours on special occasions and critiqued for its quality. Despite wartime prohibitions, Katsurai observed that people still quietly brewed their own sake; and with festive occasions nearly once a month there were many excuses for a tipple.

Villagers in Tosayamamura made wheat noodles called *hōtō* by tearing off pieces of dough and adding them to porridge or simmered dishes. More refined noodles such as sōmen were purchased for special occasions such as the Buddhist memorials for the dead at the spring and autumnal equinoxes and Obon, the festival of the dead held in August. Buckwheat was cooked whole in equal proportion with rice and made into dough that could be rolled out and cut into noodles or eaten raw, the most typical way of consuming the grain in the winter. Locals made rice cakes for funerals and wheat dumplings as offerings to the ancestors for Obon. Normally, it was fine to eat foods after they had been used as offerings, but it was thought that if children ate the dumplings meant for Obon, they would become forgetful.

The usual accompaniments to these staples, Katsurai stated, were pickles, particularly daikon preserved in salt, 'the most important side dish for the lifetimes of farmers'. Farmers made their own *konnyaku*, which they simmered with taro or mixed with mashed tofu to make a salad. Tofu, which was occasionally made at home but was more often purchased from a tofu seller, was the most highly esteemed delicacy, Katsurai wrote. It was eaten raw, boiled with taro and vegetables or added to miso soup. Tofu was also fried and then stuffed with rice to make *inarizushi*, or added to simmered dishes. Stock came from small dried fish, which were also added to children's lunches and served as a snack for adults when drinking sake. Katsurai observed that until recently farmers made their own miso and soy sauce, both of which were used locally for soup and flavouring. Sugar was hardly ever consumed.

The fresh seafood that Kōchi is famous for today was typically unavailable to residents of Tosayamamura in Katsurai's era, except for very special occasions, the village being approximately 25 kilometres from the Pacific. Katsurai wrote, 'usually most people do not eat raw fish.' For religious holidays and seasonal observances, locals purchased sardines at a local shop during the winter months. Salted mackerel – much too salty for Katsurai's taste – was also available, but it smelled so bad that even the flies avoided it and residents could purchase it only once a week or so. After the war began, mackerel became unavailable. Freshwater fish, including salmon, ayu, dace, a variety of goby called *gori* and eel, could be caught from June to mid-October in the nearby Kagami River. River crabs were a particular delicacy for farmers unaccustomed to eating seafood. On special occasions the wealthy obtained horse mackerel, *katsuo* and fatty tuna for sashimi, but these fish were available only in limited amounts after the start of the war. If someone was ill with a respiratory problem, a member of their family travelled to Kōchi City to purchase black porgy, since drinking its blood or eating it in soup was thought to cure pneumonia. Consuming eel liver was thought to be a cure for night blindness caused by malnutrition. The local accompaniment for sashimi was vinegar made from yuzu, which as noted earlier remains a local speciality of Kōchi.

In Tosayamamura before the Second World War, salted fish were rinsed and used in sushi, and the village was especially noted for its 'mountain sushi' made from ayu and salmon. Rather than pressing small cuts of fish on top of rice like the *nigiri* sushi invented in Edo that is well-known today, the description of sushi in Tosayamamura was of 'whole sushi' (*sugatazushi*), a type of sushi Kōchi is famous for today in which an entire fish, such as a mackerel, is cleaned, covered with salt and vinegar, stuffed with rice and sliced into pieces to be served so that the fish retains its shape, usually with the head and tail pointing upwards.[62] Sushi was prepared for festive occasions and seasonal observances such as the New Year and usually served with glutinous rice mixed with azuki beans.

Katsurai observed a gender disparity in meat consumption in Tosayamamura. Men often ate duck, whale, rabbit, fowl, beef and horse-meat, since these foods were served with sake at parties that men attended. Women and children might have a chance to eat meat only once or twice a year. Rabbits were hunted or raised at home for food, and occasionally dogs were also consumed. Before 1900, beef consumption was taboo, because cows were considered too valuable to eat, and when beef was consumed, in the twentieth century, people did not cook and eat it in their homes but rather did so outdoors, taking their cooking pot and utensils to soak in a stream for a while after the meal. Meat was still avoided in Katsurai's era if one planned to go to a shrine, and both meat and fish were shunned before making a pilgrimage to a temple. Eggs were reserved for the infirm, and it was auspicious to eat whale meat on the second day of the New Year. Locals caught pit vipers and pickled them in alcohol, then removed the skins and dried the snakes to preserve them to be eaten as a snack or as a restorative for the infirm and for women who had given birth. But eating too many snakes or consuming slugs could earn the scorn of other villagers. Katsurai related a rumour about one couple whose chamber pot was said to be filled with snake skins and bones.

Vegetables were more common to the diet than fish or meat, and they included daikon, pak choi, napa cabbage, lettuce, garland chrysanthemum, onion, turnip, burdock, taro and garlic. In springtime farmers gathered mountain herbs such as King Solomon's seal and *Patrinia villosa* (*otokoeshi*, called *tochina* locally, a variety of the herb *ominaeshi*), which were usually served mixed with tofu. Other gathered plants – red garlic, butterbur, ginger, *warabi*, Japanese knotweed, royal fern and bamboo shoots – made their seasonal appearances on the menu and could be pickled in salt to eat months later. Eating pumpkin at the start of winter was thought to stave off paralysis. There were only a few pear, mikan and persimmon trees locally, so most fruit had to be shipped in from locations elsewhere in Kōchi. Children of the village could gather a purple pod-like fruit with a jelly-like interior called *akebi*, as well as chestnuts and acorns.

As a scholar of folk religion, Katsurai was especially attentive to customs and taboos about food in Tosayamamura: in most homes, he reports, the woman of the household offered a small amount of rice to the deities and buddhas each day, but buckwheat was not considered a fit offering because according to legend it originated from dog faeces. Dropping chopsticks was considered bad luck, and it was thought polite to leave a little food uneaten. Leftovers from a wedding should never be fed to the cat but rather eaten by the family the next day. People from households where there had been a death or a birth were prohibited from eating and drinking with others when they worked in the mountains. It was unlucky to throw used tea leaves into the toilet. The custom when someone in the family went on a journey (or was conscripted and deployed in the armed services) was to prepare a tray of food for them after they had left home so that the traveller would not go hungry. The tray was placed in the alcove (*tokonoma*) of the home with a separate tray of offerings for the ancestral deities to ensure the traveller's safe return. On top of a separate tray, the family placed a wooden ladle, soybeans left on the vine, a pine branch and a trifoliate orange on a branch along with a serving of the first grain cooked for the day. The ladle represented calling someone home; the soybeans evoked sincerity; the orange, called *kikoku*, was a homonym for 'returning to one's country'; and the pine was a homonym for 'waiting' – all talismans that promised a family member's speedy and safe return.[63]

One of Katsurai's most compelling descriptions is of 'platter cuisine' (*sa'achi* or *sawachi ryōri*), which remains the characteristic style of formal entertaining in Kōchi and is described in cookbooks of Kōchi cuisine as well as now being available in versions for tourists at restaurants and inns.[64] The term *sawachi* refers to large ceramic plates 30–60 cm in diameter, which are usually of brightly coloured Arita or Kutani-style porcelain – the former comes from Saga and the latter from Ishikawa.[65] Historically, families did not necessarily own these vessels and lacked the expertise needed to prepare the platters, so they hired a village chef, a local man with the culinary skills and serving ware.[66] The larger platters were set out on boxes to elevate them from the floor, and guests were invited to take from them the foods that they wanted, similar to a buffet.

Sawachi banquets in Kōchi today feature raw foods, typically sashimi or *katsuo tataki*; and 'composite foods' (*kumimono*) – that is to say, prepared foods such as sushi, vegetable and seafood salads; simmered seafood

Sawachi cuisine.

with vegetables, mushrooms and tofu; sweet azuki bean jelly; and fruit. The menu varies by season. Marlin and thin sōmen noodles are typical additions for summer, although Katsurai explains that noodles were not considered appropriate for weddings since they were more typical of the food provided at wakes.[67] After the Second World War, chicken, beef, pork and Chinese-style dishes such as sweet-and-sour pork came to be included in *sawachi* cuisine, but fish and vegetables are the cuisine's historical foundation and remain *sawachi*'s focal point.[68]

Katsurai states that in Tosayama village local custom dictated that the host sat in the centre of a U-shaped arrangement of platters of food. Assisted by two or three helpers, the host poured sake for the guests seated around the outside of the row of platters and handed them small plates of food served from the larger *sawachi*.

Katsurai attended a send-off party for a draftee in November 1941 where there were about 25 guests, and plates of food each with portions enough for two to three people. He listed the contents of the nine plates as follows:

1. *Kobu* sushi [a Kōchi delicacy: the *kobu* (kombu) is simmered in vinegar and a sweetener, then used like nori as a wrapper for rice]; sliced mikan [satsuma]; *inarizushi* [fried tofu pockets stuffed with sushi rice]
2. *Makizushi*; mikan; tempura; *inarizushi*
3. Fish sushi [probably the aforementioned *sugatazushi*]; *konnyaku* simmered with vegetables
4. Mikan; *inarizushi*; tofu and vegetable salad; sweetened azuki bean jelly
5. Large sea bream 'served lifelike' [*ikezukuri*; a large bream is steamed whole and then stuffed with *okara*, tofu lees, or it is sliced into sushi while still retaining the shape of the fish]; sashimi; vegetables[69]
6. Sushi; taro
7. Apples; *konnyaku*; sweetened azuki bean jelly; *kobu*-roll [prob-ably the same *kobuzushi* as above]; tempura
8. Whale meat; tofu; *konnyaku*
9. Raw fish mixed with miso

Besides the quantity of food, especially seafood, which was a rarity for this mountainous area, the sea bream 'served lifelike' bears the hallmarks of a formal banquet and the trademark of an accomplished chef. The chef's challenge in creating *ikezukuri* is to give the appearance of a living fish using a dead one.[70] Chefs insert slivers of bamboo to support the fish from the inside, making it look as if it is jumping out of the water. Served on a platform, the fish is surrounded by vegetables carved into auspicious shapes (a pumpkin could be transformed into a lucky tortoise, representing longevity) as well as flowers and decorative bamboo or pine branches. There are perhaps as many as twenty variations of *ikezukuri* in Kōchi today, with carp being a long-accepted favourite for sashimi.[71] Katsurai commented that red fish such as carp or sea bream were essential to serve at auspicious occasions such as weddings. Conversely, mackerel and sardines, which were eaten year-round, were eschewed for celebrations and considered unlucky. On auspicious occasions, chefs would cut bamboo leaves into decorations.

Parties were a time to enjoy sake, which was the favourite delicacy available, especially for men. Formidable drinkers could polish off six 180-millilitre servings before bed – more than half of a large (1.8-l) bottle of sake – but on a real binge they could push the limit to three of those bottles, which seems impossible and might simply be included in Katsurai's narrative to attest to the fact that some villagers were prodigious drinkers. Drinking occurred before, during and after a party. It was customary for the staff preparing the festivities to have a drink and their own gathering in the food preparation area before the banquet. Parties sometimes lasted until the next day, when neighbours came over to help clean up and enjoy more food and sake. When women found themselves alone doing these tasks, they would have their own 'cleaning parties', accompanied by more drinking and eating.[72] Clearly the people of Tosayamamura knew how to enjoy life, mustering their resources even in the midst of wartime deprivation to put on fitting celebrations.

Like Saga, Kōchi today remains noted for its sake, and women of the prefecture are said to be able to match the men in drinking. The descriptor for men in Kōchi is *igossō*, which means 'spirited' or 'stubborn'. Women in Kōchi are *hachikin* – warm-hearted, gutsy and able to keep their wilful husbands under control – even if they have to sit on them to do so.[73] Today, more sake is consumed in the prefecture than in any other in Shikoku. Local preferences are for 'Tosa dry' sake, which is easier to consume in quantity than stronger-tasting sake. Representative brands include Tsukasabotan, Kame Izumi, Koshi no Kanbai, Tosazuru and Suigei ('Drunken Whale').[74] In 2012 Kōchi's citizens spent more on alcohol than did those of any other prefecture.[75]

Tosa Genji

As for Katsurai Kazuo, the mountains of Kōchi were the draw for the folklorist Miyamoto Tsuneichi (1907–1981), who travelled into them in 1941 – the same year Katsurai wrote his study – to search for representative informants. Representative for Miyamoto did not mean typical, because he wanted to give voice to the 'forgotten Japanese', the title of his publication of 1960 based on decades of research conducted while walking throughout Japan.[76] In the mountain community of Yusuhara, Miyamoto met an eighty-year-old man he nicknamed Tosa Genji, who was living in a hovel underneath a bridge. Miyamoto's narrative sheds further light on the variety of the prefecture's foodways before and during the Second World War.

As in Saga, Tosa's samurai were among the architects of the fall of the last warrior government and helped to establish the Meiji government in 1868. Most famous in this group from Tosa was Sakamoto Ryōma (1835–1867), the samurai who helped to ally Chōshū and Satsuma domains in 1866, a union that eventually led to the overthrow of the Tokugawa regime two years later. Killed by Tokugawa assassins, Ryōma is lionized throughout Japan today, especially in Tosa and particularly in Yusuhara, which identifies itself as the place where he left Tosa to make his name in national history. Visitors to Yusuhara can admire a massive statue of Ryōma and his companions and see exhibits about him and local life at Yusuhara's museum. They can stroll the paths through Yusuhara that Ryōma was said to have walked, and even take to the trails wearing socks bearing Ryōma's portrait, which are on sale in Yusuhara.

Despite the prefecture's famous samurai, the informant nicknamed Tosa Genji was by his own testimony a lover, not a fighter. Miyamoto chose the name to call to mind the Shining Prince Genji, the famed voluptuary of Murasaki Shikibu's novel *The Tale of Genji*, composed about the year 1000. Tosa Genji did not have the refinement of Murasaki's Shining Prince, but he claimed to have had a number of lovers rivalling his famous forebear.

Miyamoto met the man he nicknamed Tosa Genji on a trip to Shikoku in the early months of 1941. He had received funding for his travels from Shibusawa Keizō (1896–1963), a wealthy industrialist, leading figure in the study of folk culture and founder of the Attic Museum, home to a collection of tools and ephemera of rural life. Miyamoto had worked as a farmer and then as a schoolteacher, but he had shown a talent for ethnology, which prompted Shibusawa to lure him away from a potential teaching position in Manchuria in 1939 by offering to finance his peripatetic study of the Japanese countryside. The publication of Miyamoto's book *Wasureta Nihonjin* (Forgotten Japanese) in 1960, which contains the author's interaction with Tosa Genji, confirmed Miyamoto's talents and positioned him as the intellectual heir to Shibusawa and Yanagita Kunio as the leading scholar of Japanese folklore. Today Miyamoto's book is recognized as a classic study of oral history.[77]

Miyamoto arrived in Yusuhara just fifteen years after the first bus route linked the hamlet to Susaki, a town on Kōchi's coast. In that period the trip was a rugged four-hour drive.[78] Travelling that same route by bus today takes 75 minutes on a road that narrows at times to one lane and follows a streambed through the mountains and pocket valleys with terraces containing neat rows of well-manicured tea bushes.

Today in Yusuhara one can see the graves of samurai heroes of the Meiji Restoration, and Sakamoto Ryōma's presence seems everywhere, but tourist maps do not show where Tosa Genji lived. Miyamoto met his informant under a bridge, where he discovered him living in a shanty made of discarded mats and scrap timber, wearing a kimono so dirty that the pattern was indiscernible. Blind and toothless Tosa Genji and his wife survived on the kindness of the community. Tosa Genji reported, 'I'm given people's leftovers and I eat them; and I've been under this bridge near on thirty years now.'[79] When his wife left to beg for food, he recounted his life story to Miyamoto, complete with all of his romantic conquests, which began even before he had become an adult, lasted through his early job working as a cow trader and continued through his three-year stint selling the bark from paper mulberry trees, a local product Yusuhara had been noted for since the early modern period.[80] 'I pursued women until I finally lost my sight,' he recalled.[81] Tosa Genji was an outsider in Yusuhara in many ways, having been born in neighbouring Ehime prefecture and due to his infirmity and poverty.

The geography of Yusuhara brought challenges to the lives of any resident, not just Tosa Genji. Yusuhara is the heart of Yusuhara district, an area of northwest Kōchi prefecture that juts into and would be part of Ehime were it not for a section of the Shikoku Karst also known as the 'Goblin Plateau' (Tengu Kōgen), a rugged highpoint of weathered rock and grass 1,485 metres above sea level, which divides the two prefectures and forms Yusuhara district's northern boundary.[82] Mountains also form the district's eastern and western borders. To the east is the Shoshidai Karst. To the west are more mountains and surrounding hills, including Mount Amatsutsumi (1,110 m) and Mount Jizō (1,095 m). In the middle of the highest mountains in western Japan, Yusuhara is one of the few places in Kōchi prefecture where snow falls.

Until 1912 Yusuhara village was called Isunoki, 'trees for posts', an indication of the importance of the timber industry locally. Today 91 per cent of Yusuharachō is woodland, but much of the Japanese cedar forest dates from after the Second World War, when the trees were planted by hand on the steep slopes surrounding Yusuhara and meant to capitalize on the post-war demand for building materials.[83] The local government has been supportive of the forestry industry, as evidenced by the many wooden structures around Yusuhara, which include a traditional theatre, the Yusuhara-za, constructed in 1948; a modern primary and middle school, Yusuhara Gakuen, built in 2001; the wooden bridge leading to Tsuno Jinja, the community's principal shrine; and foremost the city hall and visitors' centre designed by the noted architect Kuma Kengo (b. 1954), in a style that combines ancient and modern materials to create a facade of irregularly alternating rectangles of wood and glass. Kuma, whose firm has designed the National Stadium for the Tokyo 2020 Olympics, also designed Yusuhara's Hotel Above the

Clouds, which has a branch in the visitors' centre; its main facility is on the outskirts of the village, about thirty minutes away by foot. The main hotel is a concrete edifice with a wooden corridor on stilts, which connects to a heated swimming pool.

As remarkable as these wooden structures is the emphasis on sustainability and responsible stewardship that are hallmarks of Yusuhara's forestry today. In 2000 the village won an international award from the Forest Stewardship Council (FSC) for environmentally conscious logging conducted in a manner both economically sustainable and socially beneficial. Yusuhara's mills market timber with the Forest Stewardship Council (FSC) seal, indicating the high standards by which it was produced; and the community was only the second place in Japan to receive the FSC designation.[84]

Before the timber industry became prominent in Yusuhara after the Second World War, paper mulberry trees such as the ones that Tosa Genji purchased were an important source of income for farmers in Yusuhara. Locals also grew paper bush for the same purpose, harvesting both plants in the first months of the year. Both plants must be chopped into pieces then boiled to remove the fibres from the bark to make the principal ingredient for Tosa paper, which has been recognized nationally for its high quality since the Heian period and which won recognition as a 'national traditional craft' in 1976.[85]

Miyamoto did not reveal what Tosa Genji's wife brought back when she returned from begging for food, but from Tosa Genji's other statements readers can imagine the types of food the couple longed to eat. Tosa Genji's narrative indicates that dishes such as sticky rice cooked with azuki beans were reserved for auspicious occasions, such as when a girl menstruates for the first time. So Tosa Genji tells of his astonishment when he met a wealthy married woman who fed her cow azuki beans with rice and sake. The lavish attention she gave her cow – and the absence of her husband – were a powerful draw for Tosa Genji. He seduced her, convincing her to meet him at a nearby temple on a hill. Such memories of sex and steamed rice are a sharp contrast to the leftovers his spouse, whom he refers to as Grandma, collects from locals.[86]

In 1941 when Miyamoto met Tosa Genji, steamed glutinous rice with azuki beans would have been even more of a luxury given wartime restrictions on rice consumption and rationing, and particularly in Yusuhara, where rice was not the main staple owing to the mountainous geography. The rugged terrain of Yusuhara did not allow much flat land for paddies except in valleys near riverbeds or where terraces could be created; and due

Yusuhara visitors' centre and city market (*machi no eki*) designed by Kuma Kengo, 2013.

to excessive rain and poor drainage, farmers in Yusuhara could grow only one crop of rice each year.[87]

Instead of rice, Yusuhara's farmers relied on dry fields and slash-and-burn agriculture to clear the mountain slopes. Corn, called 'millet' or Chinese millet locally, was the main staple, with some buckwheat and ordinary millet consumed as well. Corn became an important foodstuff throughout Shikoku after its arrival in the seventeenth century, gradually displacing barnyard millet.[88] In Yusuhara corn was harvested between August and September. Corn was sometimes steamed or grilled on the cob as a snack, but most often it was dried. Farmers boiled the ears to remove the husks, exposing the kernels underneath, then tied the ears into bundles, which they hung to dry for two months. Then they removed the kernels by striking the cobs with sticks. Before eating, women cracked the kernels using a rotating mortar, an essential tool for every home in the area. Farmers who owned paddies could add rice to their corn, but typical proportions were still 80 to 90 per cent corn. Boiled, the taste of the dish was fine while it was served warm, but cold or reheated it became unpalatable, especially if there were no rice or barley included. Grinding the kernels created cornmeal, which could be prepared as gruel or used as flour to make into dumplings. Corn mixed with a little rice remained the dominant staple in Yusuhara for some residents until the early 1960s, and farmers ate four times a day, as recalled in a publication of interviews from 2004 with seven of Yusuhara's older citizens who were born in or before the mid-1930s.[89]

After rising, residents in Yusuhara typically consumed a breakfast of rice mixed with corn (or perhaps with barley if it was summer, before the corn harvest) along with miso soup and pickles – sometimes with white or sweet potatoes or with a side of cornflour if more nourishment was needed. A second breakfast, called 'first tea', was at 10 am and was usually packaged for eating at a work site. A typical first tea consisted of corn with rice packed in a bamboo container with a separate container of pickles and miso for flavouring. 'Second tea', consumed in the afternoon between 2 and 3 o'clock, consisted of the same types of food – usually the leftovers from first tea. During the winter, ground buckwheat was made into porridge by adding it to boiling water. The familiar staple of corn with rice and/or barley returned for dinner, with the addition of a side dish of simmered vegetables such as daikon, aubergine, burdock or pumpkin. Rivers added some diversity to the diet by providing fish such as local varieties of salmon and carp, which were eaten grilled with salt. Spring brought gathered herbs and vegetables such as Japanese knotweed, *warabi*, bamboo shoots, *udo* and red garlic.[90] These plants needed to be blanched or processed before eating to remove their bitterness. Some vegetables, such as royal fern, could be dried to preserve them for winter.[91] *Warabi* was added to miso soup and simmered dishes and cooked in oil; on special occasions it was seasoned with small fish and soy sauce and mixed with mashed tofu.[92] Besides gathered herbs and vegetables, nuts were once prevalent in the diet of people who lived in the mountainous parts of Kōchi, and are the reason why the foodways in this area were called a throwback to Neolithic times. Horse chestnuts in particular were an important source of energy in the local diet.[93]

If life was difficult in Yusuhara, it was even more of a challenge 40 kilometres north in the hamlet of Teragawa, where Miyamoto found another informant on his trip to Kōchi in 1941.[94] Teragawa was the northernmost village in Kōchi prefecture, located some 800 metres above sea level in a place where the mountainous terrain did not allow for paddies. Rice was so precious in Teragawa that it was said by outsiders that the people of the hamlet encountered the grain only on their deathbed, when someone would rattle a bamboo container filled with rice in an act believed to facilitate their rebirth in a place where rice was abundant. Haruki Shigenori (1713–1780), a domanial official who spent a year in Teragawa in 1751, confirmed this observation in his description of life in the hamlet, *Teragawa kyōdan* (The Story of Teragawa), reporting that locals did not even have rice to eat at the New Year. He explained, 'there is no rice in this hamlet so people cannot eat it; they don't make rice cakes or set up New Year's displays in their doorways – they only have dumplings made from barnyard millet.'[95] To purchase rice and other supplies meant the villagers of Teragawa had to travel to the closest city, which was Saijō in Ehime prefecture, almost 10 kilometres over the mountains (closer than Kōchi City, which was some 145 km away).[96]

On the steep paths near Teragawa, Miyamoto met a woman suffering from leprosy who had stuck to lonely trails in the mountains to avoid meeting people on her journey across Shikoku. Miyamoto's encounter sets the stage for his description of this remote locale. He describes Teragawa as a community of just seventeen households, with homes built in clusters of three or four. Even cows were a rarity in Teragawa, Miyamoto noted, because they had to be carried up the narrow winding footways to the hamlet. When the first cow arrived, in 1902, one woman thought that it was a horse with horns.[97]

Miyamoto described the prevalence of slash-and-burn agriculture in paddy-less Teragawa, whose villagers recounted how during times of famine people from neighbouring Ehime prefecture came to the Teragawa area to cut down trees and plant millet on the sloping fields arriving so hungry that they even ate millet husks.[98] Similar types of farming are evident in *The Story of Teragawa*, in which Haruki wrote that the villagers began farming around April, setting fire to brush and trees, clearing the land and relying on the ash to fertilize fields of azuki and barnyard millet. Plots were often 4 kilometres from the villagers' homes, necessitating that they build small huts where they could stay and tend their crops until harvest. Barnyard millet was a much more suitable crop for the area's poor soil and colder temperatures than rice or millet. After the harvest, barnyard millet was boiled and hulled before being dried and milled in a mortar. Without boiling, the grain was hard, lacked its characteristic yellow colour and did not taste as good. Typically, farmers grew barnyard millet in fields for two or three years before converting to azuki or soybeans for two to three years, then returning to millet for another three years. After nine years, the soil became overworked and the land would be allowed to return to forest, requiring that the farmers move to a different plot. Like the people of Yusuhara, residents of

Teragawa made use of gathered herbs and vegetables. They also hunted deer at night during the farming season, and boar in the early spring along with rabbit, pheasant and pigeon, according to *The Story of Teragawa*. Horse chestnuts and acorns were also important sources of carbohydrate.[99] As with gathered plants such as *warabi*, horse chestnuts needed to be soaked in lye to leach out their bitterness to make them edible. They were then ground to make flour that could be used to make dumplings.[100] On the border with Ehime (called Iyo province in the early modern period), Teragawa village was the site of a domanial checkpoint. Villagers in Miyamoto's time recalled the need to guard against timber thieves from Iyo. Besides timber, tea, honey and beeswax were other sources of income that could be sold to the few merchants who came to the area.[101]

Visitors to Yusuhara today may not know the story of Tosa Genji; they come instead either to trace Sakamoto Ryōma's footsteps or to see how a remote mountain community with a population of just over 4,600 has transformed itself into an eco-village. Besides its sustainable timber industry, Yusuhara is a model for the use of renewable sources of energy. In 1999 the community constructed wind turbines at the crest of Shikoku Karst on its border with Ehime. The wind turbines generate approximately 3.4 million kilowatt hours yearly, powering Yusuhara's streetlights and supplying about 18 per cent of local electricity needs.[102] Solar cells on the town hall provide 40 per cent of the building's required energy; and Yusuhara Gakuen, the primary and middle school, derives its power from a nearby hydroelectric dam.

With these innovations, Yusuhara today is a far cry from the impoverished hamlet it was before the Second World War. The only reminder of the prominence of corn in the diet are small bags of ground corn that are sold in the city's visitor's centre, which operates a *machinoeki*, an urban version of the michinoeki mentioned previously. Visitors can also purchase such 'local' products as honey, frozen pheasant meat, vegetables and fruit muffins. Local cuisine can be sampled at restaurants such as Gallery's Kitchen, a ramen shop on the main street that sells 'mountain ramen' made with pheasant, providing a luxurious interpretation of the Chinese-style noodle dish.

Some 3 kilometres outside town, the modern Kumo no Ue no Hoteru (Hotel Above the Clouds), offers a glorious view of the surrounding mountains over a reflective pond near the dining area, where a version of a multi-course *kaiseki* meal is offered for dinner. The *kaiseki* meal manages to avoid most references to local food except that ayu or salmon is offered on alternate nights and there is a soup of gathered herbs whose flavour is lost in pork stock. In the morning guests receive a small dish of simmered local knotweed to augment an otherwise typical Japanese breakfast of rice, miso soup, grilled fish or sausage, omelette and pickles. Across the street from the hotel is a small area dedicated to a cluster of traditional farm buildings called Furusato Hiroba (Hometown Square), where a few older wooden dwellings have been moved for preservation and to attract tourists. One of these early farmhouses is now the restaurant Kusabuki (Thatched Hut), which serves set meals of local dishes that includes a lunch platter of country-style soba noodles, rice cooked with pheasant, simmered black soybeans, a selection of mountain vegetables, grilled aubergine and pickles, introducing the local cuisine to visitors.

Wind turbines on Shikoku Karst, 2013.

Japan's Tibet

Like her contemporary Miyamoto Tsuneichi, the folklorist Ema Mieko wanted to introduce disenfranchised people from rural areas to a wider readership; but instead of wandering all over Japan as Miyamoto did, she and her husband, the novelist Ema Shū, settled in the mountainous Hida region of Gifu prefecture to write about the lives of people living in the Japanese Alps, the mountain range that divides Japan's main island down the centre. Miyamoto was a disciple of Shibusawa Keizō, and Ema Mieko was a student of the other giant of twentieth-century folklore studies, Yanagita Kunio. Yanagita encouraged Mieko and her husband to focus their studies on the Hida region and the two settled in Takayama, the area's largest city, where they founded the journal *Hidabito* (People of Hida). Ema Shū served as editor of the journal from 1935 until 1944, and the publication contained many of the couple's own writings, sometimes presented under pseudonyms. Ema Shū applied his research to adding ethnographic details to his massive novel in two volumes, *Yama no tami* (Mountain Folk). *Mountain Folk* relates the story of the armed opposition of locals to the reformist policies of Umemura Hayami (d. 1870), who was appointed governor of Hida by the Meiji regime shortly after the 1868 Restoration.[103] Ema Mieko's articles in *Hidabito* were republished in her book *Hida no onnatachi* (The Women of Hida) in 1942.[104]

Ema Shū aptly described the Hida region as 'a land of mountains and still more mountains', adding that the people of Hida were, without exception, mountain folk.[105] Hida forms the northern part of Gifu (population 2.03 million), which is the fifth most mountainous prefecture in Japan and entirely landlocked. Modern Gifu prefecture is comprised of Hida in the north and Mino in the south. In the early modern period Hida was a single domain while Mino was an aggregate of several small fiefdoms, the largest being Ōgaki. Hida briefly became a prefecture from the period of the Meiji Restoration in 1868 until 1876, when it was joined with Mino to make Gifu.

Mountain topography formed a natural division between Hida and Mino. The mountainous Hida area extends 150 kilometres north to south and about 340 kilometres east to west, with elevations ranging between 1,000 and 2,990 metres. Parts of the Mino area are at sea level and do not experience as much snowfall or as cold temperatures as Hida, where in some parts there are as few as seventy frost-free days a year. One-third of Hida is forested, contributing to Gifu's status as the second most heavily forested prefecture in Japan.[106]

Hida's settlements are in its valleys, the largest being Furukawa and Takayama, site of Takayama City.[107] The latter is in the Takayama Plain (570 m above sea level) and it was the location of the castle of Kanamori Nagachika (1524–1608). After he defeated the Mitsuki clan, which had risen to dominate Hida province during the sixteenth century, Kanamori's control of Hida was affirmed by Toyotomi Hideyoshi in 1586. In 1600 Kanamori fought on the winning side at the Battle of Sekigahara, waged in the southern part of Gifu prefecture, which helped reconfirm his tenure of Hida; and he constructed his castle in Takayama in 1605. He encouraged merchants and artisans to settle in the town near his fortress. Kanamori was an avid student of the tea ceremony, a practice also of his adopted son Yoshishige (1558–1615) and his son Kanamori Sōwa (1584–1656), the latter of whom went on to promote his own style of tea among the aristocracy in Kyoto. Sōwa's presence still resonates in the tea utensil supply shops and high-end restaurants of Takayama, a town that justifiably advertises itself as a 'little Kyoto', for its historic areas and preserved streets, called the Sanmachi Suji.

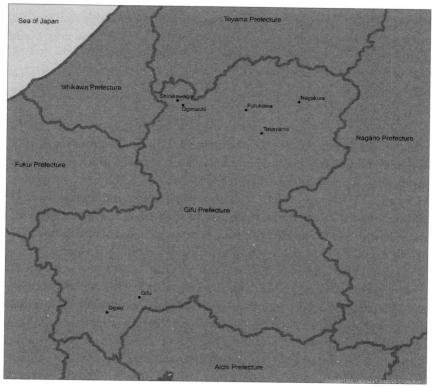

Map of Gifu.

In 1692, craving the timber and mineral resources of Hida, the central warrior government ordered that the Kanamori house be transferred to another, far less wealthy, domain in modern Yamagata prefecture and took direct control of Hida, levelling Nagachika's castle and administering the territory through a magistrate in Takayama. Takayama remained Hida's largest city and it was the largest city in Gifu until 1879, when it was surpassed by Gifu City, the prefectural capital.

Despite its larger settlements like Takayama, the perception before the Second World War was that the Hida region was remote, a place that Ema Mieko referred to as 'Japan's Tibet'.[108] Railways linked Hida with Nagoya in 1934, but the journey took two days to complete.[109] Today, the trip from Gifu City to Takayama is just over two hours and is one of the most scenic rail journeys in Japan, since the train follows the Hida River northwards through narrow gorges. With the completion of the Takayama Bypass in 1972, a motorway connected Takayama with the northern city of Hida and then on to Toyama prefecture, Gifu's neighbour to the north. The road allowed for the first time the operation of a bus route from Takayama into the Hida mountain range. The road climbs to altitudes almost 2,745 metres.[110] Before the construction of this highway, heavy snowfalls would cut off access to villages in the north of Hida during the winter.[111]

The Question of Rice in the Diet of Hida

Hida is well known among historians of Japanese food because it is ground zero in the scholarly debate about how much rice Japanese people consumed at the end of the early modern period, thanks to a remarkable record of food production from the area called *Hida gofudoki* (The Latter Gazetteer of Hida, 1873).[112] Though other prefectures made similar attempts to research and report on local products, customs and industries, *The Latter Gazetteer of Hida* is unique for its level of detail. It provides a survey of three districts in Hida, encompassing 415 villages. Compiled by the prefectural official Tomita Ayahiko under orders from the governor of Hida, it is part local history and part demography. Most importantly for historians, the work includes data about agricultural products. Tomita and his staff undertook the survey from 1869 to 1870, relying on some older records and sending out requests for information from village officials in charge of collecting taxes.[113]

The Latter Gazetteer of Hida lists 168 foodstuffs that were produced or gathered in the region, including 42 varieties of vegetable, 24 species of fish, 24 types of fruit, fourteen different mushrooms, twelve types of nut, ten different grains, eight mammals, seven birds, seven types of tuber and three varieties of bean. Close to half these items were gathered rather than farmed foodstuffs. For the local diet, staple grains were a primary energy source according to this record, and of these rice was grown in the largest quantity, amounting to over 8.7 million litres, followed by barnyard millet at about 5 million litres, barley at 1.9 million litres, wheat at 500,000 litres, foxtail millet and buckwheat each at 270,000 litres and ordinary millet at 17,000 litres. According to the gazetteer, money from the sales of locally manufactured goods was used to purchase 255,000 litres more rice from outside the region and 1.4 million litres of other grains.[114]

Based on these figures, Koyama Shūzō and his colleagues at the National Museum of Ethnology have argued in a series of publications that rice was the main staple for the Hida region. Grains accounted for 90 per cent of the calories consumed in Hida, according to Koyama, and rice was the chief of these at 52 per cent of the total, followed by barnyard millet at just 21 per cent.[115] That rice could play such an important role in the diet in a region as mountainous as Hida has provoked scholars to extrapolate that rice was eaten by ordinary people by the end of the early modern period, if not earlier.[116] In other words, *The Latter Gazetteer* supports the contention that peasants, who made up most of the population, consumed rice and did not just grow it to pay taxes. Adding rice to the other food products listed in *The Latter Gazetteer* and measuring the amount against the population of the area has allowed scholars to estimate the average per capita food supply for Hida at 1,850 calories per day.[117] Consequently, although the diet of Hida was lacking in many ways, as described below, the prevalence of rice provides evidence to support the view of food scholars such as Ishige Naomichi, Koyama's colleague at the National Museum of Ethnology, that rice has long been the main staple food for the population of Japan.[118]

However, the estimates created from *The Latter Gazetteer* are for food supply, not consumption, which leaves open the question of what the people of Hida actually ate. *The Latter Gazetteer* was not a survey of eating habits or a record of the actual diet. Some scholars have cited the same research on *The Latter Gazetteer* as evidence of the prevalence of rice consumption in the Hida area, but with far less enthusiasm. The cultural geographer Arizono Shōichirō agrees that the study undertaken by scholars at the National Museum of Ethnology indicates that rice was an important part of the diet in Hida, but he places the amount of rice consumed in the region per capita daily at about 285 grams, amounting to slightly less than two bowls of cooked rice.[119] Harada Nobuo, a leading food scholar, reviewed the findings of the *Latter Gazetteer* studies, and he contends that the grains listed as produced in Hida were intended not to describe consumption but were meant instead to assess taxes.[120] According to Harada, officials would have taken all of the rice away from local cultivators, leaving Hida's farmers to subsist on other grains, tubers, game, fish and whatever else they could find to eat.[121]

Despite attempts to hypothesize per capita estimates of food supply for the entire Hida area, diet in the region was hardly uniform. *The Latter Gazetteer of Hida* indicates variations in the diet in Hida depending on the locale. Of the 415 villages included in the survey, 403 grew barnyard millet but only 343 grew rice.[122] In contrast to the low-lying area of Mino in the southern part of Gifu prefecture, which was a centre for paddy agriculture, rice growing faced many more challenges in Hida due to the mountainous topography. Villages 800 metres above sea level could not grow rice at all and could rely only on barnyard millet. Even those located at around 600 metres had difficulty growing rice with the varieties available at the time.[123] Farmers in locales where rice could be grown built terraced paddies connected to irrigation channels and shallow ponds, using sunlight to warm the water to raise the temperature in the paddies and thus facilitate rice growing. To boost production further, farmers planted faster growing varieties of rice in cooler sections of the paddies and higher yielding but later varieties in warmer spots in the same paddy.[124]

Settlements deeper and higher in Hida's mountains that could not grow rice in paddies undertook slash-and-burn agriculture. Writing in the 1930s, Ema Mieko described this mode of farming in Hida:

> In the villages in the interior, barnyard millet comprises half of the agricultural products grown: there are dry fields of it cultivated and paddies. Such paddy in lands in high areas even today will not produce rice and grows barnyard millet just like dry fields. Barnyard millet is also grown in *nagi*. *Nagi* is a term in Hida referring to fields for slash-and-burn agriculture: mountain slopes too steep for regular fields are burned and cleared and barnyard millet, buckwheat and soybeans are grown without fertilizer following a primeval method of farming. Even today this is widely practised in mountain villages deep in the interior such as Shirakawa and Nyūkawa.[125]

Slash-and-burn agriculture of this sort was undertaken in the small mountain hamlets of Hida until the early 1960s. In Nagakura, a small community of 46 farm households in Kamitakarachō, 30 kilometres northwest of Takayama City, where the topography was unsuitable for paddy land, farmers grew barnyard millet, foxtail millet, soybeans and azuki for four or five consecutive years on fields that they had burned and cleared. Thereafter they planted buckwheat.[126]

A twenty-year cycle of cultivation for slash-and-burn fields was typical for the Hida region. After selecting an area of land for clearing, in the summer farmers cut trees and grasses, allowing them to dry for a few days before setting them alight. The ash became fertilizer for a crop of buckwheat or turnips sown in the early autumn and harvested in November. Barley would be planted the next year, followed in subsequent years by crops of foxtail millet, azuki or sesame; then the field would be devoted to mulberry trees to provide leaves to feed silkworms. After two decades of use, the land would be abandoned. As in Teragawa village in Shikoku, farmers in Hida maintained scattered plots often far from their homes, sometimes requiring the construction of a small hut near their fields for them to stay in while tending their crops.[127]

Whereas the studies of the National Museum of Ethnology provide an overview of the entire Hida region, of the 415 villages listed in *The Latter Gazetteer*, only the entries for 28 villages give enough detail to enable a closer look at the connections between specific populations and production levels. Examining these sites, the food scholar Ehara Ayako concluded that only a quarter of the 28 villages would have produced more rice than the amount estimated by the National Museum of Ethnography scholars, and even those locales would have needed more grain beyond rice in their diet to support their population. According to Ehara, this gap in food energy would have had to be bridged by importing food in exchange for other products from the Hida area. *The Latter Gazetteer* lists the major products produced in Hida as silk thread, which was sold to Kyoto's Nishijin textile area as well as to Yokohama, pongee, floss silk, timber, mulberry paper and saltpetre, along with silver and copper.[128] These resources provided revenue with which to purchase foods needed in the Hida region.

Whether or not rice played an important role in the diet in Hida may be a question of minor importance compared to the fact that according to estimates of the scholars from the National Museum of Ethnology based on *The Latter Gazetteer*, there were more pressing health concerns caused by malnutrition. National estimates for food supply in the year 1900 are 2,100 calories per capita, a diet so lacking in nourishment that it resulted in stunted growth.[129] Given that Hida's per capita average for 1873 is pegged at 1,850 calories in an area with a harsh climate that demanded that its residents labour heavily to survive, one might conclude that Hida's population hovered just around starvation. Specifically, scholars using the National Museum of Ethnology study have pointed to deficiencies in vitamins A and C, calcium and iron, causing deaths in childbirth and stroke.[130] Even in the late 1930s, Hida's high rate of infant mortality contributed to an average life expectancy of between 32 and 34 years – more than a decade lower than the rest of the nation.[131]

But *The Latter Gazetteer of Hida* may not reveal the entire story about the diet in the northern part of Gifu prefecture. Nuts such as horse chestnuts and acorns have been suggested as providing a food supply for the population of Hida that was underestimated in official records because these foodstuffs, except for chestnuts, were not taxed and had little commercial value. *The Latter Gazetteer* lists some 254 villages that harvested horse chestnuts and acorns. Locals soaked the nuts in water with lye from ash to remove their astringency before pounding them into flour to be used to make *mochi* or cooked with grain. Production totals from these 254 villages suggest that there was sufficient supply of nuts to support some 3,000 people in Hida annually, providing a larger supply of energy than either buckwheat or foxtail millet.[132] Reviewing the data provided by *The Latter Gazetteer*, the scholar Matsuyama Toshio has estimated a population of 92,600 for the year 1870 and concludes that only some 59,420 people could have had a 2,000-calorie per capita food supply. Imported foodstuffs supported an additional 13,500 people. In other words, close to 20,000 people still would not have had enough food.[133] According to *The Latter Gazetteer* two villages harvested *warabi*; the rhizomes were blanched and ground to create a starch that could be made into *mochi*. But nuts were a more significant source of food energy, according to Matsuyama, who lists six edible varieties found in the Hida area: chestnuts, horse chestnuts, acorns, walnuts, hazelnuts and Japanese nutmeg. Potentially a greater amount of these nuts could be gathered than the grains harvested in the region. As an example from the data available, Matsuyama presents the data in *The Latter Gazetteer* for Kanagido village in Yoshiki district, where 1.4 times as much chestnuts and horse chestnuts was harvested as rice, barnyard millet, foxtail millet and soybeans the village grew. Chestnuts were an important cash crop and were the largest nut crop for Hida, according to *The Latter Gazetteer*. Farmers boiled them and sold them dried, for a value 1.2 times the amount for which rice sold. Chestnuts had the advantage of being ready to eat once their shells were removed, unlike acorns and horse chestnuts, which needed to be processed before eating and had no commercial value. Yet acorns and horse chestnuts ranked second and third in terms of the amounts of foodstuffs gathered in Hida, according to Matsuyama's interpretation of *The Latter Gazetteer*, although the total quantity of nuts collected remains unknown, since many villages did not report this information. Of the 254 villages in *The Latter Gazetteer* said to have collected nuts, totals are available for only 78 locales. Based on these available numbers, Matsuyama estimates that the amount of chestnuts, acorns and horse chestnuts gathered in Hida amounted to about one-quarter of the quantity of rice and barnyard millet grown – enough to support 25 per cent of the population through gathered foods, which is close to bridging the aforementioned gap between population and food supply he calculated.[134]

Once an essential food, nuts – except for chestnuts, which are incorporated into dishes and confectionery throughout Japan as an autumnal delicacy – are no longer part of the local diet in Hida or elsewhere, due to the effort needed to process them to remove (most of) their bitter taste. Making *mochi* from horse chestnuts is labour-intensive and requires gathering the nuts, soaking them in water for a day to kill any insects and drying them in the sun for several days to preserve them. Before cooking, the nuts are again soaked in water for several days to soften the shells so that they can be hulled. Then the nuts are placed in a large sack to be soaked in water for an additional ten to fifteen days. Transferred to a bucket and covered in ash and warm water, they are allowed to sit for an additional two to three days, or even longer, to leach out the astringency. Then, once washed, the nuts can be added to glutinous rice, then steamed and pounded in a mortar to make *mochi* that can be grilled or added to miso soup. Horse chestnut cakes are said to be tastiest if they are 70 per cent rice and only 30 per cent nuts.[135] But the bitterness of the horse chestnuts, if eaten on a daily basis, is said to linger on the palate and they do not make for an enjoyable meal, according to Ema Mieko's account.[136] A similar process is needed to make acorns edible, but they are still not rendered very palatable; consumption of acorns in the Hida region had ceased entirely by the end of the Second World War, with horse chestnuts disappearing from the diet not long afterwards.[137]

This diet of barnyard millet and nuts once set the people of Hida apart from those in the rest of the country and contributed to images of the area's perceived dissimilarity from national norms. Ema Mieko feared that readers of her and her husband's publication *People of Hida* 'from other prefectures will look at that journal and will simply conclude that Hida is a mountainous country where people live like monkeys'.[138] Ema's concern about prejudice against the people of Hida was not groundless. People from the Hida area spoke with a distinct accent, and in the twentieth century, women from Hida were called 'rope-making women', referring to the rural custom whereby women were consigned to parturition huts while they menstruated, where they made rope to pass the time. Men of Hida were described as 'wood haulers', speaking to one of the economic activities of the area. Both sexes were collectively termed 'beggars from Hida'.[139] Ema Mieko felt compelled to challenge the erroneous views of city-dwellers about Hida:

> If someone from the cities is asked whether they know about the diet of people in mountain villages, I think they will be puzzled and undoubtedly reply that they imagine the diet is without doubt terribly crude. Most people not only don't realize that even today barnyard millet is among the daily staples, but they also don't even know what barnyard millet is.[140]

Though she was quick to correct such misconceptions about Hida, Ema's constant reference to prejudice against the people of Hida reinforced the exoticism of the region she dubbed 'Japan's Tibet'. Hida's otherness piqued the interest of Ema's readers and by attributing misinformation about Hida to anonymous people in the cities, she could claim a role for herself as an expert on the region.

The Women of Hida

In her book *The Women of Hida*, instead of introducing readers to individual women, Ema presented the life of a hypothetical woman from birth through childhood to adulthood and motherhood. She sometimes included the voices of anonymous informants but more often drew comparisons between life for women in Hida and for women in urban areas. For example, unlike women in cities, Ema noted that women from Hida could not buy milk for their babies and instead fed them rice gruel.[141]

Rice was a relatively recent part of the diet in Hida, Ema explained, prevalent only since the late 1920s. Before then barnyard millet was the most important staple, especially in the early modern period, when taxes had to be paid in rice. Ema relied on her informants, not *The Latter Gazetteer of Hida*, to make this argument. Even in the early 1940s, Ema reported how barnyard millet remained the staple in the furthest reaches of Hida, though the grain was mixed with rice in a ratio that varied from as little as

20–30 per cent rice to 50 per cent rice. Dishes of pure white rice remained reserved for special occasions such as the New Year and agricultural festivities accompanying the transplanting of rice seedlings. The rarity of white rice was epitomized for Ema in the actions of one elderly woman from the village of Kitani, who on New Year's Day would raise her bowl of white rice to her forehead and say, 'how impious for us to eat white rice consumed by the emperor'.[142]

But even barnyard millet was precious for some people, observed Ema, extrapolating further on the humble diet of Hida and in mountain villages. Only the wealthy ate pure barnyard millet, she wrote. Poorer farmers consumed millet mixed with bran, 'a food that not even a horse would be glad to eat today'. Ema reported that the elderly of Hida recalled to her how warm barnyard millet bran was palatable, but cold it was positively dreadful.[143]

Barnyard millet was only one of the staples eaten seasonally in Hida according to Ema Mieko, who confirmed the importance of horse chestnuts and acorns in the local diet. One elderly informant in the Adano area of Hida informed her that his family had at one time consumed upwards of ten large bales of acorns a year, and they were once an important part of his diet. *Warabi* and kudzu (arrowroot) were collected and made into starch, and even poisonous mistletoe was reportedly eaten, although Ema did not explain how it was processed and consumed.[144]

Girls had to learn how to prepare miso, make pickles and do other housework as well as help with the farming, but a mother's role in the household in Hida was defined to a large part by her role in food preparation, according to Ema. Most of the first of Ema's two chapters on mothers focuses on food preparation. She observes that the local term for mother was 'controller of the cauldron', meaning that the mother managed the cooking area, supervising younger women in the household in preparing food. At mealtimes, the mother sat with pots of cooked grains in front of her, and no one else was allowed to touch them. She doled out the appropriate grains and amount to each person. She would eat the leftovers, after everyone else was finished.[145]

The mother was tasked with preparing the barnyard millet, which needed to be milled every day using a waterwheel-driven mortar that often froze in winter. She had to prepare it in three different ways every day: barnyard millet mixed with an equal amount of or twice as much rice; barnyard millet alone; and the same grain mixed with its bran. Holidays necessitated making an additional small pot of rice to be used as a religious offering. The different methods of grain preparation were required because people in the family ate different proportions of barnyard millet depending on their gender and status, a custom prevalent in other regions of Japan, as explained in Chapter Three. The male heir, elderly men and young children in the household ate barnyard millet and rice. The dish of pure barnyard millet was for male servants and elderly women related to the heir. The mother consumed the worst-tasting grain mixed with bran, and did so without complaint, according to Ema.[146]

Life in Hida required hard work, which necessitated eating at least seven times daily in the summer; all these meals would be prepared by the mother of the household. Ema recorded the times of these meals and their typical contents, which did not show much variation:

Breakfast	4:00	Grain dish, miso soup, pickles, flour, horse chestnut cake
Morning snack	9:00	Grain dish, miso soup, pickles
Lunch	11:00	Grain dish, miso soup, pickles
Midday tea	12:00	Flour, horse-chestnut cake, pumpkin
Snack	15:00	Grain dish, miso soup, pickles
Supper	18:00	Grain dish, miso soup, pickles
Dinner	before bedtime	Horse-chestnut cakes, flour, white potato

Ema indicated that the family skipped the morning snack in the winter, because breakfast was eaten later than during the rest of the year.[147]

The 'flour' dish mentioned above was made from Shikoku millet (Shikokubie), called 'Chinese millet' (*karabe*) locally. The flour was placed in a bowl and hot water added to make dough that was eaten raw.[148] Pickles made from red turnips remain a noted speciality of Hida today, but locals in Ema's time also pickled daikon and other vegetables, as they do today. Apart from the kabocha squash served at noon, the only side dishes were pickles and miso soup. Ema recounted that it was typical for farmers in the region to say, 'miso and pickles are the best delicacies; if you got 'em, you don't need anything else.'[149] It was the mother's responsibility to make miso and pickles. 'A mother who is bad at preparing miso and pickles is said to be worse than a mother who can't sew,' according to a local saying Ema recorded.[150] In sum, cooking defined the role of motherhood in Hida as Ema viewed it.

Shirakawagō, Provincial Food and World Heritage

Though remote even just fifty years ago, Hida's Shirakawagō is now a frequent stop for overseas tourists after it was granted UNESCO World Heritage status in 1995. Shirakawagō refers to an amalgam of 42 villages north of the Shirakawa River.[151]

Ogimachi, on the banks of the Shō River, is the hamlet that is the main tourist draw to Shirakawagō, due to its distinctive traditional farmhouses of three or four storeys with steeply pitched roofs, called *gasshō zukuri* because their shape is reminiscent of two hands joined in prayer. Houses several centuries old survive in Ogimachi thanks to the area's remoteness and lack of economic development, but Ogimachi is hardly isolated today. A bus ride from Takayama takes less than an hour and Ogimachi is a frequent stop for chartered tourist buses; about 1.5 million tourists visit Shirakawagō annually.[152]

The multistorey farmhouses of Ogimachi and the surrounding area were dwellings for large households of upwards of 30 people, consisting of the family head, the heir and his wife and all their children, who would remain unwed all their lives. Large households such as these were typical of Hida until the first decade of the twentieth century, when greater economic opportunities allowed unmarried sons to leave their parents' homes to find work and thereby establish their own families.[153] In Ogimachi's farmhouses, the family would live on the ground floor of the house and the upper floors would be devoted to raising silkworms.

Shirakawagō is also the name used for a brand of sake brewed by Miwa Shūzo, located two hours by road south of the Hida region in Ōgaki, a city in Gifu's rice belt. Prior estimates of rice production derived from *The Latter Gazetteer of Hida* say nothing about the amount of rice used in sake brewing, but surprisingly the rice-poor region of Hida had many breweries historically and several are still in operation. Rice merchants in Takayama often turned to brewing sake as a way to maintain the demand for rice by transforming their rice reserves into this profitable beverage.[154] Takayama alone has six sake breweries, located in the historic district, including Niki Shuzō, established in 1695, and Hirase Shuzō, makers of the brand Kusudama and operated by the same family for fifteen generations. Other popular brands based in Gifu prefecture include Chiyogiku, a famous aged sake named Daruma Masamune, Kozaemon, Michizakari, Nagaragawa, Reisen and Tenryō. Local demand helps sustain these breweries. In 2014, Gifu ranked second from the bottom of Japan's 47 prefectures in alcohol

Ogimachi, Shirakawagō, 2013.

consumption, but sake is nonetheless a local favourite. Gifu ranks eighteenth in terms of per capita sake consumption, but at the bottom of the list for beer drinking – a sure sign of local preference for the rice beverage.[155]

Ogimachi has a reputation for its home-brewed sake called *doburoku*, or what one elderly resident called 'rice oil'.[156] Brewing *doburoku* with rice or barnyard millet was yet another task for the mothers of Shirakawagō, according to Ema Mieko.[157] After the sake laws of 1896, communities were allowed to produce only up to 180 litres of sake tax-free, so the custom of home brewing became a clandestine activity. Today, Ogimachi celebrates a *doburoku* festival annually in mid-October, following what is claimed to be a 700-year-old tradition. A museum dedicated to the festival provides visitors with samples of the cloudy brew, which is sweeter than non-alcoholic *amazake*, 'sweet sake', brewed from a blend of warm water, rice and *kōji*. Local shops also sell *doburoku manjū* – azuki-stuffed buns flavoured with the home-brewed sake.[158]

Visitors to Ogimachi who try to find dishes made from horse chestnuts and acorns will be disappointed as these are not offered to tourists. Ema Mieko described how families in Shirakawagō once ate fifteen or sixteen large bags of horse chestnuts yearly and because nut trees were so important, children were scolded for playing on or climbing them.[159] One elderly resident told me that he liked the taste of grain mixed with horse chestnuts, but that acorns were too bitter.[160] But references to the prominence of nuts in the diet historically are absent from the displays in the restored farmhouses.

In 1942 Gifu prefecture ranked fourth nationally in the amount of barnyard millet it produced, but today the grain does not even figure in the prefecture's production totals.[161] Even as late as the 1960s, according to one government survey, the main staples in Nagakura village in Hida, mentioned earlier for its slash-and-burn agriculture, were barnyard millet, Shikoku millet, buckwheat and millet along with soybeans and azuki. Locals there also gathered horse chestnuts and acorns to mix with glutinous rice to make *mochi*.[162] Gifu is nationally recognized for its persimmons, of which it produces more than any other prefecture. 'Hida beef' is also well known; and the Mino area is famous for ayu (sweetfish), which is the prefectural fish. But barnyard millet has disappeared as a staple food.

Ogimachi's Doburoku Museum and some of its historic farmhouses display labelled examples of barnyard millet and foxtail millet. Both grains can last for decades if properly preserved, so one wonders when the samples were originally affixed to the museum walls. An inn in Ogimachi called Furusato (Home Town) in a centuries-old farmhouse serves barnyard millet and rice for breakfast and dinner, but the white rice is just dusted with tiny millet grains that are hardly noticeable and a far cry from the proportions of barnyard millet once consumed, according to Ema Mieko's data. An open-air museum across the river from Ogimachi grows some ancient grains, but in Ogimachi proper, the beautiful farmhouses are surrounded by rice paddies.

A taste of Hida's local cuisine is available at Kissa Satō, run by the local food expert Satō Naoko. Her recommended lunch in late June 2013 consisted of soup with dumplings made from buckwheat and a mixture of glutinous and non-glutinous rice served in a clear broth with tofu and shiitake. Accompanying this was a salad of daikon and carrot; a serving of sliced kabocha topped with black sesame seeds; a slice of hard tofu (*katadōfu*, called *ishidōfu*, 'stone tofu', in Ogimachi, where it is a speciality); daikon pickled with red turnip, which is another classic of local Hida food; and a small serving of okra topped with *katsuobushi* flakes.

Asked to describe the traditional cuisine of Hida, Satō Naoko drew attention to the book she co-wrote, *Honkosama no omotenashi: Shirakawagō no hō'onkō ryōri* (Meals for Honkosama: The Hō'onkō Cooking of Shirakawa Village, 2012). Honkosama is an annual observance of the passing of Shinran (1173–1262), founder of Jōdo Shinshū, the True Pure Land sect of Buddhism, which historically had many adherents in the Hida area. Shinran died in the eleventh lunar month, but in Hida the anniversary of his death is celebrated between November and January. Families in Shirakawamura invite a priest to chant sutras and they serve vegetarian food called *osai* or *toki* to the priest, relatives and neighbours assembled. The feast is simple in terms of its ingredients, but Satō states that it takes a year of preparation. Few families in Shirakawa maintain the full tradition today, which is what prompted Satō and her co-authors to survey the *hō'onkō* cooking of four families and compile their book.[163]

Hō'onkō meals follow a set structure. At one time food was served when people assembled and then the priest chanted sutras and offered a short sermon, but today food and sake appear only after the priest has finished. The meal is quite filling, to the point that it is said that one does not need to eat for a week afterwards. Each person is served two trays of food and guests are also given additional prepared dishes to carry home, usually wrapped in magnolia leaves, another standard of Hida cuisine.[164] Today, hosts purchase miso, tofu and sweets, but these were once all homemade. Some dishes require gathering wild vegetables such as royal fern, *warabi* and aster in the spring and preserving them in salt; other dishes require mushrooms and nuts collected in the autumn. These season-specific preparations explain why the meal is said to take a year to make.[165]

In Ogimachi today, the Kabuchi family serves two trays of food for each guest for its *hō'onkō* banquets. The first tray features rice sprinkled with boiled azuki beans (Shinran is said to have liked beans); soup with *nameko* mushrooms and homemade tofu; black-eyed beans pan-fried and then simmered until soft; and pickled Chinese cabbage, daikon and the ubiquitous red turnip. Two more dishes threaten to spill off the first tray. The first, called *chatsu*, features a long piece of grilled tofu topped with boiled carrot, burdock and royal fern next to a tofu salad of Japanese butterbur and aster in sesame dressing. For the second dish, various foods are hidden in a bowl beneath another slab of grilled tofu; these dishes consist of fried sweet potato and simmered delicacies sweetened with mirin and sugar – bamboo shoots, taro and shiitake. The second tray holds a small pile of round white mochi on a plate, and two other dishes are composites of separate snacks.

The first is a bowl containing a whole persimmon; fried *warabi* and ostrich fern mashed with sesame then blended with sugar and soy sauce; *maitake* mushrooms (hen-of-the-woods) simmered with sake, soy sauce and sugar; sweet potato tempura; myoga ginger simmered in soy sauce and sesame oil; a variety of lily called *amana* blended with tofu; *udo* (a pale, asparagus-like vegetable) simmered with light soy sauce, sake and mirin; and cloud ear fungus in a walnut dressing. A selection of sweets arranged on a large magnolia leaf includes slices of sweet potato; walnuts; a bitter persimmon; peanuts; dried nuts; glutinous rice steamed with soybeans; chestnuts; and regular and sweetened steamed soybeans.[166]

Though *hō'onkō* was once a home-cooked meal, some people in Shirakawagō now have their *hō'onkō* meals catered, and there is even one establishment that prepares a *hō'onkō* menu by prior arrangement for tourists. Satō Naoko is happy to see local culinary traditions adapt to the times, commenting,

> It is one matter simply to inherit a tradition and another to make 'local ingredients' and 'health' paramount while also taking into account outside information and trends to do things like [operate] restaurants and increase the variety and adapt the taste to create something original. Offering people the kind of food one can take pride in will inspire and please visitors, who will be sure to say 'this is the taste of Shirakawagō'.[167]

Unlike the barnyard and foxtail millet that have become museum pieces in Hida, aspects of the traditional banqueting cuisine can be successfully adapted to please guests to the region.

The daily diet in the locales surveyed in this chapter – Saga, Kōchi and Hida – has transformed so much since the Second World War that the everyday fare of fifty years ago is no longer visible. The local foods people once ate for every meal – the mixed grain dishes, nut *mochi* and pickled mustard greens – are dishes that local people themselves now find largely unpalatable and presume to be unmarketable to outsiders. Local cuisine today, then, is the select representation of an area's food culture, updated and dressed up to appeal to visitors. In some instances locally sourced ingredients such as crab in Tarachō in Saga serve as the basis for creating a cuisine in a place where seafood has long figured prominently in the coastal diet but was rare in communities just 3 kilometres inland. Other attempts to raise the gastronomic profile of an area are found in roadside stations – *michinoeki* – such as Tarafukukan in Taracho and the market in the visitor's centre in Yusuhara, which sell foodstuffs grown, gathered and manufactured in the nearby area. Today the *sawachi* cuisine of Kōchi is more marketable for its beloved seafood delicacies such as *katsuo tataki* than the heartier and more labour-intensive *hǒonkō* meals of the Hida area, which survive in the ritual culinary repertoire of only a few families. But both forms of banqueting cuisine represent local efforts to present native culinary traditions in the most positive light to outsiders, to correct any lingering notions that the foods from these regions are somehow lacking compared to dominant culinary norms.

Local food also reveals what is missing in the rhetoric of national dietary cultures. The prominence of sake in the culinary cultures of Saga, Kōchi and Hida points to the puzzling absence of any discussion of sake or any other beverage in the definition of *washoku* as the traditional dietary cultures of the Japanese. The examples of food life in these regions make the salient point that people not only eat in a dietary culture, they also drink; and beverages should be considered alongside food in discussions of diet at the national level as well. The enjoyment that many in Saga, Gifu and Kōchi have drinking local sake serves as a reminder that regardless of what central authorities and scholars who write about local food might say, and despite what is labelled and sold as 'local' food to tourists, local food also serves local needs and satisfies local preferences.

Hǒonkōsama cuisine of the Kabuchi family, Ogimachi.

CONCLUSION

This book has examined the most prominent cuisines of Japan, from the recent articulation of traditional dietary cultures (*washoku*), to its predecessor in wartime national people's cuisine (*kokumin-shoku*), to the older *kaiseki* cuisine of the tea ceremony, to the *obentō* cuisine of the boxed lunch and the proliferation of local cuisines in national culinary discourse today. Rather than describe objective realities, these cuisines represent the efforts of authorities to guide citizens' behaviour by delimiting idealized consumption habits.

Although these cuisines have become the dominant ways in which people talk about Japanese food, as attempts to shape behaviour they have only limited success because of their great divergence from the more complicated realities they supposedly describe. The story of the Japanese government's campaign for a UNESCO listing for 'traditional Japanese dietary cultures', which began this study, has helped publicize Japanese food abroad and even boosted exports of Japanese ingredients, but whether or not the promotion of *washoku* can change eating habits domestically to encourage more Japanese citizens to eat 'Japanese food', by the government's definition, remains to be seen. As Chapter One indicated, a survey undertaken in 2013 by the beverage maker Takara Shuzō asked 3,000 people in Japan between the ages of twenty and sixty about whether or not the UNESCO listing of *washoku* would change their attitudes to traditional Japanese dietary cultures: more than half (54.1 per cent) said that it would not.[1] *Washoku*'s predecessor, national people's cuisine, was a more audacious example of the government's attempt to use cuisine to support national objectives. National people's cuisine lost all salience in the closing years of the Second World War in the face of people's struggle to obtain enough food simply to survive. The post-war redefinition of national people's cuisine as 'people's food', referring to inexpensive popular dishes such as ramen and Japanese curry, shows how a once hegemonic term was repurposed in popular usage to domesticate beloved foreign foods. As with the state-imposed national people's cuisine, the categories of local food and local cuisine that developed in national culinary discourse had very little to do with how the people who supposedly ate these foodstuffs construed their own dietary lifestyles. Popular stereotypes about life in localities that were viewed as peripheral to national trends presented challenges for the people living in these areas to overcome, but they have done so in part by laying claim to their own local culinary traditions, as the examples in Chapter Seven drawn from Saga, Kōchi and Hida demonstrate. In these locales, culinary traditions were identified and promoted to the benefit of actual local pride and economy.

Cuisines are abstract and prescriptive and food is concrete and malleable, but one continuity that the identity of cuisine shares with the realty of feeding and eating is the onus placed on women in a food culture that they are not always allowed an equal share in. The invention of lunch and its expression in *bentō*, the homemade boxed lunch, provide examples of how innovations in culinary habits placed new burdens on women as homemakers not just to feed their families but to follow specific nutritional and aesthetic guidelines in crafting new types of dining experience. Similar gender disparities long affected the daily meals produced and consumed in many households. Some farming and fishing households designated as the 'woman's meal' the dregs from the grain pot. In the Hida region, mothers prepared different pots of grain for members of their family depending on age, status and gender, but they ate leftovers themselves. The current insistence of the promoters of traditional dietary cultures on cooking more 'Japanese' food places greater demands on female homemakers, who are often blamed for the failings of the contemporary diet. Popular complaints listed in Chapter One, that *washoku* is too time-consuming and difficult to cook, reflect the burden of Japanese cuisine on women charged with preparing it. Cuisines may not create gender disparities, but they do enhance those related to food preparation and consumption, which have long and wide-reaching historical roots.

From the standpoint of the diner, Japanese cuisine in its local, national and other forms deserves the international acclaim it has received, but the 'Japanese' foods generally available today are only a fraction of the nation's diverse culinary heritage, as this book has also revealed. A myopic focus in media and scholarship on white rice has meant that the different types of grain – most notably varieties of millet – once consumed in Japan are no longer to be found except as animal feed. Gone too is the corn-based diet of rural parts of Kōchi, and the barley and rice once eaten in cities and the countryside. On the one hand, such a loss is understandable if these food-stuffs and others that have disappeared are not worth preserving. According to some experts, they simply taste bad. On the other hand, for a country so intent on documenting and preserving its heritage, including its culinary past, the fact that some foods once consumed as staples by large portions of the population have practically disappeared represents a great loss for a land so devoted to food. Without the chance to sample barnyard millet, foxtail millet, cornmeal mixed with rice, nut dumplings and other recipes, we may not know the taste of what we are missing; but, looking at the broad history of food in Japan in comparison with the current food scene, notwithstanding the plurality of today's 'traditional dietary cultures', we can know what foods are now missing.

Taste is the reason why some local foods survive as local cuisines, as Chapter Six explained, but not all the cuisines available today locally are in good taste or necessarily taste good. Saga prefecture, for example, has many fine culinary treasures, but its local food scene is uneven. For centuries the city of Arita in Saga has been synonymous with its fine ceramics, which provide a colourful base to enhance culinary creations, as the *sawachi* cuisine of Kōchi exemplifies well. Before the Second World War, Arita was known as an 'eater's paradise', and it makes sense that a place that values fine china would have an equal appreciation for the delicacies served on it.[2] Visiting local museums in Arita today one can certainly deepen one's appreciation of the city's fine porcelain, and one can even take some modern examples home thanks to the numerous shops that line the main thoroughfare. But the local food scene in Arita is wanting. The tourist centre displays hundreds of handmade coffee mugs on its walls and allows visitors to select one example to drink from. After the choice is made, a helpful volunteer fills the ¥100,000 ($1,000/£700) cup with ¥100 ($1/£0.65) instant coffee made from a machine, which seems an injustice in a country well known for its coffee connoisseurs and skilled baristas.[3] The restaurants in Arita have similar schemes that allow customers the chance to sample a drink from the many beautiful cups on hand, but their food does not distract much from the tableware, proving that the local culinary movement still has room for growth.

Food cultures are far more complicated than the terms, such as cuisine, that are used to describe them, especially when a cuisine is defined on the basis of a few dishes alone. And for an outsider to use taste as the basis for evaluating a local cuisine seems particularly fraught with problems because taste varies by individual. Rather than judging what is lacking according to some imagined standard, what is there deserves appreciation in its own right. If the people of Arita wanted me to remember the local porcelain, which is far more integral to the city's history and economy today than the local food ever was, then they certainly succeeded, because nowhere else have I used a ¥100,000 cup to drink a ¥100 cup of coffee. The critical study of the cuisines of modern Japan made in this book should not provoke us to abandon terms such as tea cuisine or Japanese dietary cultures, but neither should we be confined by them as we enjoy the many foods available in Japan and as we try to imagine, and perhaps one day even recover, those that seem to have been lost.

REFERENCES

Note on Translation

1 Satohiro Serizawa, 'Regional Variations and Local Interpretations of the National Food: The Case of Japanese Noodles', in *International Conference on Foodways and Heritage: A Perspective of Safeguarding the Intangible Cultural Heritage*, ed. Sidney C. H. Cheung and Chau Hing-wah (Hong Kong, 2013), pp. 94–5.
2 Seijō Daigaku Minzokugaku Kenkyūjo, ed., *Nihon no shoku bunka hoi hen: Shōwa shoki, zenkoku shokuji shūzoku no kiroku* (Tokyo, 1995), pp. 309–10.
3 John D. Keys, *Japanese Cuisine: A Culinary Tour* (Tokyo, 1966), p. 136.

Introduction

1 As an example of the first approach, see Rachel Laudan, *Cuisine and Empire: Cooking in World History* (Berkeley, CA, 2013), p. 4. For the second, see, for example, Katarzyna Cwiertka, *Modern Japanese Cuisine: Food, Power and National Identity* (London, 2006).
2 For this approach to cuisine, see Eric C. Rath, *Food and Fantasy in Early Modern Japan* (Berkeley, CA, 2010).
3 George Carlin, *When Will Jesus Bring the Pork Chops?* (New York, 2004), pp. 123–4, 127.
4 Kristin Surak lists 2.3 million tea practitioners in Japan in 2006, some 90 per cent of whom are women, which is less than 2 per cent of the population. Kristin Surak, *Making Tea, Making Japan: Cultural Nationalism in Practice* (Stanford, CA, 2013), p. 135.
5 Arizono Shōichirō, *Kinsei shomin no nichijōshoku: Hyakushō wa kome o taberarenakatta ka?* (Ōtsu, 2007), p. 1.
6 Takeuchi Yukiko, 'Chōri to jendā', in *Shokubunka kara shakai ga wakaru!*, ed. Harada Nobuo (Tokyo, 2009), p. 122.

1 What is Traditional Japanese Food?

1 Other terms for Japanese food include *honpō ryōri* and *Nihon shoku*. The former, which literally means 'our cuisine', is no longer generally used, and the latter

does not appear as frequently today as *washoku* and *Nihon ryōri*. For a history of the usage of these terms, see Chapter Six, n. 2.

2 Abe Koryū, *Kokoro no keshōbako* (Tokyo, 2002), p. 102.

3 The food historian Harada Nobuo also distinguishes between *washoku* and *Nihon ryōri*: the former he identifies as a particular meal structure and the latter he links to national identity that changes over time. Harada Nobuo, *Washoku to Nihon bunka: Nihon ryōri no shakaishi* (Tokyo, 2005), pp. 9, 12–13. For more on the complexity of defining the term *ryōri*, see Eric C. Rath, *Food and Fantasy in Early Modern Japan* (Berkeley, CA, 2010), pp. 28–31, 36–7.

4 For a discussion and critique of the effectiveness of Japan's soft-power initiatives as they relate to food in particular, see Gabriella Lukacs, '*Iron Chef* Around the World: Japanese Food Television, Soft Power, and Cultural Globalization', *International Journal of Cultural Studies*, XIII/4 (2010), pp. 409–26.

5 Rumi Sakamoto and Matthew Allen, 'There's Something Fishy about that Sushi: How Japan Interprets the Global Sushi Boom', *Japan Forum*, XXIII/1 (2011), pp. 100, 110, 112.

6 'Washoku, Traditional Dietary Cultures of the Japanese, Notably for the Celebration of New Year', www.unesco.org, accessed 26 August 2014.

7 Santōsha, *Shoku seikatsu dēta sōgō tōkei nenpyō 2014* (Tokyo, 2014), p. 255.

8 Ibid.

9 Kumakura Isao, 'Nihon shokubunkashi no kadai', in *Kōza shoku no bunka*, ed. Ishige Naomichi and Kumakura Isao (Tokyo, 1999), vol. II, pp. 3–5.

10 UNESCO, 'Nomination file no. 00869 for Inscription in 2013 on the Representative List of the Intangible Cultural Heritage of Humanity', www.unesco.org/culture/ich/en/lists, accessed 26 August 2014, p. 14.

11 Video Research Ltd, 'Kuppu nūdoru wa washoku?! – Washoku chōsa kara miru, washoku no fukuzatsu no jittai', www.videor.co.jp, 25 June 2015.

12 Harada, *Washoku to Nihon bunka*, p. 230.

13 Naomichi Ishige, 'Japan', in *The Cambridge World History of Food*, ed. Kenneth F. Kiple and Kriemhild Coneè Ornelas (New York, 2000), vol. II, p. 1176.

14 Kumakura, 'Nihon shokubunkashi no kadai', p. 18; Nagayama Hisao, *Naze washoku wa sekai ichi na no ka* (Tokyo, 2012), p. 4.

15 Murai Yasuhiko, 'Kaiseki ryōri no rekishi', in *Kaiseki to kashi*, ed. Tsutsui Hiroichi (Kyoto, 1999), p. 24.

16 Nihon Shoku Bunka no Sekai Muke Isan Bunka Tōroku ni Muketa Kentōkai, 'Nihon shokubunka no muke bunka isan kisai teiansho no gaiyō', www.bunka.go.jp/seisaku/bunkazai/shokai/mukei_bunka_isan/pdf/syokubunka_120925.pdf, February 2012, accessed 25 April 2012.

17 Santōsha, *Shoku seikatsu dēta sōgō tōkei nenpyō 2014*, p. 336.

18 Ibid.

19 Matsushita Sachiko, *Zusetsu Edo ryōri jiten* (Tokyo, 1996), p. 114.

20 Santōsha, *Shoku seikatsu dēta sōgō tōkei nenpyō 2014*, p. 336.

21 The survey also asked about the positive virtues of *washoku*, and those were the top three responses; ibid.

22 Ibid.

23 Stephanie Assmann has described how food education campaigns that promote *washoku* seek to steer Japanese consumers away from Western-style dishes. She writes, 'the food education campaign can only be understood

as a defensive reaction to the realities of dietary globalization in Japan.' See Stephanie Assmann, 'The Remaking of a National Cuisine: The Food Education Campaign in Japan', in *The Globalization of Asian Cuisines: Transnational Networks and Culinary Contact Zones*, ed. James Farrer (New York, 2015), p. 171.

24 Vaclav Smil and Kazuhiko Kobayashi, *Japan's Dietary Transition and its Impacts* (Cambridge, MA, 2012), pp. 175, 189.

25 UNESCO, 'Nomination file no. 00869 for Inscription in 2013 on the Representative List of the Intangible Cultural Heritage of Humanity', p. 3.

26 Kumakura Isao, 'Nihon no dentōteki shokubunka to shite no washoku no inkikata', in *Nihon no shoku no kinmirai*, ed. Kumakura Isao (Kyoto, 2013), p. 10.

27 For a comprehensive study of the way the Japanese government supports agriculture in return for the political backing of the nation's farmers, see Aurelia George Mulgan, *The Politics of Agriculture in Japan* (New York, 2000).

28 Smil and Kobayashi, *Japan's Dietary Transition and its Impacts*, p. 196.

29 Ibid., p. 26.

30 Ibid., p. 17.

31 Ichikawa Takeo, 'Shokubunka ni miru chiikisei', in *Zenshū Nihon no shokubunka*, ed. Haga Noboru and Ishikawa Hiroko (Tokyo, 1996), vol. XII, p. 17. Kumakura Isao agrees that the ideal version of *washoku* was widely available only after the Second World War, as a result of Japan's strong economic growth; Kumakura, 'Nihon no dentōteki shokubunka to shite no washoku no inkikata', p. 15.

32 Harada Nobuo, *Rekishi no naka no kome to niku: Shokumotsu to tennō, sabetsu* (Tokyo, 1993), p. 282.

33 Simon Partner, *Toshié: A Story of Village Life in Twentieth-century Japan* (Berkeley, CA, 2004), p. 13.

34 Toda Hiroyoshi, *Shokubunka no keisei to nōgyō: Niō chūkan no bāi* (Tokyo, 2001), pp. 248–9; Ministry of Agriculture, Forestry and Fisheries, *Heisei nijūnen shokuryō jikyūristu*, www.maff.go.jp/j/zyukyu/fbs/index.html, accessed 25 May 2012, p. 2.

35 Katarzyna Cwiertka, *Modern Japanese Cuisine: Food, Power and National Identity* (London, 2006), p. 24; Smil and Kobayashi, *Japan's Dietary Transition and its Impacts*, p. 2; Toda, *Shokubunka no keisei to nōgyō*, pp. 248–9.

36 Eric C. Rath, 'New Meanings for Old Vegetables in Kyoto', *Food Culture and Society*, XVII/2 (2014), pp. 205, 208.

37 Kōsaka Mutsuko, 'Kyōdo ryōri no chiriteki bunpu', in *Zenshū Nihon no shokubunka*, ed. Haga Noboru and Ishikawa Hiroko (Tokyo, 1996), vol. XII, pp. 28–9.

38 Cwiertka, *Modern Japanese Cuisine*, p. 159.

39 For a discussion of the global sourcing of fish in Japan's sushi trade, see Sasha Issenberg, *The Sushi Economy: Globalization and the Making of a Modern Delicacy* (New York, 2007).

40 Smil and Kobayashi, *Japan's Dietary Transition and its Impacts*, p. 17.

41 On the positive side, the *washoku* boom has been credited with boosting Japan's agricultural exports to record levels in 2013 and 2014. 'Washoku Boom Helps Japan's Farm Exports', *Japan News*, 11 February 2015, available at www.newsonjapan.com.

42 Eric J. Hobsbawm and Terrence O. Ranger, eds, *The Invention of Tradition* (New

York, 1983); Stephen Vlastos, ed., *Mirror of Modernity: Invented Traditions of Modern Japan* (Berkeley, CA, 1998).

43 Theodore C. Bestor, *Tsukiji: The Fish Market at the Center of the World* (Berkeley, CA, 2004), pp. 124, 150.

44 Segawa Kiyoko, *Shoku seikatsu no rekishi* (Tokyo, 2001), p. 38; Ehara Ayako, Ishikawa Naoko and Higashiyotsuyanagi Shōko, *Nihon shokumotsushi* (Tokyo, 2009), p. 9.

45 Some examples include Yamada Junko, *Edo gurume tanjō: Jidai koshō de miru Edo no aji* (Tokyo, 2010); Watanabe Zenjirō, *Kyodai toshi Edo ga washoku o tsukuta* (Tokyo, 1988); Ōkubo Hiroko, *Edokko wa nani o tabeteita ka* (Tokyo, 2005); Hayashi Shunshin, *Edo, Tōkyō gurume saijiki* (Tokyo, 1998); and Watanabe Shin'ichiro, *Edo no shomin ga hiraita shokubunka* (Tokyo, 1996).

46 Kumakura observed that this tendency was especially common in scholarship published before the 1980s. Kumakura, 'Nihon shokubunkashi no kadai', pp. 13–16.

47 Matsushita, *Zusetsu Edo ryōri jiten*, p. 298; Nakamura Kōhei, *Shinpan Nihon ryōri gogenshū* (Tokyo, 2004), p. 674.

48 Emiko Ohnuki-Tierney, *Rice as Self: Japanese Identities through Time* (Princeton, NJ, 1993), p. 15.

49 Arizono Shōichirō, *Kinsei shomin no nichijōshoku: Hyakushō wa kome o taberarenakatta ka?* (Ōtsu, 2007), p. 1.

50 Susan B. Hanley, *Everyday Things in Premodern Japan: The Hidden Legacy of Material Culture* (Berkeley, CA, 1997), p. 166.

51 Arizono, *Kinsei shomin no nichijōshoku*, p. 1.

52 Smil and Kobayashi, *Japan's Dietary Transition and its Impacts*, pp. 20, 134. In 1900 Japan was 97 per cent food self-sufficient, but by 1925 it was a significant importer of rice, wheat and sugar; ibid., pp. 139, 141.

53 The lack of seafood in the pre-war diet is mentioned in several studies. See Seijō Daigaku Minzokugaku Kenkyūjo, ed., *Nihon no shokubunka, hoi hen: Shōwa shoki, zenkoku shokuji shūzoku no kiroku* (Tokyo, 1995), p. 289; B. F. Johnston, *Japanese Food Management in World War Two* (Palo Alto, CA, 1953), p. 85; Takeuchi Yukiko, 'Chōri to jendā', in *Shokubunka kara shakai ga wakaru!*, ed. Harada Nobuo (Tokyo, 2009), p. 122.

54 The scholar Koizumi Kazuko offers these typical examples of urban and rural meals, and examines their nutritional content. She writes that according to the contemporary standards set by the National Institute for Nutrition, an adult man doing hard labour such as farm work requires a diet of 2,400 calories daily and 80 grams of protein, but the typical caloric intake in the late 1930s was only 2,345 calories and 74.1 grams of protein; Koizumi Kazuko, *Chabudai no Shōwa* (Tokyo, 2002), pp. 68–70.

55 Matsuyama Toshio, *Ko no mi* (Tokyo, 1982), p. 33. See also Chapter Three.

2 Tea Cuisine and the Origins of Japanese Cuisine

1 Both restaurant and tea *kaiseki* evolved as abbreviations of 'main tray' (*honzen*) style banqueting cuisine, which was the most formal mode of dining in the medieval and early modern periods. Main tray cuisine serves three, five, seven or more trays simultaneously, each with a soup and side dishes. See Eric C.

Rath, '*Honzen* Dining – The Poetry of Formal Meals in Late Medieval and Early Modern Japan', in *Japanese Foodways Past and Present*, ed. Eric C. Rath and Stephanie Assmann (Urbana, IL, 2010), pp. 19–41. Tea *kaiseki* shows more restraint in the number of trays and dishes. A typical modern tea menu begins with rice, soup and *mukōzuke* – sliced fish served by itself as sashimi or in a fish salad (*namasu*) with other ingredients and a vinegar dressing – followed by a simmered dish (*nimono*, also called *wanmori*) and grilled foods (*yakimono*). Next, a soup to cleanse the palate (*suimono*) is a prelude to delicacies (*chinmi*) from the sea and mountains. Pickles (*kō no mono*) and hot water from the rice pot (*yutō*) conclude the meal, which precedes the consumption of sweets (*kashi*) and the drinking of tea. During a tea ceremony, the components of the meal are brought out simultaneously, but in the restaurant version of *kaiseki* the dishes are enjoyed one at a time, and the meal concludes with rice and soup rather than beginning with them. Richard Hosking, *A Dictionary of Japanese Food: Ingredients and Culture* (New York, 1996), pp. 31, 67–8.

2 For a discussion of the beginnings of the restaurant trade in the pleasure quarters of late seventeenth-century Edo, see Eric C. Rath, 'Sex and Sea Bream: Food and Prostitution in Hishikawa Moronobu's *Visit to Yoshiwara*', in *Seduction: Japan's Floating World: The John C. Weber Collection*, ed. Laura W. Allen (San Francisco, CA, 2015), pp. 30–32.

3 Michael Ashkenazi and Jeanne Jacob, *The Essence of Japanese Cuisine: An Essay on Food and Culture* (Philadelphia, PA, 2000), p. 140.

4 Hosking, *A Dictionary of Japanese Food*, pp. 210, 226. Perhaps the earliest example of this phrase is found in *Ryōri mōmoku chōmishō*, published in 1751. See Shōsekiken Sōken, *Ryōri mōmoku chōmishō*, in *Nihon ryōri hiden shūsei: Genten gendaigoyaku*, ed. Issunsha (Kyoto, 1985), vol. I, p. 322.

5 Kumakura Isao identifies tea *kaiseki* as the origin of modern Japanese cuisine, repeating a view that appears in earlier scholarship as described below. Kumakura Isao, *Nihon ryōri bunkashi: Kaiseki o chūshin ni* (Kyoto, 2002), p. 13. For another prominent Japanese scholar making similar claims, see Ebara Kei, *Edo ryōrishi kō: Nihon ryōri (sōsōski)* (Tokyo, 1986), p. 52. In her groundbreaking book *Modern Japanese Cuisine: Food, Power and National Identity*, Katarzyna Cwiertka observes, '*kaiseki* aesthetics functioned as a vital homogenizing component in the process of the making of Japanese national cuisine.' Katarzyna Cwiertka, *Modern Japanese Cuisine: Food, Power and National Identity* (London, 2006), pp. 112–13.

6 The belief that Rikyū's tea embodied the rustic style is a commonly held one, as expressed in Theodore Ludwig, 'Chanoyu and Momoyama: Conflict and Transformation in Rikyū's Tea', in *Tea in Japan: Essays on the History of Cha no yu*, ed. Paul Varley and Kumakura Isao (Honolulu, HI, 1989), pp. 71–100.

7 Kumakura Isao, 'Sen no Rikyū: Inquiries into his Life and Tea', in *Tea in Japan*, ed. Varley and Kumakura, pp. 55–9.

8 Cwiertka, *Modern Japanese Cuisine*, p. 110. Cwiertka's singling out of one individual for praise is incongruent with the conclusions in her landmark study, which traces the rise of modern Japanese cuisine in processes beyond the diffusion and standardization of *kaiseki* aesthetics to include the spread of urban meal patterns, the introduction of Western foods and the role of institutions such as the Japanese military in homogenizing Japanese taste. Ibid., especially pp. 79, 176.

9 In a paperback book for a popular audience, *The Wisdom of Kaiseki Cuisine* (*Kaiseki ryōri no chie*), the food scholar Kushioka Keiko offers, 'the tea cuisine that Rikyū refined had a tremendous impact on pre-existing banquet cuisine and even ordinary meals.' Kushioka Keiko, *Kaiseki ryōri no chie* (Tokyo, 1999), p. 30. A recently published history of Japanese food includes a section on the foundation of Japanese cuisine with a short discussion of tea cuisine, which focuses entirely on Rikyū's contributions. The authors cite passages from two sources said to express Rikyū's philosophy of *kaiseki* to explain that tea cuisine in Rikyū's period marked a pinnacle in the development of earlier forms of Japanese cuisine; Ehara Ayako, Ishikawa Naoko and Higashiyotsuyanagi Shōko, *Nihon shokumotsushi* (Tokyo, 2009), pp. 95–6.

10 This observation is adapted from Priscilla P. Clark, who describes French cuisine as an incarnation of the nation in her article, 'Thoughts for Food I: French Cuisine and French Culture', *The French Review*, XLIX/1 (1975), pp. 32–41.

11 Katarzyna Cwiertka, 'Culinary Culture and the Making of a National Cuisine', in *A Companion to the Anthropology of Japan*, ed. Jennifer Robertson (New York, 2005), p. 417.

12 Kristin Surak, *Making Tea, Making Japan: Cultural Nationalism in Practice* (Stanford, CA, 2013), pp. 8–9.

13 Murai Yasuhiko, 'Kaiseki ryōri no rekishi', in *Kaiseki to kashi*, ed. Tsutsui Hiroichi (Kyoto, 1999), pp. 18–19.

14 In their discussion of tea cuisine, the authors present several menus served to warlords in 1584, 1588, 1592 and 1593, which they describe as tea cuisine, defined as an abbreviated form of banqueting cuisine. Sasagawa and Adachi list Rikyū as well as other tea masters being in attendance at one such meal in 1584; and the authors cite *Nanpōroku*, a collection of teachings attributed to Rikyū, but otherwise Rikyū does not receive special mention in their narrative. Sasagawa Rinpū and Adachi Isamu, *Kinsei Nihon shokumotsushi* (Tokyo, 1973), pp. 67–75.

15 Sekishū taught the tea ceremony to the first Tokugawa shogun, Ieyasu (1542–1616). He was also a warlord (*daimyō*) and founder of the Sekishū school of tea, rival to the Sen families that claimed descent from Rikyū. That Sasagawa and Adachi draw attention to this *daimyō* tea master presents the notion that Rikyū did not have the final word about tea cuisine. Sasagawa and Adachi, *Kinsei Nihon shokumotsushi*, p. 72. The authors attribute Sekishū's statement to *Illustrious Examples* (*Meiryō kōhan*) by Sanada Zōyo, an early eighteenth-century collection of anecdotes in 40 volumes about the first five Tokugawa shoguns and their highest-ranking vassals.

16 Sen Sōshitsu XIV and Sen Sōshu, eds, *Chadō zenshū* (Tokyo, 1936), vol. VII.

17 Sen Sōshu, 'Kaiseki no yurai oyobi hensen', in *Chadō zenshū*, ed. Sen Sōshitsu XIV and Sen Sōshu, vol. VII, pp. 3. 11, 12.

18 Sen Sōshitsu XIV, 'Kaiseki shukaku no kokoroe', in *Chadō zenshū*, ed. Sen Sōshitsu XIV and Sen Sōshu, vol. VII, pp. 17, 19.

19 Uotani Tsunekichi, 'Cha ryōri no jidai shoku', in *Chadō zenshū*, ed. Sen Sōshitsu XIV and Sen Sōshu, vol. VII, pp. 165, 166–7.

20 Saitō Tokio, *Nihon Shokubunka jinbutsu jiten: Jinbutsu de yomu Nihon shokubunkashi* (Tokyo, 2005), p. 57.

21 Surak, *Making Tea, Making Japan*, p. 103.

22 Morisue Yoshiaki and Kikuchi Yūjirō, *Shokumotsushi: Nihonjin no shoku seikatsu*

no hatten (Tokyo, 1952), pp. 107–11.

23 Morisue Yoshiaki and Kikuchi Yūjirō, *Kaikō shokumotsushi: Nihonjin no shoku seikatsu no hatten* (Tokyo, 1965) pp. 128–9, 130–31.

24 That Watanabe's text was often used in secondary schools and women's colleges is a point made in Nishiyama Matsunosuke, ed., *Tabemono Nihonshi sōkan* (Tokyo, 1994), p. 385.

25 Watanabe Minoru, *Nihon no shoku seikatsushi* (Tokyo, 1964), pp. 175–6.

26 Surak, *Making Tea, Making Japan*, p. 93.

27 Morgan Pitelka, *Handmade Culture: Raku Potters, Patrons, and Tea Practitioners in Japan* (Honolulu, HI, 2005), p. 14.

28 Biographical information about Endō Genkan appears in Eric C. Rath, *Food and Fantasy in Early Modern Japan* (Berkeley, CA, 2010), pp. 128–31.

29 Endō Genkan, *Cha no yu kondate shinan*, in *Nihon ryōri hiden shūsei: Genten gendaigoyaku*, ed. Issunsha (Kyoto, 1985), vol. XI, pp. 5–208.

30 Matsuya Hisashige, *Matsuya kaiki*, in *Chadō koten zenshū*, ed. Sen Sōshitsu XV (Kyoto, 1967), vol. IX. This work covers three generations of tea masters of the Matsuya family, wealthy lacquer merchants, spanning the years 1533–1650. The authors were Matsuya Hisamasa (d. 1598), Hisayoshi (d. 1633) and Hisashige (d. 1652).

31 Mary Elizabeth Berry, *The Culture of Civil War in Kyoto* (Berkeley, CA, 1994), p. 269.

32 Rath, *Food and Fantasy in Early Modern Japan*, pp. 53–7.

33 Tani Akira, *Chakaiki no kenkyū* (Kyoto, 2001), p. 28. The Tsuda family tea journal is called *Tennōjiya kaiki*. See Sen Sōshitsu XV, ed., *Tennōjiya kaiki takaiki*, in *Chadō koten zenshū*, vol. VII; and Sen Sōshitsu XV, ed., *Tennōjiya kaiki jikaiki*, in *Chadō koten zenshū*, vol. VIII.

34 Tsutsui Hiroichi, *Kaiseki no kenkyū: Wabicha no shokurei* (Kyoto, 2002). In the introduction and afterword to his annotated version of *Nanpōroku*, Kumakura Isao betrays his ambivalence about *Nanpōroku* as a historical record of Rikyū's teas. On the one hand, he admits that it has little value historically except as an indication of Tachibana Jitsuzan's ideas, yet at the same time he affirms that *Nanpōroku* expresses Rikyū's way of tea. See Kumakura Isao, *Nanpōroku o yomu* (Kyoto, 1983), pp. I, 397–8. The former leader of the Urasenke school of tea also nodded to the historical problems surrounding *Nanpōroku* but nonetheless equated the text with Rikyū's teachings. See Sen Sōshitsu XV, *Tea Life, Tea Mind* (New York, 1979).

35 Tani, *Chakaiki no kenkyū*, p. 28.

36 Kumakura, *Nanpōroku o yomu*, p. 390.

37 Sen Sōshitsu XV, ed., *Rikyū hyakkaiki*, in *Chadō koten zenshū*, vol. VI, pp. 405–73.

38 Iguchi Kaisen and Nagashima Fukutaro, eds, *Chadō jiten* (Kyoto, 1978), p. 802.

39 Tani, *Chakaiki no kenkyū*, p. 47.

40 Kumakura, *Nanpōroku o yomu*, p. 241.

41 Tsutsui, *Kaiseki no kenkyū*, pp. 91–2.

42 Kumakura, *Nihon ryōri bunkashi*, p. 19; Tani, *Chakaiki no kenkyū*, p. 348.

43 Kumakura, *Nihon ryōri bunkashi*, pp. 18–19.

44 Sen Sōshitsu XV, ed., *Yamanoue Sōjiki*, in *Chadō koten zenshū*, vol. VI, p. 104.

45 Citation from online version of *Nihon kokugo daijiten*, through Japan Nareji,

www.japanknowledge.com, accessed 12 January 2010. Many of the first tea practitioners also studied linked verse (*renga*), which might account for their adoption of the term *kaiseki*.

46 Tsutsui, *Kaiseki no kenkyū*, pp. 89–90.

47 Kumakura, *Nihon ryōri bunkashi*, p. 19.

48 Kumakura Isao, 'Senkeryū no kaiseki', in *Chadōgaku taikei* (Kyoto, 1999), vol. IV, p. 137.

49 Instead of *kaiseki*, Tani Akira advocates using different words for tea cuisine, *cha ryōri*. Tani, *Chakaiki no kenkyū*, p. 348.

50 The sociologist Priscilla Parkhurst Ferguson contends that published cookbooks laid the foundation for the establishment of French cuisine in the early modern period: 'French cuisine becomes French not so much through the food eaten as through the texts written and then avidly read.' Priscilla Parkhurst Ferguson, *Accounting for Taste: The Triumph of French Cuisine* (Chicago, IL, 2004), p. 34. For a discussion of the implications of print culture for early modern Japanese cuisine, see Rath, *Food and Fantasy in Early Modern Japan*, pp. 112–20.

51 *Kurome* is possibly a young mullet fish but more likely a variety of black kombu. Nakamura Kōhei, *Shinpan Nihon ryōri gogenshū* (Tokyo, 2004), p. 217. *Horomiso* is said to have originated in the Heian period (794–1185). Served to monks attending long religious debates at Tōdaiji temple, it was later used for fish and vegetable salads (*aemono*). Mixed with the miso are sesame, hemp seed, walnuts and *sanshō*. Ibid., p. 635. *Mizuae* recipes call for dried squid, small dried fish (*iriko*) used for making soup stock, dried cod and other types of dried fish, which are softened in water, mixed with vegetables and then covered in a vinegar dressing. Matsushita Sachiko, *Zusetsu Edo ryōri jiten* (Tokyo, 1996), p. 109. *Yakimiso* is something cooked over wood coated with miso. Expensive to make, the dish is a metaphor for something costly and wasteful. *Misoyaki* is something cooked in miso. *Atsumejiru* was a rather lavish soup that appeared on the menus of formal banquets for warriors in the early sixteenth century. Typical ingredients included small dried fish, abalone, wheat gluten, soybeans and sweet seaweed (*ama nori*). Nakamura, *Shinpan Nihon ryōri gogenshū*, p. 33. Ebara notes its rarity in tea ceremony menus in Ebara, *Edo ryōrishi kō*, p. 63. Today, *tataki* refers to sashimi that is seared briefly over a fire and then has seasonings pounded into it. See Chapter Seven for a description of *katsuo tataki*. The figures in this section are derived from Tsutsui, *Kaiseki no kenkyū*, p. 106.

52 The Buddhist vegetarian cuisine Tsutsui refers to is *shōjin ryōri*. Ibid., p. 90.

53 There is no evidence that Rikyū himself was a vegetarian. Not only did he prepare meat for others, but it was served to him as well, according to a record of tea gatherings, *Tennōjiya kaiki*, which lists a meal on the eighth day of the New Year in 1577 when Tsuda Sōkyū served Rikyū two types of sashimi – carp and swan – accompanied by a crucian carp soup. See Sen, *Tennōjiya kaiki jikaiki*, pp. 243–4.

54 Kumakura, 'Sen no Rikyū: Inquiries into his Life and Tea', p. 58.

55 Tsutsui Hiroichi, 'Chanoyu no kashi: Sono seiritsu to tenkai', in *Kaiseki to kashi*, ed. Tsutsui Hiroichi (Kyoto, 1999), p. 303.

56 Sen, *Rikyū hyakkaiki*, pp. 451–60.

57 Ibid., pp. 422–40.

58 The duck dish is called *senba ire*. Ibid., pp. 435–8.

59 Scholars have contended that the rules of *toriawase* so important in modern Kyoto cuisine hark back to tea *kaiseki*. See Murai Yasuhiko, *Buke bunka to dōbōshū* (Tokyo, 1991), p. 312.

60 Kumakura, *Nanpōroku o yomu*, p. 54.

61 Sen, *Rikyū hyakkaiki*, pp. 407–22.

62 This style of dining featured multiple short trays. Guests sat on the floor with a main tray (*honzen*) in front of them and with a second and third tray to the right and left of the main tray. Depending on the occasion and the guest's rank, additional trays could be added behind the second and third trays. For a description of this mode of dining, main tray cuisine (*honzen ryōri*), see Rath, '*Honzen* Dining'.

63 Kumakura, *Nanpōroku o yomu*, p. 141.

64 Kusumi Soan, *Chawa shigetsushū*, in *Nihon no chasho*, ed. Hayashi Tatsusaburō, Yokoi Kiyoshi and Narabayashi Tadao (Tokyo, 1972), vol. II, pp. 16–17.

65 Sen, *Rikyū hyakkaiki*, p. 411.

66 Kumakura, *Nanpōroku o yomu*, p. 9.

67 Tsutsui, *Kaiseki no kenkyū*, p. 90.

68 Kumakura, *Nanpōroku o yomu*, p. 54.

69 Tsutsui, *Kaiseki no kenkyū*, p. 105.

70 Tani, *Chakaiki no kenkyū*, p. 351.

71 Tsutsui, *Kaiseki no kenkyū*, pp. 96–9.

72 We can compare this hypothetical number of 3,431 tea ceremonies, which estimates 73 tea ceremonies a year, with the 50 to 60 teas per year that Tsuda Sōkyū (d. 1591), one of the authors of *Tennōjiya kaiki*, attended in the 1570s (Berry, *The Culture of Civil War in Kyoto*, p. 342). If Rikyū hosted only 50 to 60 teas per year over the course of his 47-year career (1544–91), that would yield between 2,350 and 2,820 tea ceremonies in all, with extant records for just 3 or 4 per cent of the total. Tea practitioners recorded only the more remarkable tea events in their journals, so Tsuda may have attended many more teas that he did not record. Ibid., pp. 271–2. Clearly, the records we have for teas for Rikyū represent a fraction of the many ceremonies he presided over.

73 Unfortunately, *Rikyū's Hundred Teas*, which begins on the seventeenth day of the eighth month of 1590 and ends two months into 1591, does not represent an entire year's worth of tea ceremonies. Thus, we cannot estimate how many tea ceremonies with meals a tea master of Rikyū's stature might have held in a year.

74 Tsutsui, *Kaiseki no kenkyū*, p. 9. In a publication that pre-dates Tsutsui's study, the cultural historian Murai Yasuhiko also commented that this menu was representative of the tea master. Murai, 'Kaiseki ryōri no rekishi', p. 45.

75 Tani, *Chakaiki no kenkyū*, p. 349.

76 Sen Sōshitsu XV, *The Japanese Way of Tea: From its Origins in China to Sen Rikyū*, trans. V. Dixon Morris (Honolulu, HI, 1998), p. 155.

77 Yabe Yoshiaki, *Takeno Jōō: Cha no yu to shōgai* (Kyoto, 2002), pp. 150–58.

78 Harada Nobuo, '"Cha kaiseki" kaidai', in *Nihon ryōri hiden shūsei*, ed. Issunsha, vol. XI, pp. 263–77.

79 Tani, *Chakaiki no kenkyū*, pp. 362–3.

80 Kumakura, 'Sen no Rikyū', p. 58.

81 Kumakura, *Nihon ryōri bunkashi*, p. 116.

82 My translation of 'sake-drenched wheat gluten with kombu' (*sake fu konbu*)

is a literal one, since I have not found a recipe for or a description of this dish elsewhere. The second soup, called an *atsumono*, and the accompanying foods were served at a later stage in the meal and so they were not counted as part of the initial number of dishes. Endō, *Chanoyu kondate shinan*, p. 107.

83 Ibid., pp. 7–8.
84 Ibid., pp. 93–4. The translation is from Rath, *Food and Fantasy in Early Modern Japan*, p. 150.
85 Endō, *Chanoyu kondate shinan*, p. 192.
86 Ibid., pp. 193–4.
87 Kumakura, *Nihon ryōri bunkashi*.
88 Tsutsui, *Kaiseki no kenkyū*, pp. 147, 197, 202.
89 Endō, *Chanoyu kondate shinan*, p. 188.
90 Ibid., p. 94.
91 See Rath, *Food and Fantasy in Early Modern Japan*, pp. 128–47.
92 Endō, *Chanoyu kondate shinan*, p. 120.
93 Ibid., p. 140.
94 Rath, *Food and Fantasy in Early Modern Japan*, p. 141.
95 The 'Akita' bracken (*warabi*) may be from that northern province or it could be another variety. The text indicates 'deep-fried leaves' (*yakiage ha*); that these are perilla leaves is my guess. Imperial Palace persimmons were also called Yamato persimmons in light of their association with that ancient province, which forms modern Nara prefecture. Endō, *Chanoyu kondate shinan*, p. 166.
96 Ibid., p. 189.
97 This translation is adapted from Kumakura, 'Sen no Rikyū', p. 57. The anonymous translator equates (tea food) *kaizen* (literally 'tray for the gathering') in the original text with *kaiseki*, and that correspondence is problematic. See Yabunouchi Chikushin, *Genryū chawa*, in *Chadō koten zenshū*, ed. Sen Sōshitsu, vol. III, p. 438.
98 Sen, *Tea Life, Tea Mind*, p. 74.
99 Gary Sōka Cadwallader and Joseph R. Justice, '*Kaiseki*, Stones for the Belly: Cuisine for Tea during the Early Edo Period', in *Japanese Foodways Past and Present*, ed. Eric C. Rath and Stephanie Assmann (Urbana, IL, 2010), p. 68.
100 These publications include Kumakura, *Nanpōroku o yomu*; Tsutsui, ed., *Kaiseki to kashi*; Tsutsui, *Kaiseki no kenkyū*; and Paul Varley and Kumakura Isao, eds, *Tea in Japan: Essays on the History of Chanoyu* (Honolulu, HI, 1989).
101 Ludwig, 'Chanoyu and Momoyama', pp. 72–3. *Tea in Japan* was partially funded by Urasenke and also contains an essay by the former head of the Urasenke school.
102 Yasunosuke Fukukita, *Cha no Yu: The Tea Cult of Japan* (New York, 1935).

3 Rice and its Identities

1 Historian Harada Nobuo, for instance, partially attributes the prominence of rice in the Japanese diet to the fact that it tastes good. Harada Nobuo, '"Kome shikō" saikō', in *Shokubunka kara shakai ga wakaru!*, ed. Harada Nobuo (Tokyo, 2009), p. 17.

2 Suge Hiroshi, *Ine* (Tokyo, 1998), p. 15.

3 Emiko Ohnuki-Tierney, *Rice as Self: Japanese Identities through Time* (Princeton, NJ, 1993), p. 6.

4 Vaclav Smil and Kazuhiko Kobayashi, *Japan's Dietary Transition and its Impacts* (Cambridge, MA, 2012), p. 13.

5 Masuda Shōko, *Zakkoku no shakaishi* (Tokyo, 2011), p. 63.

6 Miyazaki Yasusada, *Nōgyō zensho*, in *Nihon nōgyō zensho* (Tokyo, 1978), vol. XII, pp. 130–32. The list of types of rice in this source could refer to the same varieties by different names, or the same name could refer to different varieties. Kimura Shigemitsu, *Nihon nōgyōshi* (Tokyo, 2010), p. 187.

7 Susan B. Hanley, *Everyday Things in Premodern Japan: The Hidden Legacy of Material Culture* (Berkeley, CA, 1997), p. 80.

8 *Japan Yearbook* lists 4,000 varieties of rice in cultivation in 1912. Y. Takenob [sic] and K. Kawakami, *Japan Yearbook: Complete Cyclopedia of General Information and Statistics on Japan for the Year 1912* (Tokyo, 1911), p. 302.

9 Jennifer Robertson, 'Sexy Rice: Plant Gender, Farm Manuals, and Grass-roots Nativism', *Monumenta Nipponica*, XXXIX/3 (1984), pp. 233–60.

10 Suge, *Ine*, p. 55.

11 Ehara Ayako, Ishikawa Naoko and Higashiyotsuyanagi Shōko, *Nihon shokumotsushi* (Tokyo, 2009), p. 66.

12 Black rice is different from 'red rice', which has undergone something of a revival in recent years in Japan for its associations with the Nara period (710–784) when it is said to have been widely planted and eaten.

13 The revived versions of red rice such as Beni no Miyako, Kan'nio and Beniroman are said to be much tastier than the varieties grown in premodern Japan. See Ogura Kumeo, Komatsuzaki Takeshi and Hatae Keiko, eds, *Nihon ryōri gyōji, shikitari daijiten* (Tokyo, 2003), vol. I, p. 7.

14 Kimura, *Nihon nōgyōshi*, pp. 233–4.

15 Suge, *Ine*, pp. 65–6.

16 Ōmameuda Minoru, *Okome to shoku no kindaishi* (Tokyo, 2007), p. 6.

17 Alan Davidson, *The Oxford Companion to Food*, 3rd edn, ed. Tom Jaine (New York, 2006), pp. 342–3, 665.

18 Ichikawa Takeo, 'Kaisetsu', in *Zenshū Nihon no shokubunka*, ed. Haga Noboru and Ishikawa Hiroko (Tokyo, 1996), vol. XII, p. 7.

19 Asaoka Kōji, *Nabe, kama* (Tokyo, 1993), p. 71.

20 Except as noted, the following description of processing rice is from Miwa Shigeo, *Usu* (Tokyo, 1978), pp. 107–8.

21 Kimura, *Nihon nōgyōshi*, p. 183.

22 Miwa, *Usu*, p. 112.

23 Grinding 1 *koku* (180 litres of rice) in a revolving mortar typically damaged 1 *shō* and 5 or 6 *gō* (2.7–2.9 litres) of kernels; Miwa, *Usu*, pp. 116, 120.

24 Ehara, Ishikawa and Higashiyotsuyanagi, *Nihon shokumotsushi*, p. 255; Seijō

Daigaku Minzokugaku Kenkyūjo, ed., *Nihon no shokubunka: Shōwa shoki, zenkoku shokuji shūzoku no kiroku* (Tokyo, 1990), p. 266.

25 Arizono Shōichirō, *Kinsei shomin no nichijōshoku: Hyakushō wa kome o taberarenakatta ka?* (Ōtsu, 2007), p. 51.

26 According to the *Agricultural Text from Aizu*, which describes the process, if a farmer threshed from morning to mid-afternoon and then used a rotating mortar for hulling, he could finish 60–70 sheaves of rice, but if a farmer simply threshed all day he could thresh between 90 and 100 sheaves. See Sase Yojiuemon, *Aizu nōsho*, in *Nihon nōgyō zensho*, vol. XII, p. 77. A sheaf of rice consists of eight smaller bundles of rice called *wa*, each of which is made up of eight to twelve rice stalks. Thus a sheaf contains between 64 and 96 stalks of rice. See Yabu Shinobu, *Satoyama, satoumi kurashi zukan: Ima ni ikasu Shōwa no chie* (Tokyo, 2012), pp. 77–8.

27 The core of a rice kernel consists of the endosperm (comprising 91–92 per cent of the kernel) and the embryo, which amounts to 2–3 per cent; Kurosawa Fumio, *Kome to sono kakō* (Tokyo, 1982), p. 21.

28 Ibid., pp. 29–35.

29 Te-tzu Chang, 'Rice', in *The Cambridge World History of Food*, ed. Kenneth F. Kiple and Kriemhild Coneè Ornelas (New York, 2000), vol I, p. 44.

30 Alexander R. Bay covers the debate among Japanese medical professionals and branches of the military about the causes of beriberi in the late nineteenth and early twentieth centuries. See Alexander R. Bay, *Beriberi in Modern Japan: The Making of a National Disease* (Rochester, NY, 2012).

31 Kurosawa, *Kome to sono kakō*, p. 36.

32 Besides brown rice, the government also distributed partially milled rice and rice mixed with other grains such as cracked corn. See Koizumi Kazuko, *Chabudai no Shōwa* (Tokyo, 2002), pp. 46–7.

33 Okumura Ayao, *Nihon men shokubunka no 1300 nen* (Tokyo, 2009), p. 452.

34 Hammer-shaped pestles can be found in Japan dating from the Yayoi period (300 BCE–300 CE), but these did not become widespread until the late seventeenth century; Ishige Naomichi, *Men no bunkashi* (Tokyo, 2006), p. 106. With a hammer, it takes a person two hours to mill 18 litres of rice; Miwa, *Usu*, p. 78.

35 Stone mortars make their appearance during the middle part of the Kamakura period (1185–1333) as tea mortars (*chausu*) used to make powdered tea (*matcha*), however use of these was restricted to the elite. Ibid., p. 105.

36 Ishikawa Hiroko, ed., *Shoku seikatsu to bunka: Shoku no ayumi* (Tokyo, 1988), p. 16; Ōkubo Hiroko, *Edokko wa nani o tabeteita ka* (Tokyo, 2005), p. 13.

37 The technology for both standing mortars and waterwheels to mill grain dates from as early as the eighth century in Japan, but neither became widespread until the early modern period and their use was restricted to urban areas for professional rice millers, flour mills or sake brewers. See Miwa, *Usu*, pp. 70, 73; Okumura, *Nihon men shokubunka no 1300 nen*, p. 290.

38 Yunoki Manabu, *Sakezukuri no rekishi shinsōpan* (Tokyo, 2005), pp. 160–62.

39 Frederick L. Dunn, 'Beriberi', in *The Cambridge World History of Food*, ed. Kiple and Ornelas, vol. I, pp. 915, 917.

40 Barak Kushner, *Slurp! A Social and Cultural History of Ramen – Japan's Favorite Noodle Soup* (Leiden, 2012), p. 94.

41 Bay, *Beriberi in Modern Japan*, p. 7.

42 Dohi Noritaka, *Edo no komeya* (Tokyo, 1981), p. 31.

43 The cost of rice was very volatile in the early modern period, so generalizations are difficult to make and modern equivalents are almost impossible to calculate. In 1829 the price of a little less than eight cups of rice was 124 coppers; in 1834, however, the same amount of rice cost 180 coppers, rising to 250 coppers in the second month of 1837 due to the devastating Tenpō Famine, which drove the price for the same amount of rice to 396 coppers by the seventh month of that year. See Ōkubo, *Edokko wa nani o tabeteita ka*, pp. 13, 26.

44 Takahashi Mikio, *Edo ajiwai zufu* (Tokyo, 1995), pp. 17–18.

45 Arizono, *Kinsei shomin no nichijōshoku*, p. 113.

46 Milling away all of the bran to create the 'white rice' preferred in Japan today further reduces the size of the kernel by 2 per cent. Kurosawa, *Kome to sono kakō*, p. 38. Modern sake making uses even more highly refined rice, where up to 65 per cent of the kernel is milled away to remove undesirable lipids and proteins that might affect the flavour.

47 Ehara, Ishikawa and Higashiyotsuyanagi, *Nihon shokumotsushi*, p. 239. When rice is polished there is about a 1 per cent reduction in protein: 100 grams of brown rice contains 338 calories, 7.4 grams of protein and 71.8 grams of carbohydrate, but the same amount of uncooked white rice yields 352 calories, 6.8 grams protein and 75.8 grams of carbohydrate. The amounts are almost the same for glutinous rice. Kurosawa, *Kome to sono kakō*, p. 29.

48 An early twentieth-century mode of polishing rice to remove all of the bran except for the germ created a type of semi-polished rice called *haigamai*, but the taste was found wanting. *Haigamai* is polished to leave 91–93 per cent of the kernel, and the result retains more B-complex vitamins than are present in white rice.

49 See Bay, *Beriberi in Modern Japan*, p. 128.

50 Ōshima Akeo, 'Shōwa shoki ni okeru kome no suihanhō to yōgu: Jikyoku no kakawari kara', in *Shoku no Shōwa bunkashi*, ed. Tanaka Nobutada and Matsuzaki Kenzō (Tokyo, 1995), p. 163.

51 The amount used to calculate per capita consumption also includes unpolished seed rice. Ōmameuda, *Okome to shoku no kindaishi*, p. 43. With premodern growing techniques, an estimate of the amount of rice crop that must be held back for seed is 1 to 2 per cent; Hanley, *Everyday Things in Premodern Japan*, p. 68.

52 Arizono, *Kinsei shomin no nichijōshoku*, p. 48. The Portuguese Jesuit João Rodrigues observed that in the last decades of the sixteenth century, one-third of the rice grown was used for sake making; cited in Harada Nobuo, '"Kome shikō' saikō", p. 20.

53 Nakayama Keiko, *Wagashi monogatari* (Tokyo, 1993), p. 13.

54 For a discussion of *mochi*, particularly their symbolism, see Eric C. Rath, 'The Magic of Japanese Rice Cakes', in *Routledge History of Food*, ed. Carol Helstosky (New York, 2015), pp. 3–18.

55 Ichikawa, 'Kaisetsu', p. 6.

56 Segawa Kiyoko, *Shoku seikatsu no rekishi* (Tokyo, 2001), p. 36.

57 Matsuyama Toshio, *Ko no mi* (Tokyo, 1982), p. 193.

58 Okumura, *Nihon men shokubunka no 1300 nen*, p. 290.

59 Masuda Shōko, *Awa to hie no shokubunka* (Tokyo, 1990), p. 12.

60 Masuda Shōko, *Zakkoku no shakaishi* (Tokyo, 2011), p. 53.

61 Regarding the impact of the rice cooker on cooking and household labour, see Helen Macnaughtan, 'Building up Steam as Consumers: Women, Rice Cookers and the Consumption of Everyday Household Goods', in *The Historical Consumer: Consumption and Everyday Life in Japan, 1850–2000*, ed. Penelope Francks and Janet Hunter (New York, 2012), pp. 79–104.

62 Suzuki Shigeo, 'Mochi no hanashi are kore', *Koko chishin*, 15 (1978), p. 27.

63 Glutinous rice becomes pasty when boiled, as we have seen.

64 Ehara, Ishikawa and Higashiyotsuyanagi, *Nihon shokumotsushi*, pp. 27, 29, 33.

65 Matsushita Sachiko, *Zusetsu Edo ryōri jiten* (Tokyo, 1996), p. 10; Ōshima, 'Shōwa shoki ni okeru kome no suihanhō to yōgu', p. 146. Ehara, Ishikawa and Higashiyotsuyanagi, *Nihon shokumotsushi*, p. 61; Asaoka, *Nabe, kama*, pp. 19, 41.

66 In some instances this pasty slime was eaten in a dish called *omoyu* as a food meant for sick people and infants. See Seijō Daigaku Minzokugaku Kenkyūjo, ed., *Nihon no shokubunka, hoi hen: Shōwa shoki, zenkoku shokuji shūzoku no kiroku* (Tokyo, 1995), p. 270.

67 Matsushita, *Zusetsu Edo jidai ryōri jiten*, p. 33.

68 Seijō Daigaku Minzokugaku Kenkyūjo, *Nihon no shokubunka, hoi hen*, p. 268.

69 Shōsekiken Sōken, *Ryōri mōmoku chōmishō*, in *Nihon ryōri hiden shūsei: Genten gendaigoyaku*, ed. Issunsha (Kyoto, 1985), vol. I, p. 251; Ōshima, 'Shōwa shoki ni okeru kome no suihanhō to yōgu', p. 147.

70 Murakami Akiko, *Daidokoro tomodachi: Nabe, kama, shichirin, hōchō, manaita, suribachi, shokudai* (Tokyo, 1987), pp. 51–2.

71 Kurosawa, *Kome to sono kakō*, p. 69.

72 *Meihan burui*, in *Nihon ryōri hiden shūsei*, ed. Issunsha, vol. IX, pp. 219–20.

73 Asaoka, *Nabe, kama*, p. 78; Koizumi Kazuko, *Shōwa daidokoro natsukashi zukan* (Tokyo, 1998), pp. 94–5. An earlier version of this passage about cooking rice appears in Eric C. Rath, 'Sex and Sea Bream: Food and Prostitution in Hishikawa Moronobu's *Visit to Yoshiwara*', in *Seduction: Japan's Floating World: The John C. Weber Collection*, ed. Laura W. Allen (San Francisco, 2015), pp. 40–41, 43.

74 Asaoka, *Nabe, kama*, p. 47.

75 Mitamura Yoshiko, 'Nabe, kama, tetsubin: Imono sanchi, Kawaguchi ni okeru komono nichijōhin no seisaku gijutsu', in *Shoku seikatsu to mingu*, ed. Nihon Mingu Gakkai (Tokyo, 1993), p. 105.

76 Koizumi, *Shōwa daidokoro natsukashi zukan*, p. 94.

77 *Kamado* had spread to the eastern parts of Japan by the late sixth century. Ōshima, 'Shōwa shoki ni okeru kome no suihanhō to yōgu', pp. 145–6, 153.

78 Penelope Francks, *The Japanese Consumer: An Alternative Economic History of Modern Japan* (New York, 2009), p. 36; Koizumi, *Shōwa daidokoro natsukashi zukan*, p. 117.

79 *Kamado* used in Edo had a hole for inserting firewood at the front; people in Osaka preferred *kamado* without that opening, and they fed in firewood from the side of the stove. Ehara, Ishikawa and Higashiyotsuyanagi, *Nihon shokumotsushi*, p. 170.

80 Ehara Ayako and Higashiyotsuyanagi Shōko, *Kindai ryōrisho no sekai* (Tokyo, 2008), p. 26.

81 Shimoda Utako, *Ryōri tebikisō*, in *Kindai ryōrisho shūsei*, ed. Ehara Ayako (Tokyo, 2012), vol. III, pp. 194–5.

82 *Meihan burui*, p. 219.

83 Shōsekiken, *Ryōri mōmoku chōmishō*, p. 251. The same author also included the tip about rescuing burned rice by adding a little sake to it. Ibid., p. 251.

84 Kushner, *Slurp!*, p. 139.

85 Jordan Sand, *House and Home in Modern Japan: Architecture, Domestic Space, and Bourgeois Culture, 1880–1930* (Cambridge, MA, 2003), p. 69.

86 Murai Gensai, *Daidokoro chōhōki* (Tokyo, 2001), pp. 17–19.

87 Ibid., p. 23. Water left over from washing rice can also be used as a stock and thickener for soup, but Murai omitted these tips.

88 Ehara, Ishikawa and Higashiyotsuyanagi, *Nihon shokumotsushi*, pp. 169–70.

89 Ōkubo Hiroko, *Edo no fāsuto fūdo* (Tokyo, 1998), p. 120.

90 Kitagawa Morisada, *Morisada mankō*, ed. Asakura Haruhiko and Kashikawa Shūichi (Tokyo, 1992), vol. V, pp. 40, 43.

91 Arizono, *Kinsei shomin no nichijōshoku*, p. 113.

92 Sand, *House and Home in Modern Japan*, pp. 78–9.

93 Hanley, *Everyday Things in Premodern Japan*, p. 63.

94 Ishige, *Men no bunkashi*, p. 104.

95 Whole barley can also be roasted then boiled to make barley tea (*mugicha*). Roasted barley pounded into flour can be eaten as a dough called *hattai* or *mugikogashi* when mixed with hot water and sometimes sugar.

96 Matsushita, *Zusetsu Edo jidai ryōri jiten*, p. 32.

97 Ishige, *Men no bunkashi*, p. 103.

98 Rolled barley (*oshimugi*), which requires high-pressure processing to create, was introduced to Japan in the twentieth century; Ishige, *Men no bunkashi*, p. 104.

99 *Meihan burui*, pp. 220–21.

100 Ehara, Ishikawa and Higashiyotsuyanagi, *Nihon shokumotsushi*, p. 59; Arizono, *Kinsei shomin no nichijōshoku*, p. 5.

101 Yoshida Hajime, *Nihon no shoku to sake: Chūsei no hakkō gijutsu o chūshin ni* (Tokyo, 1991), p. 132.

102 *Meihan burui*, pp. 220–21.

103 Kitagawa, *Morisada mankō*, vol. V, p. 40.

104 *Mugimeshi o, jōzu na nyobō, gaseimono*. From Karai Sen'ryū (1718–1790), *Senryū hyōman kuawase*, published in 1761; Watanabe Shin'ichiro, *Edo no onnatachi no gurume jijō: Ezu to sen'ryū ni miru shokubunka* (Tokyo, 1994), p. 72.

105 Kitagawa, *Morisada mankō*, vol. V, p. 40.

106 See Segawa, *Shoku seikatsu no rekishi*, p. 56.

107 Koizumi, *Chabudai no Shōwa*, pp. 8–9.

108 The proportion of rice was higher in some regions, such as Shiga, where *mugimeshi* was 80 per cent rice. Arizono, *Kinsei shomin no nichijōshoku*, pp. 4–5.

109 Katrzyna Cwiertka, *Modern Japanese Cuisine: Food, Power and National Identity* (London, 2006), p. 69.

110 Koizumi, *Chabudai no Shōwa*, pp. 8–9.

111 The author also noted the cost of the gas needed to cook the grains. The cost of gas was 1 *sen* and 2 *mō*, the same as for cooking rice, but the author noted that the cost was slightly higher in the winter. Akiho Masumi, *Katei wayō hoken shokuryō: Sanshoku kondate oyobi ryōrihō*, in *Kindai ryōrisho shūsei*, ed. Ehara

Ayako (Tokyo, 2012), vol. IV, pp. 46–8, 84–5.

112 Penelope Francks, 'Consuming Rice: Food, "Traditional" Products and the History of Consumption in Japan', *Japan Forum*, XIX/2 (2007), p. 158.

113 Segawa, *Shoku seikatsu no rekishi*, p. 56.

114 Takashi Nagatsuka, *The Soil: A Portrait of Rural Life in Meiji Japan*, trans. Ann Waswo (Berkeley, CA, 1989), p. 67.

115 Segawa, *Shoku seikatsu no rekishi*, p. 19.

116 Ōmameuda, *Okome to shoku no kindaishi*, p. 67.

117 Ehara, Ishikawa and Higashiyotsuyanagi, *Nihon shokumotsushi*, p. 255.

118 Nomoto Kyōko, 'Shoku seikatsu', in *Nihon sonrakushi kōza*, ed. Nihon Sonrakushi Kōza Henshū Iinkai (Tokyo, 1991), vol. VIII, pp. 161–2.

119 John Mock, *Culture, Community and Change in a Sapporo Neighborhood, 1925–1988: Hanayama* (New York, 1999), pp. 26–7.

120 Kerry Smith, *A Time of Crises: Japan, the Great Depression, and Rural Revitalization* (Cambridge, MA, 2001), p. 46.

121 Yano Keiichi, *'Katei no aji' no sengo minzokushi: Shufu to danraku no jidai* (Tokyo, 2007), p. 35.

122 Penelope Francks provides a table of per capita rice consumption, 1878–1937. See Penelope Francks, 'Rice for the Masses: Food Policy and the Adoption of Imperial Self-sufficiency in Early Twentieth-century Japan', *Japan Forum*, XV/1 (2003), p. 131.

123 Koizumi, *Chabudai no Shōwa*, pp. 8–9.

124 Masuda Shōko, 'Zakkoku no yūretsukan', in *Shoku no Shōwa bunkashi*, ed. Tanaka Nobutada and Matsuzaki Kenzō (Tokyo, 1995), p. 48; Tanaka Nobutada, 'Gochisō to shokubunka', in *Shoku no Shōwa bunkashi*, ed. Tanaka and Matsuzaki, p. 86.

125 Cwiertka, *Modern Japanese Cuisine*, p. 79.

126 Masuda, *Zakkoku no shakaishi*, pp. 2–3, 45.

127 Nomoto, 'Shoku seikatsu', pp. 161, 164.

128 Masuda, *Zakkoku no shakaishi*, p. 45.

129 Chapter Five describes this survey in further detail.

130 Tanaka, 'Gochisō to shokubunka', p. 85.

131 Hori's essay is included in the appendix of Seijō Daigaku Minzokugaku Kenkyūjo, ed., *Nihon no shokubunka, hoi hen*, pp. 317–18. He quotes the amount of rationed rice as being 2 *gō*, 5 *shaku* (450 ml).

132 By comparison, military rations in the 1920s and 1930s amounted to about one and a half cups (350 ml) of barley mixed with rice per person per meal. See Cwiertka, *Modern Japanese Cuisine*, p. 79.

133 Seijō Daigaku Minzokugaku Kenkyūjo, ed., *Nihon no shokubunka, hoi hen*, p. 273.

134 Cited in Segawa, *Shoku seikatsu no rekishi*, pp. 36–7.

135 Nomoto, 'Shoku seikatsu', pp. 158–9.

136 Mikiso Hane, *Peasants, Rebels, Women and Outcastes: The Underside of Modern Japan* (New York, 1982), pp. 40–41.

137 Simon Partner, *Toshié: A Story of Village Life in Twentieth-century Japan* (Berkeley, CA, 2004), p. 13.

138 Presumably these were sweet potato leaves, since the leaves of white potatoes are poisonous. Seijō Daigaku Minzokugaku Kenkyūjo, ed., *Nihon no shokubunka, hoi hen*, pp. 264–5, 328.

139 Ibid., pp. 264–5.
140 Shimoda, *Ryōri tebikisō*, p. 199.
141 *Ryōri monogatari*, in *Nihon ryōri hiden shūsei*, ed. Issunsha, vol. I, p. 49.
142 Shōsekiken, *Ryōri mōmoku chōmishō*, p. 252.
143 Takeuchi Yukiko, 'Chōri to jendā', in *Shokubunka kara shakai ga wakaru!*, ed. Harada Nobuo (Tokyo, 2009), pp. 103–4.
144 Masuda, *Zakkoku no shakaishi*, pp. 4–8.
145 Masuda, 'Zakkoku no yūretsukan', pp. 48–9.
146 Masuda, *Zakkoku no shakaishi*, pp. 15–16, 24, 28, 252–3. Despite the many negative associations of barley and millets, these grains also had a positive image throughout Japan, and in some places foods made from them were used in ritual celebrations such as those at New Year. Masuda provides an exhaustive list of these places. Ibid., pp. 88–240.
147 Sand, *House and Home in Modern Japan*, p. 33.
148 Richard K. Beardsley, John W. Hall and Robert E. Ward, *Village Japan* (Chicago, IL, 1959), p. III.
149 Ohnuki-Tierney, *Rice as Self*, p. 9.

4 The Making of the Modern Boxed Lunch

1 Cited in Hirano Masaki, *Washoku no rireki: Shokuzai o meguru jūgo no monogatari* (Kyoto, 1997), p. 189.
2 Kenji Ekuan presents a meditation about how bentō encapsulate a unique technology of design central to Japanese civilization. Lacking documentation, his book is less an argument about bentō than a slide show of stunning photos and short paragraphs about the uniqueness and profundity of Japanese culture. Kenji Ekuan, *The Aesthetics of the Japanese Lunchbox*, ed. Daniel B. Stewart (Cambridge, MA, 1998), p. x.
3 Although gender roles are changing in Japan, fathers generally do not participate in the daily routine of bentō making for their children. Before the advent of a national school lunch programme in 1952, all students in the modern school system (with only a few exceptions, mentioned below), were required to bring a bentō from home, whereas today usually only kindergarten (*yōchien*) students eat homemade bentō at school.
4 Anne Allison, 'Japanese Mothers and Obentōs: The Lunch-Box as Ideological State Apparatus', *Anthropological Quarterly*, LXIV/4 (1991), p. 202.
5 Tomoko Onabe, 'Bentō: Boxed Love, Eaten by the Eye', in *Japanese Foodways Past and Present*, ed. Eric C. Rath and Stephanie Assmann (Urbana, IL, 2010), p. 210.
6 Japan's first railway connected Tokyo to Yokohama in 1872. The railway line from Ueno in Tokyo to Takazaki in Gunma prefecture was the first to sell *ekiben*, in 1883. Takada Masatoshi, 'Tetsudō no tabi to ekiben', *Tabi to shoku*, ed. Kanzaki Noritake (Tokyo, 2002), pp. 174, 176–7.
7 Shintani Takanori and Sekizawa Mayumi, *Minzoku kojiten: Shoku* (Tokyo, 2013), p. 34; Hirano, *Washoku no rireki*, p. 181; Harada Nobuo, *Edo no ryōri to shoku seikatsu* (Tokyo, 2004), p. 135.
8 Hirano, *Washoku no rireki*, p. 174.

9   Ishikawa Hiroko, ed., *Shoku seikatsu to bunka: Shoku no ayumi* (Tokyo, 1988), p. 219.

10 Ehara Ayako, Ishikawa Naoko and Higashiyotsuyanagi Shōko, *Nihon shokumotsushi* (Tokyo, 2009), p. 261.

11 Yamashita Saburō, Satō Kazuko and Nashihara Hiroshi, 'Jidai bentōbako shiryō shūsei', *Tōhoku kōgyō daigaku kiyō rikōgaku hen*, I (1981), pp. 96–140; II (1982), p. 122.

12 Ibid., p. 104.

13 Yoshikawa Seiji, 'Bentō konjaku monogatari', in *Zenshū Nihon no shokubunka*, ed. Haga Noboru and Ishikawa Hiroko (Tokyo, 1997), vol. X, p. 142.

14 The term for these leaf plates is *kaishiki*. Nakamura Kōhei, *Shinpan Nihon ryōri gogenshū* (Tokyo, 2004), p. 131.

15 Nishimura Kenji, ed., *Kikigaki Mie no shokuji*, in *Nihon no shoku seikatsu zenshū* (Tokyo, 1987), vol. XXIX, pp. 110, 185.

16 Honma Nobuo, ed., *Kikigaki Niigata no shokuji*, in *Nihon no shoku seikatsu zenshū* (Tokyo, 1985), vol. XV, pp. 22–3, 64, 89.

17 The term *warigo* appears in Ki no Tsurayuki's (*c.* 868–945) *Tosa Diary* (*Tosa nikki*). Nagayama Hisao, *Nihon kodai shoku jiten* (Tokyo, 1998), p. 444.

18 Honma, ed., *Kikigaki Niigata no shokuji*, pp. 22–3, 89.

19 Watanabe Zenjirō, ed., *Kikigaki Tōkyō no shokuji*, in *Nihon no shoku seikatsu zenshū*, vol. XIII (Tokyo, 1988), pp. 16–17.

20 Fujimoto Kōnosuke, *Kikigaki Meiji no kodomo asobi to kurashi* (Tokyo, 1986), pp. 314–15.

21 Bunkachō, *Shoku seikatsu*, vol. IX of *Nihon minzoku chizu* (Tokyo, 1988), p. 17.

22 Hirano, *Washoku no rireki*, p. 184.

23 Ehara, Ishikawa and Higashiyotsuyanagi, *Nihon shokumotsushi*, p. 182.

24 Ehara Ayako and Higashiyotsuyanagi Shōko, *Nihon no shokubunkashi nenpyō* (Tokyo, 2011), p. 164.

25 See, for example, Ishikawa, *Shoku seikatsu to bunka*, p. 159.

26 Ehara, Ishikawa and Higashiyotsuyanagi, *Nihon shokumotsushi*, p. 181.

27 Seijō Daigaku Minzokugaku Kenkyūjo, ed., *Nihon no shokubunka, hoi hen: Shōwa shoki, zenkoku shokuji shūzoku no kiroku* (Tokyo, 1995), pp. 316–17.

28 The surveys presented as the series *Nihon no shoku seikatsu zenshū* are described in Chapter Six.

29 Honma, *Kikigaki Niigata no shokuji*, p. 89.

30 Horse chestnuts had to be soaked in lye to make them edible. Ema Mieko, *Hida no onnatachi* (Tokyo, 1998), pp. 113–15.

31 Nishimura, *Kikigaki Mie no shokuji*, pp. 27–9.

32 Harada Kakurō, ed., *Kikigaki Saga no shokuji*, in *Nihon no shoku seikatsu zenshū* (Tokyo, 1991), vol. XLI, pp. 18–19, 30, 35.

33 Segawa Kiyoko, *Shoku seikatsu no rekishi* (Tokyo, 2001), p. 207.

34 Ishige Naomichi, *Ishige Naomichi shoku no bunka o kataru* (Tokyo, 2009), pp. 214–15.

35 Seijō Daigaku Minzokugaku Kenkyūjo, ed. *Nihon no shokubunka, hoi hen*, pp. 298, 328.

36 Ehara, Ishikawa and Higashiyotsuyanagi, *Nihon shokumotsushi*, pp. 169–70.

37 Watanabe, *Kikigaki Tōkyō no shokuji*, pp. 64–5, 70, 99.

38 Ehara, Ishikawa and Higashiyotsuyanagi, *Nihon shokumotsushi*, pp. 261–2.

39 For a survey of the most elaborate early modern and Meiji-period bentō

containers meant for pleasure outings, see Yamashita, Satō and Nashihara, 'Jidai bentōbako shiryō shūsei', I, pp. 96–107.

40 Ōta Yasuhiro, *Nihon shokubunka tosho mokuroku Edo – kindai* (Tokyo, 2008), p. 180.

41 Daigo Sanjin, *Ryōri hayashinan*, in *Nihon ryōri hiden shūsei: Genten gendaigoyaku* (Kyoto, 1985), vol. IV, p. 67.

42 Ibid., p. 82.

43 Ibid., p. 87.

44 Ibid., p. 96.

45 Ibid., p. 97.

46 Ibid., p. 98.

47 Ehara, Ishikawa and Higashiyotsuyanagi, *Nihon shokumotsushi*, p. 229.

48 Jordan Sand, *House and Home in Modern Japan: Architecture, Domestic Space, and Bourgeois Culture, 1880–1930* (Cambridge, MA, 2003), p. 60.

49 Anzai Komako, *Shiki mainichi sanshoku ryōrihō* (Tokyo, 1909), p. 65.

50 Ibid., p. 1.

51 Ehara and Higashiyotsuyanagi, *Kindai ryōrisho no sekai*, pp. 106, 150.

52 Akiho Masumi, *Katei wayō hoken shokuryō: Sanshoku kondate oyobi ryōriho*, in *Kindai ryōrisho shūsei*, ed. Ehara Ayako (Tokyo, 2012), vol. IV, pp. 9, 12–13.

53 Ibid., pp. 12–14, 16–21.

54 Ibid., p. 96.

55 The Japanese name of the chicken dish is *kotoretto shanpondo*. I am grateful to Ken Albala for identifying this recipe for me.

56 Vaclav Smil and Kazuhiko Kobayashi, *Japan's Dietary Transition and its Impacts* (Cambridge, MA, 2012), p. 2.

57 The name of the small kudzu crackers is *Yoshino arare*. The Yoshino area of Nara prefecture was famous for its high-quality kudzu flour. *Arare* are a type of small *senbei*, indicative of the literal meaning of *arare*: hailstone. Akiho, *Katei wayō hoken shokuryō*, pp. 90, 263–8.

58 Sand, *House and Home in Modern Japan*, p. 257.

59 Kamijima Sachiko, ed., *Kikigaki Ōsaka no shokuji*, in *Nihon no shoku seikatsu zenshū* (Tokyo, 1991), vol. XXVII, p. 110.

60 Ehara Ayako and Higashiyotsuyanagi Shōko, *Kindai ryōrisho no sekai* (Tokyo, 2008), pp. 104–5.

61 Fujimura Munetaro, *Nichiyō benri bentō ryōri annai* (Tokyo, 1905), p. 1.

62 Ibid., p. 6.

63 Ibid., pp. 2–3, 5.

64 Ibid., p. 7.

65 Ibid., pp. 57, 80, 109. Richard Hosking, *A Dictionary of Japanese Food: Ingredients and Culture* (New York, 1996), p. 92.

66 Fujimura, *Nichiyō benri bentō ryōri annai*, pp. 79–95.

67 Ehara Ayako, 'Dai kyūkan, bentō, tsukemono', in *Kindai ryōrisho shūsei* (Tokyo, 2013), vol. IX, p. 2.

68 Nishino Miyoshi, *Wayō shiki bentō ryōri kazugazu* (Tokyo, 1916), pp. 15–16, 32–3, 74–5, 87–8, 101, 118, 171, 182, 229–30.

69 Ibid., p. i.

70 Ibid., pp. 9, 45–7, 64–8.

71 Ibid., pp. 7, 165–6.

72 Ibid., pp. 10, 12–13, 20–21, 28–9, 222–3.

73 Nishino includes a recipe for whole lobster with ground pepper; see ibid., pp. 61–2.

74 Heibonsha and Miraisha, eds, *Shinpen jūdai ni nani o tabetaka* (Tokyo, 2004), pp. 345–6.

75 Nomoto Kyōko, 'Shoku seikatsu', in *Nihon Sonrakushi Kōza*, ed. Nihon Sonrakushi Kōza Henshū Iinkai (Tokyo, 1991), vol. VIII, p. 165.

76 Ehara, Ishikawa and Higashiyotsuyanagi, *Nihon shokumotsushi*, p. 264; Ishikawa, ed., *Shoku seikatsu to bunka*, p. 223.

77 Hausu Shokuhin Kabushikigaisha Hībushitsu, ed., *Meiji, Taishō, Shōwa no shokutaku* (Tokyo, 2001), p. 43.

78 Dai Nippon Ryōri Kenkyūkai, *Tsūgaku jidō eiyō bentō jūni kagetsu*, in *Kindai ryōrisho shūsei*, ed. Ehara Ayako (Tokyo, 2013), vol. IX, p. 1.

79 Ibid., pp. 1–2.

80 Ibid., pp. 3–4.

81 Ibid., p. 11.

82 Ibid., pp. 44, 45, 46, 47, 56, 70.

83 Ibid., pp. 24, 44.

84 Katarzyna Cwiertka, *Modern Japanese Cuisine: Food, Power and National Identity* (London, 2006), pp. 101–2; Dai Nippon Ryōri Kenkyūkai, *Tsūgaku jidō eiyō bentō jūni kagetsu*, p. 13.

85 Dai Nippon Ryōri Kenkyūkai, *Tsūgaku jidō eiyō bentō jūni kagetsu*, pp. 12, 13, 29, 82.

5 National People's Cuisine

1 The term *kokuminshoku* juxtaposes *shoku*, which can refer to food or a cuisine, with the word *kokumin*, meaning citizens, itself a compound word that identifies the people (*min*) with the nation (*koku*). Barak Kushner translates *kokuminshoku* as 'people's national food'. See Barak Kushner, *Slurp! A Social and Culinary History of Ramen – Japan's Favorite Noodle Soup* (Leiden, 2012), p. 146. To render *shoku* into English, I use the word cuisine instead of food to highlight the ideological dimensions of *kokuminshoku*.

2 Recent research on ramen by Barak Kushner, Satomi Fukutomi and George Solt has alerted us to the way ramen is now the 'people's food' *par excellence*. See Kushner, *Slurp!*; Satomi Fukutomi, 'Connoisseurship of B-grade Culture: Consuming Japanese National Food Ramen', PhD dissertation, Department of Anthropology, University of Hawai'i at Manoa, 2010; and George Solt, *The Untold History of Ramen: How Political Crises in Japan Spawned a Global Food Craze* (Berkeley, CA, 2014). Wartime *kokuminshoku* needs greater academic study.

3 As of October 2012, some 42 countries banned imports of select Japanese foodstuffs after the March 2011 nuclear disaster. See Kyodo News International, 'Japan Aims to Have HK Lift Ban on Japanese Food Imports', www.globalpost. com, 15 August 2013. Many of these bans still remain in place as of May 2015.

4 Native ethnologists (*minzokugakusha*), sometimes referred to as folklorists, are a different group from professional ethnologists working in universities. Prominent members of the latter group also supported Japanese militarism and imperialism as described in Kevin Michael Doak, 'Building National Identity

through Ethnicity: Ethnology in Wartime Japan and After', *Journal of Japanese Studies*, XXVII/1 (2001), pp. 1–39.

5 The conclusions of these wartime ethnologists resonate with recent studies of nationalism, which find national identity performed in the prosaic activities of daily life. See, for example, Michael Billig, *Banal Nationalisms* (London, 1995), and Tim Edensor, *National Identity and Everyday Life* (New York, 2002). Kristin Surak provides compelling reference to the ideas of these scholars in the context of modern Japan in her study of the tea ceremony. See Kristin Surak, *Making Tea, Making Japan: Cultural Nationalism in Practice* (Stanford, CA, 2013).

6 The classic account of wartime austerity and suffering is Thomas H. Havens, *Valley of Darkness: The Japanese People and World War Two* (New York, 1978). For Havens's account of the domestic food situation, see ibid., pp. 114–32.

7 'Seventy-per-cent-milled-rice' (*shichibumai*, also called *shichibu tzukimai*), which left 30 per cent of the bran, became the legal standard for rice milling in 1939. See Alexander R. Bay, *Beriberi in Modern Japan: The Making of a National Disease* (Rochester, NY, 2012), p. 128.

8 Ehara Ayako, Ishikawa Naoko and Higashiyotsuyanagi Shōko, *Nihon shokumotsushi* (Tokyo, 2009), p. 266; Jerome B. Cohen, *Japan's Economy in War and Reconstruction* (Minneapolis, MN, 1949), p. 362.

9 Yoshida Kikujirō, *Seiyōgashi Nihon no ayumi* (Tokyo, 2012), p. 350.

10 *Asahi Shimbun*, 6 October 1940, p. 7, accessed through Kikuzō II Bijuaru Dijitaru Nyūsu Ākaibu, http://database.asahi.com.

11 Benjamin Uchiyama, personal correspondence, 2 September 2013; Benjamin Uchiyama, 'Carnival War: A Cultural History of Wartime Japan, 1937–1945', PhD dissertation, University of Southern California (2013), p. 123.

12 Yano Keiichi notes the crucial role of the IRAA in popularizing the term *kokuminshoku* from 1940. Yano Keiichi, *'Katei no aji' no sengo minzokushi: Shufu to danraku no jidai* (Tokyo, 2007), p. 43.

13 See, for instance, Fujimoto Kōtarō, 'Senji Doitsu kokumin shokuryō mondai', *Kokumin keizai zasshi*, XVIII/4 (1915), pp. 89–109.

14 Lizzie Collingham, *The Taste of War: World War Two and the Battle for Food* (New York, 2011), p. 25.

15 There was considerable factionalism and disunity in the IRAA. See Havens, *Valley of Darkness*, pp. 56, 59, 61.

16 *Asahi Shimbun*, 1 March 1941, p. 4, accessed through Kikuzō II Bijuaru Dijitaru Nyūsu Ākaibu, http://database.asahi.com.

17 Ehara, Ishikawa and Higashiyotsuyanagi, *Nihon shokumotsushi*, p. 277.

18 *Asahi Shimbun*, 1 March 1941, p. 4.

19 Katarzyna Cwiertka, *Modern Japanese Cuisine: Food, Power and National Identity* (London, 2006), p. 132.

20 Nihon Sekijūjisha, *Senji kokuminshoku* (Tokyo, 1941), p. 8.

21 Taisei Yokusankai Bunkabu, ed., *Kokumin to eiyō* (Tokyo, 1942), pp. 28–9.

22 *Asahi Shimbun*, 4 March 1941, p. 4, accessed through Kikuzō II Bijuaru Dijitaru Nyūsu Ākaibu, http://database.asahi.com.

23 *Asahi Shimbun*, 5 March 1941, p. 4, accessed through Kikuzō II Bijuaru Dijitaru Nyūsu Ākaibu, http://database.asahi.com.

24 *Asahi Shimbun*, 11 March 1941, p. 4; ibid., 12 March 1941, p. 4, accessed through

Kikuzō 11 Bijuaru Dijitaru Nyūsu Ākaibu, http://database.asahi.com.

25 Nihon Sekijūjisha, *Senji kokuminshoku*, p. 10.
26 Richard J. Smethurst, *Agricultural Development and Tenancy Disputes in Japan, 1870–1940* (Princeton, NJ, 1986), p. 67.
27 The estimates for food supply are from Vaclav Smil and Kazuhiko Kobayashi, *Japan's Dietary Transition and its Impacts* (Cambridge, MA, 2012), pp. 81–3.
28 Additionally, Yano Keiichi mentions a three-part film made in 1941 titled *Kokuminshoku*. See Yano, 'Katei no aji' no sengo minzokushi, p. 44.
29 The event is mentioned briefly in Ehara, Ishikawa and Higashiyotsuyanagi, *Nihon shokumotsushi*, pp. 276–7.
30 Nihon Sekijūjisha, *Senji kokuminshoku*, pp. 48–244.
31 Katō Toshiko, *Kokuminshoku: Eiyō kondate sanbyaku rokujū go nichi*, in *Kindai ryōrisho shūsei*, vol. XI, ed. Ehara Ayako (Tokyo, 2013), p. 3.
32 Ibid., p. 49.
33 Modern recipes for *kaki zōsui* (oyster porridge) also add chopped shiitake, mitsuba and egg. See Nakamura Kōhei, *Shinpan Nihon ryōri gogenshū* (Tokyo, 2004), p. 138.
34 Kanagawaken Shokuryō Eidan, *Kessen shoku seikatsu kufūshū* (Osaka, 1944), pp. 183, 186–7.
35 Smil and Kobayashi, *Japan's Dietary Transition and its Impacts*, p. 78. A much earlier estimate pegs the average caloric intake in Japan in 1945 at 1,680 calories. Cohen, *Japan's Economy in War and Reconstruction*, p. 386.
36 Kanagawaken Shokuryō Eidan, *Kessen shoku seikatsu kufūshū*, p. 1.
37 The IRAA convened regional commissions in early 1941 to undertake study of the problems of food shortages and nutrition in the process of defining national people's cuisine. Tanaka Nobutada, '"Shoku saishū techō" to "Shokushū chōsa"', in *Nihon no shokubunka: Shōwa shoki, zenkoku shokuji shūzoku no kiroku*, ed. Seijō Daigaku Minzokugaku Kenkyūjo (Tokyo, 1990), p. 657.
38 Yokusan Undōshi Kankōkai, *Yokusan kokumin undōshi* (Tokyo, 1954), p. 381.
39 Hashiura was active in leftist politics in the first two decades of the twentieth century after which he became Yanagita's 'right-hand man'. See Alan Christy, *A Discipline on Foot: Inventing Japanese Native Ethnography, 1910–1945* (New York, 2012), pp. 32–3. Regarding folkloric research on Japanese food in the 1920s, see Tanaka, '"Shoku saishū techō" to "Shokushū chōsa"', p. 654. Yanagita's first publication about food was *Foodstuffs and the Heart* (*Shokumotsu to shinzō*), which appeared in 1932. See Yanagita Kunio, *Shokumotsu to shinzō* (Tokyo, 1977).
40 So noted Yanagita's disciple, the food scholar Segawa Kiyoko, in her afterword to Yanagita's study of food culture, ibid., p. 230.
41 Fukamizu Seisaku (also called Fukamizu Shōsaku) was born in Nagano and travelled and studied in Europe and the United States. He wrote and illustrated children's books, including, with Akiko Nitta as the author, *Chiisana hanataba* (Tokyo, 1937). From 1935 to 1940 he was a teacher at Seijō Gakuen, the middle and high school associated with Seijō University. He also taught English at Seijō Elementary School while working for the Imperial Rule Assistance Association, but his exact position within the IRAA is not clear. He was a close associate of Yanagita's from the mid-1930s. See Tanaka, '"Shoku saishū techō" to "Shokushū chōsa"', p. 657.
42 Christy, *A Discipline on Foot*, pp. 217, 221–3. For details of Hashiura's

involvement in the food survey and his interaction with Yanagita, see Seijō Daigaku Minzokugaku Kenkyūjo, ed., *Nihon no shokubunka*, p. i.

43 Tessa Morris-Suzuki, 'The Invention and Reinvention of "Japanese Culture"', *Journal of Asian Studies*, LIV/3 (1995), p. 767.

44 The preface appeared in the printed booklets sent to fieldworkers. Tanaka, '"Shoku saishū techō" to "Shokushū chōsa"', p. 656.

45 The term rural food (*kyōdo shoku*) did not appear in the study, perhaps because by the 1930s native ethnologists preferred the term *minzokugaku* to 'rural research' (*kyōdo kenkyū*). See Christy, *A Discipline on Foot*, p. 117.

46 Azio Fukuta, 'Fieldwork in Folklore Studies', *Current Anthropology*, XXVIII/4, *Supplement: An Anthropological Profile of Japan* (August–October 1987), pp. S91–2.

47 There are 85 extant volumes in this survey. Fifty-eight volumes of the survey are published in Seijō Daigaku Minzokugaku Kenkyūjo, ed. *Nihon no shokubunka*, and 27 more appear in Seijō Daigaku Minzokugaku Kenkyūjo, ed., *Nihon no shokubunka, hoi hen: Shōwa shoki, zenkoku shokuji shūzoku no kiroku* (Tokyo, 1995). The former is from the Yanagita Bunkō collection at Seijō University and the latter was from the collection of Hashiura Yasuo's son, later donated to Seijō University.

48 Tanaka, '"Shoku saishū techō" to "Shokushū chōsa"', p. 654. Yanagita set out four goals for researching eating habits (*shokusei*) in an essay, of 1935 to learn: 1) the local names of foodstuffs; 2) ways of eating; 3) the amounts consumed; and 4) utensils. Additionally, the distinction between ordinary and celebratory occasions was fundamental to Yanagita's understanding of culture. See Yanagita, *Shokomotsu to shinzō*, pp. 214–15, 226.

49 Each question usually also included several sub-questions that I have not translated here.

50 The study of vernacular terms was a preoccupation of national ethnological research. See Fukuta, 'Fieldwork in Folklore Studies', p. S92.

51 Seijō Daigaku Minzokugaku Kenkyūjo, ed., *Nihon no shokubunka, hoi hen*, pp. ix–xviii.

52 For a discussion of the ethnologists' methodological assumptions, see Christy, *A Discipline on Foot*, pp. 41, 104, 127.

53 Hashiura enlisted colleagues and students in the study and solicited the help of fieldworkers through advertisements in the September 1941 issue of the society's journal *Minkan denshō* and by postcards sent to the organization's members; Tanaka, '"Shoku saishū techō" to "Shokushū chōsa"', pp. 658–9.

54 Researchers in two locations in Miyagi prefecture spoke to just a single person in each place. In one location in Iwate prefecture five people were interviewed and in another, just one. In Gifu prefecture the informants were students. In Akita prefecture the eight informants disagreed in their responses, which prompted the interviewer to assert prerogative in deciding who was correct, although the study was explicit in its directions to fieldworkers not to interject their own ideas and to stick to the scripted questions. Seijō Daigaku Minzokugaku Kenkyūjo, ed., *Nihon no shokubunka*, pp. 10, 22, 30, 46, 65, 281; Tanaka, '"Shoku saishū techō" to "Shokushū chōsa"', p. 656.

55 Seijō Daigaku Minzokugaku Kenkyūjo, ed., *Nihon no shokubunka*, p. i.

56 Tanaka Nobutada, '"Nihon no shokubunka (hoi hen)" to Hashiura Yasuo kyūzō

shiryō', in *Nihon no shokubunka, hoi hen*, ed., Seijō Daigaku Minzokugaku Kenkyūjo, p. 334.

57 Hori Ichirō, who became a noted scholar of Japanese folk religions, wrote three of the synthetic essays. Another prominent ethnologist and historian, Wakamori Tarō (1915–1977), compiled the field report for a site within Kyoto City and contributed two essays, which he later published, dating them 25 June 1943. See Wakamori Tarō, *Nihon minzokugaku no riron, Wakamori Tarō chosakushū* (Tokyo, 1981), vol. IX, pp. 366–77. The remaining essays were not published until 1995, by Seijō University. Tanaka Nobutada, '"Nihon no shokubunka (hoi hen)" to Hashiura Yasuo kyūzō shiryō', p. 334. Both Hori and Wakamori were researchers in the National Spiritual Culture Research Center, a think tank established by the Ministry of Education in 1932 to counter left-wing ideology and support the study of Japanese culture.

58 Seijō Daigaku Minzokugaku Kenkyūjo, ed. *Nihon no shokubunka, hoi hen*, pp. 261–329.

59 Ibid., p. 324.

60 Seijō Daigaku Minzokugaku Kenkyūjo, ed., *Nihon no shokubunka*, p. 440.

61 Seijō Daigaku Minzokugaku Kenkyūjo, ed., *Nihon no shokubunka, hoi hen*, p. 318.

62 Ehara, Ishikawa and Higashiyotsuyanagi, *Nihon shokumotsushi*, p. 279.

63 The term 'substitute foods' (*daiyōshoku*) is much older than the word *kokuminshoku*. In 1919 the Ministry of Agriculture promoted wheat bread as a substitute food for rice, as described in an article of 23 July 1919 in *Asahi Shimbun*. See Katō Hidetoshi, *Meiji Taishō Shōwa shoku seikatsu sesō shi* (Tokyo, 1977), pp. 142–3.

64 Ehara Ayako and Higashiyotsuyanagi Shōko, *Nihon no shokubunka nenpyō* (Tokyo, 2011), pp. 296, 299.

65 Andrew Gordon, *A Modern History of Japan: From Tokugawa Times to the Present* (New York, 2003), p. 218. For the effects of wartime deprivation on the lives of schoolchildren in the final years of the war, see Samuel Hideo Yamashita, 'The "Food Problem" of Evacuated Children in Wartime Japan, 1944–1945', in *Food and War in Mid-Twentieth-century East Asia*, ed. Katarzyna J. Cwiertka (Burlington, VT, 2013), pp. 131–48.

66 Adachi Iwao, *Nihon shokumotsu bunka no kigen* (Tokyo, 1981), pp. 388–9.

67 Cwiertka, *Modern Japanese Cuisine*, pp. 69, 79.

68 Barak Kushner, *Slurp!*, p. 126.

69 On the post-war history of ramen, see Solt, *The Untold History of Ramen*, pp. 43–71.

70 See, for example, Harada Nobuo, *Washoku to Nihon bunka: Nihon ryōri no shakaishi* (Tokyo, 2005), p. 11.

71 The survey distinguished between ramen with a soy sauce stock and 'Chinese soba', presumably with a meat broth. The latter garnered recognition as *washoku* from only 46.4 per cent of respondents: Video Research Ltd, 'Kuppu nūdoru wa washoku?! – Washoku chōsa kara miru, washoku no fukuzatsu no jittai', Video Research Ltd, 25 June 2015, www.videor.co.jp, accessed 15 July 2015.

6 When Local Food Became Local Cuisine

1 Vaclav Smil and Kazuhiko Kobayashi, *Japan's Dietary Transition and its Impacts* (Cambridge, MA, 2012), p. 196.

2 Representing the former approach, in their study of local food, the scholars Matsushita Sachiko and Yoshikawa Seiji studied the ten major regions in Japan to chart local foods. Matsushita Sachiko and Yoshikawa Seiji, 'Nihon no kyōdo ryōri', *Chiba daigaku kyōiku gakubu kenkyū kiyō*, XXII (1973), pp. 263–98. The latter method is seen in *Nihon minzoku chizu* (Atlas of Japanese Folk Culture), described in this chapter.

3 Smil and Kobayashi, *Japan's Dietary Transition and its Impacts*, p. 141. Two Japanese words designate local food: *kyōdo shoku* and *kyōdo ryōri*. *Kyōdo ryōri* may be the earlier expression, but *kyōdo shoku* was the term that was used most in publications before and during the Second World War. Instances of the term *kyōdo shoku* in print media outnumber those of *kyōdo ryōri* before and during the Second World War in the *Asahi Shimbun* by more than three to one; in *Yomiuri Shimbun* by two to one; and in a major database of magazines and journals by six to one. The usages of both terms show their prevalence until the Second War and their disappearance until Japan had recovered from the war.

The first reference to the term *kyōdo ryōri* in the *Asahi Shimbun* is on 2 August 1934, and there are nine references between then and 1940, after which the word does not appear again until 1967. In the same publication, *kyōdo shoku* first appears on 9 September 1940, and there are 34 uses of the term from then until July 1945, after which the term does not appear again until 1956. Kikuzō II Bijuaru Dijitaru Nyūsu Ākaibu, http://database.asahi.com, accessed 22 October 2013.

The *Yomiuri Shimbun* contains an advertisement for a restaurant serving 'downhome cooking' (*zaigo/zaikyō oryōri*) – a term that does not appear again in that publication. The first entry for *kyōdo ryōri* dates to 3 March 1938, and there are eight appearances of the term between then and 1943 before it next appears in 1964. *Kyōdo shoku* first appears in 12 March 1941, and the term appears in print sixteen times to 1944, after which its next appearance is in 1973; Yomidasu Rekishikan, database.yomiuri.co.jp/rekishikan, accessed 22 October 2013.

Zasshi kiji sakuin shūsei dētabēsu, a 'database for Japanese magazines and scholarly journals published from the Meiji era to the present', offers one entry for *kyōdo ryōri* in 1924; the next grouping of entries begins in 1959. Entries for *kyōdo shoku* appear beginning in 1941 with six publications in the 1940s and there are 24 articles that mention the term in 1941–5; the next reference is in 1956. See Zasshi Kiji Sakuin Shūsei dētabēsu, zassaku-plus.com, accessed 22 October 2013.

The Japanese dictionary *Nihon kokugo daijiten* includes a reference to *kyōdo ryōri* from a 1929 publication, *Nihon ryōri tsu*. See *Nihon kokugo daijiten*, cited through Japan Nareji, www.japanknowledge.com, accessed 1 February 2013. The same database does not have an entry for *kyōdo shoku*.

4 Alix Cooper notes that the category of the 'local' is fairly recent in the European context as well; she writes, 'The ubiquity of the term "local" is itself a relatively modern phenomenon; during the early modern period, it was used only in

certain fairly narrow contexts, for example to discuss "local motion" in physics.'
Alix Cooper, *Inventing the Indigenous: Local Knowledge and Natural History in
Early Modern Europe* (New York, 2007), p. 2.

5 'Washoku, Traditional Dietary Cultures of the Japanese, Notably for the
Celebration of New Year', www.unesco.org/culture/ich/RL/00869, accessed 26
August 2014.

6 Arjun Appadurai, 'How to Make a National Cuisine: Cookbooks in
Contemporary India', *Comparative Studies in Society and History*, XXX/1 (1988),
p. 21.

7 Searching the *Asahi Shimbun* newspaper reveals the use of several terms that
can be translated as Japanese cuisine. The words *honpō ryōri* appear in 1879,
Nihon ryōri in 1880, *Nihon shoku* in 1884 and *washoku* in 1892. Kikuzō II Bijuaru
Dijitaru Nyūsu Ākaibu, http://database.asahi.com, accessed 21 May 2013. I am
grateful to Michiko Ito for alerting me to this.

8 Kumakura Isao, *Nihon ryōri no rekishi* (Tokyo, 2007), p. 124.

9 Yano Keiichi, *'Katei no aji' no sengo minzokushi: Shufu to danraku no jidai*
(Tokyo, 2007), p. 27.

10 Regarding sushi's connection with Edo, see Jordan Sand, 'How Tokyo Invented
Sushi', in *Food and the City*, ed. Dorothée Imbert (Washington, DC, 2014),
pp. 223–48. Edo was long famous for its soba, and had some 3,763 soba shops
by 1860; see Matsushita Sachiko, *Zusetsu Edo ryōri jiten* (Tokyo, 1996), p. 65.
Tempura can be traced to European prototypes, although its exact origins
are uncertain. The earliest recipes in Japan for tempura were quite unlike the
familiar modern version, which took form in Edo in the late eighteenth century.
See Eric C. Rath, *Food and Fantasy in Early Modern Japan* (Berkeley, CA, 2010),
pp. 103–6. Looking more broadly at the role of Edo in shaping modern Japanese
cuisine, one Japanese scholar titled his book *The Big City of Edo Invented
Washoku*: Watanabe Zenjirō, *Kyodai toshi Edo ga washoku o tsukuta* (Tokyo,
1988).

11 For a discussion of nuances of the term cuisine (*ryōri*) in premodern Japan, see
Rath, *Food and Fantasy in Early Modern Japan*, pp. 28–30.

12 Rice cakes (*mochi*) provide a prominent example of the ways in which ordinary
foodstuffs could take on extraordinary meanings in traditional Japanese dietary
culture. See Eric C. Rath, 'The Magic of Japanese Rice Cakes', in *The Routledge
History of Food*, ed. Carol Helstosky (New York, 2015), pp. 3–18.

13 Ichikawa Takeo, 'Kaisetsu', in *Zenshū Nihon no shokubunka*, ed. Haga Noboru
and Ishikawa Hiroko (Tokyo, 1996), vol. XII, p. 3.

14 For a comparative table of these texts and the foodstuffs each lists, see
Matsushita, *Zusetsu Edo ryōri jiten*, pp. 391–6.

15 I am grateful to Glynne Walley for helping me track down this citation.
Takizawa Bakin, 'Kiryo manroku', in *Nihon zuihitsu taisei: Dai ikki*, ed. Nihon
Zuihitsu Taisei Henshūbu (Tokyo, 1975), pp. 234, 262.

16 Thomas Satchell, trans., *Hizakurige, or Shank's Mare* (Rutland, VT, 1960), p. 277.

17 *Nihon kokugo daijiten*, cited through Japan Nareji, www.japanknowledge.com,
accessed 1 February 2013.

18 Alan Christy, *A Discipline on Foot: Inventing Japanese Native Ethnography,
1910–1945* (New York, 2012), pp. 96–9.

19 Yano, *'Katei no aji' no sengo minzokushi*, pp. 25, 27.

20 Penelope Francks, *The Japanese Consumer: An Alternative Economic History of Modern Japan* (New York, 2009), p. 88.

21 Masuda Shōko, *Zakkoku no shakaishi* (Tokyo, 2011), p. 2.

22 The Japanese term for 'new rural cooking' is *shin nōson ryōri*. The year 1920 marked the creation of the Imperial Government Institute for Nutrition, one of the first such government bodies anywhere in the world. See Katarzyna Cwiertka, *Modern Japanese Cuisine: Food, Power and National Identity* (London, 2006), p. 121.

23 Insect consumption was hardly a rarity in early twentieth-century Japan. A nationwide survey conducted in 1918 described the types of insects consumed and discovered that eleven varieties of moth, fourteen types of bee and eleven varieties of grasshopper were regularly eaten. See Nishie Masayuki, *Taberu* (Tokyo, 2013), p. 15.

24 Yano, 'Katei no aji' no sengo minzokushi, pp. 38–9, 42.

25 Taisei Yokusankai Bunkabu, ed., *Kokumin to eiyō* (Tokyo, 1942), p. 36.

26 Ehara Ayako, Ishikawa Naoko and Higashiyotsuyanagi Shōko, *Nihon shokumotsushi* (Tokyo, 2009); B. F. Johnston, *Japanese Food Management in World War Two* (Palo Alto, CA, 1953), p. 82.

27 Ichikawa, 'Kaisetsu', p. 4. The wartime Nōrinshō is the predecessor of the modern Nōrin Suisansho (Ministry for Agriculture, Forestry and Fisheries, MAFF). The study was published in December 1944 as *Honpō kyōdo shoku no kenkyū* (Research on Local Food in Japan), and subsequently republished as Chūō Shokuryō Kyōryokukai, ed., *Kyōdo shoku kankō chōsa hōkokusho* (Chiba, 1976). The study did not include all the findings of the survey. For example, portions of the reports compiled by the imperial universities in Kyoto, Kyushu and Tōhoku were omitted; ibid., p. 3.

28 Ibid., p. ii.

29 Ibid., prologue (*reigen*), pp. 1–2.

30 Ibid., p. 3.

31 Ibid., pp. 411–12.

32 Ibid., p. 435.

33 Ibid., p. 599.

34 Hida was a site for folkloric research from the 1930s, with publications that included Kawaguchi Magojirō, *Hida no Shirakawamura* (Hida Takayamachō, 1934) and scholarship by the husband-and-wife team of novelist Ema Shū and folklorist Ema Mieko, who published a journal called *Hidabito* (The People of Hida) from 1935 to 1944. Scott Schnell, 'Ema Shū's "The Mountain Folk": Fictionalized Ethnography and Veiled Dissent', *Asian Folklore Studies*, LXV/2 (2006), pp. 269–321. Hida is examined in further detail in Chapter Seven.

35 Ema Mieko, *Hida no onnatachi* (Tokyo, 1998), pp. 1, 9.

36 Barak Kushner, *Slurp! A Social and Culinary History of Ramen – Japan's Favorite Noodle Soup* (Leiden, 2012), pp. 154, 161.

37 Kimura Shigemitsu, *Nihon nōgyōshi* (Tokyo, 2010), p. 359.

38 Andrew Gordon, *A Modern History of Japan: From Tokugawa Times to the Present* (New York, 2003), p. 251.

39 Ura's book provides short descriptions of dishes organized by prefecture with some additional notes about the nutritional properties of these foods. Ura Riyo, *Kyōdo ryōri* (Tokyo, 1961). In 2002, the Institute of Public Health became part of the National Institute of Public Health.

40 Smil and Kobayashi assert that there were more profound changes in the average Japanese diet from 1950 to 2006 than in the American diet between 1909 and 2006. See Smil and Kobayashi, *Japan's Dietary Transition and its Impacts*, p. 95.

41 Bunkachō, *Shoku seikatsu, Nihon minzoku chizu* (Tokyo, 1988), vol. IX, introduction, n.p. Food was only one dimension of folk culture surveyed by Department of Education personnel under the auspices of the Agency for Cultural Affairs.

42 The amount of rice consumed in 1962 was more than double the amount of rice consumed per capita today. Naomichi Ishige, 'Japan', in *The Cambridge World History of Food*, ed. Kenneth F. Kiple and Kriemhild Coneè Ornelas (New York, 2000), vol. II, p. 1182.

43 Ishige's conclusions are based on a 1983 survey of 284 women aged 70 or over about their eating habits throughout their lives. See Ishige Naomichi, *Ishige Naomichi shoku no bunka o kataru* (Tokyo, 2009), pp. 178, 183.

44 Matsushita and Yoshikawa, 'Nihon no kyōdo ryōri', p. 297.

45 Ishige, *Ishige Naomichi shoku no bunka o kataru*, p. 192.

46 The study, written under the name Kimura Mutsuko, originally appeared in the journal *Chirigaku hyōron*, XLVII/6 (1974), and it was reprinted as Kōsaka Mutsuko, 'Kyōdo ryōri no chiriteki bunpu', in *Zenshū Nihon no shokubunka*, ed. Haga and Ishikawa, vol. XII, pp. 27–43.

47 Ibid., pp. 28–9, 34–6, 38–9.

48 Any informant born before 1868 would have been more than a century old when Kōsaka made her study, and the pre-Meiji conditions that the informant would have reported on would have been the vague recollections of life as a toddler. Kōsaka's study does not mention informants by name or age, so whether the interviewers spoke to anyone born before 1868 is unstated. See ibid.

49 Millie Creighton, 'Consuming Rural Japan: The Marketing of Tradition and Nostalgia in the Japanese Travel Industry', *Ethnology*, XXXVI/3 (1997), p. 241.

50 On the concept of hometown (*furusato*), see Jennifer Robertson, *Native and Newcomer: Making and Remaking a Japanese City* (Berkeley, CA, 1991), p. 5.

51 Ishige, *Ishige Naomichi shoku no bunka o kataru*, p. 231.

52 Zenkoku Ryōri Kenkyūkai Hiiragikai, *Nihon no kyōdo ryōri* (Tokyo, 1974), p. 3. An earlier version of the book was published as *Nihon no kyōdo ryōri: 500 shū no tsukurikata to aji no fūdoki* (Tokyo, 1966).

53 Zenkoku Ryōri Kenkyūkai Hiiragikai, *Nihon no kyōdo ryōri* (Tokyo, 1974), pp. 113–18.

54 Ibid., pp. 139, 295. Armchair culinary tours of Japan were not restricted to Japanese publications in the late 1960s. John Keys's *Japanese Cuisine* provided English readers with short descriptive sketches for 46 Japanese regions, each with an accompanying recipe and a map. See John D. Keys, *Japanese Cuisine: A Culinary Tour* (Tokyo, 1966).

55 George Solt, *The Untold History of Ramen: How Political Crises in Japan Spawned a Global Food Craze* (Berkeley, CA, 2014), pp. 73–4.

56 The advertisement for the MAFF series appears on the final unnumbered page of Mori Motoko, ed., *Kikigaki Gifu no shokuji*, in *Nihon no shoku seikatsu zenshū* (Tokyo, 1990), vol. XXI. Regarding renewed interest in traditional and local food in the 1980s, see Ehara, Ishikawa and Higashiyotsuyanagi, *Nihon shokumotsushi*, p. 329.

57 Azio Fukuta, 'Fieldwork in Folklore Studies', *Current Anthropology*, XXVIII/4, *Supplement: An Anthropological Profile of Japan* (August–October 1987), p. S92.

58 All the volumes are prefaced with a statement that indicates the descriptions will be in the present tense despite the fact that they refer to the late Taishō and early Shōwa periods. See, for example, Matsuzaki Atsuko, ed., *Kikigaki Kōchi no shokuji*, in *Nihon no shoku seikatsu zenshū* (Tokyo, 1986), vol. XXXIX, p. 3.

59 Creighton, 'Consuming Rural Japan', p. 243.

60 Matsuzaki, *Kikigaki Kōchi no shokuji*, p. 22.

61 Honma Nobuo, ed., *Kikigaki Niigata no shokuji*, in *Nihon no shoku seikatsu zenshū* (Tokyo, 1985), vol. XV; Matsuzaki, *Kikigaki Kōchi no shokuji*; Mori, *Kikigaki Gifu no shokuji*; Harada Kakurō, ed., *Kikigaki Saga no shokuji*, in *Nihon no shoku seikatsu zenshū* (Tokyo, 1991), vol. XLI.

62 On the promotion of local foods, especially traditional vegetables in Kyoto, see Eric C. Rath, 'New Meanings for Old Vegetables in Kyoto', *Food, Culture and Society*, XVII/2 (2014), pp. 203–23.

63 *Fūdo* is an ancient term expressing local climate and topography. Native food (*fūdo shoku*, 風土食), evokes another term also pronounced *fūdo shoku* but written differently (風土色), meaning terroir, the special characteristics derived from a locale.

64 The Japanese word for vegetable, *yasai*, literally means 'field plant' and once denoted greens gathered in mountains and fields, but today refers to cultivated varieties in contrast to 'mountain herbs' (*sansai*) and certain mushrooms, which are not or cannot be cultivated easily and must be gathered. See Yazawa Susumu, 'Wagakuni no yasai to bunka – Tsukena, kabu o chūshin to shite', in *Zenshū Nihon no shokubunka*, ed. Haga and Ishikawa, vol. IV, p. 153.

65 Ichikawa, 'Kaisetsu', p. 13.

66 Greg de St Maurice, 'Savoring Kyoto: Sensory Fieldwork on the Taste of Place', *Etnofoor*, XXIV/2 (2012), pp. 107–22.

67 Smil and Kobayashi, *Japan's Dietary Transition and its Impacts*, p. 17.

68 Ibid., p. 49.

69 Ehara, Ishikawa and Higashiyotsuyanagi, *Nihon shokumotsushi*, p. 299.

70 Chūō Shokuryō Kyōryokukai, *Kyōdo shoku kankō chōsa hōkokusho*, p. 411. Crow snake (*karasu hebi*) is more commonly known as *shimahebi*, Japanese striped snake. The snake is not poisonous and reaches 1.5 metres in length. It is used in traditional medicine.

71 Advertisement on final unnumbered page of Mori, *Kikigaki Gifu no shokuji*.

72 In 2013 I ate at Daikichi, a noted restaurant in Kōchi City, where the hostess touted the authenticity of the establishment's local cuisine by showing me that the dishes I had ordered were mentioned in the volume for Kōchi in the MAFF's series.

73 Ministry of Agriculture, Forestry and Fisheries, 'Nōsan gyoson no kyōdo ryōri hyakusen', www.rdpc.or.jp/kyoudoryouri100/ryouri/03about, accessed 15 January 2013.

74 One origin story of gyōza in Utsunomiya is that they were brought to Japan by returning soldiers or civilians stationed in China during the Second World War. See Kushner, *Slurp!*, pp. 167–8. Besides the interesting way that conspicuously foreign foods introduced in the post-war era are labelled as 'local' Japanese dishes, the MAFF pamphlet offers these dishes as both 'local cuisines' and 'local

foods', revealing the ambiguity in the term *ryōri*. Ministry of Agriculture, Forestry and Fisheries Rural Development Planning Commission, ed., *Japan's Tasty Secrets* (Tokyo, 2009).

75 Bunkachō, 'Hōdō happyō', 9 March 2012, www.bunka.go.jp, accessed 25 April 2012, p. 3. For a discussion of this government announcement, see Eric C. Rath, 'How Intangible is Japan's Traditional Dietary Culture?', *Gastronomica: The Journal of Food and Culture*, XII/4 (Winter 2012), pp. 2–3.

76 Bunkachō, 'Hōdō happyō', p. 3.

77 'B-grade' (*B-kyū*) foods are inexpensive dishes typically prepared and sold outside the home, such as ramen, okonomiyaki and fried noodles (*yakisoba*). See Satomi Fukutomi, 'Connoisseurship of B-grade Culture: Consuming Japanese National Food Ramen', PhD dissertation, Department of Anthropology, University of Hawai'i at Manoa (2010), p. 4.

78 Jeff Pratt describes some of the goals of local food movements in the West. See Jeff Pratt, 'Food Values: The Local and the Authentic', *Critique of Anthropology*, XXVII/3 (2007), pp. 288–9.

79 'Food and cuisine are clearly part of Japan's nationalist agenda and soft power discourse', write Rumi Sakamoto and Matthew Allen. See Rumi Sakamoto and Matthew Allen, 'There's Something Fishy about that Sushi: How Japan Interprets the Global Sushi Boom', *Japan Forum*, XXIII/1 (2011), p. 112.

7 Local Food Cultures in Saga, Kōchi and Hida

1 Harada Kakurō, ed., *Kikigaki Saga no shokuji*, in *Nihon no shoku seikatsu zenshū* (Tokyo, 1991), vol. XLI, p. 344.

2 Naruse Uhei, *Shijū nana todōfuken jiyasai, konamono shokubunka hyakka* (Tokyo, 2009), pp. 234–5.

3 Saga no 'Shoku to Nō' Kizuna Zukuri Purojekkuto Kaigi, *Saga no shoku to nō o kangaete miyō* (Saga, 2009), p. 3.

4 A different survey of the prefecture's traditional foods divides Saga into six areas: the Saga Plain, encompassing the region around Saga City; the Ariake coastal region south of Saga City, abutting Fukuoka prefecture; further south along the coast, the mountainous Tara region bordering Nagasaki; following the boundary between Nagasaki and Saga and moving northward, the Arita area noted for its ceramic workshops; the Japan Seacoast region, Saga's most northern area, which includes the outlying islands; finally, the Sefuri Mountain region, which forms a border between Saga and Fukuoka. See Harada, *Kikigaki Saga no shokuji*. The same book also contains a separate explanation of the diet of Christian communities on the outlying island of Madarajima.

5 Ibid., p. 347.

6 Akamine Jun, 'Whale Meat Foodways in the Contemporary Japan: From Fish Sausages in the 1960s to Whale Tongue in the 1990s', in *International Conference on Foodways and Heritage: A Perspective of Safeguarding the Intangible Cultural Heritage*, ed. Sidney C. H. Cheung and Chau Hing-wah (Hong Kong, 2013), p. 84.

7 Naruse Uhei, *Shijū nana todōfuken, dentō shoku hyakka* (Tokyo, 2009), pp. 262–3; Takahashi Shoten, *Karada ni oishii sakana no benrichō: Zenkoku osakana*

mappu & mannō reshipi (Tokyo, 2013), pp. 66–8; Saga no 'Shoku to Nō' Kizuna Zukuri Purojekkuto Kaigi, *Saga no shoku to nō o kangaete miyō*, p. 3.

8   In some parts of the Saga Plain, waterways cover 17 per cent of the land, but the average is about 9 per cent. See Harada, *Kikigaki Saga no shokuji*, p. 345.

9   Ibid., pp. 25, 34.

10 Ibid., pp. 345–6.

11 Sadamitsu Mitsuo, *Saga no kakure aji: Shokubunka o tazunete* (Saga, 2001), p. 58.

12 Burando Sōgō Kenkyūjo, 'Todōfuken betsu tokei to rankingu de miru kenminsei', www.todo-ran.com, accessed 18 July 2014.

13 Harada, *Kikigaki Saga no shokuji*, pp. 38, 350.

14 Nishi Nihon Shinbunsha Shakaibu, *Kyūshū wagashi kikō* (Fukuoka, 2005), pp. 38–9.

15 For a clip of the interview, see 'Ichii wa doko ni? Todōfuken "mirokudo" rankingu', www.dailymotion.com, accessed 8 July 2014.

16 The ranking was generated by a survey of 29,651 people by the Burando Sōgō Kenkyūjo. See Burando Sōgō Kenkyūjo, 'Todōfuken betsu tokei to rankingu de miru kenminsei', www.todo-ran.com, accessed 18 July 2014.

17 Shimada Yōshichi is the comedian's stage name; his given name is Tokunaga Akihiro. The original title of *The Wonder Granny of Saga* was *Look at it Differently and Be Happy* (*Furimukeba kanashiku mo naku*). The book appeared from a smaller publisher, Ōta Shuppan, in 1987 in a release of just 3,000 copies, but it was later picked by the major firm Tokuma Shoten in 2004, and that firm thereafter published several more of Shimada's books about his grandmother. Later titles in the 'Wonder Granny' series published by Tokuma Shoten include *Gabai bāchan no waraigao de ikinshai!* (Live with a Smile Like a Wonder Granny!, 2005), *Saga no gabai bāchan no shiawase no toranku* (Wonder Granny's Happy Suitcase, 2006) and *Gabai bāchan no yūki ga waku gojū no kotoba* (Fifty Words from the Wonder Granny to Raise your Spirits, 2011). Another publishing house, Shūeisha, has released other books by Shimada about his grandmother in Saga, such as *Gabai bāchan: Saga kara Hiroshima e mezase Kōshien* (Wonder Granny: From Saga Destination Kōshien in Hiroshima), published in 2007. Kōshien is the baseball stadium in Hiroshima where the famous high-school baseball competition is held annually.

18 The films have been distributed to Taiwan and Korea, and Shimada's first book about his grandmother has been translated into Bahasa Indonesia and English.

19 Shimada Yōshichi, *Saga no gabai bāchan* (Tokyo, 2004), pp. 12–22.

20 Ibid., p. 21.

21 Ibid., pp. 5, 7, 219–21.

22 Ibid., pp. 34, 36–9.

23 Shimada Yōshichi, *Saga no gabai bāchan no reshipi* (Tokyo, 2006), pp. 13, 17, 20, 97.

24 Naruse Uhei and Hori Chisako, *Shijū nana todōfuken jiyasai, dentō yasai hyakka* (Tokyo, 2009), pp. 258–9.

25 Takii Shubyō Kabushikigaisha, *Todōfuken betsu chihō yasai zenshū* (Tokyo, 2002), pp. 272–8, 282–90.

26 Shimada, *Saga no gabai bāchan*, pp. 230–31.

27 Sadamitsu, *Saga no kakure aji*, p. 17.

28 Naruse and Hori, *Shijū nana todōfuken jiyasai, dentō yasai hyakka*, p. 258.

29 Personal communication with Ikeda Yuriko, a Saga prefectural official in charge

of promoting local agricultural products; Ikeda Yuriko of the Shoku to Nō Kizuna Zukuri, 1 July 2013.

30 Sadamitsu describes how the greens are dried in the sun, placed in a container, sprinkled with salt and covered with a heavy weight for a few days to press out any moisture. They are then drained and their flavour is enhanced with pepper, persimmon peel and more salt, before they are pressed again to remove any remaining liquid from the leaves. See Sadamitsu, *Saga no kakure aji*, pp. 24–5.

31 Ibid., pp. 86–7, 114–15, 118–19.

32 Ei Shuppansha, *Nihonshū no subete* (Tokyo, 2012), p. 108.

33 *Nihon Rekishi Chimei Taikei*, 'Hamamachi', accessed through Japan Nareji, www.japanknowledge.com, accessed 18 July 2014.

34 The eighth-century *Hizen fudoki* (Chronicle of the Culture and Gazetteer of Hizen) indicates that the name Tara was derived from the original place name Tarashi, meaning affluent, thanks to the plentiful food in the area. See Michiko Y. Aoki, *Records of Wind and Rain: A Translation of Fudoki with Introduction and Commentaries* (Ann Arbor, MI, 1997), pp. 4, 267.

35 Fukuda Aiko, ed., *Tarafukan tsūshin*, 97 (June 2013).

36 Ministry of Land, Infrastructure and Transport website: Kokudo Kōtsūshō, 'Michi no eki annai', www.mlit.go.jp, accessed 16 July 2014.

37 Gavin Parker, 'Michi-no-eki: An Opportunity for the Local Economy', *Town and Country Planning* (July–August 2010), p. 345; Toshiyuki Yokota, *Guidelines for Roadside Stations 'Michinoeki'*, World Bank (2004), www.worldbank.org, accessed 18 July 2014.

38 Parker, 'Michi-no-eki', pp. 344–5.

39 Yokota, *Guidelines for Roadside Stations 'Michinoeki'*, pp. 39–40, 75. Seki Mitsuhiro, '"Michi no eki" sore wa chiiki sangyō shinkō to kōryū no kyoten', in *Michi no eki: Chiiki sangyō shinkō to kōryū no kyoten*, ed. Seki Mitsuhiro and Sakemoto Hiroshi (Tokyo, 2011), pp. 26, 27, 29, 31, 34, 40.

40 Yokota, *Guidelines for Roadside Stations 'Michinoeki'*, p. 40.

41 Nichigai Asoshiētsu, *Jiten Nihon no chiiki burando, meisanhin* (Tokyo, 2009), p. 372.

42 Takahashi Shoten, *Karada ni oishii sakana no benrichō*, p. 154.

43 Harada, *Kikigaki Saga no shokuji*, pp. 281, 290–91, 298–9, 303.

44 Takahashi Shoten, *Karada ni oishii sakana no benrichō*, p. 61.

45 Before the twentieth century, *katsuobushi* remained too expensive for daily use for most people, who instead made stock from other fish, kombu, mushrooms or different materials, depending on where they lived.

46 The cost of the season's first skipjack tuna varied each year, but the prices presented here from *Morisada mankō* are often cited. See Takahashi Mikio, *Edo ajiwai zufu* (Tokyo, 1995), p. 214. The conversions to modern currency are not exact, but are provided to give an approximation of the cost. The conversion from Edo-period coinage to modern currency appears in Yōsensha, *Edo no shoku to kurashi: Nagaya no banmeshi kara shōgun ga kononda gōka ryōri made* (Tokyo, 2014), p. 36.

47 Miyashita Akira, *Katsuobushi* (Tokyo, 2000), p. 338.

48 Burando Sōgō Kenkyūjo, 'Todōfuken betsu tokei to rankigu de miru kenminsei', www.todo-ran.com, accessed 18 July 2014.

49 Ehara Ayako, Ishikawa Naoko and Higashiyotsuyanagi Shōko, *Nihon*

shokumotsushi (Tokyo, 2009), p. 130.

50 Zenkoku Ryōri Kenkyūkai Hiiragikai, *Nihon no kyōdo ryōri* (Tokyo, 1974), p. 296; Miyashita, *Katsuobushi*, pp. 188–9.

51 Miyashita Akira, 'Katsuo', in *Tabemono Nihonshi sōkan*, ed. Nishiyama Matsunosuke (Tokyo, 1994), p. 196; Fujiwara, *Karada ni oishii sakana no benrichō*, p. 44.

52 Miyashita, *Katsuobushi*, pp. 47–51.

53 Miyagawa Itsuo, *Tosa sakana ajiwau* (Kōchi, 1999), p. 54.

54 Miyagawa Itsuo, *Tosaryū omotenashi: Sawachi, tataki, sekku* (Kōchi, 2004), pp. 50–51.

55 Burando Sōgō Kenkyūjo, 'Todōfuken betsu tokei to rankigu de miru kenminsei', www.todo-ran.com, accessed 18 July 2014.

56 *Nihon rekishi chimei taikei*, cited through Japan Nareji, www.japanknowledge. com, accessed 18 July 2014.

57 Zenkoku Ryōri Kenkyūkai Hiiragikai, *Nihon no kyōdo ryōri*, p. 295.

58 Matsuzaki Atsuko, ed., *Kikigaki Kōchi no shokuji*, in *Nihon no shoku seikatsu zenshū* (Tokyo, 1986), vol. XXXIX, pp. 161, 344.

59 The title page of Kondō Hideo's book *Shikoku: Tabemono minzokugaku* states that the diet of the stone-age Jōmon period (10,000–300 BCE) existed in Shikoku until the Shōwa 40s (1965–1974). See Kondō Hideo, *Shikoku: Tabemono minzokugaku* (Matsuyama, 1999).

60 Katsurai's account appears in Seijō Daigaku Minzokugaku Kenkyūjo, ed., *Nihon no shokubunka, hoi hen: Shōwa shoki, zenkoku shokuji shūzoku no kiroku* (Tokyo, 1995), pp. 219–36. Like the other respondents, Katsurai followed the format of questions issued by the Popular Traditions Association.

61 Katsurai Kazuo, *Tosayama minzokushi* (Kōchi, 1955), p. 4. This book does not contain the report Katsurai wrote for the Popular Traditions Association's survey.

62 Matsuzaki, *Kikigaki Kōchi no shokuji*, p. 54.

63 Seijō Daigaku Minzokugaku Kenkyūjo, ed., *Nihon no shokubunka, hoi hen*, pp. 219–30, 234–5.

64 For an example of a Kōchi cookbook featuring *sawachi* cuisine, see Miyagawa, *Tosaryū omotenashi*.

65 The term *sawachi* dates from as early as the twelfth century, but its first recorded use in Kōchi is in 1674. See Miyagawa, *Tosaryū omotenashi*, p. 6. The origin of *sawachi* cuisine is unclear but it may reflect a style of dining that warriors used while on campaign, or it could be a variation of medieval banqueting cuisine (*honzen ryōri*). Ogura Kumeo, Komatsuzaki Takeshi and Hatae Keiko, eds, *Nihon ryōri gyōji, shikitari daijiten* (Tokyo, 2003), vol. I, p. 108. A similar style of eating is evident in the pleasure district of Yoshiwara in Edo in the late seventeenth century, suggesting that samurai from Tosa domain may have learned about *sawachi* cuisine in Edo and brought the custom back home. See Eric C. Rath, 'Sex and Sea Bream: Food and Prostitution in Hishikawa Moronobu's Visit to Yoshiwara', in *Seduction: Japan's Floating World: The John C. Weber Collection*, ed. Laura W. Allen (San Francisco, CA, 2015), pp. 28–43. In the early modern period, *sawachi* dining was exclusive to the samurai in Kōchi and commoners there did not adopt the custom until the Meiji period; Matsuzaki, *Kikigaki Kōchi no shokuji*, p. 45.

66 Takeuchi Yukiko presents an interview with one of these semi-professional chefs who plied his trade part-time in Chiba prefecture. Her informant owned dedicated serving ware and had specialized knowledge of culinary customs and food preparations for banquets. Such cooks once played an important role in villages at a time when most marriage ceremonies and other important gatherings took place in the home. See Takeuchi Yukiko, 'Chōri to jendā', in *Shokubunka kara shakai ga wakaru!*, ed. Harada Nobuo (Tokyo, 2009), pp. 118–19.

67 Matsuzaki, *Kikigaki Kōchi no shokuji*, pp. 45–6.

68 Miyagawa, *Tosaryū omotenashi*, pp. 14, 21.

69 Another form of *ikezukuri* features a live fish served partially sliced to be eaten as sashimi.

70 In making *ikezukuri*, the term 'dead fish' is avoided in Kōchi. Chefs refer instead to the fish as having 'risen' (*agatta*), suggesting that the spirit of the fish may have risen to the Buddhist Pure Land or that the fish at least is rising up from the platter.

71 Miyagawa, *Tosaryū omotenashi*, pp. 38, 40–41, 47.

72 Seijō Daigaku Minzokugaku Kenkyūjo, *Nihon no shoku bunka, hoi hen*, pp. 232–5.

73 Kariya Tetsu and Hanasaki Akira, *Oishinbo*, 87 (Tokyo, 2004), p. 124.

74 Ei Shuppansha, *Nihonshū no subete* (Tokyo, 2012), p. 102.

75 Burando Sōgō Kenkyūjo, 'Todōfuken betsu tokei to rankigu de miru kenminsei', www.todo-ran.com, accessed 18 July 2014.

76 Miyamoto Tsuneichi, *Wasureta Nihonjin* (Tokyo, 1971); published in English as Tsuneichi Miyamoto, *The Forgotten Japanese: Encounters with Rural Life and Folklore*, trans. Jeffrey S. Irish (Berkeley, CA, 2010).

77 Alan Christy, *A Discipline on Foot: Inventing Japanese Native Ethnography, 1910–1945* (New York, 2012), pp. 31, 39.

78 Matsuzaki, *Kikigaki Kōchi no shokuji*, p. 344. The length of the trip is according to Tatemichi Hitoshi, an official in the Yusuharachō mayor's office, personal conversation, 8 July 2013.

79 Miyamoto, *The Forgotten Japanese*, p. 109.

80 Kōchiken Yusuharachō, *Kumo no ue de itadakimasu: Yusuhara no dentō shoku* (Yusuharachō, Kōchi, 2004), p. 130.

81 Miyamoto, *The Forgotten Japanese*, p. 126.

82 In the early modern period Yusuharachō (a name that itself dates only from 1966) was part of a much larger span of territory, 'Tsuno Mountain Township' (Tsuno *sangō*), encompassing Yusuhara, five nearby villages and three villages from neighbouring Tsunochō. The township was named after the prominent Tsuno family, which held an estate in the area in the seventh century.

83 Conversation with Tatemichi Hitoshi of the planning division of Yusuhara's local government, 8 July 2013.

84 Ōe Tadaki, *Chiiki no chikara: Shoku, nō, machizukuri* (Tokyo, 2008), p. 122.

85 Matsuzaki, *Kikigaki Kōchi no shokuji*, pp. 108, 110; Nichigai Asoshiētsu, *Jiten Nihon no chiiki burando, meisanhin*, p. 357.

86 Miyamoto, *The Forgotten Japanese*, pp. 112, 123–4.

87 Matsuzaki, *Kikigaki Kōchi no shokuji*, p. 161.

88 Kondō, *Shikoku*, p. 30. Corn arrived in Japan in the late sixteenth century from

South America through the introduction of Iberian merchants and missionaries.

89 Matsuzaki, *Kikigaki Kōchi no shokuji*, pp. 128, 130–31; Kōchiken Yusuharachō, *Kumo no ue de itadakimasu*, pp. 16, 88–9.

90 Japanese knotweed (*itadori*) has long stalks that resemble a cross between bamboo and asparagus. It can be peeled and pickled in salt as a preserved food or eaten raw; but it should be consumed only sparingly, since it contains oxalic acid, which can cause sickness and kidney failure. *Itadori* also has medicinal properties, and the origin of the plant's name has been suggested to be 'pain remover'. It is still used in traditional medicine as a coagulant and for pain relief. See ibid., pp. 32, 35.

91 Ibid., pp. 117, 131. The bitter taste of raw *warabi* indicates the presence of the carcinogenic poison ptaquiloside, which can be removed by placing the fresh herbs in a bowl, covering them with hot water and adding a spoonful of wood ash or baking soda. If the mixture is allowed to rest overnight, the bitterness leaches out of the herbs and they are ready to be consumed safely.

92 Matsuzaki, *Kikigaki Kōchi no shokuji*, pp. 151–2.

93 Japanese horse chestnut (*tochi*), *Aesculus turbinata*, is sometimes called buckeye.

94 The village is now part of Hongawamura in Tosa district.

95 Matsuzaki, *Kikigaki Kōchi no shokuji*, pp. 163, 168.

96 Ibid., p. 163.

97 Miyamoto, *The Forgotten Japanese*, pp. 217–18, 220.

98 Ibid., p. 223.

99 A 100-gram serving of horse chestnuts contains 369 calories, 3.1 grams of protein, 6.1 grams of fat and 75.4 grams of carbohydrate. By contrast, the same amount of polished rice has 352 calories, 12.9 grams of protein, 0.9 grams of fat and 76.4 grams of carbohydrate. See Matsuyama Toshio, *Ko no mi* (Tokyo, 1982), p. 62.

100 Matsuzaki, *Kikigaki Kōchi no shokuji*, pp. 163, 168; *Nihon rekishi chimei taikei*, accessed through Japan Nareji, www.japanknowledge.com, 22 July 2014. Aki, a community on Kōchi's eastern seacoast, is still noted for its tofu made from acorns.

101 Miyamoto, *The Forgotten Japanese*, pp. 218–19, 221.

102 Ōe, *Chiiki no chikara*, p. 137.

103 For a discussion of Ema's novel, published first in 1938 and then in a revised edition in 1973, see Scott Schnell, 'Ema Shū's *The Mountain Folk*: Fictionalized Ethnography and Veiled Dissent', *Asian Folklore Studies*, LXV/2 (2006), pp. 269–321.

104 Ema Mieko, *Hida no onnatachi* (Tokyo, 1998), p. 3.

105 As cited in Schnell, 'Ema Shū's *The Mountain Folk*', p. 302.

106 Mori Motoko, ed., *Kikigaki Gifu no shokuji*, in *Nihon no shoku seikatsu zenshū* (Tokyo, 1990), vol. XXI, p. 347; Gifu is ranked second in terms of rate of forestation. See Burando Sōgō Kenkyūjo, 'Todōfuken betsu tokei to rankigu de miru kenminsei', www.todo-ran.com, accessed 18 July 2014.

107 For a description of Furukawa, see Scott Schnell, *The Rousing Drum: Ritual Practice in a Japanese Community* (Honolulu, HI, 1999), especially pp. 36–44.

108 Ema, *Hida no onnatachi*, p. 9.

109 Schnell, *The Rousing Drum*, p. 270.

110 Haga Noboru, 'Sankoku Hida no hito to minzoku', in *Yama no tami no minzoku to bunka: Hida o chūshin ni mita sankoku no henbō*, ed. Haga Noboru (Tokyo, 1991), p. 5.

111 Schnell, *The Rousing Drum*, p. 37.

112 Tomita Ayahiko, *Hida gofudoki*, ed. Ashida Koreto, *Dai Nihon chishi taikei* (Tokyo, 1968), vols XLI and XLII.

113 Koyama Shūzō, '"Hida gofudoki" ni miru Edo jidai no shoku seikatsu', in *Zenshū Nihon no shokubunka*, ed. Haga Noboru and Ishikawa Hiroko (Tokyo, 1999), vol. II, p. 21.

114 Ibid., pp. 212–13.

115 Ibid., p. 293.

116 Emiko Ohnuki-Tierney, *Rice as Self: Japanese Identities through Time* (Princeton, NJ, 1993), pp. 33–4.

117 Fujino Yoshiko, 'Meiji shoki ni okeru sanson no shokuji to eiyō: "Hida gofudoki" no bunseki o tsūjite', *Kokuritsu minzoku hakubutsukan kenkyū hōkoku*, VII/3 (1982), pp. 632–54.

118 Ishige Naomichi, 'Japan', in *The Cambridge World History of Food*, ed. Kenneth F. Kiple and Kriemhild Coneè Ornelas (New York, 2000), vol. II, pp. 1175–6.

119 Arizono Shōichirō, *Kinsei shomin no nichijōshoku: Hyakushō wa kome o taberarenakatta ka?* (Ōtsu, 2007), p. 43.

120 Harada Nobuo, *Edo no shoku seikatsu* (Tokyo, 2003), pp. 178–9.

121 Ibid.

122 Koyama, '"Hida gofudoki" ni miru Edo jidai no shoku seikatsu', p. 213.

123 Matsuyama, *Ko no mi*, pp. 180, 183.

124 Mori, *Kikigaki Gifu no shokuji*, p. 349.

125 Ema, *Hida no onnatachi*, p. 37. Nyūkawa, is now part of Takayama City, a fifteen-minute drive northwest from Takayama railway station. It was the site of Kyoto Imperial University's study of rural food in 1943–4 that formed part of the Ministry of Agriculture's wartime efforts to promote national people's cuisine, described in Chapter Six.

126 Bunkachō, *Shoku seikatsu, Nihon minzoku chizu* (Tokyo, 1988), vol. IX, p. 292.

127 Mori, *Kikigaki Gifu no shokuji*, pp. 349–50.

128 Ehara Ayako, '"Hida gofudoki" ni miru Hida no kurashi', *Tōkyō kaseigakuin daigaku kiyō*, XXIX (1989), pp. 3, 5, 12–13.

129 Vaclav Smil and Kazuhiko Kobayashi, *Japan's Dietary Transition and its Impacts* (Cambridge, MA, 2012), pp. 81, 86–7.

130 Susan B. Hanley, *Everyday Things in Premodern Japan: The Hidden Legacy of Material Culture* (Berkeley, CA, 1997), p. 91.

131 The figures for life expectancy were, according to Ema Mieko, derived from surveys undertaken by hospitals and government clinics. See Ema, *Hida no onnatachi*, pp. 44–5. Average life expectancy in Japan in 1900 was 43 for men and 44 for women. See Smil and Kobayashi, *Japan's Dietary Transition and Its Impacts*, p. 113.

132 Not enough tubers were grown to serve as a sufficient source of energy in Hida. See Koyama, '"Hida gofudoki" ni miru Edo jidai no shoku seikatsu', pp. 213–14.

133 Matsuyama, *Ko no mi*, pp. 183–4.

134 Ibid., pp. 187, 189–95.

135 Mori, *Kikigaki Gifu no shokuji*, pp. 242–3.

136 Ema, *Hida no onnatachi*, p. 38.

137 Matsuyama, *Ko no mi*, p. 226. Acorns are not even listed as a traditional foodstuff in Hida in *Kikigaki Gifu no shokuji*, which purports to describe the

diet in the area in the 1920s and 1930s. See Mori, *Kikigaki Gifu no shokuji.*

138 Ema, *Hida no onnatachi*, p. 1.

139 Haga, 'Sankoku Hida no hito to minzoku', pp. 4, 11.

140 Ema, *Hida no onnatachi*, pp. 33–4.

141 Ibid., p. 33.

142 Ibid., pp. 34–6.

143 Ibid., pp. 36–7.

144 Ema did not provide any indication of the exact size of a bale. Ibid., p. 38.

145 Ibid., pp. 50, 109–10, 116, 117.

146 Ibid., pp. 114–16.

147 Ibid., p. 113; Ema provides the names of the meals; the approximate times and contents are derived from her book and supplied by Matsuyama Toshio. See Matsuyama, *Ko no mi*, p. 215.

148 Mori, *Kikigaki Gifu no shokuji*, pp. 78–9. This method of eating Shikoku millet is the same as that for buckwheat dough (*sobagaki*).

149 Ema, *Hida no onnatachi*, p. 123.

150 Ibid., p. 124.

151 The terminology is a little confusing, since *gō* usually designates a district. Shirakawamura, which seems to indicate a village, is actually a county, a larger area than Shirakawagō, within Ōno district. Shirakawamura is in the northwest corner of Gifu prefecture, bordering Ishikawa prefecture to the west and Toyama prefecture to the north.

152 Shirakawamura Shōkōkai, *Honkosama no omotenashi: Shirakawagō no hō'onkō ryōri* (Shirakawagō, 2012), p. i.

153 Mori, *Kikigaki Gifu no shokuji*, p. 90.

154 Personal communications with Hirase Katsusuke, president of Hirase Shuzō, 26 June 2013.

155 Burando Sōgō Kenkyūjo, 'Todōfuken betsu tokei to rankigu de miru kenminsei', www.todo-ran.com, accessed 18 July 2014.

156 Ibid. Personal communication with elderly informant in Ogimachi, 27 June 2013.

157 Ema, *Hida no onnatachi*, pp. 133–4.

158 Mori, *Kikigaki Gifu no shokuji*, pp. 88–9.

159 Ema, *Hida no onnatachi*, p. 118.

160 Personal communication with elderly informant in Ogimachi, 27 June 2013.

161 Chūō Shokuryō Kyōryokukai, ed., *Kyōdo shoku kankō chōsa hōkokusho* (Chiba, 1976), p. 190.

162 Bunkachō, *Shoku seikatsu*, pp. 292–3. Nagakura was hardly an outlier: a diet of grains other than rice prevailed in the other communities in Hida reported in this survey; ibid., pp. 292–7.

163 Shirakawamura Shōkōkai, *Honkosama no omotenashi*, p. 2.

164 Magnolia leaves can also serve as a cooking surface. The leaves are smeared with miso and chopped green onion and placed on a portable brazier to cook vegetables, eggs or beef.

165 Shirakawamura Shōkōkai, *Honkosama no omotenashi*, pp. 2–3.

166 Ibid., pp. 8–11.

167 Ibid., p. 4.

Conclusion

1 Santōsha, *Shoku seikatsu dēta sōgō tōkei nenpyō 2014* (Tokyo, 2014), p. 254.
2 Harada Kakurō, ed., *Kikigaki Saga no shokuji*, in *Nihon no shoku seikatsu zenshū* (Tokyo, 1991), vol. XLI, p. 218.
3 For a discussion of Japan's highly evolved coffee culture, see Merry White, *Coffee Life in Japan* (Berkeley, CA, 2012).

BIBLIOGRAPHY

Abe Koryū, *Kokoro no keshōbako* (Tokyo, 2002)

Adachi Iwao, *Nihon shokumotsu bunka no kigen* (Tokyo, 1981)

Akamine Jun, 'Whale Meat Foodways in the Contemporary Japan: From Fish Sausages in the 1960s to Whale Tongue in the 1990s', in *International Conference on Foodways and Heritage: A Perspective of Safeguarding the Intangible Cultural Heritage*, ed. Sidney C. H. Cheung and Chau Hing-wah (Hong Kong, 2013), pp. 76–91

Akiho Masumi, *Katei wayō hoken shokuryō: Sanshoku kondate oyobi ryōrisho*, in *Kindai ryōriho shūsei*, vol. IV, ed. Ehara Ayako (Tokyo, 2012)

Allison, Anne, 'Japanese Mothers and Obentōs: The Lunch-box as Ideological State Apparatus', *Anthropological Quarterly*, LXIV/4 (1991), pp. 195–208

Anzai Komako, *Shiki mainichi sanshoku ryōrihō* (Tokyo, 1909)

Aoki, Michiko Y., *Records of Wind and Rain: A Translation of Fudoki with Introduction and Commentaries* (Ann Arbor, MI, 1997)

Appadurai, Arjun, 'How to Make a National Cuisine: Cookbooks in Contemporary India', *Comparative Studies in Society and History*, XXX/1 (1988), pp. 3–24

Arizono Shōichirō, *Kinsei shomin no nichijōshoku: Hyakushō wa kome o taberarenakatta ka?* (Ōtsu, 2007)

Asaoka Kōji, *Nabe, kama* (Tokyo, 1993)

Ashkenazi, Michael, and Jeanne Jacob, *The Essence of Japanese Cuisine: An Essay on Food and Culture* (Philadelphia, PA, 2000)

Assmann, Stephanie, 'The Remaking of a National Cuisine: The Food Education Campaign in Japan', in *The Globalization of Asian Cuisines: Transnational Networks and Culinary Contact Zones*, ed. James Farrer (New York, 2015), pp. 165–85

Bay, Alexander R., *Beriberi in Modern Japan: The Making of a National Disease* (Rochester, NY, 2012)

Beardsley, Richard K., John W. Hall and Robert E. Ward, *Village Japan* (Chicago, IL, 1959)

Berry, Mary Elizabeth, *The Culture of Civil War in Kyoto* (Berkeley, CA, 1994)

Bestor, Theodore C., *Tsukiji: The Fish Market at the Center of the World* (Berkeley, CA, 2004)

Billig, Michael, *Banal Nationalisms* (London, 1995)

Bunkachō, 'Hōdō happyō', www.bunka.go.jp, 9 March 2012

—, *Shoku seikatsu, Nihon minzoku chizu* (Tokyo, 1988), vol. IX

Burando Sōgō Kenkyūjo, 'Todōfuken betsu tokei to rankingu de miru kenminsei', www.todo-ran.com

Cadwallader, Gary Sōka, and Joseph R. Justice, '*Kaiseki*, Stones for the Belly: Cuisine for Tea during the Early Edo Period', in *Japanese Foodways Past and*

Present, ed. Eric C. Rath and Stephanie Assmann (Urbana, IL, 2010), pp. 68–91

Carlin, George, *When Will Jesus Bring the Pork Chops?* (New York, 2004)

Chang, Te-tzu, 'Rice', in *The Cambridge World History of Food*, ed. Kenneth F. Kiple and Kriemhild Coneè Ornelas (New York, 2000), vol I, pp. 132–49

Christy, Alan, *A Discipline on Foot: Inventing Japanese Native Ethnography, 1910–1945* (New York, 2012)

Chūō Shokuryō Kyōryokukai, ed., *Kyōdo shoku kankō chōsa hōkokusho* (Chiba, 1976)

Clark, Priscilla P., 'Thoughts for Food I: French Cuisine and French Culture', *The French Review*, XLIX/1 (1975), pp. 32–41

Cohen, Jerome B., *Japan's Economy in War and Reconstruction* (Minneapolis, MN, 1949)

Collingham, Lizzie, *The Taste of War: World War Two and the Battle for Food* (New York, 2011)

Cooper, Alix, *Inventing the Indigenous: Local Knowledge and Natural History in Early Modern Europe* (New York, 2007)

Creighton, Millie, 'Consuming Rural Japan: The Marketing of Tradition and Nostalgia in the Japanese Travel Industry', *Ethnology*, XXXVI/3 (1997), pp. 239–54

Cwiertka, Katarzyna, 'Culinary Culture and the Making of a National Cuisine', in *A Companion to the Anthropology of Japan*, ed. Jennifer Robertson (New York, 2005), pp. 415–28

—, *Modern Japanese Cuisine: Food, Power and National Identity* (London, 2006)

Dai Nippon Ryōri Kenkyūkai, *Tsūgaku jidō eiyō bentō jūni kagetsu*, in *Kindai Ryōrisho shūsei*, vol. IX, ed. Ehara Ayako (Tokyo, 2013)

Daigo Sanjin, *Ryōri hayashinan*, in *Nihon ryōri hiden shūsei: Genten gendaigoyaku* (Kyoto, 1985), vol. IV

Davidson, Alan, *The Oxford Companion to Food*, 2nd edn, ed. Tom Jaine (New York, 2006)

Doak, Kevin Michael, 'Building National Identity through Ethnicity: Ethnology in Wartime Japan and After', *Journal of Japanese Studies*, XXVII/1 (2001), pp. 1–39

Dohi Noritaka, *Edo no komeya* (Tokyo, 1981)

Dunn, Frederick L., 'Beriberi', in *The Cambridge World History of Food*, ed. Kenneth F. Kiple and Kriemhild Coneè Ornelas (New York, 2000), vol. I, pp. 914–19

Ebara Kei, *Edo ryōrishi kō: Nihon ryōri (sōsōshi)* (Tokyo, 1986)

—, *Ryōri monogatari kō: Edo no aji kokon* (Tokyo, 1991)

Edensor, Tim, *National Identity and Everyday Life* (New York, 2002)

Ego Michiko, *Nanban kara kita shokubunka* (Fukuoka, 2004)

Ehara Ayako, 'Dai kyūkan, bentō, tsukemono', in *Kindai ryōrisho shūsei* (Tokyo, 2013), vol. IX, pp. 1–5

—, '"Hida gofudoki" ni miru Hida no kurashi', *Tōkyō kaseigakuin daigaku kiyō*, XXIX (1989), pp. 1–15

Ehara Ayako and Higashiyotsuyanagi Shōko, *Kindai ryōrisho no sekai* (Tokyo, 2008)

—, *Nihon no shokubunkashi nenpyō* (Tokyo, 2011)

Ehara Ayako, Ishikawa Naoko and Higashiyotsuyanagi Shōko, *Nihon shokumotsushi* (Tokyo, 2009)

Ekuan, Kenji, *The Aesthetics of the Japanese Lunchbox*, ed. Daniel B. Stewart (Cambridge, MA, 1998)

Ema Mieko, *Hida no onnatachi* (Tokyo, 1998)

Endō Genkan, *Cha no yu kondate shinan*, in *Nihon ryōri hiden shūsei: Genten gendaigoyaku*, ed. Issunsha (Kyoto, 1985), vol. XI, pp. 5–208

Farris, William Wayne, *Daily Life and Demographics in Ancient Japan* (Ann Arbor, MI, 2009)

Ferguson, Priscilla Parkhurst, *Accounting for Taste: The Triumph of French Cuisine* (Chicago, IL, 2004)

Francks, Penelope, 'Consuming Rice: Food, "Traditional" Products and the History of Consumption in Japan', *Japan Forum*, XIX/2 (2007), pp. 147–68

—, *The Japanese Consumer: An Alternative Economic History of Modern Japan* (New York, 2009)

—, 'Rice for the Masses: Food Policy and the Adoption of Imperial Self-sufficiency in Early Twentieth-century Japan', *Japan Forum*, XV/1 (2003), pp. 125–46

Fujimoto Kōnosuke, *Kikigaki Meiji no kodomo asobi to kurashi* (Tokyo, 1986)

Fujimoto Kōtarō, 'Senji Doitsu kokumin shokuryō mondai', *Kokumin keizai zasshi*, XVIII/4 (1915), pp. 89–109

Fujimura Munetaro, *Nichiyō benri bentō ryōri annai* (Tokyo, 1905)

Fujino Yoshiko, 'Meiji shoki ni okeru sanson no shokuji to eiyō: "Hida gofudoki" no bunseki o tsūjite', *Kokuritsu minzoku hakubutsukan kenkyū hōkoku*, VII/3 (1982), pp. 632–54

Fujiwara Masataka, *Karada ni oishii sakana no benrichō* (Tokyo, 2013)

Fukuda Aiko, ed., *Tarafukan tsūshin*, 97 (June 2013)

Fukukita, Yasunosuke, *Cha no Yu: The Tea Cult of Japan* (New York, 1935)

Fukuta, Azio, 'Fieldwork in Folklore Studies', *Current Anthropology*, XVIII/4, Supplement: *An Anthropological Profile of Japan* (August–October 1987), pp. S91–S94

Fukutomi, Satomi, 'Connoisseurship of B-grade Culture: Consuming Japanese National Food Ramen', PhD dissertation, Department of Anthropology, University of Hawai'i at Manoa (2010)

Gordon, Andrew, *A Modern History of Japan: From Tokugawa Times to the Present* (New York, 2003)

Haga Noboru, 'Sankoku Hida no hito to minzoku', in *Yama no tami no minzoku to bunka: Hida o chūshin ni mita sankoku no henbō*, ed. Haga Noboru (Tokyo, 1991), pp. 3–21

Hane, Mikiso, *Peasants, Rebels, Women, and Outcastes: The Underside of Modern Japan* (New York, 1982)

Hanley, Susan B., *Everyday Things in Premodern Japan: The Hidden Legacy of Material Culture* (Berkeley, CA, 1997)

Harada Kakurō, ed., *Kikigaki Saga no shokuji*, in *Nihon no shoku seikatsu zenshū* (Tokyo, 1991), vol. XLI

Harada Nobuo, '"Cha kaiseki" kaidai', in *Nihon ryōri hiden shūsei: Genten gendaigoyaku*, ed. Issunsha (Kyoto, 1985), vol. XI, pp. 263–77

—, *Edo no ryōri to shoku seikatsu* (Tokyo, 2004)

—, *Edo no shoku seikatsu* (Tokyo, 2003)

—, '"Kome shikō" saikō', in *Shokubunka kara shakai ga wakaru!*, ed. Harada Nobuo (Tokyo, 2009), pp. 15–58

—, *Rekishi no naka no kome to niku: Shokumotsu to tennō, sabetsu* (Tokyo, 1993)

—, *Washoku to Nihon bunka: Nihon ryōri no shakaishi* (Tokyo, 2005)

Hausu Shokuhin Kabushikigaisha Hibushitsu, ed., *Meiji, Taishō, Shōwa no shokutaku* (Tokyo, 2001)

Havens, Thomas H., *Valley of Darkness: The Japanese People and World War Two* (New York, 1978)

Hayashi Shunshin, *Edo, Tōkyō gurume saijiki* (Tokyo, 1998)

Heibonsha and Miraisha, eds, *Shinpen jūdai ni nani o tabetaka* (Tokyo, 2004)

Hirano Masaki, *Washoku no rireki: Shokuzai o meguru jūgo no monogatari* (Kyoto, 1997)

Hobsbawm, Eric J., and Terrence O. Ranger, eds, *The Invention of Tradition* (New York, 1983)

Holden, Tim, 'The Overcooked and Underdone: Masculinities in Japanese Food Programming', in *Food and Culture: A Reader*, ed. Carole Counihan and Penny Van Esterik, 2nd edn (New York, 1997), pp. 202–20

Honma Nobuo, ed., *Kikigaki Niigata no shokuji*, in *Nihon no shoku seikatsu zenshū* (Tokyo, 1985), vol. XV

Hosking, Richard, *A Dictionary of Japanese Food: Ingredients and Culture* (New York, 1996)

Hyakushō denki, annotated by Furushima Toshio (Tokyo, 2001)

'Ichii wa doko ni? Todōfuken "mirokudo" rankingu', www.dailymotion.com, accessed 8 July 2014

Ichikawa Takeo, 'Kaisetsu', in *Zenshū Nihon no shokubunka*, ed. Haga Noboru and Ishikawa Hiroko (Tokyo, 1996), vol. XII, pp. 3–14

—, 'Shokubunka ni miru chiikisei', in *Zenshū Nihon no shokubunka*, ed. Haga Noboru and Ishikawa Hiroko (Tokyo, 1996), vol. XII, pp. 17–26

Iguchi Kaisen and Nagashima Fukutaro, eds, *Chadō jiten* (Kyoto, 1978)

Ishige, Naomichi, 'Japan', in *The Cambridge World History of Food*, ed. Kenneth F. Kiple and Kriemhild Coneè Ornelas (New York, 2000), vol. II, pp. 1175–83

Ishige Naomichi, *Ishige Naomichi shoku no bunka o kataru* (Tokyo, 2009)

—, *Men no bunkashi* (Tokyo, 2006)

Ishikawa Hiroko, ed., *Shoku seikatsu to bunka: Shoku no ayumi* (Tokyo, 1988)

Issenberg, Sasha, *The Sushi Economy: Globalization and the Making of a Modern Delicacy* (New York, 2007)

Japan Nareji, www.japanknowledge.com

Johnston, B. F., *Japanese Food Management in World War Two* (Palo Alto, CA, 1953)

Kamijima Sachiko, ed., *Kikigaki Ōsaka no shokuji*, in *Nihon no shoku seikatsu zenshū* (Tokyo, 1991), vol. XXVII

Kanagawaken Shokuryō Eidan, *Kessen shoku seikatsu kufūshū* (Osaka, 1944)

Kariya Tetsu and Hanasaki Akira, *Oishinbo*, 87 (Tokyo, 2004)

Katō Hidetoshi, *Meiji Taishō Shōwa shoku seikatsu sesō shi* (Tokyo, 1977)

Katō Toshiko, *Kokuminshoku: Eiyō kondate sanbyaku rokujū go nichi*, in *Kindai ryōrisho shūsei*, vol. XI, ed. Ehara Ayako (Tokyo, 2013)

Katsurai Kazuo, *Tosayama minzokushi* (Kōchi, 1955)

Kawaguchi Magojirō, *Hida no Shirakawamura* (Hida Takayamachō, 1934)

Keys, John D., *Japanese Cuisine: A Culinary Tour* (Tokyo, 1966)

Kikuzō II Bijuaru Dijitaru Nyūsu Ākaibu, http://database.asahi.com

Kimura Shigemitsu, *Nihon nōgyōshi* (Tokyo, 2010)

Kitagawa Morisada, *Morisada mankō*, ed. Asakura Haruhiko and Kashikawa Shūichi (Tokyo, 1992)

Kōchiken Yusuharachō, *Kumo no ue de itadakimasu: Yusuhara no dentō shoku* (Yusuharachō, 2004)

Koizumi Kazuko, *Chabudai no Shōwa* (Tokyo, 2002)

—, *Shōwa daidokoro natsukashi zukan* (Tokyo, 1998)

Kokudo Kōtsūshō, 'Michi no eki annai', www.mlit.go.jp

Kondō Hideo, *Shikoku: Tabemono minzokugaku* (Matsuyama, Ehime, 1999)

Kondō, Hiroshi, *Saké: A Drinker's Guide* (New York, 1984)

Kōsaka Mutsuko, 'Kyōdo ryōri no chiriteki bunpu', in *Zenshū Nihon no shokubunka*, ed. Haga Noboru and Ishikawa Hiroko (Tokyo, 1996), vol. XII, pp. 27–43

Koyama Shūzō, '"Hida gofudoki" ni miru Edo jidai no shoku seikatsu', in *Zenshū Nihon no shokubunka*, ed. Haga Noboru and Ishikawa Hiroko (Tokyo, 1999), vol. II, pp. 211–22

Kumakura Isao, *Nanpōroku o yomu* (Kyoto, 1983)

—, 'Nihon no dentōteki shokubunka to shite no washoku no inkikata', in *Nihon no shoku no kinmirai*, ed. Kumakura Isao (Kyoto, 2013), pp. 3–25

—, *Nihon ryōri bunkashi: Kaiseki o chūshin ni* (Kyoto, 2002)

—, *Nihon ryōri no rekishi* (Tokyo, 2007)

—, 'Nihon shokubunkashi no kadai', in *Kōza shoku no bunka*, ed. Ishige Naomichi and Kumakura Isao (Tokyo, 1999), vol. II, pp. 11–23

—, 'Sen no Rikyū: Inquiries into his Life and Tea', in *Tea in Japan: Essays on the History of Chanoyu*, ed. Paul Varley and Kumakura Isao (Honolulu, HI, 1989), pp. 33–69

—, 'Senkeryū no kaiseki', in *Chadōgaku taikei* (Kyoto, 1999), vol. IV, pp. 135–75

'Kuppu nūdoru wa washoku?! – Washoku chōsa kara miru, washoku no fukuzatsu no jittai', Video Research Ltd, 25 June 2015, www.videor.co.jp, accessed 15 July 2015

Kurosawa Fumio, *Kome to sono kakō* (Tokyo, 1982)

Kushioka Keiko, *Kaiseki ryōri no chie* (Tokyo, 1999)

Kushner, Barak, *Slurp! A Social and Culinary History of Ramen – Japan's Favorite Noodle Soup* (Leiden, 2012)

Kusumi Soan, *Chawa shigetsushū*, in *Nihon no chasho*, ed. Hayashi Tatsusaburō, Yokoi Kiyoshi and Narabayashi Tadao (Tokyo, 1972), vol. II, pp. 1–58

Kyodo News International, 'Japan Aims to Have HK Lift Ban on Japanese Food Imports', www.globalpost.com, 15 August 2013

Laudan, Rachel, *Cuisine and Empire: Cooking in World History* (Berkeley, CA, 2013)

Ludwig, Theodore, 'Chanoyu and Momoyama: Conflict and Transformation in Rikyū's Tea', in *Tea in Japan: Essays on the History of Chanoyu*, ed. Paul Varley and Kumakura Isao (Honolulu, HI, 1989), pp. 71–100

Lukacs, Gabriella, '*Iron Chef* Around the World: Japanese Food Television, Soft Power, and Cultural Globalization', *International Journal of Cultural Studies*, XIII/4 (2010), pp. 409–26

Macnaughtan, Helen, 'Building up Steam as Consumers: Women, Rice Cookers and the Consumption of Everyday Household Goods', in *The Historical Consumer: Consumption and Everyday Life in Japan, 1850–2000*, ed. Penelope Francks and Janet Hunter (New York, 2012), pp. 79–104

Maruyama Yasunari, 'Kinsei ni okeru daimyō, shomin no shoku seikatsu: Sono ryōri kondate o chūshin to shite', in *Zenshū Nihon no shokubunka*, ed. Haga Noboru and Ishikawa Hiroko (Tokyo, 1999), vol. II, pp. 173–98

Masuda Shōko, *Awa to hie no shokubunka* (Tokyo, 1990)

—, *Zakkoku no shakaishi* (Tokyo, 2011)

—, 'Zakkoku no yūretsukan', in *Shoku no Shōwa bunkashi*, ed. Tanaka Nobutada and Matsuzaki Kenzō (Tokyo, 1995), pp. 39–75

Matsushita Sachiko, *Zusetsu Edo ryōri jiten* (Tokyo, 1996)
Matsushita Sachiko and Yoshikawa Seiji, 'Nihon no kyōdo ryōri', *Chiba daigaku kyōiku gakubu kenkyū kiyō*, XXII (1973), pp. 263–98
Matsuya Hisashige, *Matsuya kaiki*, in *Chadō koten zenshū*, ed. Sen Sōshitsu XV (Kyoto, 1957), vol. IX
Matsuyama Toshio, *Ko no mi* (Tokyo, 1982)
Matsuzaki Atsuko, ed., *Kikigaki Kōchi no shokuji*, in *Nihon no shoku seikatsu zenshū* (Tokyo, 1986), vol. XXXIX
Meihan burui, in *Nihon ryōri hiden shūsei: Genten gendaigoyaku*, ed. Issunsha (Kyoto, 1985), vol. IX, pp. 211–72
Ministry of Agriculture, Forestry and Fisheries, *Heisei nijūnen shokuryō jikyūristu*, www.maff.go.jp, accessed 25 May 2012
—, 'Nōsan gyoson no kyōdo ryōri hyakusen', www.rdpc.or.jp, accessed 15 January 2013
Ministry of Agriculture, Forestry and Fisheries Rural Development Planning Commission, ed., *Japan's Tasty Secrets* (Tokyo, 2009)
Mitamura Yoshiko, 'Nabe, kama, tetsubin: Imono sanchi, Kawaguchi ni okeru komono nichijōhin no seisaku gijutsu', in *Shoku seikatsu to mingu*, ed. Nihon Mingu Gakkai (Tokyo, 1993), pp. 103–15
Miwa Shigeo, *Usu* (Tokyo, 1978)
Miyagawa Itsuo, *Tosa sakana ajiwau* (Kōchi, 1999)
—, *Tosaryū omotenashi: Sawachi, tataki, sekku* (Kōchi, 2004)
Miyamoto Tsuneichi, *Wasureta Nihonjin* (Tokyo, 1971)
Miyamoto, Tsuneichi, *The Forgotten Japanese: Encounters with Rural Life and Folklore*, trans. Jeffrey S. Irish (Berkeley, CA, 2010)
Miyashita Akira, 'Katsuo' in *Tabemono Nihonshi sōkan*, ed. Nishiyama Matsunosuke (Tokyo, 1994), pp. 196–7
—, *Katsuobushi* (Tokyo, 2000)
Miyazaki Yasusada, *Nōgyō zensho*, in *Nihon nōgyō zensho* (Tokyo, 1978), vol. XII
Mock, John, *Culture, Community and Change in a Sapporo Neighborhood, 1925–1988: Hanayama* (New York, 1999)
Mori Motoko, ed., *Kikigaki Gifu no shokuji*, in *Nihon no shoku seikatsu zenshū* (Tokyo, 1990), vol. XXI
Morisue Yoshiaki and Kikuchi Yūjirō, *Kaikō shokumotsushi: Nihonjin no shoku seikatsu no hatten* (Tokyo, 1965)
—, *Shokumotsushi: Nihonjin no shoku seikatsu no hatten* (Tokyo, 1952)
Morris-Suzuki, Tessa, 'The Invention and Reinvention of "Japanese Culture"', *Journal of Asian Studies*, LIV/3 (1995), pp. 759–80
Mulgan, Aurelia George, *The Politics of Agriculture in Japan* (New York, 2000)
Murai Gensai, *Daidokoro chōhōki* (Tokyo, 2001)
Murai Yasuhiko, *Buke bunka to dōbōshū* (Tokyo, 1991)
—, 'Kaiseki ryōri no rekishi', in *Kaiseki to kashi*, ed. Tsutsui Hiroichi (Kyoto, 1999), pp. 7–64
Murakami Akiko, *Daidokoro tomodachi: Nabe, kama, shichirin, hōchō, manaita, suribachi, shokudai* (Tokyo, 1987)
Nagatsuka, Takashi, *The Soil: A Portrait of Rural Life in Meiji Japan*, trans. Ann Waswo (Berkeley, CA, 1989)
Nagayama Hisao, 'Edo no shokubunka', in *Edo jidai 'seikatsu bunka' sōkan*, ed. Nishiyama Matsunosuke (Tokyo, 1992), pp. 36–41

—, *Naze washoku wa sekai ichi na no ka* (Tokyo, 2012)
—, *Nihon kodai shoku jiten* (Tokyo, 1998)
Nakagawa Noriko, *Nihon no kyōdo ryōri* (Tokyo, 1974)
Nakamura Kōhei, *Shinpan Nihon ryōri gogenshū* (Tokyo, 2004)
Nakayama Keiko, *Wagashi monogatari* (Tokyo, 1993)
Naruse Uhei, *Shijū nana todōfuken, dentō shoku hyakka* (Tokyo, 2009)
—, *Shijū nana todōfuken jiyasai, konamono shokubunka hyakka* (Tokyo, 2009)
Naruse Uhei and Hori Chisako, *Shijū nana todōfuken jiyasai, dentō yasai hyakka* (Tokyo, 2009)
Nichigai Asoshiētsu, *Jiten Nihon no chiiki burando, meisanhin* (Tokyo, 2009)
Nihon Sekijūjisha, *Senji kokuminshoku* (Tokyo, 1941)
Nihon Shoku Bunka no Sekai Muke Isan Bunka Tōroku ni Muketa Kentōkai, 'Nihon shokubunka no muke bunka isan kisai teiansho no gaiyō', February 2012, www.bunka.go.jp, accessed 25 April 2012
Nihonshū no subete, ed. Ei Shuppansha (Tokyo, 2012)
Nishi Nihon Shinbunsha Shakaibu, *Kyūshū wagashi kikō* (Fukuoka, 2005)
Nishie Masayuki, *Taberu* (Tokyo, 2013)
Nishimura Kenji, ed., *Kikigaki Mie no shokuji*, in *Nihon no shoku seikatsu zenshū*, vol. XXIX (Tokyo, 1987)
Nishiyama Matsunosuke, ed., *Tabemono Nihonshi sōkan* (Tokyo, 1994)
Nishino Miyoshi, *Wayō shiki bentō ryōri kazugazu* (Tokyo, 1916)
Nomoto Kyōko, 'Shoku seikatsu', in *Nihon sonrakushi kōza*, ed. Nihon Sonrakushi Kōza Henshū Iinkai (Tokyo, 1991), vol. VIII, pp. 157–71
Nozagi Hiromitsu, *Washoku no oishii kotsu* (Tokyo, 1999)
Ōe Tadaki, *Chiiki no chikara: Shoku, nō, machizukuri* (Tokyo, 2008)
Ogura Kumeo, Komatsuzaki Takeshi and Hatae Keiko, eds, *Nihon ryōri gyōji, shikitari daijiten*, 2 vols (Tokyo, 2003)
Ohnuki-Tierney, Emiko, *Rice as Self: Japanese Identities through Time* (Princeton, NJ, 1993)
Ōkubo Hiroko, *Edo no fāsuto fūdo* (Tokyo, 1998)
—, *Edokko wa nani o tabeteita ka* (Tokyo, 2005)
Okumura Ayao, *Nihon men shokubunka no 1300 nen* (Tokyo, 2009)
Ōmameuda Minoru, *Okome to shoku no kindaishi* (Tokyo, 2007)
Onabe, Tomoko, 'Bentō: Boxed Love, Eaten by the Eye', in *Japanese Foodways Past and Present*, ed. Eric C. Rath and Stephanie Assmann (Urbana, IL, 2010), pp. 201–18
Ōshima Akeo, 'Shōwa shoki ni okeru kome no suihanhō to yōgu: Jikyoku no kakawari kara', in *Shoku no Shōwa bunkashi*, ed. Tanaka Nobutada and Matsuzaki Kenzō (Tokyo, 1995), pp. 143–72
Ōta Yasuhiro, *Nihon shokubunka tosho mokuroku Edo – kindai* (Tokyo, 2008)
Parker, Gavin, 'Michi-no-eki – an Opportunity for the Local Economy', *Town and Country Planning* (July–August 2010), pp. 342–6
Partner, Simon, *Toshié: A Story of Village Life in Twentieth-century Japan* (Berkeley, CA, 2004)
Pitelka, Morgan, *Handmade Culture: Raku Potters, Patrons, and Tea Practitioners in Japan* (Honolulu, HI, 2005)
Pratt, Jeff, 'Food Values: The Local and the Authentic', *Critique of Anthropology*, XXVII/3 (2007), pp. 285–300

Rath, Eric C., *Food and Fantasy in Early Modern Japan* (Berkeley, CA, 2010)

—, '*Honzen* Dining: The Poetry of Formal Meals in Late Medieval and Early Modern Japan', in *Japanese Foodways Past and Present*, ed. Eric C. Rath and Stephanie Assmann (Urbana, IL, 2010), pp. 19–41

—, 'How Intangible is Japan's Traditional Dietary Culture?', *Gastronomica: The Journal of Food and Culture*, XII/4 (Winter 2012), pp. 2–3

—, 'The Magic of Japanese Rice Cakes', *Routledge History of Food*, ed. Carol Helstosky (New York, 2015), pp. 3–18

—, 'New Meanings for Old Vegetables in Kyoto', *Food, Culture and Society*, XVII/2 (2014), pp. 203–23

—, 'Reevaluating Rikyū: Kaiseki and the Origins of Japanese Cuisine', *Journal of Japanese Studies*, XXXVIX/1 (2013), pp. 67–96

—, 'Rural Life and Agriculture', in *A Companion to Japanese History*, ed. William Tsutsui (Malden, MA, 2007), pp. 477–92

—, 'Sex and Sea Bream: Food and Prostitution in Hishikawa Moronobu's *Visit to Yoshiwara*', in *Seduction: Japan's Floating World: The John C. Weber Collection*, ed. Laura W. Allen (San Francisco, CA, 2015), pp. 28–43

Robertson, Jennifer, *Native and Newcomer: Making and Remaking a Japanese City* (Berkeley, CA, 1991)

—, 'Sexy Rice: Plant Gender, Farm Manuals, and Grass-roots Nativism', *Monumenta Nipponica*, XXXIX/3 (1984), pp. 233–60

Ryōri monogatari, in *Nihon ryōri hiden shūsei: Genten gendaigoyaku*, ed. Issunsha (Kyoto, 1985), vol. I, pp. 7–92

Sadamitsu Mitsuo, *Saga no kakure aji: Shokubunka o tazunete* (Saga, 2001)

Saga no 'Shoku to Nō' Kizuna Zukuri Purojekkuto Kaigi, *Saga no shoku to nō o kangaete miyō* (Saga, 2009)

Saitō Tokio, *Nihon Shokubunka jinbutsu jiten: Jinbutsu de yomu Nihon shokubunkashi* (Tokyo, 2005)

Sakamoto, Rumi, and Matthew Allen, 'There's Something Fishy about that Sushi: How Japan Interprets the Global Sushi Boom', *Japan Forum*, XXIII/1 (2011), pp. 99–121

Sand, Jordan, *House and Home in Modern Japan: Architecture, Domestic Space, and Bourgeois Culture, 1880–1930* (Cambridge, MA, 2003)

—, 'How Tokyo Invented Sushi', in *Food and the City*, ed. Dorothée Imbert (Washington, DC, 2014), pp. 223–48

Santōsha, *Shoku seikatsu dēta sōgō tōkei nenpyō 2014* (Tokyo, 2014)

Sasagawa Rinpū and Adachi Isamu, *Kinsei Nihon shokumotsushi* (Tokyo, 1973)

Sase Yojiuemon, *Aizu nōsho*, in *Nihon Nōgyō Zensho* (Tokyo, 1978), vol. XII, pp. 3–218

Satchell, Thomas, trans., *Hizakurige, or Shank's Mare* (Rutland, VT, 1960)

Schnell, Scott, 'Ema Shū's *The Mountain Folk*: Fictionalized Ethnography and Veiled Dissent', *Asian Folklore Studies*, LXV/2 (2006), pp. 269–321

—, *The Rousing Drum: Ritual Practice in a Japanese Community* (Honolulu, HI, 1999)

Segawa Kiyoko, *Shoku seikatsu no rekishi* (Tokyo, 2001)

Seijō Daigaku Minzokugaku Kenkyūjo, ed., *Nihon no shokubunka: Shōwa shoki, zenkoku shokuji shūzoku no kiroku* (Tokyo, 1990)

—, ed., *Nihon no shokubunka, hoi hen: Shōwa shoki, zenkoku shokuji shūzoku no kiroku* (Tokyo, 1995)

Seki Mitsuhiro, '"Michi no eki" sore wa chiiki sangyō shinkō to kōryū no kyoten', in *Michi no eki: Chiiki sangyō shinkō to kōryū no kyoten*, ed. Seki Mitsuhiro and Sakemoto Hiroshi (Tokyo, 2011), pp. 25–49

Sen Sōshitsu XIV, 'Kaiseki shukaku no kokoroe', in *Chadō zenshū*, ed. Sen Sōshitsu XIV and Sen Sōshu (Tokyo, 1936), vol. VII, pp. 15–45

Sen Sōshitsu XIV and Sen Sōshu, eds, *Chadō zenshū* (Tokyo, 1936), vol. VII

Sen Sōshitsu XV, *The Japanese Way of Tea: From its Origins in China to Sen Rikyū*, trans. V. Dixon Morris (Honolulu, HI, 1998)

—, 'Reflections on Chanoyu and its History', trans. Paul Varley, in *Tea in Japan: Essays on the History of Chanoyu*, ed. Paul Varley and Kumakura Isao (Honolulu, HI, 1989), pp. 233–42

—, *Tea Life, Tea Mind* (New York, 1979)

—, *Tennōjiya kaiki takaiki*, in *Chadō koten zenshū* (Kyoto, 1967), vol. VII

—, *Tennōjiya kaiki jikaiki*, in *Chadō koten zenshū* (Kyoto, 1967), vol. VIII

—, *Yamanoue Sōjiki*, in *Chadō koten zenshū* (Kyoto, 1967), vol. VI, pp. 49–129

Sen Sōshitsu XV, ed., *Rikyū hyakkaiki*, in *Chadō koten zenshū* (Kyoto, 1967), vol. VI, pp. 405–73

Sen Sōshu, 'Kaiseki no yurai oyobi hensen', in *Chadō zenshū*, ed. Sen Sōshitsu XIV and Sen Sōshu (Tokyo, 1936), vol. VII, pp. 1–14

Serizawa, Satohiro, 'Regional Variations and Local Interpretations of the National Food: The Case of Japanese Noodles', in *International Conference on Foodways and Heritage: A Perspective of Safeguarding the Intangible Cultural Heritage*, ed. Sidney C. H. Cheung and Chau Hing-wah (Hong Kong, 2013), pp. 92–106

Shimada Yōshichi, *Saga no gabai bāchan* (Tokyo, 2004)

—, *Saga no gabai bāchan no reshipi* (Tokyo, 2006)

Shimoda Utako, *Ryōri tebikisō*, in *Kindai ryōrisho shūsei*, ed. Ehara Ayako (Tokyo, 2012), vol. III, pp. 1–311

Shintani Takanori and Sekizawa Mayumi, *Minzoku kojiten: Shoku* (Tokyo, 2013)

Shirakawamura Shōkōkai, *Honkosama no omotenashi: Shirakawagō no hōʻonkō ryōri* (Shirakawagō, 2012)

Shōsekiken Sōken, *Ryōri mōmoku chōmishō*, in *Nihon ryōri hiden shūsei: Genten gendaigoyaku*, ed. Issunsha (Kyoto, 1985), vol. I, pp. 219–323

Smethurst, Richard J., *Agricultural Development and Tenancy Disputes in Japan, 1870–1940* (Princeton, NJ, 1986)

Smil, Vaclav, and Kazuhiko Kobayashi, *Japan's Dietary Transition and its Impacts* (Cambridge, MA, 2012)

Smith, Kerry, *A Time of Crises: Japan, the Great Depression, and Rural Revitalization* (Cambridge, MA, 2001)

Solt, George, *The Untold History of Ramen: How Political Crises in Japan Spawned a Global Food Craze* (Berkeley, CA, 2014)

St Maurice, Greg de, 'Savoring Kyoto: Sensory Fieldwork on the Taste of Place', *Etnofoor*, XXIV/2 (2012), pp. 107–22

Suge Hiroshi, *Ine* (Tokyo, 1998)

Surak, Kristin, *Making Tea, Making Japan: Cultural Nationalism in Practice* (Stanford, CA, 2013)

Suzuki Shigeo, 'Mochi no hanashi are kore', *Koko chishin*, XV (1978), pp. 22–30

Taisei Yokusankai Bunkabu, ed., *Kokumin to eiyō* (Tokyo, 1942)

Takada Masatoshi, 'Tetsudō no tabi to ekiben', *Tabi to shoku*, ed. Kanzaki Noritake (Tokyo, 2002), pp. 174–97

Takahashi Mikio, *Edo ajiwai zufu* (Tokyo, 1995)

Takahashi Shoten, *Karada ni oishii sakana no benrichō: Zenkoku osakana mappu & mannō reshipi* (Tokyo, 2013)

Takenob [sic], Y., and K. Kawakami, *Japan Yearbook: Complete Cyclopedia of General Information and Statistics on Japan for the Year 1912* (Tokyo, 1911)

Takeuchi Yukiko, 'Chōri to jendā', in *Shokubunka kara shakai ga wakaru!*, ed. Harada Nobuo (Tokyo, 2009), pp. 101–46

Takii Shubyō Kabushikigaisha, *Todōfuken betsu chihō yasai zenshū* (Tokyo, 2002)

Takizawa Bakin, 'Kiryo manroku', in *Nihon zuihitsu taisei: Dai ikki*, ed. Nihon Zuihitsu Taisei Henshūbu (Tokyo, 1975), pp. 159–303

Tanaka Nobutada, 'Gochisō to shokubunka', in *Shoku no Shōwa bunkashi*, ed. Tanaka Nobutada and Matsuzaki Kenzō (Tokyo, 1995), pp. 76–97

—, '"Nihon no shokubunka (hoi hen)" to Hashiura Yasuo kyūzō shiryō', in *Nihon no shokubunka, hoi hen: Shōwa shoki, zenkoku shokuji shūzoku no kiroku*, ed. Seijō Daigaku Minzokugaku Kenkyūjo (Tokyo, 1995), pp. 330–36

—, '"Shoku saishū techō" to "Shokushū chōsa"', in *Nihon no shokubunka: Shōwa shoki, zenkoku shokuji shūzoku no kiroku*, ed. Seijō Daigaku Minzokugaku Kenkyūjo (Tokyo, 1990), pp. 653–65

Tani Akira, *Chakaiki no kenkyū* (Kyoto, 2001)

Toda Hiroyoshi, *Shokubunka no keisei to nōgyō: Niō chūkan no bāi* (Tokyo, 2001)

Tomita Ayahiko, *Hida gofudoki*, in *Dai Nihon chishi taikei*, ed. Ashida Koreto (Tokyo, 1968), vols XLI and XLII

Trubek, Amy, *The Taste of Place: A Cultural Journey into Terroir* (Berkeley, CA, 2008)

Tsutsui Hiroichi, 'Chanoyu no kashi: Sono seiritsu to tenkai', in *Kaiseki to kashi*, ed. Tsutsui Hiroichi (Kyoto, 1999), pp. 290–318

—, *Kaiseki no kenkyū: Wabicha no shokurei* (Kyoto, 2002)

Uchiyama, Benjamin, 'Carnival War: A Cultural History of Wartime Japan, 1937–1945', PhD dissertation, University of Southern California (2013)

UNESCO, 'Nomination file no. 00869 for Inscription in 2013 on the Representative List of the Intangible Cultural Heritage of Humanity', www.unesco.org/culture/ich/en/lists, accessed 26 August 2014

—, 'Washoku, Traditional Dietary Cultures of the Japanese, Notably for the Celebration of New Year', www.unesco.org/culture/ich/en/lists, accessed 26 August 2014

Uotani Tsunekichi, 'Cha ryōri no jidai shoku', in *Chadō zenshū*, ed. Sen Sōshitsu XIV and Sen Sōshu (Tokyo, 1936), vol. VII, pp. 165–71

Ura Riyo, *Kyōdo ryōri* (Tokyo, 1961)

Varley, Paul, and Kumakura Isao, eds, *Tea in Japan: Essays on the History of Chanoyu* (Honolulu, HI, 1989)

Vlastos, Stephen, ed., *Mirror of Modernity: Invented Traditions of Modern Japan* (Berkeley, CA, 1998)

Wakamori Tarō, *Nihon minzokugaku no riron, Wakamori Tarō chosakushū* (Tokyo 1981), vol. IX

'Washoku Boom Helps Japan's Farm Exports', *The Japan News*, 11 February 2015, www.newsonjapan.com

Watanabe Minoru, *Nihon shoku seikatsushi* (Tokyo, 1964)

Watanabe Shin'ichiro, *Edo no onnatachi no gurume jijō: Ezu to sen'ryū ni miru shoku bunka* (Tokyo, 1994)

—, *Edo no shomin ga hiraita shokubunka* (Tokyo, 1996)

Watanabe Zenjirō, ed., *Kikigaki Tōkyō no shokuji*, in *Nihon no shoku seikatsu zenshū* (Tokyo, 1988), vol. XIII

—, *Kyodai toshi Edo ga washoku o tsukuta* (Tokyo, 1988)

White, Merry, *Coffee Life in Japan* (Berkeley, CA, 2012)

Yabe Yoshiaki, *Takeno Jōō: Cha no yu to shōgai* (Kyoto, 2002)

Yabu Shinobu, *Satoyama, satoumi kurashi zukan: Ima ni ikasu Shōwa no chie* (Tokyo, 2012)

Yabunouchi Chikushin, *Genryū chawa*, in *Chadō koten zenshū*, ed. Sen Sōshitsu (Kyoto, 1960), vol. III, pp. 397–497

Yamada Junko, *Edo gurume tanjō: Jidai koshō de miru Edo no aji* (Tokyo, 2010)

Yamashita Saburō, Satō Kazuko and Nashihara Hiroshi, 'Jidai bentōbako shiryō shūsei', *Tōhoku kōgyō daigaku kiyō rikōgaku hen*, I (1981), pp. 96–140; II (1982), pp. 121–40

Yamashita, Samuel Hideo, 'The "Food Problem" of Evacuated Children in Wartime Japan, 1944–1945', in *Food and War in Mid-Twentieth-century East Asia*, ed. Katarzyna J. Cwiertka (Burlington, VT, 2013), pp. 131–48

Yanagida [sic], Kunio, *Japanese Manners and Customs in the Meiji Era*, trans. Charles S. Terry (Tokyo, 1957)

Yanagita Kunio, *Shokumotsu to shinzō* (Tokyo, 1977)

Yano Keiichi, 'Katei no aji' no sengo minzokushi: Shufu to danraku no jidai* (Tokyo, 2007)

Yazawa Susumu, 'Wagakuni no yasai to bunka – Tsukena, kabu o chūshin to shite', in *Zenshū Nihon no shokubunka*, ed. Haga Noboru and Ishikawa Naoko (Tokyo, 1997), vol. IV, pp. 153–62

Yokota, Toshiyuki, *Guidelines for Roadside Stations 'Michinoeki'*, World Bank (2006), http://documents.worldbank.org/curated/en/home, accessed 18 July 2014

Yokusan Undōshi Kankōkai, *Yokusan kokumin undōshi* (Tokyo, 1954)

Yomidasu Rekishikan, www.yomiuri.co.jp/database

Yōsensha, *Edo no shoku to kurashi: Nagaya no banmeshi kara shōgun ga kononda gōka ryōri made* (Tokyo, 2014)

Yoshida Hajime, *Nihon no shoku to sake: Chūsei no hakkō gijutsu o chūshin ni* (Tokyo, 1991)

Yoshida Kikujirō, *Seiyōgashi Nihon no ayumi* (Tokyo, 2012)

Yoshikawa Seiji, 'Bentō konjaku monogatari', in *Zenshū Nihon no shokubunka*, ed. Haga Noboru and Ishikawa Hiroko (Tokyo, 1997), vol. X, pp. 141–52

Yunoki Manabu, *Sakezukuri no rekishi shinsōpan* (Tokyo, 2005)

Zasshi Kiji Sakuin Shūsei Dētabēsu, http://zassaku-plus.com

Zenkoku Ryōri Kenkyūkai Hiiragikai, *Nihon no kyōdo ryōri* (Tokyo, 1974)

ACKNOWLEDGEMENTS

This book began as a different project, and I am grateful to Michael Leaman of Reaktion Books for publishing this work instead of the one I initially promised him. Nancy Stalker and Barak Kushner graciously read and copiously commented on the manuscript and I appreciate their advice in honing my argument. The mistakes and gaps that may remain are despite their best efforts, and the meticulous assistance of my editor Aimee Selby, who helped me improve my argument and writing in many ways. Benjamin Uchiyama, my colleague at the University of Kansas History Department, read a draft of Chapter Five and his comments about wartime national people's dress and its relationship to national people's cuisine proved insightful. Wayne Farris helped me clarify this book project at an earlier stage.

I had the opportunity to present versions of several chapters at conferences on Japanese cuisine, where I gained much from the comments and observations of the attendees. I gave a version of Chapter Five at 'Devouring Japan: An Interdisciplinary Conference on Japanese Cuisine and Foodways', organized by Nancy Stalker at the University of Texas at Austin in 2014, and gave talks based on chapters One and Four at 'Emotionalizing the Nation: Conflicting Narratives in Japanese Food Identities', convened at the Royal Flemish Academy, Brussels, in 2015 by Andreas Niehaus and Tine Walravens of the University of Ghent. I also presented on the contents of Chapter Four at the University of California Santa Barbara in 2015. Chapter Six began as a conference paper in 2013 for 'Traveling Cuisines: Culinary Politics and Transnational Foodways In and Out of Asia' at the Sophia University Institute of Comparative Culture in Tokyo. I am grateful to the conference organizer, James Farrer, who has allowed me to publish here an extended version of that chapter, which appeared earlier in the conference volume as: 'The Invention of Local Food', in *The Globalization of Asian Cuisines: Transnational Networks and Culinary Contact Zones*, ed. James Farrer (New York, 2015), pp. 145–64. An earlier version of Chapter Two appeared as 'Revaluating Rikyū: Kaiseki and the Origins of Japanese Cuisine', *Journal of Japanese Studies*, XXXIX/1 (2013), pp. 67–96.

Travel in Japan in 2013 for this study was made possible by the University of Kansas Center for East Asian Studies, the Department of History, and Office for International Programs, the College of Liberal Arts and Sciences and by a travel award from the Japan-United States Friendship Commission and Northeast Asia Council of the Association for Asian Studies. My investigation was further supported by the University of Kansas General Research Fund, allocation number 2301735.

I appreciate the time and knowledge of the government officials and food specialists who discussed with me the food culture of their home regions. In Gifu I met with the prefectural government officials Aotani Hideki, Matsunami Kumi, Nikawa Tomomi and Sugihara Ryōtarō, who proved especially eager to assist me. In Takayama and Hida, I gained knowledge from my conversations with the staff of the Takayama city office, Futamura Noriko, Hayashi Tokushi and Ushimaru Takehiko, who included the scholar of local food Kamide Kayoko in our discussions. Hirase Katsusuke told me about the history of sake brewing in Takayama and gave me a personal tour of his family brewery, Hirase Shuzō. Satō Naoko was an invaluable reference about traditional foods in Hida and a marvellous cook in her restaurant, Kissa Satō in Ogimachi. Ikeda Yuriko and Shibahara Kensuke of the Saga prefectural government helped me understand the variety and depth of that prefecture's food culture, while Ikeda Yukito and Ishibashi Takeharu introduced me to the operation of the Tarafukan in Tarachō. I am grateful to Hara Shōko, Sugimoto Hisanori and Tabata Kazushi of the Kōchi prefectural government, who shared their expertise and who introduced me to Professor Matsuzaki Atsuko of Kōchi Women's University, offering me the chance to learn from an expert who made an appearance in the famous food manga *Oishinbō* by Kariya Tetsu and Hanasaki Akira. Tatemichi Hitoshi was especially generous with his time when I toured Yusuhara in Kōchi and I am grateful for his showing me the community, sharing in the local history and disclosing the best places to eat there. Less formal conversations also enlivened my study, and I am thankful for the hospitality of the Iki Iki Kan in Hamashuku and Tsurusō Inn in Saga, the Murasaki Inn in Takayama, the Doboroku Festival Museum and the inn Furusato in Ogimachi Shirakawagō, and for the staff and customers of the indoor eatery Hirome Ichiba and the restaurant Daikichi in Kōchi.

For many years on many different occasions I have benefited from the advice and often shared the joy of commensality with a number of colleagues in the world of Japanese studies, food studies and beyond, including Ken Albala, Stephanie Assmann, Ted Bestor, Katarzyna Cwiertka, Greg de St Maurice, Higashiyotsuyanagi Shōko, Tomoko Onabe, Jonah Salz, Jordan Sand, Samuel Yamashita, Takeshi Watanabe and Merry White. Thank you all.

At the University of Kansas, my greatest debt is to the superb librarian Michiko Ito, who has built up a marvelous collection of resources on Japanese food culture without which this study would not have been possible, and for her in obtaining rights for some of the images included in the volume. Also in the University of Kansas Watson Library, GIS Specialist Rhonda S. Houser helped me create the maps for this book. My colleagues in the History Department and Center for East Asian Studies also deserve my thanks, in particular Devon Dear and Megan Greene, and Tom Lewin for his friendship and perspective on so many matters. I have also had the fortunate opportunity to work with talented graduate students, including Andrew Kustodowicz, Mindy Landeck and Chikako Mochizuki, who provided some suggestions for Chapter Seven.

The Lawrence Trail Hawks helped me to burn off the calories from enthusiastic indulgence in things edible and potable that are the side benefits and risks of too much 'food scholarship'. My mom has indulged my fascination with sushi since I was in high school, and my friends at the time, who know who they are, will remember some of our ulterior motives in seeking out Japanese food. I shared many good meals and conversations with my stepfather Phil Balsamo, to whose memory this book is dedicated. My daughter Dana and wife Kiyomi help me to 'keep it real' and provide support to me in ways too numerous to list.

PHOTO ACKNOWLEDGEMENTS

The author and publishers wish to express their thanks to the below sources of illustrative material and/or permission to reproduce it.

Created using ArcGIS with data from DIVA-GIS (diva-gis.org): p. 166; created using ArcGIS with data from DIVA-GIS (diva-gis.org) – base map credit to Esri, HERE, DeLorme, MapmyIndia, © OpenStreetMap contributors, and the GIS user community: pp. 167, 185, 203; author photos: pp. 147, 175, 179, 197, 201, 214; from Dai Nippon Seikatsu Kyōkai [with assistance from the Ministry of Finance Department for the Promotion of National Savings and the Imperial Rule Assistance Association Bureau of Public Welfare], *Chochiku o umidasu seikatsu no gōrika* (Tokyo: Dai Nihon Seikatsu Kyōkai, 1942), photo courtesy of the Tokyo Metropolitan Edo-Tokyo Museum: p. 135; courtesy of Jyoseikan, Kōchi City, Kōchi: pp. 182, 191; courtesy of the Kita City Asukayama Museum, Tokyo: p. 109; courtesy of *Kumamoto Nichinichi Shimbun*: p. 81; courtesy of *Mainichi Shimbun*: pp. 22 (22 November 2014), 35 (18 January 1954), 97 (22 March 2010), 144 (1 November 1945); courtesy of the Ministry of Agriculture, Forestry and Fisheries and the Rural Development Planning Commission: p. 162; courtesy of the Nagasaki University Library: pp. 71, 73; from Shirakawamura Shōkōkai, *Honkosama no omotenashi: Shirakawagō no hōonkō ryōri* (Shirakawagō, Gifu, 2012) – reproduction courtesy of Satō Naoko: p. 218; courtesy of the Tokyo Metropolitan Edo-Tokyo Museum (collection of the Sō Clan of Tsushima Domain, early Edo period): p. 107; courtesy of Wada Yūko of Syowabento.blog: p. 122; courtesy of the Yatsushiro Municipal Museum: pp. 77, 101.

INDEX

Page numbers in *italic* refer to illustrations